Storing & Preserving Garden Produce

FOR DUMMIES®

by Pammy Riggs

A John Wiley and Sons, Ltd, Publication

Storing & Preserving Garden Produce For Dummies®

Published by
John Wiley & Sons, Ltd
The Atrium
Southern Gate
Chichester
West Sussex
PO19 8SQ
England
www.wiley.com

For general information on our other products and services, please contact our Customer Care Department within the U.S. at 877-762-2974, outside the U.S. at 317-572-3993, or fax 317-572-4002.

For technical support, please visit www.wiley.com/techsupport.

Wiley publishes in a variety of print and electronic formats and by print-on-demand. Some material included with standard print versions of this book may not be included in e-books or in print-on-demand. If this book refers to media such as a CD or DVD that is not included in the version you purchased, you may download this material at http://booksupport.wiley.com. For more information about Wiley products, visit www.wiley.com.

British Library Cataloguing in Publication Data: A catalogue record for this book is available from the British Library

ISBN 978-1-119-95156-8 (pbk); ISBN 978-1-119-95387-6 (ebk); ISBN 978-1-119-95388-3 (ebk); ISBN 978-1-119-95389-0 (ebk)

Printed and bound in Great Britain by TJ International, Padstow, Cornwall

10 9 8 7 6 5 4 3 2 1

About the Author

Pammy Riggs' younger years were spent on Scottish farms where growing, storing and preserving – everyday parts of life – went on around her. Her teenage years were spent in a Georgian house in Wiltshire with over an acre of walled garden and orchards tended manically and efficiently by her father. Helping in the garden, orchard, apple loft and kitchen was expected and much storing and preserving knowledge rubbed off in an organic manner.

Always with a vegetable garden of her own, and now a 17-acre smallholding (www.providencefarm.co.uk) where home-grown sustainable food is the main focus, Pammy is an active member of the Transition Town movement. This movement has instigated the first Communal 'Potato Plot' for Tavistock TT, where successful group growing and harvesting of organic potatoes is hosted by the generous Laura at Tregillis Farm in Cornwall.

Believing that now is the time for getting reconnected with a more natural and creative life, Pammy's website, www.providencefarm.co.uk, plans to open up the knowledge of the countryside and sustainability to a wider group. Pammy's passion is to empower us all to get out from behind our computers and desks and get our hands dirty in the rich soil of life. This book is one step on the way to achieving that.

Dedication

To the generations who taught us how.

Author's Acknowledgements

Firstly, my thanks go to the *For Dummies* team – especially Claire Ruston, Steve Edwards and Andy Finch. Also, to my sister, Di Quinn at Punch's Pickles for sharing her lifetime of expertise, and to the Queens of Preserving – Mo Rice, Jill Gigg and Bathford Communty Shop – for their help.

My friends who shared their recipes and knowledge with me were: my husband and partner in preserving, Ritchie Riggs; Neil, my favourite seedsman at www.tamarorganics.co.uk; Arjen Huese, for special biodynamics info; Diana Lee, my herbalist friend, and her partner, Rob Meredith for supplying heritage seeds; Linda Travis of Westlake Apple Juice and Cider with her vinegar lore; Gill of www.bangorsorganic.co.uk for all things physalis and other recipes; Joy Moore for the original bean chutney recipe; John Bennett for remembering his Mum's Marrow Rum; Jenny Brooks and Malcolm at www.hogsbot.co.uk for endless discussions around the subject; Mike Sealey, my Environmental Health Officer, for educating me in food safety; Rosie Beat for her technical review; and last but never least, my Mum's old and tattered recipe books with all their memories attached.

Publisher's Acknowledgements

We're proud of this book; please send us your comments at http://dummies.custhelp.com. For other comments, please contact our Customer Care Department within the U.S. at 877-762-2974, outside the U.S. at 317-572-3993, or fax 317-572-4002.

Some of the people who helped bring this book to market include the following:

Acquisitions, Editorial, and Vertical Websites

Project Editor: Steven Edwards

Commissioning Editor: Claire Ruston

Assistant Editor: Ben Kemble

Development Editor: Andy Finch

Copy Editor: Charlie Wilson

Technical Editor: Rosie Beat

Recipe Tester: Emily Nolan

Nutritional Analyst: Patty Santelli

Proofreader: Kim Vernon

Production Manager: Daniel Mersey

Publisher: David Palmer

Cover Photos: © iStock / j Viktorija Kuprijanova

Cartoons: Ed McLachlan

Composition Services

Project Coordinator: Kristie Rees

Layout and Graphics: Carl Byers, Timothy C. Detrick, Lavonne Roberts

Indexer: Estalita Slivoskey

Special Help

Brand Reviewer: Jennifer Bingham

Publishing and Editorial for Consumer Dummies

    Kathleen Nebenhaus, Vice President and Executive Publisher

    Kristin Ferguson-Wagstaffe, Product Development Director

    Ensley Eikenburg, Associate Publisher, Travel

    Kelly Regan, Editorial Director, Travel

Publishing for Technology Dummies

    Andy Cummings, Vice President and Publisher

Composition Services

    Debbie Stailey, Director of Composition Services

Contents at a Glance

Recipes at a Glance

Table of Contents

Introduction

● ●

*N*o doubt about it: growing your own food is hugely satisfying and great fun, which is why more and more people are digging up their lawns to make vegetable patches, building raised beds on them or becoming allotmenteers. Although watching nature's cycle of growth and decay over the year is fascinating, seeing your lovingly home-grown crops going to waste is frustrating when all your fruit or vegetables are ready at one time and you can't eat everything.

This book steps into the space between growth and decay with some simple and some slightly more involved methods to store and preserve your food and make use of it for longer. Our ancestors knew all about the importance of storing food, working out safe ways to preserve the fruits of their labours. Today, though, you've the advantage of modern appliances to help with home drying, freezing and preserving, and you can use this technology in conjunction with the wisdom of times gone by. People no longer build homes with apple lofts and root stores, but you can find ways to improvise whatever your situation.

About This Book

Storing and preserving food isn't rocket science; with a bit of confidence and practice, this book helps you fill your store cupboards with your own home-made jams and chutneys. You need only the desire to experience your own home-grown food for as long as possible around the year to make a start. Some solutions are really simple: for example, save up a few brown paper bags and you've all the equipment you need to dry herbs and seeds. For those preserving methods that do require specialist equipment, I explain what you need and when. I also lead you through the processes and techniques that ensure that you do the best job with the produce you have, such as the following:

- ✔ Choosing the best, freshest fruit and veg for preserving

- ✔ Finding the most suitable equipment you already have in your kitchen and knowing which essential tools you need to buy

- ✔ Recognising what's safe practice in the preserving line and knowing when to discard any dubious results

✔ Describing and explaining the main methods of preserving, all written in a fun-to-follow way

✔ Providing recipes and methods of storage for commonly grown fruit and veg

✔ Setting out extra knowledge for the more adventurous in spirit who like to get out and forage in wild places or even travel the world in search of food and preserving-related knowledge

I guide you from the garden to the store cupboard, upstairs to the apple loft and downstairs to the root cellar, including a trail of delicious preserve recipes and hints on how to organise your methods. With this book, you can make the most of your own lovely home-grown food and any that you glean from the wider world.

Conventions Used in This Book

The recipes in this book include preparation times, processing times and the yield you can expect from your efforts. When a recipe is a little less straight-forward, I explain any unusual timings clearly. Here are details that apply to each recipe but aren't repeated every time:

✔ Always use vinegar with at least 5 per cent acidity.

✔ Use salt with no additives: sea salt or preserving salt is best.

✔ Use heavy-bottomed, preserving pans for all cooking.

✔ Always use non-corrosive non-reactive materials (such as stainless steel, glass or ceramic equipment and utensils), because vinegar and fruit acids react with certain metals.

✔ Use purpose-made jars, lids and new rubber seals when working with heat-treated preserves.

✔ Note that times for heat-treating or boiling start when the liquid reaches the boiling point: you see this moment in the bubbling movement of the liquid.

✔ Test for a vacuum seal on every jar when heat-treated foods cool down.

I use degrees Celsius (Fahrenheit) for temperatures, with Gas Marks for oven temperatures. Fan ovens may run at a slightly higher temperature: look at your appliance maker's instruction booklet and adjust accordingly. Gas hobs react quicker when lowering temperatures than electric or stove heating units, which is particularly important when reaching the crucial setting point for jams and jellies; be sure to understand your equipment and work out a system of removing the pan safely from the heat if necessary.

I also use the following typographical conventions to make navigating your way around the book's content even easier:

 ✔ *Italic* highlights new terms that I define nearby.
 ✔ **Boldfaced** text indicates the action part of numbered steps.
 ✔ `Monofont` shows website addresses.

Foolish Assumptions

In writing this book, I made the following assumptions about you:

 ✔ You view growing and preserving food as an honourable task that's worth taking time over. You know that it gives you common-sense access to fresh food and exercise, and a way to relax and connect with 'real' life and similarly minded people.

 ✔ You're growing your own fruit and veg based around what's available in an ordinary seed catalogue and in a natural way, using no poisonous chemicals.

 ✔ You want to make the best of your outdoor efforts by preserving all the food you grow in a simple, straightforward way using additional ingredients you choose yourself (and therefore trust).

 ✔ You're familiar with basic food preparation and cooking methods and have access to an average kitted-out kitchen.

 ✔ You haven't made jams or other preserves before or recently and want basic, easy-to-follow instructions and knowledge to make sense of what you're doing.

How This Book Is Organised

I organise this book into six parts. The first part gives you the basic message, encouraging you to embark upon the road to storing and preserving your home-grown produce. The next four parts run you through all the different methods that have traditionally been the backbone of every gardening year, with a visit to the orchard, soft fruit area and greenhouse if you have one. I take you round your vegetable beds, herb garden and hen house, and on a trip down country lanes for wild harvest foraging just like your grandparents did as a matter of course.

Along the way, I provide recipes for every taste, sweet tooths and savoury lovers, and if these recipes whet your appetite for foody adventures farther afield, you find the information to set you on the right track. Good luck for your next adventure!

Part 1: Understanding Preserving

Sometimes you need a bit of motivation to start a new pursuit, and so Chapter 1 gives you plenty of that. You get to look at the kinds of equipment you need in Chapter 2 – most tools may already be in your kitchen and are inexpensive to buy anyway. If food safety worries you, Chapter 3 gives honest information about potential problems, but also the knowledge and tools to make informed judgements on the safety of the large variety of food you can preserve and the confidence to give it a go. I suggest starting with something low risk and easy, and building up from there. You can pop back to these three chapters for a reminder at any time.

Part 11: Discovering Storing and Preserving Methods

This part contains the nitty-gritty of preserving, sometimes describing such basic methods that you wonder why you need a book at all (things are always simple when you know, right?) and at other times providing you with the enjoyment of discovering how a process works. I cover all the standard preserving methods: basic storage (Chapter 4); sweet and sour preserving techniques (Chapters 5 and 6, respectively); freezing (Chapter 7); drying, salting and modern vacuum-packing (Chapter 8); and making drinks (Chapter 9). With some experience behind you and when the logic of a method is clear, you can use this part to adapt recipes to the particular fruits, vegetables or combinations that your garden provides. A natural element like a garden doesn't stick to a rigid timetable, so expect to deal with surprises.

Part 111: Working with Home-Grown Fruits

This part describes, and provides a huge range of recipes for high-up orchard fruits such as apples (Chapter 10), lower-bush plants headed by berries and currants (Chapter 11) and a mouth-watering range of exotic-tasting fruiting vegetables, where tomatoes and aubergines conspire to bring the Mediterranean into your home (Chapter 12).

Part IV: Keeping and Eating Garden Vegetables

You can easily store your rooting plants with just a few guidelines; or take a more complicated approach if you prefer to transform them into unlikely and delicate heady brews (Chapter 13 has all the info). I also discuss beans (Chapter 14) and the best of the rest of other vegetables (Chapter 15), whether they go into the jam pan or chutney and relish jars. Throughout this part, I provide recipes for every occasion from a royal visit to a ploughman's lunch.

Part V: Preserving and Using Herbs, Eggs and Wild Extras

I get a bit eccentric, a truly British trait, in this part. I show you how to save handfuls of your herbs for adding taste to meals and as a bit of gentle beauty treatment in Chapter 16. Hens are appearing at the bottom of lots of gardens (in pens usually!), so preserving eggs and understanding how to smooth out their flow is an important part of lots of lives nowadays (check out Chapter 17). Going outside your garden and into the countryside allows you to find free food treats and the recipes I include show you how to turn your gathered bounty into delicate treats (Chapter 18).

Part VI: The Part of Tens

No *For Dummies* book is complete without these short chapters. They help you succeed in your preserving endeavours (Chapter 19) and guide you around some common pitfalls (Chapter 20). Chapter 21 is for the adventurous among you, helping you to open doors to experiencing a wider world of food, growing and processing.

Icons Used in This Book

The following four icons appear throughout this book and point out specific aspects and information that you don't want to miss.

Of course, this book is filled with great tips, but this icon directs you to a particularly useful hint or shortcut born from my experience, thus helping you to smooth the way to perfect preserving.

This icon indicates something that's important enough to really commit to your memory.

When you see this icon, pay special attention: it helps you to avoid potential problems, keeps your food safe and helps your recipes succeed.

I keep the technical stuff to an absolute minimum in this book, but sometimes bulking out a method with deeper understanding is helpful. But skip these paragraphs if you're impatient to get cracking with the hands-on material.

Where to Go from Here

I want you to be able to use *Storing and Preserving Garden Produce For Dummies* as a reference book of chapters that you can read in any order you like. If one aspect of a method is unclear in a recipe, simply flick to the appropriate chapter of Part II to get the method clear in your head.

If you've just gathered in your biggest harvest ever of one fruit or veg, use the comprehensive contents or index to go straight to the section you require. For example, if your crop is apples, visit Chapter 10 for recipes and pointers, read Chapter 6 if you fancy making chutney and check out Chapter 5 for jam-making information.

If you want to use this book while sitting by the fireside on a cold January evening studying a seed catalogue, cross-reference the different fruits and vegetables. I provide hints on good specific varieties for storing to take the hard work out of your decision-making and Chapter 21 contains innovative ideas for filling your pockets with free seeds.

If you spot a recipe that looks jolly tasty and want to get on with it, do so, but please flick to Chapter 3 first for a run through of safety procedures. This chapter covers basic safety practices, such as avoiding cross-contamination with raw meats and produce and keeping pets out of the kitchen, to help reinforce safe preserving and keep your family's food safe.

Just remember that having fun and enjoying the fruits (and veg) of your own labour is the most important thing, whichever page you start on.

Part I
Understanding Preserving

'Just how <u>much</u> wine did you make, Nigel?'

In this part . . .

This part focuses on the reasons you may want to go down the route of storing and preserving the home-grown produce that you so lovingly tended throughout the year. After all, nature never stands still and no sooner is your fruit and veg ready to harvest than it begins to deteriorate. The chapters in this part motivate and encourage you to begin preserving, even if you have only basic kitchen equipment to hand. And because you often give some of your preserves away (which is all part of the tradition), having enough basic knowledge to enable you to feel confident in the safety aspects of preserving means that you can do so without worry.

Chapter 1

Experiencing the Good Life with Good Reasons

In This Chapter

▶ Discovering good reasons for storing and preserving

▶ Planning ahead and choosing wisely

▶ Looking at the different ways to store and preserve

▶ Deciding what works for you

Getting back to nature and growing your own vegetables has become fashionable these days and with good reason. Not many generations ago, humans had to preserve the food they grew in the clement months to feed them through the rest of the year. With modern shopping, storing and packing techniques (and the fact that most people now live in larger urban areas with less garden space), that knowledge hasn't been passed on from kitchen to kitchen as it used to be . . . which is where this book comes in. It can even help you decide what to plant in the first instance, right down to the details about which fruit and veg varieties make best use of your space and time.

If you still need a bit of encouragement to set off on the preserving adventure, you can find it in this chapter because I provide some compelling reasons. I also summarise some of the different methods by which you can preserve your home-grown food and introduce you to the content of this book as a whole, to help you make the best use of all the information it contains.

Reaping the Rewards of Preserving

This section provides loads of reasons for storing and preserving your own produce. Here, I describe the physical and psychological benefits, the financial advantages and how the whole activity can help you and your family achieve a healthy balance in life. Preserving has traditionally been a kitchen table activity that involves young and old members of the family. Making time to connect with each other and pass on the family traditions and stories in this way is a valuable bonding experience.

Wanting the good life

Many people have a dream about giving up the rat race and moving towards a simpler, more straightforward way of life. As someone who grows your own food, you've already made a great start. And if the rat race is still a part of your life, and realistically looks like staying so, you can still take solace from your growing area, no matter how small; growing, storing and consuming your own food immediately puts you in touch with nature, providing you with a bit of the good life.

For example, if you've children, showing them exactly where their food comes from – grounding them, getting them out into the fresh air, exercising their bodies and providing solid, useful knowledge for their minds – is one of the single most important things you can do for them in their lives.

Working in the soil involves healthy bending and carrying, stretching ligaments and tendons with a food-rewarded workout. Soaking in a hot bath after a day in the garden, reflecting on the food to come, just has to be the best form of relaxation possible.

With all these benefits to gain, you don't want to miss out. Whatever stage you're at as a home-produce grower, this book can now help you to make best use of your newfound lifestyle.

Saving for a rainy day: Thrifty ways

Knowing that you've the right knowledge to preserve your hard-earned harvest has the great knock-on effect of helping you to produce healthy food in a thrifty manner. Your very own produce made into food for friends and family is unique and impossible to better.

Saving money by making your own food is a first-class way to stretch the pennies, especially if your family is 100 per cent behind you in your preserving project. A new venture like this involves changing the eating habits of a lifetime for the family, and persuading children (and some adults – you know your own family best!) to change to a more wholesome diet of home-grown fruit and vegetables (preserved or fresh) can take a little guile. Remember, your preserves are made to last, and so use your judgement, gently shoehorning preserves into family life in creative ways.

As well as the obvious uses, here are few ideas on how to make preserves fun as well as thrifty and tasty:

- Have a special 'pub meal' – a ploughman's lunch – at home using your own pickles and preserves. Serve the adults beer and the children home-made cordial (with fizzy water sometimes), or open up a bottle of home-made wine for a special occasion.

- Brighten up economical meals by stirring a generous dollop of chutney into baked beans to put on toast or casseroles (especially those made with your own dried beans).

- Eat fresh bread and butter with jam instead of buying sweets, or have a cream tea with home-made scones and jam. Splash out on clotted cream if you like to have scones as well as bread and jam: an authentic West Country treat.

- Look in old-fashioned cookbooks (find them in second-hand shops or on your grandparents' dusty shelves) for the basics such as jam roly-poly and jam tarts. Rediscover milk puddings, rice pudding, sago and tapioca with a spoonful of jam to sweeten and colour it up, turning back the clocks to enjoy 'real' food.

Making food from scratch creates less waste all round, and less packaging keeps your bins emptier, which has to be good for everyone and the planet.

Take the long view. After all, your preserves are made to last, so introduce them to the family gradually. Over-exposure to a new taste can sometimes cause a stubborn streak to emerge in even your closest family members, so use your insider knowledge to best advantage.

For anyone with a host of family and friends, supplying birthday and Christmas presents becomes a nightmare, and sometimes an expensive nightmare. The perfect solution to giving useful but thrifty gifts is to give small amounts of home-made produce, uniquely packaged, for just the right occasion. So when you're potting up jams and chutneys, put aside a few small or fancily shaped jars especially for gift wrapping. (Chapter 6 contains more great gift ideas, as does Chapter 16, which looks at ways to preserve flowers, transforming them into sweet-smelling lavender bags or beauty treatments for friends and family.)

Satisfying your soul with home-grown therapy

As well as providing good physical exercise, growing your own also increases your self-confidence and provides a sense of satisfaction that comes from the feeling of independence and control that you gain from your endeavours.

Working with fruit and vegetables, whether in the garden or in the kitchen, is a rewarding occupation. Losing yourself in a task while peeling and chopping and stirring and sieving returns you to the tasks performed by millions of people for thousands of generations, and your finished product is sure to make you glow with pride, even if your first try is a bit wobbly round the edges to start with.

You're uniquely creative, so be proud of your achievements and smile every time you see your laden cupboards and shelves; this produce is food for the stomach *and* the soul; the perfect way to build up self-esteem and a well-stocked larder simultaneously.

Passing on the knowledge

Growing, preserving and using your own food is a highly social activity, helping to strengthen families and even increasing understanding across nations. Traditionally, recipes travel with people, in their heads, their hearts and their cravings for dishes to remind them of home. Giving gifts of preserves opens up the opportunity for cross-fertilisation of ideas and opens a new avenue for conversation. The Mediterranean seeps more and more into the UK's diet, and many of the plants once thought exotic are everyday items in store cupboards. Therefore, discover how to grow your own 'exotics', swap experiences with friends and neighbours, and bring your own piece of another country to the table. Chapter 12 provides a lot more information in this area.

When receiving recipes from friends or neighbours that you enjoy, continue the traditional ritual by naming your version in their honour: for example, 'Aunt Mary's Chutney', 'Elizabeth's Jam' and 'Uncle Henry's Marrow Rum' may not mean much to strangers, but the names keep memories alive, giving the opportunity to relive past experiences and remember friends and family who are no longer with you.

Planning Ahead in a Down-to-Earth Way

The key to successful storing and preserving is planning ahead, because you're working with nature here and, in nature, things don't always go smoothly.

When you take over an existing garden or allotment, you find some established plants already in place. After a season of tasting their fruits, you may love them and decide to keep them, or find that the variety you inherit doesn't suit your taste. Even if you're organising a completely new venture, creating a garden in a new house, re-organising an existing growing area or planning some guerrilla gardening (yes, you read that correctly; see Chapter 21), you need to plan. For example, if you intend to replace all the tomato ketchup (a recipe is in Chapter 12) that your family eats in a year with a home-made version, your choice of tomatoes (a dry, pasty type) is going to be different from tomatoes that are right for the Summer Vegetable Pickle recipe in Chapter 13 (sweet, tiny cherry tomatoes).

Develop the gardener's habit of sitting round a roaring fire in the winter months with seed catalogues spread about you. Match up the varieties you grow to the preserves you intend to make, choosing quantities that you're capable of storing. You won't benefit growing peas to satisfy a frozen pea habit if you don't own a freezer; you're better off considering peas that dry well and changing your eating habits a little too.

Healthy plants store best and are the tastiest too.

Rotating your crops

One thing you definitely can't control is the weather, which influences how your plants grow, develop and mature during the seasons. Thankfully, there exists a well-known crop rotation regime that you can control. This regime is worth following and it helps you to achieve the healthiest crops. And, of course, the best quality disease-free produce has the highest chance of storing well for the longest time. So, whatever the size or shape of your growing area, take time to think through a *crop rotation* plan.

The idea of crop rotation is to ensure that two years elapse before you grow the same crop in the same ground again. Different plants take different amounts of goodness from the soil, so rotating your crops maintains the mineral balance of your soil. Crop rotation also reduces the risk of lingering disease and makes the best use of your hard-won compost. You can develop a rotation for your own unique growing area based on these principles; just remember that the longer the time you can leave between growing similar crops on the same ground, the better.

For a basic three-year rotation, mentally divide your growing area – be it raised beds or a straightforward vegetable garden or allotment – into four roughly equal plots numbered 1, 2, 3 and 4, and allocate one of the following crop types to each plot:

- ✓ **'A' crops:** potatoes, carrot, beetroot, parsnips, onion, shallots, leeks, tomatoes, courgettes, marrows, pumpkins, celery, Florence fennel, aubergines, peppers, cucumbers, melons, celeriac, salsify and scorzonera

- ✓ **'B'crops:** beans, peas, sweetcorn, spinach, swiss chard, globe artichokes

- ✓ **'C' crops:** cabbages, cauliflower, Brussels sprouts, kale, kohl rabi, swedes and turnip

- ✓ **'D' crops:** permanent crops such as rhubarb, asparagus, fruit bushes, and herbs

You can add in fast-growing crops like lettuce where you've space.

Each year, shuffle the A, B and C types along by one plot, leaving plot 4 the same to accommodate the permanent 'type D' plants that over-winter and regenerate the following year. In this way, you get a system that flows:

- ✓ Year 1: Plot 1: 'A' crops; Plot 2: 'B' crops; Plot 3: 'C' crops; Plot 4: 'D' crops
- ✓ Year 2: Plot 1: 'C' crops; Plot 2: 'A' crops; Plot 3: 'B' crops; Plot 4: 'D' crops
- ✓ Year 3: Plot 1: 'B' crops; Plot 2: 'C' crops; Plot 3: 'A' crops; Plot 4: 'D' crops
- ✓ Year 4: Plot 1: 'A' crops; Plot 2: 'B' crops; Plot 3: 'C' crops; Plot 4: 'D' crops

Check out *Growing Your Own Fruit & Veg for Dummies* by Geoff Stebbings (Wiley) and *Organic Gardening For Dummies* by Sue Fisher, Ann Whitman and Suzanne DeJohn (Wiley) for more growing wisdom.

Remembering what and where you've planted from year to year is really hard, so draw out a plan to refer to year after year. You don't have to be a brilliant artist to sketch out a rough plan of your growing area on a bit of paper.

Selecting what to grow and how to preserve it

The range of produce that you can choose to grow in your own garden or allotment is vast, as is the huge variety of options for preserving it. You put a lot of effort into your garden or allotment, so making the most of the resulting fruit and veg is only sensible.

If you love orchard fruits (apples, pears and so on), Chapter 10 has everything you need for enjoying and preserving these tree-top treats. Cooking apples, for example, form the basis of more than just apple pie. Lots of jams and chutneys combine cooking apples with other ingredients. And although the wrinkly little storeroom apple may look humble from the outside, nothing is better that its sweet surprise to your taste buds, or peeled, quartered, cored and presented to a child in place of sweeties.

If berries are more your thing, Chapter 11 contains loads of great ideas and recipes. Berries are among the most colourful fruits you can grow – pale greens and yellows from gooseberries, pillar-box reds from redcurrants, raspberries and strawberries and the darkness of blackcurrants – and you can use them in loads of great recipes.

Playing at gooseberries . . . in a good way!

My son took over an allotment that had obviously been well loved by its previous owner. The perennial herbs were there, albeit a bit straggly and in want of a bit of care. He also inherited some excellent soft fruit bushes, including the most delicious dessert gooseberry I've ever tasted: sweet, yellow, plump and juicy. The straggly herbs went, but the gooseberry bush is definitely staying and he's looking out for other allotment owners who may know what this variety is called.

Fruit or vegetable . . . vegetable or fruit? Does it matter? I call them fruiting vegetables in Chapter 12 and they're delicious whatever their name. Tomatoes and garlic feature here (along with their more exotic friends). Living without these two flavours seems impossible nowadays, but just a few generations ago they hardly featured in the store cupboard at all. Chapter 12 helps you choose which varieties are best for your preserving plans.

You may not think that root vegetables are the most exciting of plants, but Chapter 13 may well just prove you wrong. Take potatoes, for example. Potatoes are the true root vegetable – hiding away from the light of day and easy to store in a dry dark place, but when unearthed and unleashed in your kitchen, the humble potato is the king of versatility! You can bake it, roast it, mix it, mash it, smash it, cream it, pipe it, use it as a topping or as the bottom of a pie. Root vegetables are a great crop choice, and Chapter 13 shows you what to do with your harvest.

Beans and peas (or *legumes* to those in the know) sometimes suffer from a bad press, but check out Chapter 14 to see the other side of the coin. These plants come in as many forms as you can dream up, from tall climbers that require support to free-standing dwarf varieties that are great for small growing spaces. Most can be dried as well as eaten fresh and they provide a great source of protein, too. Meals based around beans are healthy and nutritious, but don't think that you have to stop there. Tasty chutneys and a special bean hummus are on the menu too.

If you think that Chapters 10 to 14 are exhaustive, think again. Chapter 15 serves up a truly diverse selection of produce to play with – all those tricky plants that stubbornly refuse to fit into neat categories; in other words (as the chapter title says) 'the best of the rest'. Plants like squashes need a frost-free environment to store well, and offer unusual storing possibilities. For example, you can group any of the wide variety of intriguingly coloured and beautifully shaped squashes available around the house as edible decoration in place of vases of flowers in the winter months. Alternatively, if you enjoy having your senses assaulted, go for the 'true Brit' option of scorching hot fresh horseradish pickle or sauce. Conversely, try soothing yourself with the sensuous, silky asparagus soup, brimming with sophistication.

Another group of plants that can slip under the radar where preserving is concerned are herbs: Chapter 16 ensures that they get their due attention as well. You're probably already familiar with pots and bunches of dried herbs for jollying up everyday meals – you do find that information here – but to encourage you to stray from the kitchen towards the boudoir you can also find recipes from yesteryear. Try, for example, dabbing a little home-made lavender water behind your ears or creating a rosemary rinse to add extra sheen to your hair – both natural beauty treatments of their day. Visit Chapter 16 and recreate yourself naturally – go on, you're more than worth it!

Growing your favourites

If your time and growing space is limited, you have to make choices about what you can grow. On the one hand, giving space over to exotic plants that you never find in your local shops is an option, with the assumption that you can buy the more mundane staples from a trusted supplier. But, on the other hand, the staples – freshly pulled or dug from the garden and whether for fresh eating or preserving – are always going to be in some mysterious way your own, and nothing beats ordinary fresh vegetables beautifully prepared.

What a wonderful dilemma it presents: write a 'must have' list of your favourites, ordering them first to last. This list can help you to gain a perspective and make decisions you're happy with in the long term.

Ensuring that you have the right amount: Multi-method preserving

Growing your own food isn't an exact science, of course, and at times you're bound to find that you've produced too much of a particular fruit or veg. Of course, this situation is where effective storing and preserving comes into its own.

You can use several methods for preserving one type of plant: for example, if you find yourself with a 'madness' of marrows, use several different ways of preserving them. That's the beauty: you may hate cooked or stuffed marrow, but love Marrow and Ginger Jam (Chapter 15 has the recipe). Or you can use marrow as one of the bulking up ingredients in a chutney, thus transforming what you hate into what you love. And of course if the whole marrow thing turns out to be a disaster, make a note to yourself about that too and don't grow much, or any, next year.

Look to your successes and plan your new growing seasons around your (and your family's) favourites, making room for even more of the best-loved treats.

When starting out on your preserving adventure, you benefit by staying realistic in your ambitions. Preparing and making preserves takes time, so if you're a busy person, be realistic. If you struggle to juggle a full-time job, three children and three evening classes a week, start small – perhaps with a small chutney or cordial-making project using equipment you already have in your home. As you gain in experience, and perhaps ditch one of the evening classes, you can build up to buying specialist equipment over time and getting more ambitious. Remember, too, that you need storage space for jars of jams and chutneys and places to stand fermenting containers of wines – sometimes for months at a time – especially if space is already an issue in your home.

Egg-zamining egg-stra information

More and more people are keeping chickens at the bottom of the garden (at last a useful, fruitful pet!), but hens live by the seasons too so you need help to work out a strategy that enables you to keep enjoying home-grown eggs, even when your hens are having a rest. Chapter 17 has loads more info – how to extend the egg harvest if you keep your own chickens and are fed up with omelettes every day and a reminder to record, however briefly, what works – but that's only a snippet. If you want even more chickeny information, take a look at *Keeping Chickens For Dummies* by Pammy Riggs, Kimberley Willis and Rob Ludlow (Wiley) and get the whole story.

In addition, the book you're holding now also has a whole chapter (Chapter 18) on dealing with wild food that you find when you're out and about. Keeping your eyes peeled when you're on a country walk can really be rewarding. Harvest time, which is usually in the autumn, is the best time of year, but you can come across a few surprises in other seasons too.

Overviewing Storing and Preserving Methods

Storing and preserving wouldn't be possible without using some well-tried methods. Here's a snippet of what I cover in Part II:

- ✓ **Clamping and other simple storage:** Easy peasy as long as you have the space to store; Chapter 4 tells you more.

- ✓ **Using sweetness for preserving:** Reducing moisture with a period of cooking, and then adding enough sugar to hold your mixture in a kind of suspense, is the basic idea; for wider interpretation, go to Chapter 5.

✔ **Making good use of vinegar:** The acid in this ingredient creates an environment where bacteria can't thrive. Uses range from straightforward cold pickling to interesting sweet and sour combinations, designed for their taste and beauty; Chapter 6 expands upon this theme.

✔ **Freezing:** This modern invention allows you to plug into your cold side and keep your delicate vegetables in suspended animation. Read about this highly efficient approach to preserving in Chapter 7.

✔ **Drying, salting and vacuum-packing:** Drying exposes food to a temperature high enough to evaporate moisture but low enough that the food doesn't cook. You can use the sun as your heater (after all, the sun is free), but sometimes that's unreliable; or buy a purpose-made food dehydrator for perfect results every time. Salting reduces moisture content in a different way and is usually a preliminary process before pickling, but it can be useful in its own right. Vacuum-packing excludes air and any attendant micro-organisms halting deterioration, but it does involve a cost element (read all about it in Chapter 8).

✔ **Making drinks suitable for children and adults:** Make children's fruity cordials without nasty additives and wines (for the parents) with flavours you never find in any shop. You find making drinks easier with a little specialist equipment to make life easy and a little patience to allow wines to mature. Drink to your health and new-found skills in Chapter 9.

Choosing What Works for You

Home preserving takes time and commitment. You already have the growing to look after, so seeing your lovely produce go to waste feels like a sin; instead, put by some time especially for preserving. Each recipe has a guide time, but individual skills vary and a lot depends on the initial quality of the produce you're preserving. Salvaging the good apple flesh from a basketful of *windfalls* (apples blown down onto the ground by the wind) takes much longer to sift through than straightforward cutting of a pristine basketful.

Factor in the time you need to sterilise your preserving jars too, although often this task can run alongside your cooking time. Getting ahead of yourself by buying the two main preserving ingredients, sugar and vinegar, in bulk (as long as doing so is cost effective and you've somewhere to keep the ingredients safe and dry) adds convenience and allows you to get on with preserving at the drop of a hat when an opportunity occurs.

Sharing a snippet on safety

The ability to preserve food is the main reason for the success of the human race, but the natural route for food is to deteriorate, and bacteria and other micro-organisms play a major part in this deterioration. So be aware and don't unwittingly add any potential dangers to your working area. Follow these tips for a safe and happy preserving experience:

- **Understand that cross-contamination is the number one potential problem.** Never mix raw food preparation or fridge storage space, especially not raw chicken, with preparation or stored ingredients for preserving. Use different shelves or closed containers if you've both in the house at the same time. Ideally, keep separate utensils and chopping boards for each; failing that, reach for the antibacterial spray often and regularly, using it as the manufacturer recommends. Pay attention to the details.

- **Shoo the pets out into the garden.** Even the best-groomed and loved pets carry bacteria. They probably don't want to share your preserves (unless you've a Labrador dog who eats anything), so don't let them share in the making.

- **Do let your children help you.** Give them something simple to do, but make them aware of the dangers of hot pans and sharp knives. Even small children can help with weighing out ingredients and preserving is a good forum for discussion about all the good things in life. Keep a few plasters handy, though, just in case.

- **Keep your environment free from clutter.** Make interested children welcome in the preserving area, but not their stray skateboards and toy cars. You're likely to be carrying and pouring hot liquids at some time, so having a pre-planned strategy (for example, drink and biscuit time sitting up at a table) to keep children where you can see them while you carry out these operations is a good idea.

Chapter 3 contains loads more on safety and hygiene issues, and may just be the most important chapter in this book.

Handling handy tools of the trade

Of course, to do anything successfully, you need to have the right basic equipment available. You may well *want* all the fancy equipment that makes life easy to hand, but that's the luxury end of the market and not possible for everyone. But with a good large stainless steel pan, somewhere to heat it up, a stirring implement and recycled jam jars, you're halfway to your first batch of preserves. And if you enjoy your first efforts in the preserving line, make sure that you put the basic equipment on the next Christmas present list: Chapter 2 helps you prioritise as regards getting all tooled up.

You may start with little and achieve good results, but if the preserving bug hooks you, you can make life much more rewarding and easy by tooling yourself up with the following:

- ✔ The first investment has to be a preserving pan; without one, you're restricted in the amount you can safely and easily make in one batch.

- ✔ Two inexpensive, but excellent tools are the extra-long-handled wooden spoon (to keep your hands and arms away from hot splashes) and a jam funnel. Potting up preserves is altogether easier and less messy with this simple device.

- ✔ Wine-making without a demijohn and fermentation trap is too difficult to consider; look into Chapter 9 for more tipple advice.

- ✔ Freezers are part of most households these days but serious freezer storage for the avid grower comes in the form of a chest freezer hidden away in a place where you open it less frequently than the one for everyday use standing in the kitchen.

- ✔ A notebook for jotting down recipe tips, problems to watch out for next time and your successes ends up as a family treasure. The dog-eared pages, jammy fingerprints and stains exude a personal family history and it becomes a much-loved working document, something a computer file can never impart, no matter how informative.

Expanding your preserving possibilities

Life needn't stop with storing and preserving your own home-grown produce. Chapter 21 provides ideas to help satisfy that yearning for more food experiences or when you want to become part of something bigger. Here, you find ideas, community projects and international organisation in place already, just waiting for your enthusiastic input to make them work. Stay at home and join a gardening club, put your name down on the allotment list, find a Community Supported Agriculture scheme and go part-time farming; or travel the world looking at worldwide wine-making with WWOOF (if you're intrigued to know what that means, skip to Chapter 21).

That's what this book is all about: you can find the information you need between these pages but you don't need to follow it in an ordered way. Most importantly, enjoy yourself in whatever adventure you follow.

Chapter 2

Equipping Yourself and Your Kitchen

*A*ny job is easier with the right tools, and storing and preserving your home-grown produce is no different. The advantage you have is that in an ordinary, well-stocked kitchen you already own most of what you need, although a few specialist extras make everything run smoothly and efficiently. (Don't forget that recipes are essential tools too, in their way!) This chapter reminds you of what's useful and already in your kitchen cupboards and drawers, and also helps you when you're choosing where to invest in new equipment, from the basic to the downright luxurious.

Choosing good quality, even if you have to save up a little, always pays you back in the end.

Examining Your Existing Equipment at Home Sweet Home

Your cooking area is highly personal to you, but you can turn it into a small but efficient jam or chutney factory with the minimum of effort. If you can feed a family of four by cooking everyday meals, you probably have enough equipment around to make a start on preserving home-grown produce.

Seeing a row of neatly labelled preserved goodies in the store cupboard rightly brings with it a sense of pride, as well as a source of food, when you've put the effort into creating them.

Studying your kitchen space

Your kitchen space is already likely to feature the following:

- **Cupboards and drawers:** For keeping preserves out of bright sunlight.
- **Oven and hob:** For heating and cooking (not that you need me to tell you that!).

Get to know your hob and how it 'behaves', because some recipes need precise heat control. Gas hobs react more quickly than electric, so be ready to remove pans physically from the heat when your mixture reaches the correct temperature if your hob reacts slowly. Just like angry humans, some hobs boil over quickly out of nowhere and others simmer away for ages!

- **Sink:** For washing up and cleaning down.
- **Worktops:** To chop, prepare, pour and label.

You make use of all this space and equipment when you preserve your own food at home. Storing food needs space too, but apart from cupboards storage is usually elsewhere in your home. (Visit Chapter 4 for more details on storing food.)

Going potty with pans and bowls

Check out the tools you have in your kitchen, especially if you inherited old-fashioned pans and bowls or bought interesting-looking equipment in second-hand shops. Some tools may be more useful than others. Make sure that you understand what materials they're made from *before* launching into using them for making preserves.

The following is a list of materials that are safe to use as kitchen equipment:

- **Ceramic** is ideal for all ingredients. All sizes are useful at some time; although ceramic isn't suitable for heating over direct heat, you can use it as the container part of a *bain-marie* (a boiling-water bath with an inner pan for gentle heating) for melting and at a gentle heat.
- **Glass** is useful for all types of ingredients, but it can't withstand direct heat and may crack.

- **Plastic** is excellent for specific uses and withstands all types of ingredients, including acid vinegar and fruit acid, but isn't meant for heating; it may also stain with some fruits, vegetables and spices.

- **Pyrex** is a useful, heat-resistant, glass-like material that's often transparent, white or patterned. Look at the base for a statement about specific uses: heat resistance and dishwasher and oven safe is good. But if it doesn't state so, don't use for anything other than cool and gentle heat.

- **Stainless steel** equipment is extremely useful in the kitchen. The brightness of the shine on the metal and the heavy weight are the first clues that something is made of stainless steel. Most, but not all, stainless steel tools carry a stamp simply stating 'stainless steel'; see this label and you're in the clear. All stainless steel is non-corrosive and suitable for cooking safely with vinegar and acid fruits.

Looking for any maker's guarantees or statements about the usefulness of the item is a good idea. You're full steam ahead if you see 'stainless steel', 'heat resistant' or other similar claims.

Don't use new or second-hand equipment made from:

- **Aluminium:** Often inexpensive, these lightweight items are a giveaway with their dull metallic sheen (when comparing them to good stainless steel). They're often on sale in second-hand and charity shops as people swap to better-quality tools; err on the side of caution and don't buy them. (See the sidebar 'Aluminium alarms' for more details.)

- **Copper and brass:** Many old-fashioned jam pans are made from these materials, but times move on; don't invest here because copper and brass pans aren't acid-resistant.

- **Enamel:** Although common in years gone by, few enamel tools survive totally intact and any tiny cracks or chips reveal a ferrous (iron-based) metal underneath. This metal reacts with acids including vinegar, so avoid these items. If you don't, at best your food will taste metallic and at worst you may even poison yourself – or someone else.

- **Galvanised equipment:** You find this sturdy weatherproof coating, more suited to animal feeding and drinking equipment, on robust gear, but galvanised equipment is fit only for outdoor use. So while you may be eyeing up the horse's drinking bucket because of its handy size, keep it well out of the kitchen. The zinc coating breaks down in the presence of acid, releasing toxins that you really don't want in your preserves.

Avoid all the materials in the preceding list in any of your preserving equipment: at the very least, they can taint your food and in a worse-case scenario, they're downright poisonous.

Aluminium alarms

I have a firm memory as a child of watching a boiling pot of chutney cooking in an aluminium pan and staring at a silvery sheen on the top bubbling away. I'm only guessing, but most likely the boiling vinegar was stripping a layer of aluminium from the inside of the vessel. What worries me now is that I most likely ate all the chutney, oblivious to the health risk!

Certain metals – see the list in the earlier section 'Going potty with pans and bowls' section – corrode and in doing so may release toxins, especially when heated in the presence of an acid. For this reason, make sure that you choose stainless steel or non-metallic materials when cooking and mixing acidic foods.

Tooling up

Equipping yourself well makes life during a preserving session much easier. You probably already own most of the equipment in the following lists.

The following are some essentials to wear:

- ✔ **Apron, sensible shoes, rolled-up or short sleeves, long hair ties:** To keep you clean.

- ✔ **Cotton under-gloves:** If you plan to attempt hot-bottling. (See the later section 'Using preserving jars and bottles from specialist suppliers'; I describe hot-bottling in detail in Chapter 5.)

- ✔ **Rubber gloves (medium or industrial strength):** To protect your hands when washing with hot water or moving around hot jars.

The following are some more essential pieces of kitchen equipment:

- ✔ **Antibacterial spray:** Use as the instructions say, before starting your preserving, if you also use the surfaces for meat or muddy vegetable preparation.

- ✔ **Bain-marie:** This water bath has an inner pan for gentle heating with no risk of burning.

Improvise this useful piece of equipment by floating a stainless steel pan inside a large preserving pan, creating a non-direct heating system.

- ✔ **Chopping board:** Use thoroughly disinfected wooden or plastic boards for non-meat use; also handy for placing hot jars on.

- ✔ **Colander:** Preferably, use a colander made of stainless steel (check out the preceding section to find out why).

✔ **Funnels:** Use a small-mouthed funnel for filling bottles and a wide-mouthed one for jam-pot filling (see Figure 2-1).

If you need a funnel in a hurry, make your own by chopping a plastic bottle in half. The top, when upended, makes a good funnel, but make sure that your improvised tool's material withstands the heat of whatever you're pouring.

✔ **Measuring jugs:** Large and small capacities are useful.

✔ **Pestle and mortar:** This useful piece of equipment is for grinding spices.

✔ **Preserving pan:** This large, open-mouthed stainless steel pan with a heavy bottom for even heat distribution must be the king of preserving equipment. It needs to be open-mouthed for good evaporation and have a high handle for safely carrying hot liquids (and often a side handle too). These pans also have a pouring indent and are scored with capacity measurements to help you gauge quantities. Preserving revolves around this piece of equipment and many of the recipes in this book involve using one. You can make the largest single batches in a home-preserving environment with this type of pan (usually 4.5 kilograms maximum) safely and efficiently.

This essential preserving tool is well worth investing in (if you borrow one, you won't want to give it back!).

Figure 2-1:
A wide-mouthed funnel for filling jars.

✔ **Scales:** Simple spring scales or electronic scales, the choice is yours.

✔ **Timer:** Yours may be an integral part of your cooker, an app on your mobile phone or a free-standing item (see Figure 2-2).

Following is a selection of useful handheld implements to keep available:

✔ **Graters:** Two types – a box grater and a flat one – give plenty of scope for different size parings (see Figure 2-2).

✔ **Knives:** Use sharp, stainless steel knives and keep several sizes available. Make sure that the size is comfortable in your hand for the task; chopping is part of food preparation fun!

Efficient use of your knives follows on from having sharp knives, so keep a knife sharpener handy, too.

✔ **Lemon juicer:** Lemons feature often in preserve-making for their acid juice (see Figure 2-2).

✔ **Measuring spoons:** Use purpose-made measures for accuracy and have more than one set (see Figure 2-2).

✔ **Scissors:** Use to cut packaging.

✔ **Sieve:** Plastic and metal are both useful for straining and hand pureeing.

✔ **Stainless steel spoons:** Spoons include teaspoon, tablespoon, slotted spoon and ladle.

✔ **Vegetable peeler:** Use with or without coring attachment and masher.

✔ **Wooden spoons and other utensils:** You need short, medium and extra-long handled wooden spoons; and especially for jam- and jelly-making, heat-resistant spatulas (see Figure 2-2).

✔ **Zester:** This tool makes easy work of removing the *zest* or thin parings of lemon skin, but the finest side of your box grater can do the job too.

Here are a few more mundane, yet essential, bits and pieces:

✔ **Compost bin:** Invest in a sturdy bucket with a carrying handle and work out a good composting system, because you always have plenty of vegetable and fruit waste when you take your preserving seriously. Fortunately, when you grow your vegetables too, you'll probably have a good compost heap in your garden or allotment already – the perfect place to put all that vegetable waste. Remember to empty the bucket containing your vegetable and fruit trimmings on your compost heap regularly, but don't mix in your cooked food waste. Save cooked food and meat waste for the sealable bin provided by your local council.

✔ **Labels and writing tool:** Make your own or buy sticky labels to write on with a permanent marker, and never mix up your preserves again.

✔ **Oven gloves:** Use to carry hot items.

Figure 2-2: Miscellaneous useful kitchen utensils.

- ✔ **Paper and kitchen towels:** Use to mop up spillages and wipe rims of jars and hands.

- ✔ **Tea towels and dishcloths:** Use clean cloths, permanent and disposable types, for all the usual reasons, and for carrying hot dishes when oven gloves are too cumbersome.

Buying new jars or recycling old ones

Both new and recycled jars are handy: buy new jars from cooking or catering shops or order them online. This section points out the various uses for jars.

Sterilise both new and recycled jars before use.

Recycling jars and bottles

You're doing what generations before you did when recycling bottles and jars for your preserves. Use good-quality, un-chipped ones in all sorts of sizes for everything except heat-treating (also referred to as hot-bottling; Chapter 5 hots things up for you on this subject).

- ✔ **Everyday jars:** For your jams, jellies and chutneys. Collect various sizes of glass jars and raid the recycling bins of friends and neighbours for handy sizes. In particular, keep an eye open for small, straight-sided pots, which are especially handy when making fruit cheeses (you may prefer to turn out the preserve whole; Chapters 10 and 11 contain suitable recipes).

✔ **Screw-top, clamp-top or bottles needing corks:** For wines, flavoured vinegars and untreated cordials.

✔ **Wide-mouthed bottles:** For ketchups and runny sauces.

Topping off with new and old lids

You may have lids with your recycled jars that are perfectly good to reuse. New jars come with new lids, but sometimes at an extra cost, so be sure that you order both.

Sterilise lids and tops as you would jars:

✔ **Cellophane jam-pot closures:** An excellent alternative to metal lids, the packs contain wax disc, cellophane tops, elastic bands and labels. They're an inexpensive way to seal your pots and they're available in cooking shops as well as online. Buy the correct size, follow the instructions on the label and you can't go wrong.

✔ **Non-corrosive lids:** Buy these new lids in a cooking shop, or reuse as long as plastic coatings aren't scratched or chipped or retain lingering smells (check the recycled curry paste ones especially).

Using cellophane jam-pot closures is so simple that even a child (or husband!) can do it, and so can be the perfect job to give responsible children to do with warm, freshly made pots of preserves. Properly done, the cellophane stretches to a tight convex drum before the child's eyes, just like magic.

Chapter 3 has plenty of sterilising methods to choose from.

Using preserving jars and bottles from specialist suppliers

When heat-treating (also called hot-bottling – see Chapter 5 for an explanation) jars or bottles, use only jars made especially for that purpose: that is, heat-resistant ones with rubber-sealed tops.

Two main types of preserving jars are available:

✔ Preserving jars with removable (usually glass, but sometimes metal) tops, screw bands and rubber seals

✔ Preserving jars and bottles with clamp tops and rubber seals

Use the jars or bottles over and over again, replacing the rubber seals each time you heat-treat.

Good high-street catering and cooking shops (or online ones) carry a supply of new rubber seals, but make sure that you take one of your old ones with you when you buy new (or measure up carefully) because plenty of different sizes exist.

Whatever the purpose of your jars, they need to be free from chips, cracks or any other blemishes.

Obtaining Useful Specialist Tools and Handy Extras

The previous sections in this chapter describe all the essentials that you need to get storing and preserving. But, of course, you can also buy plenty of other items to help things go smoothly or to reduce the physical effort involved. This section looks at some options, priced from a couple of pounds upwards.

The important specialist piece of equipment is a large heavy-bottomed preserving pan, but that's so essential that I describe it in the earlier section 'Tooling up'.

Buying specialist equipment

In this section, I list a selection of useful items for preserving enthusiasts that aren't exceptionally expensive. You find most of them in a good cooking or catering shop, or online (so why not add to your Christmas wish list?):

- ✔ **Cheese cloth:** This special food-grade cloth has a looser weave than butter muslin (see later in this list). Line a sieve or colander with one or more layers to make a handy straining tool. Cheese cloth is inexpensive to buy in cooking or catering shops.

- ✔ **Food mill:** If your favourite recipe includes sieving food to a puree, you may find a food mill cuts down your time and effort by half (see Figure 2-3).

- ✔ **Jelly bag:** Made from various materials (often flannel), a jelly bag is an open-mouthed cone attached to a circular frame, usually with long ties. The more modern versions have plastic legs for suspending the jelly bag over a bowl or bucket to catch the straining liquor.

- ✔ **Muslin cloth:** Also called butter muslin, this cloth is a tight-weave, food-grade cloth suitable for straining food and people often use it to make herb pouches for adding flavour to preserves. Muslin clothes are inexpensive to buy in cooking or catering shops.

New cloth equipment needs washing, rinsing well and scalding with boiling water before using for any type of straining. Also, liquids run better through damp cloth.

Figure 2-3:
A food mill.

FOOD MILL

Some preserving books advise using disposable dishcloths for straining food. If you buy top-quality disposable coloured cloths and are sure that dye won't leak into your preserve, go ahead. But some lesser-quality cloths leak dye, so pay attention when you use these dishcloths for other tasks. If you see any hint of colour leaching, stick to a purpose-made, food-use grade of material as a straining cloth, or a well-washed and well-worn dishcloth, or a clean pillow case.

✔ **Sugar thermometer:** A good-quality sugar (or jam) thermometer accurately registers the higher temperature of boiling sugary liquids. Markings for the setting points for jam and toffee are clearly set out. Suspending the bulb of the thermometer in the centre of the liquid with a clip, or protective support, gives the most accurate readings; look out for ones made from stainless steel or other heat-resistant material.

✔ **Wine-making equipment:** Whole shops and online sites devote themselves to this subject. For a starter pack on home wine-making, stagger along to Chapter 9 where you can find a list of vital equipment.

Getting serious: Specialist equipment to die for

For serious preservers who have the means, go to town with the following:

✔ **Automatic dehydrator:** Chapter 8 has more information about this item and a home-made solar drying tool too.

✔ **Blender and liquidiser:** For pulverising and pureeing food, these items are especially good for making smooth soups.

✔ **Electronic scales:** Small or large, and from simple and inexpensive to large industrial models, electronic scales are an accurate way to measure. Do check their accuracy from time to time, however, by weighing something familiar; they 'drift' over time and don't stand getting wet.

Get to grips with the 'Tare' facility, which can take a little working out but which is a useful way to speed up measuring time. At the press of a button, this facility automatically subtracts the weight of any container you place on the scales, giving you an accurate weight reading of only the produce inside.

✔ **Food processors:** This piece of equipment cuts down the chopping time (as well as your vegetables) but raises the noise levels. It also takes away the uniqueness of cutting and chopping by hand, which some people consider a relaxing part of the job of preserving. You must decide what matters most to you –speed or peace and quiet.

✔ **Vacuum packer:** Table-top vacuum packers are now available; order one in your cooking or catering shop, or online.

Gathering Together Recipes

This book contains a good range of recipes, but don't restrict yourself. Many of the best recipes can come from friends and relations, who are only too happy to supply them and any handy tips too. Books, television programmes and the Internet are other sources – and don't forget your local library, which may be able to order books that you request.

Reading and understanding recipes

Understanding the basic terms and conventions for preserving recipes is similar to any other recipe; read your recipe several times and refer to it at each stage in the process. Times given with recipes are approximate, depending on many factors, so don't use them as a fill-in activity before an important appointment or train journey: hurrying and preserve-making don't go together well. Approaching your preserving tasks in a calm and relaxed manner gives the best results.

Some terms that you come upon in preserving recipes are:

✔ **Adding a quantity of sugar to a measured weight of fruit pulp:** Weigh and write down in your notebook the precise weights of all your most frequently used pans. Then weigh your pan with the ingredients inside and subtract the weight of the pan, thus leaving you with a accurate weight for the content of the pan. You can then work out the quantity of sugar you need, with no messy sticky transferring of ingredients from one place to another.

✔ **Adding a quantity of sugar to a measured capacity of prepared liquid:** Pour your liquid into a measuring jug (especially with small quantities) and work out the quantity of sugar before returning both to the pan for further cooking; or read the calibrations on your preserving pan if they're clear.

✔ **Rapid boil:** On a high heat, your boiling substance is foaming and breaking the surface of the liquid. The boiling may slow down from the edges when nearing setting point and show as a more sluggish 'plopping'. Watch out for splashes with this technique: time to use the long-handled wooden spoon, I think. (See the earlier section 'Tooling up'.)

✔ **Reducing:** You can drive off liquid by boiling for a length of time.

When the recipe states to reduce by half, jot down where on the calibration of your preserving pan your liquid is, and simmer until half that liquid remains.

✔ **Rolling boil:** A harder boil with larger bubbles rolling over each other, but without plopping or foaming.

✔ **Setting point:** The temperature at which your jams begin to thicken. (I describe how to test for it in Chapter 5.)

✔ **Simmering:** Boiling with small bubbles that hardly disturb the surface of the water.

Indulging in quality ingredients

However well you store and preserve something, you can't improve the ingredients you start with. If you want the best, pick at the optimum time, discarding what's not good enough (the compost heap isn't fussy) and keeping the best for your preserves.

For jams and jellies, use perfect, just ripe or under-ripe fruit; chutneys need good, firm produce (cutting around bruises and blemishes of damaged produce is fine). Delicious wines and ciders come from all sorts of quality, and even vegetable peelings, and so can be a really thrifty way to use up the dregs.

You always have to buy additional things to complete the recipe ingredients, and when you do, choose the best you can afford. Sometimes the recipe states a definite type of sugar or vinegar, particularly where colouring is important (piccalilli has to be bright yellow, for example, and so needs a clear white vinegar). At other times, you're left to choose the type yourself.

If you take care to be chemical-free in your garden, make sure that you also seek out extra ingredients with a chemical-free or organic label; otherwise all your efforts are for nothing.

Chapter 3

Preserving Garden Produce Safely

Getting down and dirty in the vegetable patch is one of life's joys. Plunging your hands into the soil and crumbling earth between your fingers connects you to the basic building blocks of life itself. The old adage 'you'll eat a peck of dirt before you die' is all the more true when you regularly poke around in a veg plot. And as you pile up peelings, stalks, leaves and weeds into friable, sweet-smelling compost, remember that none of this process can happen without the help of billions and trillions of bacteria.

Although these micro-organisms are essential and often beneficial to life on earth, some specific bacteria can get out of balance in situations where they aren't wanted and attack your lovingly home-produced food. Therefore, knowing how to store your garden produce safely and how to avoid *cross-contamination* (unwittingly moving bacteria from place to place) is vital, and not at all difficult when you're aware of the potential pitfalls. . .

. . . Which is where this chapter comes in. Here I describe how to keep 'bad' bacteria at bay, using your knowledge to fend off unwanted nasties, creating environments where they can't thrive and promoting your own healthy hygiene and storage habits to ensure that you and your food stay safe.

Cleaning Up with Commonsense Safety Guidelines

Don't let safety worries make you timid about having a go at preserving and storing your home-grown food. All you need to do is take basic, common-sense precautions and follow a regular and safe routine, as I describe in this section. If your ancestors hadn't preserved food to survive (and they managed without refrigeration and fancy packaging materials), you wouldn't be here at all! So preserving food without killing off everyone who eats it is obviously do-able!

You gain confidence when you discover a little about the problems you face (see the later section 'Recognising and Dealing with Nasties') and what's appropriate for the kind of food preservation you want to do. In fact, preserving itself is built specifically around lowering the possibility of spoilage bacteria and their teeny weeny friends getting in and munching their way through your produce, leaving problems in their wake. When you store and preserve food properly, using good materials and ingredients, you aren't going to experience many problems.

Following a sensible hygiene routine (as I describe in the later section 'Cultivating good practices') and keeping things simple helps a lot. For example, if you never carry out the more complicated preservation and storage procedures that have more potential for mistakes to happen, you can certainly avoid many of the pitfalls. If you decide to freeze portions of cordials until you need them (Chapter 9 tells you how to make cordials), you don't have to worry about lurking bacteria in bottle tops. And if your badly behaved cat is likely to walk mucky footprints all over the kitchen surfaces while you're chopping up ingredients, just shut it outside until you finish (however much it whines to come in!).

If you're worried that any of your stored produce is unsafe to eat, take a look at Chapters 19 and 20. These short chapters can set your mind at rest or help you realise that your suspicions were right and that produce isn't safe to eat.

If you don't want to eat something yourself, don't give it to anyone else, unless of course you just hate the taste!

Boxing clever with first aid

Preparing your own food means sometimes using sharp implements and boiling substances, some that boil at a higher temperature than water. Splashing scalding-hot sugar syrup calls for immediate attention, and because your pickled beetroot already has its own lovely colour, you don't want to add in your own blood-red colouring from any cuts or grazes!

Stocking a simple first-aid kit and keeping it to hand is common sense. Your kit needs to contain the following basic items:

✔ Eye wash

✔ Plasters (get the special food-grade blue plasters from chemists)

✔ Scissors

✔ Wound dressings

Cover cuts and grazes completely; bacteria live on the edges of wounds.

Occasionally, you need to reach for something stronger than soap and water for cleaning, so keep an antibacterial spray handy but be careful with chemicals (see the later section 'Taking care with chemicals' for the precautions to take).

Gathering up the cleaning tools

Humans, of course, can make mistakes, get distracted and forget things; and sometimes your equipment fails you, breaks or wears out, leaving room for trouble to brew.

Following an unintended occurrence, you need to decide whether the problem is just a question of mopping up or whether the consequences are serious enough to set your alarm bells ringing; perhaps you do need to err on the side of caution and ditch the offending article (or at least relegate it to the compost bin).

No doubt you've most of the following items in the house anyway, but here's a reminder to jog your memory in case stocks are running low:

✔ Antibacterial spray or other sterilant

✔ Bowls or buckets for washing up: plastic ones are as good as any

✔ Clean cloths: need to be really clean or even disposable ones

✔ Clean drying cloths

✔ Hand soap and nailbrush

✔ Newspaper for collecting compostables

✔ Overall or apron

✔ Paper towels for any sticky mopping-up jobs

✔ Rubber gloves: strong ones

✔ Washing-up liquid, unperfumed

✔ Water, both hot and cold: lashings of it

All these items are, of course, in addition to your specialist tools and implements, which need to be clean and ready for the job. (Chapter 2 has the low-down on equipment.)

Cultivating good practices

Deciding on and sticking to a sensible hygiene routine, leading from the vegetables in the ground to your preparation and cooking areas, gives you the best results with the fewest problems.

Knowing what to do before starting with the food

Clear away any unwanted clutter in your preparation area and around the sink and surfaces where you plan to work, making room for bulky fresh garden produce. You need plenty of space for manoeuvring when you're processing food and the last thing you need is to be tripping over toys and shoes left on the floor while you're carrying boiling-hot jam pans. (I cover jam-making in Chapter 5.)

Carry out a general wash-down of the area with hot, soapy water (wear rubber gloves so that you can have the water piping hot). Use a clean cloth on any surfaces or sinks that you plan to use. Don't forget the taps.

Choose good-quality, perfume-free washing-up liquid in the kitchen alongside food; the perfume doesn't clean anyway. You don't want to make a delicate, naturally flavoured mint jelly that contains the lingering whiff of lemon from a strong washing-up liquid. Pick your liquid for its ability to shift grease and grime and save the pongy soaps and squirts for the bathroom.

Raw meat, especially raw chicken, and your fresh vegetables *don't* mix. To avoid cross-contamination, keep any chopping or cutting boards, knives and so on for raw meat preparation only, and use a different set for vegetables only. Remember that cross-contamination works both ways: you can contaminate meat with soil-borne bacteria and vegetables with meaty contaminants.

Use some sort of code to recognise your different implements. For example, try buying a chopping board shaped in the outline of a hen for your meat preparation and keep a potato-shaped one for veg chopping. Alternatively, colour code: keep red-handled knives for meat and green for vegetables.

If you really do have to use the same implements for meat and veggies, now is the time for a really hot, soapy wash, allowing implements to drip dry and spraying them afterwards with an antibacterial preparation. Follow the instructions on the label carefully.

Poor hygiene and cross-contamination from raw meat or pets are the most common source of problems. Wash your hands and keep pets out of working food preparation areas (flip to the later section 'Grappling with pesky pests' for more details).

Bringing the garden produce to the kitchen area

You can use plastic buckets to carry your fruit and veg to the kitchen, but garden trugs are particularly handy and designed specifically for carrying gathered fruits and vegetables. *Trugs* are flat, open baskets traditionally made from natural materials such as wicker or split-wide shavings of wood woven into a wicker frame. Using these purpose-made baskets is the first step in bringing in perfect crops for processing.

Trugs have a wide, flat bottom so that the long fruits, such as runner beans, don't get damaged. They gather garden produce without damage or bruising, thus avoiding quicker spoilage.

Using trugs for gathering the garden and orchard produce is a joy. A trug-full of freshly picked produce is well worth recording with a photograph for posterity: you can look back with pride at your gardening efforts while eating bread and home-made jam by the fireside in the dead of winter.

You can never avoid dirt entirely, of course, but you can prevent bringing the majority of the earth and any unused outer leaves into the preparation area. As you walk past the compost heap on the way to the kitchen, do a once-over of the veg. Most gardeners carry a penknife in their pocket for such jobs. Scrape off any clods of earth and whip off any woody stalks and scruffy or obviously damaged parts of the plant that you aren't going to use in the finished produce. You also avoid blocking up the sink pipes with soil when you do this task outside.

Whereas most shop-bought fruit and vegetables have been through preparation stages (washed, irradiated, bagged, sorted and sifted for size until they hardly look like the real thing), your garden produce is as fresh as fresh can be, which also means covered in mud, blemishes and creepy crawlies. Muddy leeks or carrots drop and smear mud everywhere in your clean kitchen area, especially if they come in from a wet garden. Therefore, resting them on newspaper by the sink before preparing them makes easy work of clearing up later. And you can screw up the muddy paper with any chopped-out bad bits together and pop them into your compost afterwards. You don't need to waste anything; just recycle.

Changing roles from outside worker to inside worker

When you're inside with your produce, you need to change from outdoor gardening clothes to indoor clothes. (Wellington boots are exactly right for the garden but lose points on style and usability in the kitchen!)

From a safety point of view, remember that footwear that's fine for, say, a sunny day in the garden (such as open-toed sandals) isn't appropriate when working with hot substances.

Covering up with an apron or overalls saves on washing clothes later.

Handling Personal Cleanliness and Food Safety

In this section, I describe how to keep yourself, your food containers and your food clean and safe in order to banish bacterial baddies. For details on the micro-organisms themselves (and such knowledge is a vital part of winning the battle) turn to 'Unmasking spoil-sport bacteria and micro-organisms', later in this chapter.

Washing your hands

You may be wondering why I cover hand-washing here rather than under the earlier 'Cleaning Up with Commonsense Safety Guidelines' section. After all, you wash your hands several times a day anyway (I hope!), and so what's more commonsensical than that? But the question is, do you really get your hands clean?

Most people wash their hands as follows. They wet their hands under running water or in a basin of water, apply soap and then rub their palms together to spread the soap around. They attend to the tops of the hands and often interlace their fingers to clean in-between them with the rubbing. They then rinse off the soap and hopefully any dirt, visible or otherwise. Job done.

If that process sounds familiar, you're the same as millions of other people. Tests, using UV-sensitive material, find that most people carry out a hand-washing routine like this one. Unfortunately, studies also show that on average people don't wash their hands effectively and that the hands are, consequently, the main carrier of bacteria. The tips of the fingers and thumbs get the least attention in such hand-washing.

Some people, however, wash their hands more thoroughly: those who are trained to have clean hands. Surgeons, for example, spend a long time on a scrub-down routine before going into the operating theatre. Preserving food generally isn't as life threatening as removing someone's appendix, but just being aware that you may leave out finger and thumb tips should encourage you to act differently.

So, in your next hand-washing session, be aware of your actions. Pay special attention to thumbs and fingertips; after all, they're the parts of your hands that you use every time you pick anything up or do anything delicate or fiddly.

Keep a nailbrush beside the sink to remind you of your new, more thorough hand-washing technique and to help polish up the tips of your fingers as well as removing grime from under your fingernails.

Sterilising your food jars

You need to use containers to store your preserves. If you use glass bottles and jars, even brand new ones, sterilising them first is essential to stop any bacteria becoming trapped inside the jars with your preserves.

The method you choose for effective sterilisation depends on the equipment you feel happiest using and have access to, but all the methods that I describe in this section result in clean, safe jars.

You need to get used jars and bottles completely free from debris before the sterilising process begins. Otherwise, the sterilisation method simply bakes old food onto the container.

For awkward-shaped bottles and jars, use a bottlebrush to get into inaccessible corners, or tip loose tea leaves into the container with a little detergent and shake vigorously. This mild, food-friendly abrasive removes obstinate debris. For really tough jobs, allow a time for soaking first.

Oven method

Here's how to sterilise food storage jars and bottles in your conventional oven:

1. **Gather up your glass jars and bottles, examining for cracks or chips and discarding anything imperfect.**
2. **Put on rubber gloves and wash jars and bottles in hot, soapy water.**

3. Rinse in hot, clean water.

4. Place in a cold, clean oven and heat to 120 degrees Celsius (250 degrees Fahrenheit/Gas mark $^1/_2$) for 30 minutes.

5. Leave to cool slightly and remove with oven gloves; avoid touching the rim of the jar.

6. Fill the sterilised containers while still warm.

Microwave method

You can use your microwave oven to sterilise containers as follows:

1. Gather up your glass jars and bottles, examining for cracks or chips and discarding anything imperfect.

2. Put on rubber gloves and wash jars and bottles in hot, soapy water.

3. Rinse in hot, clean water.

4. Half fill each bottle or jar with water and heat on full power in the microwave until the water has boiled for at least one minute.

5. Remove with oven gloves; avoid touching the rim of the jar.

6. Swirl the water in the jars and pour away; drain the jars upside down on a clean tea towel until dry.

7. Fill the sterilised containers while warm.

Dishwasher method

Sterilising en masse is easy with a dishwasher:

1. Clean your jars and bottles first using the first steps from the earlier 'Oven method' section.

2. Place jars and lids in the dishwasher, run at its hottest setting without detergent and use the drying mode on your machine if you have it.

3. Remove with protective gloves and fill the sterilised jars and bottles while still hot.

Sterilising tablet method

People use this method mainly to sterilise babies' drinking bottles but you can also use it where you're dealing with a restricted supply of clean running water. Use it when storing robust chutneys, but not for delicately flavoured preserves because it may leave a slight taste.

The tablet method certainly sterilises your jars and bottles. Buy the sterilising tablets from a chemist and follow the instructions precisely, dissolving the tablets and soaking the jars.

Ensure that you sterilise food storage jars and bottles even if they're brand new.

Spotting the rotten apple

The easiest and quickest way to deal with your stores of fruit and vegetables is at harvest time. They need hardly any preparation work: just pop them into the appropriate bags, boxes, cellars or lofts and you're done. (See Chapter 4 for details of this type of cool storage.)

In an ideal world, you've kept absolutely perfect specimens of your fruit and vegetables, but in reality a bruise, bug or blemish begins to grow when you're not looking. Checking your stored crops from time to time gives you the chance to weed out and use up anything that seems to be 'on the turn', and to check whether the temperature of your storage rooms is right for the produce. If lots of produce is deteriorating, you've one of the following problems:

- **Too much heat:** Check whether you recently turned the heating on in the house or whether the low winter sun is coming in through a window directly onto your stores, warming them up. Extra warmth accelerates microbial growth and triggers a 'spring' response in some cases, shooting to seed. Roots go woody as the energy stored starts to grow a new plant.

- **Too cold:** Store rooms such as wooden garden sheds can freeze solid at any time. Although it may take a little while to deteriorate, produce that has been frozen through doesn't keep. Salvage what you can and use it up quickly before the rot sets in.

- **Too dry:** Fruits like a mildly humid atmosphere. Leave a bowl of water near them, or if you've earth floors in a stone or brick shed, dampen them slightly for orchard fruit storage.

- **Too wet:** Leaking roofs or walls running with condensation encourage moulds. Fix the problem and then space out your produce. If you've access to a dehumidifier, use it on full power to remove water from the atmosphere and then judge whether it needs to be a permanent fixture.

Rotten fruit and vegetables aren't palatable or visually appealing and so no one (except perhaps a mouse, a problem I address later in the section 'Grappling with pesky pests') is going to want to eat them. Also, mould and fungal spores soon infect adjacent stores, so take them right out of the vicinity.

Wrapping your favourite fruits individually in greaseproof paper or even newspaper puts a physical barrier between them and airborne spores, keeping them usable longer.

Expect the stored vegetables and fruit to change in look and texture from when you first stored them. Inevitably, the skins suffer evaporation and wrinkling, which is fine from an eating point of view.

In other cases, some produce improves with storing. You may have put away pears or apples that felt like hard bullets and tasted dry and astringent in the autumn, only to find that by the New Year they're bursting with sweetness and soft enough to bite into easily. When you have a pleasant surprise like that, record it for future reference; if you don't know the name of the variety, take a photo. Someone else may be able to identify it for you.

Check your boxes, bags, lofts and cellars regularly and weed out rotten produce.

Keeping your food safe: Tried and tested methods

Preserving food is all about creating an environment in which spoilage can't occur. People have used the following methods (ordered from the more traditional to the more modern) to store food safely for thousands of years:

- ✔ **Drying:** Includes the ancient practice of sun-drying, and applying direct heat, gently over a period of time, fiercely or by removing moisture from the atmosphere using modern equipment such as dehumidifiers (Chapter 8 has more on drying). Bacteria can't grow without water.

- ✔ **Salt:** Draws moisture out of substances and creates an environment hostile to bacteria (as I explain in Chapter 8).

- ✔ **Sugar:** Preserves with a high proportion of sugar or mixes with other bacteria inhibitors (look at Chapter 5 for jammy treats and Chapter 9 for drinkable sweets).

✔ **Acid:** Acid preserves using, or combining, vinegar with other substances (Chapter 6 has plenty more about this subject).

✔ **Freezing:** A modern method, unless you count the odd frozen mammoth caught up in a glacier! (Chapter 7 contains all the necessary info.)

✔ **Vacuum packing:** Removes the air and any airborne contaminants (again, turn to the ever useful Chapter 8).

Smoking is another form of drying, but people rarely use it for home-grown vegetables or fruit. Trendy smoked garlic tends to add flavour rather than preservation, although smoking fish really does preserve it for a long period of time.

Some bacteria are *anaerobic*, which means that they can survive without oxygen in a vacuum pack; check out the later section 'Sizing up "bad" bacteria'.

Taking care with chemicals

Keep an antibacterial spray handy to clean surfaces or tools that come into contact with raw meats (for handling precautions, flip to the earlier section 'Knowing what to do before starting with the food'). If your garage or garden shed doubles up as a store room, you may need to carry out a through wash-down with a sterilant such as hypo-chloride or a weak bleach solution.

Always read and precisely follow the instructions and amounts to use on the product labels.

Make sure that no leaky tins or containers are lurking in the vicinity. Any obvious leaks or spillages onto foodstuffs are a food hazard; take them seriously and throw out anything in direct contact with chemicals.

Strong chemicals can eat through plastic containers and impart an unpleasant smell and taste even when they aren't in direct contact with the food. Petrol-tainted carrots just don't make for a good dinner!

Recognising and Dealing with Nasties

Each single gram (0.035 ounce) of soil contains on average 1,000,000 bacteria!

Now that I have your attention and you can see how the numbers stack up against you, here's the gen on bacteria and related micro-organisms. These tiny creatures make up the majority of the world's living creatures. Because they're miniscule and you can't see, or often even smell or taste them, you can only spot bacteria down the sights of a microscope and with training in microbiology. But they glue together much of human life, invisibly doing all sorts of essential jobs quietly and efficiently in the background.

In the wrong place at the wrong time, however, certain bacteria and other micro-organisms can jeopardise food safety, and in turn your health and that of your family too.

Most commonly, food poisoning causes a quick 24 hours of unpleasant symptoms before your life can continue as normal. Much, much rarer, but worth knowing a little about, are the serious food-borne illnesses that can be debilitating or even life threatening.

Although occasional situations do arise with food-related illnesses, and some can be serious for the very young, frail or elderly, these occurrences are fortunately rare.

Here are the four main spoilers of food:

- ✔ **Contamination:** Anything objectionable on your produce may constitute contamination. Even if not necessarily a food safety risk, it may still render the produce unusable or impossible to clean effectively. Contaminants such as spilt chemicals are a food hazard and shards of glass or metal are certainly a physical risk.

- ✔ **Enzymes:** Chemicals produced by living organisms sometimes carry on working even after a plant is dead, producing unpalatable or unpleasant compounds. The signs are usually pretty obvious – patches or whole decomposing fruits and vegetables – when enzymes have been at work for any length of time.

- ✔ **Micro-organisms:** Including bacteria, mould and fungal spores, and viral infections, these can live and multiply on fresh produce or use it as a carrier to a human host. I deal with the main culprits in more detail in the next section 'Unmasking spoil-sport bacteria and micro-organisms'.

- ✔ **Oxidation:** You see oxidation working at first hand when you cut an apple open and the cut surface turns brown. Although not in itself dangerous, oxidation is unsightly and speeds up spoilage.

Unmasking spoil-sport bacteria and micro-organisms

Bacteria or other micro-organisms cause food poisoning and food-borne infections. They've different ways of infecting you and different levels of seriousness in their effects.

Food poisoning

Short-term (24–48 hours) vomiting and/or diarrhoea are your body's way of getting rid of a poison effectively. The body ejects water alongside the poisons, so you need to top up with plenty of liquids (to stop the body becoming dehydrated) even if you don't really feel like drinking. Food poisoning bacteria have grown on the food, multiplying into millions at a vast rate. Although certainly unpleasant, you don't usually suffer any long-term side effects.

Clostridium botulinum is particularly nasty, though. Check out the later Table 3-1 for more detailed information.

Food-borne disease

Long-term illnesses are caused by food-borne infections. These diseases work in a different manner to food poisoning, using food or water as a carrier to get themselves into your body, where they then multiply and do damage. It can take a long time before symptoms of a food-borne illness appear. Ingesting just a low dosage of these nasties can cause a serious illness. They're also transmitted by hands and in airborne droplets.

Fortunately, preserving food well creates an environment where these bugs can't thrive. You can also get clues about how to tame and dispel them before they cause problems by knowing in advance the circumstances in which they lurk.

Sizing up 'bad' bacteria

Table 3-1 lists the most commonly found micro-organisms that can become a food hazard.

The 'at risk' groups that I refer to in the table are the very young, pregnant women and their foetuses, the elderly and people with suppressed immune systems, such as those having chemotherapy treatments, AIDS patients, diabetics and alcoholics.

Table 3-1		Some Common 'Bad' Bacteria			
Bacteria	**Found In**	**Dangers**	**Avoidance Measures**	**Symptoms**	**Other Info**
Campylobacter jejuni	Wild birds, farm animals, pets	Pet-to-human transmission, cross-contamination, raw and cooked foods, sewage, anaerobic conditions; survives vacuum packing	Separation of raw and cooked food, personal hygiene especially in household with pets, correct pasteurisation or cooking, prevention of cross-contamination	Sporadic gastro-enteritis and acute, infectious diarrhoea lasting up to seven days but further bouts can occur	
Clostridium botulinum	Soil and water	Anaerobic conditions, vac pack, canning, bottling	High temperatures (canning temperature determined by spore destruction)	Neurotoxic effects and death	Spore forming
Clostridium perfringens	Cooked meat and gravy	Cross-contamination, anaerobic conditions	Separation of cooked and raw foods	Diarrhoea and abdominal pain	Spore forming
Eschericia coli (E. coli) 0157	Animal dung, soil, unpasteurised apple cider, contaminated water	Highly persistent bacteria, low infective dose, produces dangerous toxins	Separation of raw and cooked meats, strict personal hygiene particularly when dealing with animals; maintain home sewerage outlets, avoid leakage into well or bore hole water	Fever, vomiting, abdominal pain and blood in diarrhoea	Potential complications; a second stage sometimes follows with kidney failure and death

Bacteria	Found In	Dangers	Avoidance Measures	Symptoms	Other Info
Listeria mono-cytogenes	Chilled and delicatessen products, soft cheeses and pre-prepared salads; but any human or animal can harbour the bug	Survives in salt, tolerates dryness and alkaline situations, multiplies at low temperatures	Wash salads thoroughly, 'at risk group' (see warning) avoid raw milk products, pasteurisation	Fever, septicaemia, meningitis	Not dangerous in healthy adults but dangerous for 'at risk' groups and causes miscarriage in pregnant women
Salmonella	Eggs, poultry raw meat, raw milk	Cross-contamination, carriers	Strict personal hygiene, separation of raw and cooked foods	Diarrhoea, vomiting, fever, abdominal pain	
Staphylococcus aureus	Human nose, throat, hair, hands, pimples, boils; also in animals with problems such as mastitis	Poor hygiene practices	Strict personal hygiene, hand-washing; avoid working with food during illness (for example you have a cold)	Diarrhoea, acute vomiting, nausea, abdominal pain, collapse and fall in body temperature	

Spoiling the work of spores

Spores are reproductive cells. They're the dormant, survival form of some bacteria that arise when conditions threaten the original bacterium. Spores are dangerous because, in spore form, bacteria can survive extreme conditions. When conditions become favourable again, the bacteria emerge and begin again to multiply. One example is the *botulinum* bacteria; the danger lies in their ability to withstand freezing conditions, normal cooking temperatures, low acid and alkaline concentrations and *anaerobic conditions* (where oxygen is absent). The 'botulinum cook' is a high-pressure canning temperature set expressly to eliminate these persistent spores. Depending on the food, the temperature reaches 121 degrees Celsius (250 degrees Fahrenheit) and is carried out as an industrial process with highly specialised equipment when canning foods.

The canning process I mention in Table 3-1 involves specialist equipment to achieve high temperatures under pressure. I don't cover the specialist pressure-canning process in this book, but this process is a more extreme method of heat treatment than hot bottling, which I do deal with in Chapter 5.

Using an ordinary domestic pressure cooker doesn't produce the same results as pressure canning.

Doing bacteria out of a job

Most dangers of food poisoning come from cross-contamination with raw foods, animals and their dung.

As the earlier Table 3-1 shows, the most common hazards are carried from contaminated surfaces. Therefore, paying attention to the following aspects is crucial:

- ✔ **Cross-contamination:** Keep raw meat and vegetables separate, use different chopping boards and scrupulously clean shared equipment. Be aware that pets, although loveable, are carriers of bacteria; keep them out of food-preparation areas.
- ✔ **Personal hygiene:** Wash hands thoroughly with soap and water.

Grappling with pesky pests

Your stored produce isn't just food that you want to eat; many pests are more than happy to treat your stores as their own. Fortunately, unlike bacteria, you can see these larger creatures, from little fruit flies to rodents. This section provides a few hints on what may be nibbling at your stores.

All your beloved pets also carry bacteria, which is often harmless unless it gets into the wrong place at the wrong time (check out the earlier Table 3-1).

Chapter 4 gives you detailed info on who to trust and who to shun (and how to go about doing so) in the world of pets and pests, but here's a summary:

- ✔ **Cats:** Your moggie can be helpful for patrolling and discouraging rodents.

- ✔ **Dogs:** Your best friend can be a real boon in sniffing out rodent trouble before humans ever spot the signs. Believe the dog if he's excitable and sniffing at a hole or corner (as I discuss in Chapter 4).

- ✔ **Frogs and toads:** Encourage these creatures into your garden because they reduce the numbers of insects and other creepy crawlies and do no harm.

- ✔ **Mice:** Don't let their cuteness fool you, they're incontinent blighters leaving trails of urine and small (0.25-centimetre) droppings as they go.

- ✔ **Rats:** Rats travel over a wide area and use the same run over again. Watch for small tracks and nibbled wooden doors and sacks.

- ✔ **Slugs and snails:** They munch their way inside fruit and veg; biting into one isn't much fun!

- ✔ **Wild birds:** Most birds aren't particularly interested in your food stores, although they may peck at an apple or two, but do worry about them roosting and contaminating your stores with their droppings.

Part II
Discovering Storing and Preserving Methods

'His wife did the embalming-she's an expert in pickling and preserving.'

In this part . . .

This group of chapters covers the best-known methods of storing and preserving, all proven generation after generation for thousands of years. Understanding a bit about what the method is, and sometimes even how it works, is a confidence-building exercise. Certain methods are really simple – just a matter of putting your produce in the right place and checking from time to time that all's well – whereas other methods involve cooking and adding different ingredients to enhance keeping times and quality. Use this part together with the recipes in this book or others that you come across.

Chapter 4

Boxing, Bagging and Clamping: Cool Storage Options

*I*n this chapter, I discuss some straightforward ways of storing your produce at ambient temperatures; that is, in naturally cool situations as opposed to artificially cold storage (which I describe in Chapter 7).

People have successfully kept root vegetables and the more robust varieties of orchard fruits down in root cellars and high up in fruit lofts for generations. Old farmhouses and cottages have these storage places built into the design of the buildings or surrounding grounds. If your house is of an old-fashioned construction, or has a range of brick or stone-built outhouses that you've managed to fill up with rubbish, you may just have found the impetus for a good clear out so that you can return these areas to their intended use.

In contrast, most modern houses lack these built-in storage spaces or are constructed from materials that don't withstand the fluctuations in temperature from one season to another. But don't despair, I'm sure that you can find a hidey-hole somewhere that, with a bit of adaptation, does the job just as well. Failing that, and if you're handy enough, you can build one that doesn't need planning permission and yet is just as good for the right crops.

With a regular routine of checking and ways of keeping the peskiest of pests at bay (don't let out of sight become out of mind!), you can extend your harvest successfully.

Shelving Your Storage Problems: Easy Ways Out

Imagine that one of your crops does particularly well or the orchard flourishes unexpectedly. In such cases, you may well want to store your produce without resorting to much in the way of chopping or cooking first. This section discusses a few quick and easy kinds of storage that are right for this situation: boxes, bags and sacks among others.

The way in which you store your home-grown harvest, however, depends on a number of factors:

- ✔ **The amounts you grow:** Clearly, a good harvest requires more space for a longer period.

- ✔ **The type and varieties of produce you choose:** For example, some fruits store well almost anywhere and others are fussier.

- ✔ **The quality of your produce:** For example, undamaged fruits store more effectively than bruised ones.

- ✔ **Weather and disease considerations when the produce was harvested:** Wet fruits and vegetables don't keep as well as dry ones and diseases affect the keeping quality.

- ✔ **Whether you want to use several different methods for one type of produce:** You may want to store a certain variety of produce for using straight away and other varieties for later use. Apple varieties differ widely in their keeping qualities, for instance.

- ✔ **The amount and type of space available to you.**

- ✔ **Your access to boxes, bags and other suitable containers.**

But whatever you store, make the most of the existing spaces around you. For example, take a good look indoors at any shelves that have held the same piles of children's games, comics (if the children have moved onto new age digital gaming) or stacks of old magazines for years. Be brave and chuck stuff out to make way for the fruits of your garden and allotment harvests.

Reusing and recycling for effective storage

A great way to start solving your storage problems is to collect vegetable sacks that have an open weave fibre. The old type of greengrocer shops that sell fresh fruit and vegetables may give you their used bags and containers if you ask.

'No, that's the onion cupboard!'

One year, I successfully kept the whole of my onion harvest in an underused kitchen cupboard. A cupboard full of onions may have surprised guests looking for pots and pans, but it was dry, spacious enough to stack them just two high and easily to hand so that I was able to check daily whether any onions were going bad or sprouting green tops: I just made sure to use those ones up first.

A warm kitchen may not be the ideal place to store large amounts of produce, but I only had a small garden plot and harvested the onions in August. They were harvested in dry weather and kept extremely well; I didn't buy an onion for at least three months. They lasted until Christmas when I got my kitchen space back to fill with junk all over again!

The following types of open-weave synthetic nets with a drawstring are particularly useful for storing veggies:

- ✔ **Green and white nets:** Originally used for leeks
- ✔ **Orange nets:** Originally used for carrots
- ✔ **Purple nets:** Originally used for swedes and turnips

If commercial growers are using these nets, you can be sure that they work well. Although you don't need to stick to the colour coding, which just enhances the look of the produce, the nets are strong and durable and allow an air flow. You can hang them from rafters or nails in an airy shed, to keep produce away from pests and off the damp floor, or stack them on top of pallets (which I discuss later in this section) to get an airflow underneath.

In addition, make sure that you gather up the following useful items:

- ✔ **Cardboard boxes:** Thick or double-corrugated cardboard boxes are useful, and many shops are glad to offload them.
- ✔ **Chest of drawers:** You can create useful storage space from old wooden chests of drawers, or just remove the drawers and handles and use the drawers as boxes.
- ✔ **Hessian sacks:** These rough jute bags are made from a natural fibre. Seed potatoes come in these or you can find them in pet food shops and anywhere selling peanuts as wild bird food. They used to be common but are now more difficult to find. Treasure them if you find a source, because they're extremely useful for storing all sorts of vegetables and even apples. You can also use them as interim storage for damp vegetables that you want to sift through before clamping. The natural fibre is tough and natural produce-friendly.

✔ **Pallets:** These rough wooden structures (used for stacking and moving commodities around with a forklift truck) are generally made from untreated timber. Use them to keep your bagged or boxed produce off the floor to deter pests and allow air to circulate.

Wooden pallets are useful in a garden and allotment situation (see Figure 4-1). Use them as sides to make a neat composting area by lashing three together on edge. Layer your compost into the space in the centre. (Check out *Organic Gardening For Dummies* by Sue Fisher, Ann Whitman and Suzanne DeJohn (Wiley) for more about composting.)

✔ **Paper sacks:** You can reuse potato bags or animal feed sacks. Examine them to see how many layers of paper are in each sack and (if you've a choice) pick the ones with at least three layers of thicknesses.

✔ **Wooden boxes:** These aren't that easy to come across but are useful because they hold their shape and can be stacked. If you're handy with a hammer and saw and want to take storing your produce seriously, make some up. They're going to be most useful if they fit into a storage space neatly, and so spend a bit of time thinking it through before starting to build. Consider reusing wood from old pallets; they're usually made from untreated timber.

You can use sand in conjunction with your wooden boxes. The sand keeps the vegetables cool, moist and in the dark while holding them apart, thus preventing further contamination – handy if you've got a bad apple in the batch. Find a store of clean, moist sand (although people used to use peat, most gardeners are weaning themselves off it for environmental reasons and sand works just as well). Spread the sand out on a plastic sheet if you find it too wet; it needs to be just moist.

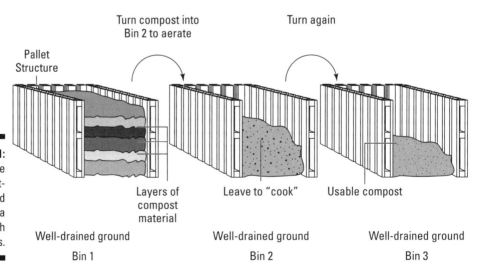

Figure 4-1: A simple compost-making and storing area made with pallets.

Turn compost into Bin 2 to aerate

Turn again

Pallet Structure

Layers of compost material

Leave to "cook"

Usable compost

Well-drained ground

Bin 1

Well-drained ground

Bin 2

Well-drained ground

Bin 3

Creating a pallet-built compost area

Pallets have slatted walls that allow air to circulate, speeding up the composting action and cooking up a great heat; you can see steam rising after just a couple of days. This heat converts all your garden and kitchen waste into friable usable fertiliser. Use more pallets to add extra 'compartments' and 'turn' your half-cooked compost from one section into another when it stops steaming; doing so adds more air and the process of heating up begins again.

You can store your compost in this way until you need to use it. Test whether it's finished by checking for worms: if the worms have left the compost, it's ready to go. Make a rough roof over your compost harvest – to stop the rain from leaching the nutrients away – by covering it in corrugated iron or a plastic sheet or nailing a wooden board to the top. The pallets are made from untreated timber and so don't leach nasty chemicals into your compost, and rot down quite quickly, but you can find plenty of new ones around to replace them.

Storing fertility in the earth for your next year's crop is just as important as storing the produce itself. Taking vegetables out of the ground is the equivalent of work for the soil and if you don't feed it with compost in return for your harvest, you end up with miserable, unhealthy crops wide open to disease.

Keeping Things Dry and Safe: What Not to Use for Storing

The preceding section shows you what items you can safely use for storing your produce, which of course implies that you're best avoiding some materials. One danger is accumulating moisture, which can happen in two ways:

- **From outside:** Weather-related water can enter your storage area, through leaks and so on, or from condensation forming on the underside of, say, corrugated roofs and dripping down. To avoid, store produce inside and insulate the roof space.

- **From inside:** The moisture within your stored produce (for example, vegetables are 70 per cent water) can be encouraged to 'sweat' out. This sweating can have as much of a detrimental effect, if not more, than a drop of rain. So, ironically, going over the top and covering your stored produce to stop exterior water getting to it can cause this problem. Instead, use breathable materials or create a vent to allow moisture to escape (see the 'Clamping It Up' section later in the chapter).

Here are some items not to use for produce storage:

- **Flimsy cardboard boxes:** Most garden produce is heavy and flimsy boxes soon sag and split.

- **Plastic pallets:** Useful to a degree, but being non-biodegradable means that they're difficult to get rid of when broken.

- **Plastic sacks:** These sacks are plentiful but make your produce sweat by setting up a humidity that encourages mould and spores to multiply and spoil your harvest.

- **Thin paper sacks:** The bottoms of these sacks take a lot of strain, and one suddenly giving way, leaving your lovingly produced vegetables all over the floor, is disheartening.

- **Woven synthetic sacks:** Although you buy fresh produce in these sacks, manufacturers intend you to use up the enclosed fruit and veg quickly (it probably has a best before date): they're not best suited for storing. If you really can't find a better alterative, use them for the produce you intend to eat first and find a better alternative for a longer timescale.

Although recycling is a great way to get hold of valuable storage equipment at a low cost, do make sure that the pre-use of the item is suitable for reusing as food storage. If you go to the trouble of growing chemical-free delicious vegetables, the last thing you want to do is spoil them by using a tainted container.

For example, commercially speaking, 'food grade' paper and plastic must be used if it touches food. You don't get your fish and chips wrapped in newspaper any more because the inks may be toxic and rub off. Also, certain plastics can impart chemicals and flavours if in direct contact with food items.

Generally speaking, if sacks or bags have been used previously for human food (such as those you glean from a greengrocer), they're safe for your produce. But be wary of animal-feed sacks. Dried dog food bags may look exactly the right size and be made of a wonderful material, but you may not want your main crop potatoes to have a light coating of dried meat residue (especially if you're a vegetarian) that taints the flavour of food that you grew yourself for a better taste in the first place!

Similarly, if you go to great lengths to grow your own produce without using chemicals in your garden or allotment, you don't want to use any bags, boxes or sacks that previously held toxic ingredients.

For example, although paper animal feed sacks from an organic farm don't impart any dangerous substances, you can't be sure that any nonorganic animal feed sacks weren't used for genetically modified animal feed (unless it states so clearly on the outside of the bag). So, if you've any concerns about eating scientifically 'tampered with' food, leave animal feed sacks alone.

Taking the Best of the Old and the New

Storing produce was a way of life for our ancestors: if they didn't store, they didn't eat. In this section, I show you how to use tried and tested methods, while also incorporating new ideas and materials, to allow you to eat your home-grown goodies around the seasons.

Getting the job done quickly and easily

A lot can be said for getting your produce straight out of the ground and into the final storage place. Sort out in advance where you can keep boxes and sacks, thus giving you time at the crucial moment to pick the freshest crops in their optimum glory. When your crops are 'past it', they're already on the track to rotting down; you're witnessing the natural growth and dying back of any biodegradable object.

Boxing excess veggies

Layer clean(ish) vegetables, such as carrots and beetroots (tops and all), into wooden boxes in moist sand to keep them fresh and edible for months. Add the sand after you've found a final resting place: boxes of sand are heavy and you need to save your back for more vegetable growing. Do pay attention to the warning about cats misunderstanding the purpose of the sand in the later section 'Hiring friendly help'!

Using washed builder's sand or playpen sand is fine, but leave the salty beach sand back beside the sea. It harms your vegetables and you never quite know what's happened to it before or where the nearest sewerage outlet is!

'Drawering' green tomatoes

Tomatoes can present a particular storage problem. Ending the season with lots of green tomatoes can be a depressing thought and you can only eat so much green tomato chutney (see Chapter 12 for the recipe).

'One rotten apple'

Checking all your stored produce regularly is necessary if you want to make the most of your crops. The old adage 'one rotten apple can spoil the barrel' is true because the tiniest blemish can increase slowly under the best of storage conditions. This spoilage is always worse where the fruits are touching each other, so give as much space as you can to individual items or wrap or layer them with paper or sand.

Here's a really simple solution to the problem. Pop extra green tomatoes in a dark drawer in a warmish place (a kitchen drawer is ideal) and allow them plenty of room to breathe, checking them regularly. One by one they ripen, just like magic. Open the drawer one day and nothing has happened; open it a few days later and you get a delicious surprise.

This simple method can keep you in fresh red tomatoes right up until Christmas. If you really want to hurry a few tomatoes along, put them in a bag with a banana. The tomatoes that aren't going to 'make it' are quickly obvious, so you can ditch them.

Leaving frost-hardy vegetables in place

Storing leeks, swedes and parsnips the natural way is easy: these frost-hardy plants have their own home-grown version of antifreeze and parsnips and swedes are all the better to eat after a frost when they taste sweeter. Just leave them in the ground until you need them. You can be eating leeks in May a whole year after sowing them: an ideal work-free storage solution. So, for an easy life, check your seed catalogue for 'frost-hardy' plants.

Leave any of these plants long enough and you can harvest their seeds too (more about seed-saving in Chapter 8).

Going up high

Somehow, the fact that your apples and pears are best suited to storage high up (for example, in an *apple loft* – a high-up storage area often built into the attic of old barns or outhouses, and yes, your pears will be happy there too) seems natural. Lay your apples (or pears) out individually, stalk up and not touching each other. On sunny warm days, open the apple loft wooden shutters to let air in and moisture out; otherwise, keep the fruit in the shade.

Your apple loft smells heavenly; the apples shrivel a little but are all the sweeter with a concentrated taste.

Discover which apples are local to your area. Different varieties have different keeping qualities and sometimes their names are a giveaway: 'Long Keeper', for example, says it all, but you have to guess whether 'Pig's Snout' or 'Katy' store well. All regions are bringing back a pride in their local varieties and hold Apple Days in autumn where you can take samples of your orchard fruits for an expert to assess.

If storing in the loft isn't possible, store your apples and pears on high shelves or in boxes; wooden ones are ideal but a sturdy cardboard box is fine. Wrap each apple separately in clean paper. Kitchen paper, tissue paper and the kind of paper chip shops use (which is effectively newspaper before it goes to print) are all excellent – just be sure that the fruit is dry when you wrap it. Newspaper is out of favour nowadays because of the toxic quality of certain inks. Keep your wrapped fruit well out of the way of bananas, unless you want to force a quicker ripening on them.

Yellow bananas give off a gas called ethylene, which encourages fruit near them to ripen.

Knocking in plenty of nails wherever you've a storage space gives you options for storing produce by hanging, from strings of vegetables such as onions and individual fruits such as squashes, or in bags and sacks of other produce. You can keep some of the less durable crops, squashes and even a cauliflower in this way for a few weeks.

Nothing withstands being frozen after it has already been picked. Looking lovely in the frozen state soon gives way to a soggy mess when the thaw sets in.

Rooting underground

Being dark, dry and underground, with a fairly constant temperature all year, a root cellar is the ideal frost-free area to store sacks, bags or boxes full of your rooty harvest. If you're lucky and have a home with a built-in cellar, clear out the junk and keep your harvest in there; even boxes of fruit store really well.

Benefiting from bricks and stones

Brick and store outhouses are better than wooden garden sheds for storage purposes. Their solid construction is slower to heat up and cool down, keeping the contents at a more regulated temperature; but they're not immune to freezing.

If you've a lot of precious stores to look after, keeping a thermometer handy and checking it daily may prove that you need to light a candle or nightlight in the outhouse in the depths of winter. Even a small amount of heat can make a big difference to whether an insulated space dips below freezing. Remember, however, that this measure may cause condensation, and so opening the doors on a fine, cold, blowy day to give the shed a healthy airing helps to dry things out.

Adapting to modern life

Modern houses are much less airy than older properties; porches and conservatories have plastic-framed glass windows and plastic doors and in general people live in a much more heated environment. Your stored vegetables can all too easily think that spring has sprung when stored in a warm porch or conservatory and begin to sprout new shoots. At this point, they're past their best for eating.

The best storage comes from a state of 'suspended animation'. Achieving this state in a modern centrally heated house is impossible.

Garages, garden sheds and cold porches are the modern-day outhouses. You can also use a coal bunker or perhaps construct something similar against a north-facing wall.

Leaving the car outside and using the garage may seem a good option to create more storage space, but don't store your vegetables next to smelly paint pots and oily petrol cans.

A wooden garden shed freezes much more quickly than a stone or brick build outhouse; bear this fact in mind if you have to use a garden shed and increase any insulation to compensate. Sheds also heat up quickly in the spring, so make sure that you leave the insulation in place after winter is over.

Employing state-of-the-art inventions

The more modern innovations are usually attached to an electricity supply: freezers (see Chapter 7), dehydrators and vacuum packers (I discuss both in Chapter 8).

Storing your produce in a *single skin* (or un-insulated) building when you live in a damp area can be a bit nerve-wracking. Two items in particular can make all the difference as to whether your crops last through the murky days of a wet winter or not:

- ✔ **Dehumidifier:** If a naturally occurring green mould appears as a regular feature on the walls of your storing area, investing in a dehumidifier may be worthwhile, at least for the dampest months.

- ✔ **Greenhouse heater:** You can buy these small appliances that give off a dry heat; using one to maintain the temperature just above freezing can save your produce.

Clamping It Up

This section shows you how to build an indoor and an outdoor root *clamp* (a heap of stored veggies covered with straw for protection). You need this information if your root harvest comes up trumps and provides a good load of potatoes, carrots or beets.

Although parsnips can be left in the ground over winter (you may want to clamp up a few for the coldest winter spells; plenty of people have broken garden forks attempting to dig parsnips out of stone-hard, frozen soil!), most root crops need to be lifted and stored in frost-free conditions.

Sacks and boxes filled with sand are fine for storing smaller amounts of veggies. Generally, you make clamps when you have at least the sort of amount that would fit into a 25-kilogram sack; right the way up to a farmer making field-scale clamps using farm machinery. Clamping is a good old-fashioned farming storage solution scaled down to a level to suit your garden or allotment proportions.

Digging up and sorting out

Prepare your vegetables (see Chapter 13 for detailed crop by crop information) for clamping by digging them up on a dry day. Remove anything obviously bruised or diseased and anything that you've stabbed with the fork; you're bound to have a few casualties in the lifting process. Take these imperfect veggies home for using up first, because they rot in the clamp and spoil their next-door neighbours.

Depending on your type of soil, you may have to brush off some of the dirt. Don't make too much work of it; farmers don't have time to examine every single plant and this system has worked for hundreds of years. But removing any large clods keeps the humidity in the clamp low, which is what deters fungal growth.

Leave potatoes on the ground to dry off for a few hours; plants with green tops need to be left to wilt or 'sweat' for at least 24 hours, reducing the moisture you introduce into your clamp.

Finding the ideal clamp spot

Clamps can be successfully built under cover or in the open ground. The basic principles for creating a successful clamp are that it should be

✔ Breathable

✔ Cool

✔ Dark

✔ Free-draining

✔ Frost-free

✔ Insulated

✔ Weatherproof

A well-constructed root cellar meets all these conditions (see the earlier section 'Rooting underground'), but tunnelling under your house to make a root cellar is probably impractical. You can achieve similar conditions above ground, however, with a bit of forethought.

Indoor clamps

The ideal place to build an indoor clamp is a stone or brick-built outhouse with an earth floor, but as long as you get the insulation right, the corner of a garage or shed works fine.

Your vegetables may still have mud on them, but essentially you're making a food area and petrol-flavoured chips from the garage aren't on anyone's favourite menu.

After you make your clamp, you really don't want to have to move it. Think out a design that shrinks and that you can dismantle piece by piece as you use up the stored produce. A straw bale clamp (see Figure 4-2) can reduce in size and give you back your garage for more conventional uses. Make sure that the clamp is in a place that doesn't obscure anything important and check that any water run-off, especially in a garage situation, tracks away from your clamp.

Outdoor clamps

You can build your clamp in an out-of-the-way corner of your garden or allotment. Keep it out of the way of paths and leave enough room for wheelbarrows to pass by. Estimate the size of the crop you're going to clamp: it may be better to choose two sites and have smaller clamps.

The really important thing is to keep your clamp out of waterlogged ground. Even if it's been a dry summer and autumn, any dip in the ground pools water even for a short time after a heavy downpour, so build on a hump rather than in a dip. Keep an eye on the weather, too. If you're aware that a really cold spell is coming, add a few layers to your clamp or open it up and revert to sacks indoors. All produce ruins if it becomes totally frozen through.

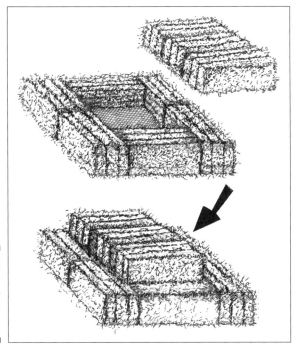

Figure 4-2:
Illustration for indoor straw bale clamp.

Building in the lee of trees or a hedge is fine but give your clamp room to breathe without a dripping umbrella of branches over it; and don't put it so far out of the way that it's awkward to get to and you forget about it.

Building 'au natural'

Indoor clamps already have the weatherproof aspect looked after, as long as you pick the right spot, and so you just need to attend to the insulation and work out a way to keep the light out. In contrast, when you're building outdoors, you have to take weatherproofing from all sides, up and down included, into consideration.

Staying indoors

Construct walls for your indoor clamp from natural material: straw bales are perfect. Small bales are around 105 x 60 x 18 centimetres (3½ x 2 x 1½ feet) and provide adequate insulation all around your clamp. Just pile your root harvest into the centre. If you can close a door to keep out the light, that may be all you have to do (especially if the floor of your shed is earth).

Finding small straw bales isn't so easy these days: farmers have gone in for bigger equipment and so the straw bales have grown too. You can peel off slices of larger straw bales and use these slices as your insulating material for walls and a floor covering if you have to store straight onto concrete. Dried bracken is a good natural material to use. Wool wall insulation material has good insulating and breathing properties but, depending on the type, may leach fire retardant chemicals.

Use only natural materials right next to your food crop; fibreglass loft insulation material may be great for the insulation but is less good for your digestive system when you come to eat your harvest.

Covering your clamp keeps the light out, depressing the urge to keep on growing. Your plants are still living things, only lying dormant for the winter, so keep the clamp dark and cool. If plants sense warmth and light, they assume that spring's in the air and come back to life. The next stage for the plant is to set seed, and unless you get on and eat it, it puts its energies into shooting up a flowering spike or in the case of spuds, sprouting or *chitting*.

Straw is the dried stalks of the grain crops (wheat, barley and oats). Hay is dried field grasses, and has thin stalks. Well-made straw is shiny and almost dust-free with larger diameter stalks and hollow centres allowing better aeration. Both insulate well but hay contains a lot of spores, which can cause moulds to grow so use straw in preference.

Find straw by speaking to farmers or buy it through horsey friends and the local riding stables. Don't get pet bedding straw from a pet shop; a tiny amount is really expensive (rabbits don't need a big bed).

Going outside

After you've found your ideal spot, dried (or sweated) your crop and gathered the insulating materials of your choice, grab your spade and flex your muscles: you need both for building a brilliant outdoor clamp.

Taking a look at Figure 4-3 and following these steps makes the process easy:

1. **Starting with a good layer of straw or bracken, make a base, about 15 centimetres (6 inches) deep.**

2. **Pile your roots in a pyramid shape onto your base.**

3. **Cover the pile with another layer of straw or bracken and leave to sweat again for a day or two, thus allowing more moisture to evaporate.**

4. **Using loose dry earth, cover the straw to a depth of 15 centimetres (6 inches) and pat it down. While you're working, pull out a few tufts of straw to make little 'chimneys' for moisture to escape on the sides and along the bottom. Then pat the earth down with the spade so that it's a smooth pyramid that the rain runs off.**

5. **Check from time to time that the outside of your clamp is still water-tight. Add more earth and pat down again after any heavy downpours or ingress by wildlife.**

No matter how well you build your clamp, if it's sitting in a puddle it won't work. In fact, the straw acts as a wick and draws water up into the clamp, so choose your site carefully.

Step 1

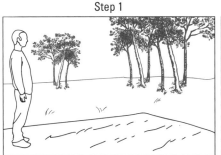

Find a well-drained spot.

Step 3

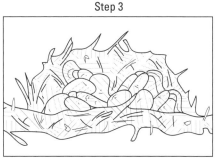

Pile up clean, dry root veg and cover with straw.

Step 2

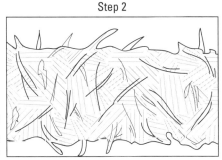

Figure 4-3: Steps to building an outdoor clamp.

Lay down a thick 10-15 centimetre (4-6 inch) straw base.

Step 4

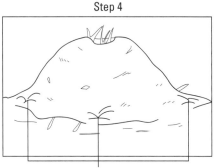

Straw breathing holes

Cover whole pile with dry earth. Leave breathing holes at base and chimney.

Sizing up perfectly

Deciding what size clamp to build depends on how much of a crop you need to store.

As long as your indoor clamp is in a convenient place, you can make it any size you like. Just peel back the cover (or remove one bale if you made a clamp similar to Figure 4-2), taking stores as you need them. You may find that it's more convenient to bag up a quantity of spuds at a time and keep them in the kitchen, but you don't harm your clamp by opening it.

Of course, home-made clamps never need to be as big as a farmer's clamp and you can never re-make an outdoor clamp properly watertight after you open it. Therefore, try building several smaller-sized piles, corresponding to a sackful of goodies; doing so allows you to dismantle one at a time with less likelihood of springing a leak. Just transfer the contents into a sack for convenience.

Letting the Right Creatures In

You can't stand guard constantly over your precious stored crops after they're in a clamp or in bags and boxes high up on shelves and in lofts. And yet, just as you want to consume this stored produce during the winter months, so do hoards of other hungry mouths. The fact is that some creatures help to guard your stores and others spoil them.

Hiring friendly help

The following animals can help you preserve your stored produce:

- ✔ **Bats:** Being bat-friendly is a good idea: they're voracious insect eaters and aren't interested in your food.

- ✔ **Cats:** Whether it's your own cat or a neighbour's, allowing puss to patrol your storage areas can deter both rats and mice.

   Be aware that any cat may look upon your sand storage boxes as cat litter trays; you don't need this sort of surprise when unearthing your best stored carrots!

- ✔ **Dogs:** Find out who owns a terrier or get one yourself; they're small and bred to chase and kill rats and other vermin. Many terrier owners like to see their dogs working and the terriers consider it a real treat. Even the scent of a dog can keep your stores free from vermin, so let them patrol regularly to maintain a hot scent.

✔ **Frogs and toads:** Both these creatures usefully eat flies, slugs and snails, although too many frogs can indicate that you've picked a wet spot, which isn't going to help your storage.

✔ **Hedgehogs:** Consider yourself honoured if a hedgehog takes up residence near your stored produce. They eat any slugs, bugs and creepy crawlies in the vicinity, and may want to make a nest in the corner of your straw bale or under dried leaves. Leave them alone because they act as an onsite caretaker.

Discouraging unwanted guests

Keep an eye out for the following unwanted visitors:

✔ **Crawling insects:** Insects, such as beetles and woodlice, usually enjoy dark, damp corners. If you've enough room, leave a gap around stored bags or raise them on pallets.

Cockroach infestations are a sign of really unhygienic circumstances. You're unlikely be troubled by these bugs in a home storage situation unless your next door neighbours run a disreputable food outlet and the bugs explode into your property too.

The presence of cockroaches calls for immediate action. Contact the environmental officer at your local council or a recognised pest controller and get to the root of the problem.

✔ **Flies:** Fruit flies breed in fermenting fruit, so check and remove rotting produce. Here's a clue: when you move such fruit, a cloud of flying insects appear, and you usually detect a sweet smell around decomposing fruit.

✔ **Mice:** Despite their sweet little faces and twitching whiskers, mice are even more of a nuisance than rats (see the next bullet point). They're incontinent and dribble urine as they busily scamper all over your produce. You notice their presence in the form of tiny black droppings or chewed up sacking and other materials. Set spring traps baited with peanut butter (I don't know why they like peanut butter, but it works better than cheese!), making sure that no children's or adults' fingers are likely to be caught. Alternatively, use a humane live trap, but if you're successful with this method you then have to take a long walk before you let the naughty mouse free to ensure that you don't get a return visit.

✔ **Rats:** Keeping these fellows away is a full-time job. They're excellent scavengers and when they've access to a food supply, they return again and again to raid it. See the preceding section for using cats and dogs as a chemical-free solution.

You can bait with rat poison if you've an infestation, but remember that rats killed with poison are a hazard to pets and wild creatures. Use any poison wisely and sparingly and as a last resort; remove any dead rats as soon as you see them.

Rats are clever animals. They gnaw their way through wood, so check your wooden doors and structures regularly for gnaw marks and look out for black oval droppings about 1-centimetre long. Rats also travel; the ones causing problems may not be 'your' rats. Allowing a dog to sniff them out may lead you to their nesting area where you can deal with them more effectively. Trapping rats is a possibility, but generally they're too canny to fall for a trap.

As with cockroaches, if you see rats anywhere near your produce, call your environmental officer or a recognised pest controller.

✔ **Slugs and snails:** Seeing shiny trails over your produce means that you're sharing your harvest with slugs and snails. A guest hedgehog soon sorts them out, or you can leave an empty *grapefruit skin housie* nearby, with a door cut into it, and see if you can trap them. This 'housie' is an old solution to a perennial garden problem. Why slugs like grapefruit is a mystery, but if you check your traps daily you'll find them lurking there. What you do to them afterwards is your business!

✔ **Wild birds:** Turfing a robin out into the cold would be a sin, but any number of wild birds (pigeons, for example) can ruin a stored loft of apples. They do so less by the few they peck and more by roosting above your stored goods and splattering them with large quantities of bird pooh! Exclude them by placing grills on the windows to maintain your air flow.

No matter how clean and organised you are, rats travel to your store from other premises, as do cockroaches. Flying insects and wild birds are also always on the move and you're never completely immune from their visits. Constant vigilance is your best weapon.

Chapter 5

Preserving With Sweetness: Jams, Jellies and Syrup

In This Chapter

▶ Choosing quality right from the start

▶ Making jams and jellies

▶ Bottling fruits safely

▶ Treating yourself with fruity butter and cheese

*N*othing brings back childhood memories more clearly than jams and jellies. The intrigue of the jelly bag suspended over a bowl and the shout from Mother to leave well alone; the temptation to squeeze the juice out was almost overwhelming, but I'd have spoiled the clarity of the end product every time. My absolute favourite job as a child was putting on the cellophane jam-pot covers. My reward for doing this fun work was watching in wonder while the at-first crinkly top stretched taut and perfect over the warm jam-pot top – magic.

This chapter reveals all the sticky secrets of using jams and jellies, and helps you to work out what's best for preserving your home-grown produce successfully into these sweet treats. I also take a look at other sweet-tooth methods – bottling in syrup and making fruit butter and cheese – which produce different textures and consistencies.

If you just want to get on with it, grab yourself a tried and tested recipe and follow it to the letter (I include a few great ones in Chapters 10 and 11, among others). Plenty of people have been on the jam trail before you, making and recording their successes, and good recipes allow you to take advantage of that wisdom.

Starting Off on the Right Foot

Before starting on your fruit-preserving adventure, collecting the right implements for the job is important. You probably have most of the required tools in your kitchen, but a few specialist items come in handy time and time again – Chapter 2 gives you the handle on what's really worth investing in.

If you're dying to get going or have a ready and ripening fruit tree beckoning, just start off by making small quantities using your normal household pots and pans.

Choose the largest heaviest bottom pans for anything involving heating up sugar: sugar's pure energy with its own properties. It boils at a higher temperature than water so splashes burn fiercely, and the hotter you go the harder the sugar becomes, until you've tooth-breaking toffee, so take care. The one specialist tool worth acquiring that doesn't cost a packet and keeps you in the mix is a long-handled wooden spoon to avoid painful, hot, sugary splashes.

Working on quality

Just as you can't make a silk purse out of a sow's ear, neither can you make good sweet preserves from inferior ingredients. The best jams and jellies come from dry, slightly under-ripe or just ripe fruit; check out Chapter 7 if you've a dilemma on whether to pick or leave your fruit to over-ripen.

Some lesser-quality produce can help you out, however – flip to the later section 'Working with pectin' to find out how you can redeem some of your scruffier fruits.

Putting your money where your mouth is

The biggest cost input for preserving with sweetness – apart from the energy to cook with – is the sugar. The fruit is of course your own, home grown and free, except for the labour of love you spend on it.

Unless a recipe requests a specific sugar – for example, demerara or soft brown sugar – always use granulated sugar. The small pieces or granulations dissolve quickly. Taking time to dissolve sugar completely before bringing it to the boil in a sweet recipe is really important – sugar burns and changes consistency on cooling. You can use a *sugar thermometer* – a specialist tool with different gradations marking the various points at which sugar sets: soft set, for jams and jellies; a harder set for fudges; and a tooth-breaking brittleness for toffee. Chapter 2 explains how to use a sugar thermometer in more detail.

Choose the type of granulated sugar that suits your taste, ethics and budget:

- ✔ **White refined granulated sugar:** the least expensive and without its own character. Find also a large crystal-white refined 'preserving' sugar for making jam with fruit high in pectin, or 'jam' sugar with added pectin. Use the latter type of sugar only if your recipe dictates or you're doing a pectin test (which I describe in the later section 'Testing for pectin').

- ✔ **Unrefined granulated sugar:** a golden sugar with a natural aroma, may come as a Fair Trade item, organic – that is, grown without the use of chemical fertilisers or sprays – or both.

Getting out of a Fruity Jam with Jams and Jellies

When your garden trees and bushes are jammed full with fruits, why not preserve them as preserves and conserve them as conserves! This section talks you through the processes of creating your own jams and jellies. In fact, the methods are similar; the main contrasting item is the texture of the fruity part:

- ✔ Jams retain their fruits, perhaps having undergone a bit of cleaning-up preparation.

- ✔ Jellies use fruits that are cooked unprepared, using only the liquid after thorough straining, and therefore losing bulk.

With jelly, extracting the juice of the fruit or combination of fruits gives the characteristic flavour and clear look with no lumps – see the section 'Using a jelly bag', later in this chapter, to find out how to keep your jelly clear.

Working with pectin

Understanding and working with pectin is essential to great jams and jellies; you need to ensure that you've pectin and acid available with the right proportion of sugar (the details for sugar come later in the chapter in 'Spooning in the sugar, with precision') for the right consistency.

Mentioning marmalades

Marmalades are jams made with citrus fruits, usually leaving the peel for taste and texture. The basic method is the same as for making jam and the texture depends on how thick or thin you cut the peel. Chapter 10 contains a recipe for Seville Marmalade, but you can mix and match with other citrus fruits for a change of flavours.

Pectin – a gummy substance and natural setting agent found in the cells of fruit – and *acid* – anything with a low pH value universally recognised by a taste you describe as 'tart' or 'sharp' – are available in some combination in all fruits. In order to achieve a *good set* – the gel-like, spreadable consistency, not too stiff and sticky or running off the knife when you try to spread it – you have to get the right balance.

Aided by the acid content, pectin is released in the simmering stage of jam-making. Often, the recipe asks for the pips or stones to be left in to provide pectin – see the Seville Marmalade recipe in Chapter 10 as an example. Pectin and acid levels are usually present in equal amounts: an exception is quince, however, which is high in pectin but low in acid. You can easily overcome such an acid imbalance by adding a quantity of lemon juice – that's high in acid – to the recipe. (Check out Chapter 10 and the Quince Jelly recipe.)

Always add extra acid at the beginning of the simmering stage because it aids the release of pectin. Many jam-making recipes employ this common theme, where lemon juice (bought in shops or, better still, squeezed from a lemon yourself) or citric or tartaric acid (both available at a chemist or cooks' shop) add both acid and enhance, rather than overpower, other flavours.

Using pans and implements made of materials that aren't attacked by the acid in the fruit avoids the possibility of taste taints. Use stainless steel for pots and pans for cooking and for cutting implements, and stainless steel, ceramic, glass or plastic for dripping and straining acid fruits.

Finding a good recipe, perhaps one that your friends and family recommend and that works for them, means that you're reassured that the pectin/acid balance and sugar combine for a good set. Notice that often recipes use a mix of fruit – for example, Blackberry and Apple Jam (the recipe for this jam is in Chapter 18). Picking your blackberries late in the season results in them having a low pectin content, and the cooking apple's naturally high pectin content compensates so that your jam sets and stores well.

Fruits are categorised by their pectin content, as follows:

- **High pectin level:** Cooking and crab apples, all the currants and citrus fruits, tart plums, damsons, gooseberries and quince (needs added acid, though) set easily. Sometimes recipes recommend adding water to dilute their pectin levels.

- **Medium pectin level:** Greengages, fresh blackberries, under-ripe apricots, loganberries and raspberries. You can expect a reasonably good set from these fruits; testing the pectin level (as I describe in the next section) helps determine whether you do need extra pectin.

- **Low pectin level:** Sweet or dessert apples and pears, strawberries, elderberries, rhubarb and any vegetable used in jam-making, such as marrow. Pectin levels also reduce in any aging and over-ripe fruit. Combine low- and high-pectin fruits, and add commercial pectin if necessary. You can buy the latter in supermarkets; be sure to follow the instructions precisely or use a portion of pectin stock – which gives a high-pectin boost to your jam. (Check out the sidebar 'Using pectin stock'.)

Testing for pectin

If you've concerns about the levels of pectin in your fruit – wetness, ripeness and juiciness all affect pectin levels as does the aging and freezing of the fruit – carry out a simple pectin test after the simmering stage and before you add any sugar:

1. **Using a small, transparent container, spoon in 5 millilitres (1 teaspoon) of your simmered fruit or jelly liquid and allow to cool.**

2. **When your liquid is cold, tip in 15 millilitres (1 tablespoon) of methylated spirit.**

3. **Swirl these together and study the result.**

Here's what to look for:

- **One jelly-like clot:** Denotes high pectin levels – use no extra pectin.

- **Two or three clots:** Means medium pectin levels – you probably don't need extra pectin. Continue to reduce your mixture by simmering and test again.

- **No clots or lots of little ones:** Indicates low pectin levels. If after further simmering and reducing the result remains the same, you need to add extra pectin.

Adding extra pectin after a low pectin test result

If your fruit is registering a low pectin level, you rectify it as follows:

- Use commercially prepared pectin at the precise amount the manufacturer recommends.
- Use 'jam' sugar, which has added pectin; you can buy jam sugar at a supermarket.
- Use a quantity of pectin stock, allowing 150 millilitres (¼ pint) per 1.8 kilograms (4 pounds) of fruit used in the recipe – see the sidebar 'Using pectin stock' for some different versions of pectin stock.

Preparing and pulping fruit

Preparing fruit for beautifully clear jellies can be quick – you don't have to remove pips, peel or even stalks if you don't want to; just clean off any obvious debris and the jelly bag catches the rest, but when you're eating your fruit-textured jam you don't want to come across a stalk or a stray pip, so preparing your ingredients carefully for the jam pan is important. Here's what to do for particular fruits if you use them for jams:

- **Destalking and cleaning:** Blackberries, raspberries, loganberries
- **Halving and de-stoning:** Plums, greengages, apricots, peaches and cherries
- **Peeling and slicing:** Rhubarb
- **Slicing, peeling and de-seeding:** Marrow
- **Topping and tailing:** Currants and gooseberries
- **Washing, cutting out any bad bits, peeling, coring and chopping:** Crab and cooking apples, pears and quinces

Jam and jelly-making follow a basic pattern tweaked to accommodate the particular fruit or combination of fruits you're using. *Conserves* usually have larger pieces of fruit and a softer set and *syrups* are runnier still; the recipe that you choose holds the key to success.

After preparation comes the simmering, which softens the fruit, breaks down skins and releases the pectin (flip to the earlier section 'Working with pectin' for all about this gummy substance and its interaction with acid).

Use a wide, open pan, ideally a preserving pan (Chapter 2 gives more information about equipment). Doing so helps with evaporation, reducing the fruit and concentrating the flavour. Never cover your simmering fruit.

Using pectin stock

Here are two methods of producing pectin stock; use the fruits that are most abundant in your garden. Two highly experienced preserve makers from Bathford let us into their secrets:

- Jill Gigg's method for making pectin stock is to take sour cooking apples, crab apples (windfalls, the wind-blown ones scattered about under the tree are fine) or sour gooseberries if they're in season. Wash and cut up 900 grams (2 pounds) including peel, cores and pips. Cover with 600–850 millilitres (1–1½ pints) of water. Stew gently for around 45 minutes (30 minutes for gooseberries). Strain through a jelly bag or several layers of net curtain fashioned into a bag.

- Mo Rice has a more abundant supply of currants and makes her stock using 1.3 kilograms (3 pounds) of redcurrants. Wash, leaving on tops, tails and any stalks, simmer with 600–850 millilitres (1–1½ pints) of water for 30 minutes and strain through a cloth. Allow 150 millilitres (¼ pint) of water for 1.8 kilograms (2 pounds) of fruit if you're using it straight away. Pot up in 150-millilitre (¼ pint) amounts, refrigerate or freeze until you need.

For your home jams, make small amounts up to a maximum of 4.5 kilograms (10 pounds) finished weight. Most home jam-making equipment is geared up to this scale and if something goes wrong you don't waste too much.

Using a jelly bag

A jelly bag is for fine straining, extracting juice from your already cooked fruit. Don't hurry or force this process. In order to get a completely clear juice, patience is the name of this game – any poking, prodding or squeezing results in tiny bits of pulp being forced through your bag and then your jelly is no longer clear.

Catering shops and the cookery departments of big stores sell jelly bags, which are made of cloth. Old-fashioned jelly bags are made with thick flannel material sewn into a cone shape and attached to a framework to hold the bag open. You suspend this kind of jelly bag above a collecting dish, bucket or pan – sometimes difficulties occur when you can't find an easy place to suspend the jelly bag; in a doorway with people pushing past is certainly not ideal! Modern jelly bags overcome this problem by having a plastic frame and legs that you fold down, thus suspending it over the pan or dish for collecting juices.

Each time you use your jelly bag, even a brand new one, scald it by pouring boiling hot water through it.

Scald your jelly bag before you use it each time and allow your fruit juices – fruit that sets well has to be quite acidic – to drip into a container that isn't attacked by acid: use china, plastic or stainless steel.

If you don't own a jelly bag, don't worry; people have been improvising successfully for years. Inventing a way of allowing your cooked fruit to strain undisturbed through a fine mesh isn't that hard, but make sure that you find somewhere where it isn't in the way:

✔ For larger amounts of fruit, turn a stool upside down. Securely attach several layers of muslin to the legs in such a manner that the cloth droops down over a dish, pan or bucket when the fruit is draining. If you don't have muslin – which you can buy at catering shops or through a cheese maker's website – use a clean white cotton pillowcase.

✔ For smaller amounts of fruit, use a large colander, or line a smaller colander or sieve with muslin, cloth or even a couple of thicknesses of clean, disposable dishcloth.

Some dark fruits – such as blackcurrants – stain a plastic bucket and any cloth you use – and so don't use the best pillowcase from the guest room!

Spooning in the sugar, with precision

Sugar draws moisture out of the fruit, thus inhibiting moulds and bacteria. The simmering of the fruit and a rapid boil, taking the temperature beyond the boiling point of water to 105 degrees Celsius (220 degrees Fahrenheit) or a little more, makes anything processed in this way a sterile food. (Check out Chapter 3 if you're hankering to know more about food safety.)

Add to your personal safety by using a special long-handled wooden spoon for stirring boiling sugar to avoid splashes – Chapter 2 has more about jam-making equipment.

Often a recipe doesn't give a specific amount of sugar, and you don't know exactly how much to use until the preparing and pulping stage is complete. If your recipe is a runny liquid ready for jelly – see Quince Jelly in Chapter 10 – the instruction to 'measure' means pouring the liquid into a suitable measuring container or jug, noting down exactly how much liquid you have and working out how much sugar you need. Usually – but always use your recipe as the final guide – for each 600 millilitres (1 pint) of prepared strained liquid, add 450 grams (1 pound) of sugar.

Some recipes request that you weigh the prepared fruit and others just state how much sugar to use. If you make up your own recipe, use the guide of 60 per cent sugar and 40 per cent fruit; for example, if you've 1.8 kilograms (4 pounds) of fruit to start with, use 2.7 kilograms (6 pounds) of sugar.

Stirring up to avoid trouble

Stirring the required amount of sugar helps it to dissolve in the warm fruit. Often the sugar is warmed too, speeding up the dissolving process (some people say stirring keeps a better colour in the jam too). You then bring the whole sugary mixture rapidly to the boil until it sets.

When adding sugar to your well-cooked, whole fruit, strained liquid or pureed fruit, don't allow the mixture to boil before all the sugar completely dissolves.

When your mixture of fruit pulp or liquid comes rapidly to the boil, looking like a colourful frothing and foaming mass, watch carefully and resist the urge to stir. All sorts of factors affect the setting time of your jam – wet fruit, over-ripe, the pectin content – and your recipe may guide you. But when the boil slows down, starting at the sides and looks more sluggish, plopping instead of foaming, remove it from the heat to test for a set.

Adding a small knob of butter 2.5 centimetres square (1 inch square) to your frothing pan reduces the scum.

Testing times

In this section, I describe several ways to test for the 'set' or consistency of your jam or jelly – using a flake test, sugar thermometer or wrinkle method, or a combination:

- ✔ **Flake test:** Coat a spoon in the preserve and hold the spoon on its side, allowing the preserve to run off. If, instead of trickling off, the jam/jelly forms a flake, you're ready to go.

- ✔ **Sugar thermometer:** Have a jug of hot water ready. Dip your thermometer into it briefly and then into your jam, moving it through the hot mixture without touching the base of the pan. If it reads 105 degrees Celsius (220 degrees Fahrenheit) you're ready; a degree below sets your jellies or anything that requires a softer set – for example, conserves – and whole fruit in set syrup.

- ✔ **Wrinkle test:** Store a few saucers or small flat ceramic dishes in the fridge. If, after spooning a little spot of your preserve onto a cold plate and pushing it with your finger, you can make wrinkles on the top, your preserve is ready. If the wrinkles are slight, you're close; return the pan to the heat for a further couple of minutes and test again.

Gas flames are more immediately responsive for heating up and cooling down. If you're using an electric hob or stove, remember the time lag in temperature control. Removing the whole jam pan from the heat puts a stop to the thickening process, and you can always return it to the heat if needs be.

Making freezer jam

When your fruit, especially berries, are a little too ripe for jam-making but still delicious and you have to deal with them quickly, make freezer jam. Follow these guidelines to make a fresh no-cook jam that you preserve in the freezer – Chapter 7 gives tips on freezer storing.

Use Chapter 11's Strawberry Freezer Jam recipe or substitute other soft ripe fruit, making freezer jam in a similar same way:

✔ Mash up clean soft fruit with caster sugar (quantities as per Strawberry Freezer Jam), cover and leave standing for one hour, mashing occasionally.

✔ Using a commercial liquid pectin and lemon juice, mix thoroughly into the sugar fruit mix for several minutes. Allow to stand for four hours and pot up into clean freezer pots.

✔ Chill for 24 hours before freezing, use within 6 months after defrosting at room temperature. Keep any leftovers in the fridge and using them up within a day or two.

Going potty and potting-up

After setting, and while the jam or jelly is settling, you may see scummy bubbles accumulating on the top. Simply spoon this layer off with a slotted spoon. (You can eat it too; the layer is still jam, just with a bit of air in it, but use it up straight away because it doesn't keep for long.) Stirring one last time to distribute the fruit evenly within the jam or any extra ingredients – sometimes a recipe calls for a measure of whisky or brandy at this stage – is a last action before potting-up into sterilised warm jars. Chapter 3 contains loads of sterilising information.

Although not absolutely necessary, a jam funnel is a great help with potting-up. Its large opening sits on top of the jar, helping to keep everything clean (getting into a sticky mess is all too easy with jam-making).

Pot up warm jam into warm jars and seal straight away.

You've several options for covering pots:

✔ Cellophane jam-pot covers, held on with an elastic band

✔ New or reused plastic-coated lids

✔ Preserving jars with clamp-top lever lids

✔ Screw-on bands over a glass top

The cellophane jam-pot covers come with wax discs – use them wax side down – to place on the top of the jam. After excluding any air, dampen the cellophane with a clean, damp cloth before placing centrally onto your pot and sealing as tightly as possible. The preserve and jar cools, sucking the top into a neat concave shape, denoting a mild vacuum seal.

Tilt your jars sideways while filling with jelly and allowing the jelly to run down the sides, so preventing air bubbles from forming.

Home-made preserves are a great personal gift, and so go for the rustic look with a scrap of gingham cloth tied over the top of the lid, create a mini hamper, or fancy up and personalise a label.

Coming Over All Syrupy! Hot Bottling

In supermarkets, you see fruits in jars stored at an ambient temperature – not in a fridge or freezer. Industrial methods make this possible because they heat commercially bottled vegetables and fruit to a high temperature under pressure, something that you can't achieve in a home kitchen with ordinary equipment.

Other home hot-bottling methods do exist, however, to enhance the storage time of some of your goodies. This section gives you the information you need to achieve safely stored bottled food by excluding harmful micro-organisms, expelling every last puff of air and creating a sound vacuum inside your bottles or jars. Whole fruits in syrups and cordials (I describe the latter yummy drinks in Chapter 9) give the best results.

Choosing suitable produce and generating syrup

Before starting, here are a couple of points to bear in mind:

✔ With the exception of tomatoes (which are really fruits, but many people think of them as veggies), never bottle vegetables. Stick to high-acid fruits. Use other methods for preserving your low-acid vegetables.

✔ The dangerous Clostridium Botulinum bacteria is associated with home-bottled foods, but if you follow the guidelines in Chapter 3 and always preserve your low-acid vegetables with other methods you can avoid the problem altogether.

In reality, problems with hot bottling are rare. Home storing for vegetables tends to revolve around other methods, such as natural storage, freezing and preserving with vinegars or even in jams, which I discuss in the other chapters in this part.

Hot bottling uses syrup. Covering fruit in a syrup or other prepared liquid tastes nice and helps to keep the fruit's colour. Poaching in the syrup before bottling keeps the fruits from disintegrating, but works best with larger fruits such as apricot halves or pears. Lay these fruits out in one layer in a pan, pour in the syrup to cover, keeping the fruits immersed under a piece of greaseproof paper, and cook until just tender. The less movement in the pan from the hot syrup, the better, but you may want to clear the syrup afterwards by running it through a sieve before putting it into your jars.

Make your syrup according to the recipe you're following, or use this guide:

- **Light syrup use:** 110 grams of (4 ounces) sugar to 600 millilitres (1 pint) of water; suitable for whole and hard fruit such as pears and plums. (Chapter 10 has a Mulled Pear recipe.)

- **Medium syrup use:** 175 grams (6 ounces) of sugar to 600 millilitres (1 pint) of water for figs, peaches and apricots.

- **Heavy syrup use:** 350 grams of (12 ounces) sugar to 600 millilitres (1 pint) of water for soft fruits such as strawberries and raspberries.

Stir the water and sugar together at a low heat to completely dissolve the sugar, before bringing to the boil and simmering for one minute.

Enhancing the colour of your bottled fruit by 'borrowing' colour from elsewhere is a legitimate cheat. Use beetroot water to make your syrup pink, for example; you don't taste the beetroot in the finished article. Or add raspberries and blackcurrant juice. Just remember to remove the equivalent amount of water to compensate.

Getting up a head of steam

Home hot bottling follows two basic methods, but before you start, take the following preparations:

- For working with the hot bottles and jars, use a good pair of protective gloves – cotton gloves under a thick pair of household rubber gloves, for example.

✔ Make sure that your bottles and jars are up to the job and never use chipped or cracked jars and bottles. Buy purpose-made preserving jars with lever-top clips or two-stage screw tops – a glass or metal top and separate screw band; both have rubber seals. Use rubber seals only once. You can buy replacement rubber seals in good catering or cookery shops.

Take your old rubber seals with you to match the size: lots of different brands are available.

Use one of the sterilising methods outlined in Chapter 3 before you start.

✔ Protect table tops by having layers of newspaper or wooden boards to stand your heated bottles on.

Pack your chosen fruits into jars, and top up with syrup. Use warm syrup and heat-treat straight away. Tap the sides of the jars or run a knife around the inner edge to release any lurking air bubbles. Shut lever-top jars *before* heat treatment – the metal expands to allow steam to escape. Place screw lids on top and do up lightly, completely tightening *after* heat treatment.

The following two methods are suitable for heat-treating cordials and fruit juices too and the same rules apply. Chapter 9 has the 'how to' on making small amounts of pure fruit juice – one or two litres of apple juice, for example. Go to Chapter 10 if you're dealing with wheelbarrow-loads of fruit for juicing.

Heat-treating in the oven

When using your oven for heat-treating, the process is as follows:

1. **Pre-heat your oven to 150 degrees Celsius (300 degrees Fahrenheit, Gas Mark 2). Line a baking tray or roasting pan with newspaper or a cloth, and space your jars out without touching, about 5 centimetres (2 inches) apart. Place into the centre of the oven; you get only three or four jars comfortably into a normal-sized oven.**

2. **Heat 600-millilitre (1 pint) jars for 30–35 minutes (or as your recipe requires).** Larger 1-litre (1¾ pints) jars need 40–55 minutes (or as per your recipe).

3. **Take the hot jars out of the oven wearing your protective gloves; place onto a wooden board and seal completely.** Test for a vacuum seal after 24 hours.

For two reasons, be particularly careful when using this method:

✔ Sugar boils at a higher temperature than water, and burns naked skin.

✔ Minute chips or cracks not visible to the naked eye are put under extreme pressure and jars may crack.

If you're at all doubtful about your jars or your ability to lift and carry hot objects, use the water bath method in the following section where less strain is put on the jars at the boiling point of water.

Heat-treating using a water bath

Use the top of your cooker and a deep pan of water for heat-treating as follows:

1. **Using dishcloths or newspaper to wrap your jars, stand them in a deep pan on a *wedge* of the same, or a *trivet* – both items provide a layer that holds the jars away from the base or sides of the pan or each other – which stops the jars cracking.** Fill the pan so that the jars are submerged by 2.5 centimetres (1 inch) or at least up to the top of the filled ingredients, and cover the pan.

2. **Bring slowly to the boil (taking about 25–30 minutes) and simmer for the time stated in your recipe.** As a guide, allow 2 minutes for soft berry fruits and apples, 10 minutes for medium-hard gooseberries, apricots and rhubarb, 20 minutes for peaches and up to 40 minutes for whole pears. You can't test them and time depends on whether you poached your fruit first.

3. **Turn off the heat, and ladle out some of the hot water so that the jars are easier to get hold of.** Remove them to a protected worktop while wearing your thick gloves or clasping them with sturdy tongs to move them. Tighten screw tops immediately. Test for a vacuum seal after 24 hours.

Testing, testing for a vacuum

Testing the vacuum is the most important part of the process for both oven and water-bath methods. Leave your heat-treated produce to cool for 24 hours, and then undo the lever-top clamp or the screw top part of your jar. Lifting the weight of the jar by holding onto the lid shows you whether a good vacuum has formed. (When using metal lids instead of glass ones, a vacuum is formed when the slightly domed centre of the lid is sucked inwards, making an audible 'click'.) If so, and all's well, tighten the seal and store your produce in a cool dark place until you want to use it.

If the seal breaks, *don't store the produce*; instead, use or freeze the contents and review your heat-treatment method. If, after a period of storage, you open the jars and the seal has released, or any discoloration or smelliness is apparent, discard the produce immediately.

Staying Out of the Dairy with Fruit Butters and Cheeses

The difference between fruit butter and fruit cheese is in the consistency:

- *Butters* are a spreadable paste for scones and pancakes or a topping for puddings.

- *Cheeses* are cooked to a more solid consistency, potted up like jams into straight-sided jars or ramekins and turned out to be cut like a cheese on its own – a dairy-free alternative – or as an accompaniment to hot and cold savoury dishes.

Chapter 10 has recipes for Damson and Medlar cheeses (reduce the sugar content guided by the method below for a butter version). Or create something with fruits or combinations of fruits and spices of your choice, using this basic method:

1. **Cut your fruits up into small pieces.** Create a pulp by first simmering the fruit in a heavy-bottomed saucepan with up to half its own volume of water (depending on the juiciness of your fruit) until really soft.

2. **Work the cooked pulp through the sieve – pliable nylon sieves work best – leaving any seeds, pips, stones or hard skin behind and discard them.** Using a food processor or hand-held blender, blitz it to a puree.

   The metal strands of poor-quality sieves may not withstand this treatment and break.

3. **Stirring all the time, re-cook the puree until the mixture is thick, adding half as much sugar as fruit.** You have to weigh the mixture to work it out: for example, 225 grams (8 ounces) of sugar per 450 grams (1 pound) fruit. Keep stirring all the while until the mixture is thick and creamy for butters. (Match weight for weight of fruit and sugar for cheeses and keep cooking until the mixture is stiff before potting.)

   Here's an easy way to weight the mixture. Jot down the weight of the pan you use, weigh the lot – pan and sieved fruit – and then subtracting the weight of the pan leaves you with the weight of the fruit mixture; much easier than spooning thick puree onto weighing scales! Alternatively, use the 'tare' button on your scale to do the sums for you.

4. **Pot up into sterilised jars with a waxed disc on the top to exclude air.** Chapter 3 gives options and advice on sterilising.

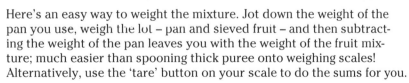

Making leathery treats

You can take the drying one stage further by using a food dehydrator – Chapter 8 airs this subject more thoroughly. By spreading a fruit butter mixture, you can make a *fruit leather – a layer of dried fruity mixture*; perfect for lunch-box treats and healthy snacks.

Chapter 6

Using Vinegar to Preserve Your Produce

Although I describe some great sweet-tooth treats for your fruity harvest in Chapter 5, if you're like me you can only eat so much sweet stuff before the craving for something a bit more savoury kicks in. If you're at that stage, this chapter is the one for you. Here I show you how to make and use vinegar to preserve your piles of, as yet, unripe tomatoes or that marrow mountain. Whether you choose to chuck together some chutney or pick a fight with pickles, just make sure that you relish (groan!) the whole process.

To avoid the problems associated with preserving low-acid foods such as vegetables (issues that I discuss in Chapter 5), this chapter describes how to add in acid (via vinegar), the vital ingredient in preserving food without losing out on flavour or variety while keeping you and your family safe from food-related hazards.

Figuring Out the Vinegar Treatment

Most fruit is high in acid; your taste buds instinctively tell you what's acidy when you bite into, for example, a sharp cooking apple by mistake. However, you don't get the same reaction in your mouth from eating a raw carrot. The difference is the low-acid content of most vegetables; and yet acid is essential to safely preserving foods. In this section, you find plenty of ways to get around the low-acid issue by using vinegar as a preserving ingredient.

Defining the different vinegar preserves

The most popular material for preserving vegetables and other low-acid foods is vinegar, which is made when fruit or grain-based alcohol – wine or cider, for example – is exposed to air and the alcohol turns to acetic acid due to a bacterial reaction. Acetic acid helps to prevent unwanted micro-organisms from thriving, so the natural acidy condition allows you to keep foods in all sorts of ways and for long periods. Vinegar is the main ingredient in all the following preserves:

- **Chutneys:** *Chutneys* are vegetable and fruit mixtures cooked together, minced to make a smooth, pulpy mix or retaining some lumpy texture within the mixture. Vinegar, sugar and spices in different combinations give huge possibilities for creativity in the kitchen. Chutneys have other benefits too: their nature means that they're exactly the right place for transforming your less than perfect produce into a delicious condiment. See the later section 'Chunking up for chutney' for more on chutneys.

- **Pickles:** When making *pickles* – made up of liquid, usually clear and made with vinegar, salt or both, and the veg or fruit steeped in this liquid – retaining the colour, texture and shape of the vegetables, fruits or eggs is important: you use whole pickled onions and cauliflower florets, for example. Often, but not always, dry or wet salt (*brine*) preparations start the process off, reducing the moisture content of the ingredients, thus ensuring a crisp texture. Recipes differ as to time and methods. See the later section 'Getting in a pickle and other states' for more on pickles.

- **Relishes:** Although similar to chutneys in some ways, with *relishes* you preserve fruit and vegetables in a smaller proportion of vinegar and sugar relative to the bulk weight. Relishes, therefore, have a looser texture, and some are made with raw ingredients and others cooked. See the later section 'Relishing your relishes' for more.

- **Ketchup and others sauces:** All *sauces* can be thick or thin, possibly even a puree, with vinegar as the preserving agent always making a final consistency resembling something between single and double cream, which is pourable from a bottle. *Ketchups* can be thick or thin sauces which you can usually pour from a bottle. Such sauces are used for accompanying, contrasting and enhancing other dishes. The later section, 'Catching up with ketchup', contains more details on ketchup.

- **Flavoured vinegars:** You can produce *flavoured vinegars* by simply steeping herbs or spices in vinegar or combining a slightly syrupy feel by steeping fruit as a first stage and boiling up with sugar later. Uses vary from flavourings for desserts to a hot concoction for soothing painful throats, with all sorts of drizzling uses in between. Flip to the later section 'Making your own flavoured vinegar' for a great Raspberry Vinegar recipe.

Using the right acid-resistant equipment

Chapter 2 has loads of info on obtaining and using preserving equipment, but in this section I provide a few specific pointers to the best materials for storing acidy preserves:

- ✔ **Jars and bottles:** Glass is the most reliable container for preserving acidic foods. Unlike when brewing alcohol (see Chapter 9 for tipple advice) or when hot bottling in syrup (Chapter 5's hot topic), your vinegar-preserved goodies rely on the acid environment within the preserve for their longevity, and so put no great physical pressure on the body of the jar. Therefore, although you can certainly use special preserving jars and bottles with special lids if you have them (I describe these tools in Chapter 2), ordinary jars and bottles are fine to reuse for vinegar preserves. Check carefully that they're whole, clean and sterilised, discarding any with chips or cracks. (Chapter 3 gives plenty of options for jar and bottle sterilisation.)

- ✔ **Lids:** Lids need to be plastic-coated, glass or cellophane tops because the acid in the vinegar corrodes most metals (except stainless steel) and causes taste taints; also, some metals can release toxins into your food (zinc, for example). For any lids from the jars and bottles that you're reusing, check that the inner plastic coating is still totally intact. If the lids are lost or imperfect, buy cellophane jam-pot covers (you can find them in cook shops or supermarkets, usually near the sugars).

  You can also buy purpose-made preserve-pot covers. This simple but effective solution comes in a neat flat-pack with wax discs for excluding air from the top of the preserve and cellophane circular covers to place over the rim of the still warm jar (held in place with provided elastic bands). The dampened cellophane dries to a perfectly smooth top if you apply it correctly. Sometimes, these packs even include labels.

- ✔ **Pots and pans:** For an easy life, choose a good-sized, heavy-bottomed pan: ideally a preserving or jam pan. Also useful is a wide-necked funnel, because potting up chutney can be a sticky job, especially if you're messy by nature.

When dealing with hot produce, do the potting up straightaway. The cooling down and subsequent shrinkage of ingredients creates a vacuum that excludes air and micro-organisms.

Before storing any vinegar-preserved foods, always check that your equipment is acid-friendly.

Assembling the preserving ingredients

Ingredients for any preserves using vinegar can be as varied as you like; most fruits, home-produced and wild, have a place here and vinegar is the safest medium for preserving vegetables at ambient temperatures. Although pickles call for perfect specimens, for any of the other acid preserves the techniques of mincing, pureeing or cooking to a pulp, and salvaging the ingredients from less than perfect produce make this art a thrifty one.

Your home-made produce makes up the bulk of the ingredients but some purchases are necessary:

- ✔ **Vinegar:** Many options are available (see the following section 'Choosing the right vinegar for the job').

- ✔ **Sugar:** Granulated sugar is usually best because it dissolves easily, or use what the recipe demands. Buy Fair Trade sugar if you like your purchasing power to be ethically and environmentally informed.

- ✔ **Sweet fruits:** Traditionally raisins or sultanas, but sometimes a more exotic fruit, such as dates, are required in a recipe.

- ✔ **Spices:** You can use whole spices for the pickling jar; buy a ready mix or make up your own. Ground spices render the mixture cloudy. Whole or crushed garlic and pieces of ginger often appear in recipes too. Add ground spices if the recipe suggests them or tie up a little muslin bag of your favourites and, stirring it around during the cooking time, remove it when you reach the strength of flavour you want.

  Make your own pickling vinegar (see the next sections 'Choosing the right vinegar for the job' and 'Making your own flavoured vinegar' for more info) a couple of months ahead of time, or put the whole spices straight into your pickle jars where the flavours continue to strengthen over time.

- ✔ **Salt:** Most recipes call for at least 5 millilitres (1 teaspoon) of salt, but pickling recipes may need more help from the salt's properties. Follow the recipe carefully because this stage is important. Table salt has additives to help it to flow and may impart a cloudiness to the finished article; if you're looking for purity, go for sea salt and dissolve it well. Read Chapter 8 to understand the role that salt plays in your preserved foods.

  Make up extra brine to the same strength for topping up. Total immersion of the veggies is key.

Choosing the right vinegar for the job

The vinegar you use for preserving has a great bearing on the finished preserve and on ensuring that the final product is safe to eat.

Make sure that the vinegar you choose for preserving food has an acidity of at least 5 per cent; you find this information on the label (take a magnifying glass because the writing can be small!). Five per cent acetic acidity is the minimum for successful preserving, because it creates a safe environment, inhibiting or preventing the growth of most dangerous micro-organisms. Read Chapter 3 to put your mind at rest about food safety.

Vinegar supplies the acidity that creates the environment in which unwanted enzyme activity (which breaks down food ingredients) or spoilage micro-organisms and bacteria (which render your food inedible and sometimes poisonous) can't exist. This process is really important when preserving food-stuffs that are naturally low in acid, such as most vegetables.

Here are the most common vinegars you find in UK shops:

✔ **Malt vinegar:** An offshoot of the beer-brewing industry, malt vinegar is an inexpensive choice but none the worse for that in the right place. It comes as a brown liquid with a distinctive 'malty' smell and flavour or in a distilled clear liquid form, often called 'white' vinegar.

You can take advantage of the 'whiteness' as part of your end result. For example, using white vinegar and white sugar in a recipe preserves the vibrancy of the colour of a particularly red tomato chutney. Check out Chapter 5 for more about sugar types.

✔ **Pickling vinegar:** This product is a fine way to start your own pickling adventure, especially if you're unsure. You buy it straight from the shelf in a shop and it contains the following in one inexpensive package (just add your suitable home-grown produce):

- A suitable vinegar (sometimes already concentrated, but this process isn't necessary if you make your own)

- Jar and lid

- Recipe

This confidence-boosting set up shows you that making your own pickling vinegar is the next easy step. You can steep whole peppercorns, juniper berries, mace, cinnamon, mustard seeds or other flavours of your choice in vinegar, straining them out before use – in this way, the spice flavour doesn't get any stronger – at ratios of about 40 grams (1½ ounces) to every litre (1¾ pints) of the chosen vinegar. Just get a month or two ahead of yourself by starting the pickling vinegar off before the pickling/chutney season is underway.

✔ **Cider vinegar:** This type comes from a fruit base and so the fruitiness is mixed with the acidity. Traditionally, this vinegar is the one for fruit preserves, but if you love it or have easy access to it, use it in other preserves too.

- ✔ **Wine vinegar:** Can be red or white depending on the original wine. This vinegar is a classy alternative to use for your delicate dishes or as part of a colour scheme.

- ✔ **Balsamic vinegar:** With its smooth mellow flavour, this vinegar is more a 'recipe specific' flavouring element, or as part of a combination, than the main preserving ingredient.

- ✔ **Non-brewed condiment:** You may think that you've found a fantastic source of cheap vinegar for sale in a chip shop, but check it out carefully and ask questions. The clue is in the name: avoid using this 'mock' vinegar, which is sometimes a by-product of the paper industry! Generally at 4–6 per cent acetic acid and with the addition of caramel colouring, it looks and smells similar to real malt vinegar, but true vinegar is brewed and your lovingly produced home-grown food deserves the real thing.

Unpasteurised (that is, not heat-treated) vinegars have 'a haze of mothers' floating in them. This rather gloopy mass is a completely natural phenomenon that comes from a breakdown of the cellular wall of the original fruits from which the vinegar derives and happens during fermentation at the vinegar stage only. Artisan vinegar producers transfer 'mothers' from one batch to another as a form of starter culture to preserve the uniqueness of their product.

If you can find vinegar with 'mothers', you're using a real artisan product just like human ancestors did in the days when preserving was a life-saving skill. If you don't want the gloopy bits in your pickles, just sieve the vinegar as you use it.

Making your own flavoured vinegar

Fruit vinegars are easy to make and perfect for bottled fruits, among other uses. Colourful fruits, such as raspberries, help liven up the look as well as the flavour of other preserves.

Raspberry Vinegar

As well as a flavouring, you can also add a dash of this vinegar (and indeed other flavoured vinegars) as the fruity part to a hot toddy (whisky with a dash of hot water), in order to chase away colds and the flu. See Chapter 3 for more on sterilisation.

Special tools required: *Jelly bag*

Preparation time: *10 minutes*

Processing time: *5 days standing, 24 hours straining*

Yield: *about 700 millilitres (1¼ pints)*

450 grams (1 pound) fresh red raspberries   *600 millilitres (1 pint) cider or white wine vinegar*

1 Steep raspberries in a bowl with cider or white wine vinegar. Cover the bowl, leaving it to infuse for five days, stirring daily.

2 Strain the vinegar once through a sieve, discarding the raspberries, and again through a scalded jelly bag (pour boiling water through it first), leaving to drain.

3 Collect the raspberry vinegar, pour into sterilised bottles and seal.

4 Store in a cool, dark place for up to one year.

Per 100-milllilitre serving: 14 calories; 0 grams protein, 4 grams carbohydrate, 0 grams fat, 0 grams saturated fat, 0 milligrams cholesterol, 0 grams fibre, 1 milligrams sodium.

Mixing Vinegar with Other Ingredients

On its own, vinegar is sharp. Even when used as a health tonic, you water it down first: 15 millilitres (1 tablespoon) in a wineglass of water is probably strong enough for most people. But when you mix vinegar with other ingredients and (usually) a little sugar, you produce a savoury delicacy, supplying the sour quality in sweet and sour.

This section describes the main types of vinegar preserves that you find in a well-stocked kitchen. Of course, you can find these preserves already made for you on the supermarket shelves as well, but none has the authenticity of chutney, pickle, relish or ketchup made with your very own home-grown produce.

Chunking up for chutney

When making chutney, you can use large chunks or mince up your ingredients for a smoother pulpier feel; the choice is yours. Either way, though, chutneys often require quite a lot of preparation work.

If you're happy using a food processor, of course, you can whiz through some of the chopping chores. Many people, however, enjoy working with vegetables to get the full satisfaction of chutney production. They accept that vegetable and fruit preparation is a satisfying and fun hands-on task, and make a space for it in their busy lives.

Put the radio or favourite music on and enjoy being 'at one' with the fruit and veg from your garden, knowing that generations of kitchens before yours have hummed to the task of preserving food.

For specific chutney recipes, check out Chapter 10 (Apple, Date and Walnut Chutney), Chapter 13 (Year Round Chutney) and Chapter 14 (Various bean chutneys).

Obtaining the perfect chutney proportions

You can often find that chutney recipes provide a little wriggle room, which is useful because you can't know exactly what yield you get from your original weight, especially if you're using up less perfect fruits and vegetables. If you come across more caterpillar munches than you originally bargained for and have to do a little remedial cutting, add some other bulking up material such as marrow, carrot or apples – in fact, whatever fruit or vegetable is in season in your growing plot – to come up to the required weight. The beauty of a chutney is that it all works!

The basic proportions of sugar, vinegar and salt are important in relation to the bulk: keep to these proportions and you can't go wrong, even if you substitute all the main bulk ingredients and make up an entirely new recipe. Whether it then tastes delicious is for you to decide!

Always dissolve sugar slowly and never be afraid to turn the heat off from under a bubbling pan while attending to a telephone call or unforeseen incident. The types of chutney recipes that I give in this book give you leeway in this respect: taking a little more time to get to the end of a recipe is better than allowing the mixture to burn onto your pan.

You can't, however, leave jam-making in this way, because the sugar and gummy pectin are changing state and so need your constant attention until the end of the process. (Chapter 5 goes into jammy detail.)

Boiling up and simmering down

The general chutney method that I describe in this section uses vinegar for the acid content and sugar for sweetness.

General Chutney

This chutney is the one to use when you've a glut of vegetables and fruit. In this recipe (which you can call Major or Colonel Chutney if you prefer!), choose your favourite vegetables and any cooking apples, pears and so on that you like. Also choose sweet, dried fruit, adding salt and spices for flavour. Varying the spice mix or the type of dried fruit makes a completely different chutney, even though your main ingredients stay pretty much the same. See Chapter 3 for more on sterilisation.

Special tools required: *Acid resistant jars, non-corrosive lids*

Preparation time: *40 minutes*

Processing time: *2–3 hours*

Yield: *approximately 3.5 kilograms (7 pounds)*

3 kilograms (6 pounds, 12 ounces) vegetable/ fruit mix (try to include at least three varieties – say, 1 kilogram (2 pounds, 4 ounces) of each as a rough guide)

500 grams (1 pound, 2 ounces) sweet dried fruit

600 millilitres (1 pint) vinegar

225 grams (8 ounces) sugar

10 millilitres (2 teaspoons) salt

10 millilitres (2 teaspoons) spices tied in a muslin bag (try a variation on peppercorns, mustard seeds, coriander, ginger root, garlic in as creative a mixture as you like)

1 Boil the toughest vegetables, for example onions, placing enough water in the base of the pan to prevent burning. Add those that soften next, for example apples and tomatoes, and cook for a further 10–20 minutes.

2 Place half the vinegar and all the salt, spices and fruits into the pot. Boil and stir the mixture to a pulp.

3 Add the other half of the vinegar and the sugar. Remove from heat or reduce heat while the sugar dissolves, and then return to a gentle simmer, stirring from time to time. When all 'loose' liquid is gone from the surface and a wooden spoon dragged along the base of the pan leaves a clear run behind it (expect this stage to take a minimum of one hour and up to two and half hours, depending on your unique mix), the chutney is ready for potting up into warm, sterile containers.

4 Leave to cool before labelling and storing out of bright sunlight. Leave for one month or even longer for the full flavour to develop.

Per 30-gram serving: 34 calories; 0grams protein, 9 grams carbohydrate, 0 grams fat, 0 grams saturated fat, 0 milligrams cholesterol, 1 grams fibre, 45 milligrams sodium.

Getting in a pickle and other states

Jars with visible chunks of whole fruits, vegetables or even eggs (Chapter 17 has a recipe for Pickled Eggs) look really impressive on your kitchen shelves, but in order to keep the crunch and wholeness an extra processing step is sometimes necessary.

If you just want to get on with pickling, go straight to Chapter 13 and follow the instructions for Pickled Beetroot, Radish Pickle and Summer Vegetable Pickle.

For a wider take on what gets your produce into a pickle, read through the whole of this section.

Pickling in two different ways

Essentially, two pickling methods exist (recipes should guide you about what's best for each type of vegetable):

- ✔ **Clear pickles:** The Ploughman's Lunch is the home of the pickled onion and one of the most famous examples of the clear pickling method. Choose whole, small vegetables: the ideal and most usual are onions, tiny beetroots (flip to Chapter 13 for beet varieties) and gherkins (don't forget to add in dill for the classic pickle combination). Cut larger vegetables into similar chunks or slices.

Vegetables are made up of 70 to 90 per cent water, so keep them crunchy by salting as a first step. Salt, a natural dehydrator, removes some of the water content of the vegetables. Watery vegetables go flaccid in your pickle jar and may leach water into your vinegary pickle, rendering it less effective at preserving. Your recipe will advise you if salting is a necessary step on the way to perfect pickles.

- ✔ **Sweet pickles:** This method is more useful for fruit preserves. It gives a savoury sweet taste, lending itself to accompanying savoury dishes, cold meats and hams, plus as pickled fruit. The delicate flavour of the fruit needs a light or fruity vinegar, so avoid the malt variety. If your fruit has a tendency to discoloration, use a red vinegar (perhaps red wine or the home-made raspberry vinegar for which I provide a recipe in the earlier section 'Making your own flavoured vinegar') to paint a picture. You don't need brining.

Clearing the way for clear pickling

Clear pickles need brining first. Use dry salt to cover layers of your chosen vegetable or make a brine by dissolving 50 grams (2 ounces) of salt in 600 millilitres (1 pint) of water. Immerse the vegetables for 24 hours using an upturned plate to keep the produce under the brine. Chapter 8 expands on the salting theme.

Clear Pickle

Here's a recipe for making clear pickle, after brining as discussed earlier.

Special tools required: *Acid-resistant jars; non-corrosive lids*

Preparation time: *20–30 minutes depending on the vegetables used*

Processing time: *Brining time only*

Yield: *1 kilogram (2 pounds, 4 ounces)*

1 kilogram (2 pounds, 4 ounces) vegetables   *Spices/flavourings as you choose*

700 millilitres (1¼ pints) vinegar

1 Rinse your vegetables swiftly in lots of clean water (a large, stainless steel colander is perfect for this task). Pat dry with clean paper towels to avoid the vegetables reabsorbing any rinsing water, and then pack your vegetables, not too tightly, into wide-topped jars.

2 Pour your cold vinegar into the jars with your spices and extra flavourings, and fill to the brim, tapping the jars to dislodge and remove any air bubbles.

3 Seal with non-corrosive – that is, plastic-lined or glass – lids. Store in a cool, dark place for a couple of months to allow the flavour to mellow.

Vary it! *Home-pickled produce can be quite sharp. To counter this tendency, add 15 millilitres (1 tablespoon) of sugar or honey to each 300 millilitres (½ pint) of vinegar. Mix it in well, adjusting the quantity to your family's taste.*

Per 30-gram serving: 14 calories; 0 grams protein, 3 grams carbohydrate, 0 grams fat, 0 grams saturated fat, 0 milligrams cholesterol, 1 grams fibre, 16 milligrams sodium.

 If you're feeling thrifty, when the pickle jar is empty of veg, don't throw away the vinegar. Instead, strain any remaining pickling spices out and pour the vinegar into a bottle for sprinkling onto your fish and chips. The result's an altogether better flavour than the non-brewed condiment masquerading as vinegar that you get in some chip shops!

Getting fruity with sweet pickles

When producing sweet pickle, plums or cherries benefit from being pricked all over to allow the vinegar syrup to penetrate and preserve from the inside too.

Sweet Pickle

In this sweet pickle recipe, use whole spices and flavourings because ground spices make the syrup cloudy. Try fine citrus parings, cinnamon sticks, star anise and cloves as attractive and exotic additions. The more robust, hard-leafed herbs (such as rosemary and bay) work well for their taste and good looks. See Chapter 3 for more on sterilisation.

Special tools required: *Sterilised jars*

Preparation time: *30–40 minutes depending on the fruit you use*

Processing time: *35 minutes*

Yield: *1 kilogram (2 pounds, 4 ounces)*

1 kilograms (2 pounds, 4 ounces) fruit, peeled

600 millilitres (1 pint) cider or wine vinegar

400 grams (14 ounces) granulated sugar for every 300 millilitres (½ pint) of vinegar

Spices/flavourings as you choose (for example, 1 or 2 cinnamon sticks, 6 cloves, or two star anise and up to 3 bay leaves at a time)

1 Put the vinegar, into a stainless steel pan, adding the flavourings. Bring it to the boil and simmer gently for five minutes.

2 Add your prepared fruit to the hot vinegar and cook for five to ten minutes until it just begins to tenderise. Hot syrup continues to cook the fruit after potting, so pack your sterilised warm jars when the fruit is still firm; a slotted spoon is really useful here. Decorate as you go with the spices and citrus parings.

3 Using your hot vinegar (strain it to clear any tiny bits of fruit if necessary), measure and mix in the sugar. Stirring over a low heat, dissolve the sugar completely.

4 Bring the mixture to a rapid boil for five minutes or until the syrup reduces and thickens slightly.

5 Pour this liquid over the packed fruit. Check and release air pockets as you go.

6 Seal, leave to cool and label. Store in a cool place out of direct sunlight.

Tip: If your fruits have a stalk, leave it in place when you're peeling, halving (or quartering for large ones): a little 'handle' looks pretty and is useful at the eating stage too.

Tip: Run a flat blade around the edge of the jars to dislodge air pockets before sealing.

Per 100-gram serving: 333 calories; 0 grams protein, 87 grams carbohydrate, 0 grams fat, 0 grams saturated fat, 0 milligrams cholesterol, 2 grams fibre, 1 milligrams sodium.

Don't forget the labelling!

You may think that your memory is on the ball and you've burned those chutney or sauce ingredients into your mind, but believe me, when you return to the store cupboard a few months later, an anonymous jar of brown 'goo' may not reveal many clues as a reminder before opening. Therefore, always label and date your preserves as soon as they cool down.

Put as much information on labels as possible. Note which kind of vinegar you used or which book the recipe comes from. Jot down the ingredients and remind yourself of any problems or shortcuts with this batch. Naming 'hand-me-down' recipes is a long-standing tradition. Writing, for example, 'Aunty Patsy's Green Bean Chutney' on the label evokes memories as well as taste, passes on family history and helps to make creating preserves a time-honoured, family occupation. And names are a compliment too . . . as long as the chutney turns out well!

For the artistic among you, or those with children to occupy, be creative: the inner product is unique to you, so make the outside unique too. (Check out the later section 'Jazzing Up Jars and Giving Gifts' for ideas.)

Relishing your relishes

When is a pickle not a pickle and a chutney not a chutney? When it's a relish!

Relishes are really a halfway house between pickle and chutney. They use the tanginess of a vinegar (usually the fruity variety rather than the more prosaic malt) with lower proportions of both vinegar and sugar than other savoury preserves and a mixture of vegetables chopped into small sizes. The vegetables retain some of their original crunch, however, so you can eat relishes straight away. Store them in the fridge for up to six weeks or use the hot-bottling technique from Chapter 5 for a longer shelf-life at ambient storage.

For relish recipes, turn to Chapter 12 for Sweetcorn and Cabbage Relish and Pickled Dill Cucumber, and Chapter 15 for and Piccalilli and Bloody Mary Relish.

Catching up with ketchup

You're as likely to hear a person ask you to 'pass the tomato sauce' as 'pass the tomato ketchup', so expect some crossover in terms here (slip to Chapter 12 for a wonderful home-made Tomato Ketchup recipe – when something tastes this great, what's in a name!).

You can rustle up mint sauce (see the recipe in Chapter 16) in a few minutes to accompany a roast lamb dinner. It has a watery consistency and keeps in the fridge for one to two weeks. You thicken other sauces with flour, often mixed with mustard powder and cook to achieve the creamy consistency of a runny double cream. And you make others by pushing softened vegetables through a sieve or blasting and blitzing with a food processor or liquidiser.

Whichever way you approach sauce-making, you get a runny product to pour from a bottle. Check out Chapter 10 for a Savoury Plum Sauce recipe.

Maturing your vinegary preserves

Vinegar takes, infuses, blends and matures with other ingredients, subtly changing taste over time:

- **Chutney:** Leave at least one month before using, but with good seals and storing facilities you can leave for up to two or three years. Refrigerate after opening.

- **Pickles:** Use the texture and size of the pickled ingredient as a guide for how long to leave before eating to allow the flavour to mature. Here are a few examples:

  Finely shredded cabbage: one week

  Small pickling onions or shallots: two weeks

  Eggs: one month

  Hard walnuts: six weeks

  You can keep for a year or even longer if storing conditions are good: a cool, dark place. Refrigerate after opening.

- **Relishes:** Eat straightaway if you like, or store in the fridge for up to six weeks. If you apply heat treatment (Chapter 5 tells you how to go about hot bottling), you can extend storage up to a year in a cool, dark place. Keep refrigerated after opening.

- **Ketchups and sauces:** Without heat treatment, keep refrigerated and use up within two months. You can keep heat-treated bottles in a cool, dark place for a year or more.

Jazzing Up Jars and Giving Gifts

Jars and bottles bursting full of your delicious, preserved goodness are ripe for decorating. Here are a few ideas to dress up your home-made foods:

✔ For a low-key, 'rustic' look, cut out circles of brown paper or rough hessian, making sure that they're large enough. Use a template for precision before securing your cover with natural garden twine or plain raffia. A strip of brown paper around the middle of the bottle or jar becomes a matching label.

✔ Achieve a 'country garden' feel if appropriate with a pair of pinking shears (scissors with a zigzag cutting edge), coloured gingham cloth (the standard tablecloth checked pattern) and plain contrasting ribbon to hold the cloth in place. Decorate your label with pictures or cut-outs of the main garden ingredients.

✔ Go 'over the top' if you so desire. The sky's the limit. Encase your lovingly prepared preserves in little gauze bags tied up with madly coloured ribbons. Go 'masculine' by choosing understated chocolate and cream décor, and stick a classy hand-made chocolate to the top of the jar for effect.

✔ Dip bottles and corks in melted wax, using a single or double dip to increase the intensity of the colour.

The fancy stuff is an extra: secure it on top of an existing strong seal, not as a replacement. The real gift is the preserve, the rest just window dressing.

Making thrifty gifts

You can give a jar of homemade preserve as a gift for any occasion (and preserves are available all year round). Such gifts make good conversation starters, and so if you're going to someone else's house for a meal, use one as a cut above a shop-bought 'bottle of plonk'. You never know, your preserve may turn out to be just the right complement to the meal, in which case don't be shy; open it up straight away.

If a special celebration is looming and you need the perfect and unique gift, try the following. Buy or make baskets or other containers (for example, cover a humble cardboard box with pretty paper), stuff with straw or shredded paper and pack with preserves. Better still, encourage friends to start their own line in preserving by making up a preserving kit for them: a bottle of vinegar, packet of pickling spices, bag of sugar, a copy of *Storing & Preserving Garden Produce For Dummies* (!) and a jar of your homemade chutney, all beautifully decorated and labelled.

Chapter 7

Freezing and Refrigerating Home Produce

The most common method for storing food is to use cold (especially very cold) temperatures. You can preserve some foods effectively and for long periods at –18 degrees Celsius (–0.4 degrees Fahrenheit), although others lose their freshness and charm.

In this chapter, I describe the equipment that you need, the refrigerating and freezing processes, and how to prepare your home produce for cold storage.

Chilling Out: Cooling and Freezing Food for Longevity

Lots of the supermarket food that you see was kept in cold storage and is still under refrigeration when you buy it. Keeping most vegetables and fruit cool – between 1 and 4 degrees Celsius (34–40 degrees Fahrenheit) – inhibits enzyme and bacterial growth (which I discuss in Chapter 3), hence the longer shelf-life; but the food tends to go off quickly when returned to room temperature.

The ideal situation with freshly picked produce is to be able to take the next step of preservation straightaway. But doing so isn't always possible or practical, which causes the following dilemma: whether to pick at the peak of condition, despite not having time to preserve, or to leave the produce to ripen further with the consequent danger of it going past its best.

Of course, this situation is where refrigerated and frozen storage comes into its own. If you pick your fruit at its best, before it becomes over-ripe and mushy, you can make more use of it: for example, jams are better made from slightly under-ripe fruits; age affects the taste and texture of vegetables. Therefore, you can store the produce in your fridge until you're able to process it further.

Pick fruit and vegetables at the peak of their condition instead of allowing them to become over-ripe on the stem. Ideally, freeze them straightaway – peas and sweetcorn are particularly prone to losing sweetness quickly. (See the section 'Preparing for the Big Freeze' later on in this chapter. If you're jamming or pickling, check out Chapters 5 and 6, and if you're after a tipple, get the lowdown in Chapter 9.)

If you've had to pick unripe fruits, you've stored them in the fridge and then you need them to ripen in a hurry, remove them from the fridge and place them in a plastic bag with a banana: the natural ethylene that bananas give off speeds up the ripening process.

The recommended temperature for home freezing is (–18 degrees Celsius/–0.4 degrees Fahrenheit). This temperature places produce into a kind of 'suspended animation' and, as long as your packaging is robust and as free from air as possible, keeps your food in good order for up to a year, by which time you've grown a new crop.

Before freezing produce, check its reaction to the cold. Fruits and vegetables differ in how they tolerate low temperatures. Some come out of the freezer as deliciously as they went in – for example, freshly picked peas and broad beans – whereas others can't stand the cold at all – for example, cucumbers. Others keep their taste but lose something of the texture – for instance, carrots become spongy. You can pick up hints on individual produce from the relevant chapters on fruits and vegetables.

Having taken the trouble to grow your own produce, make sure that you store only the best – if you find stringy beans unappetising before they're frozen, I guarantee that they don't improve after freezing!

Refrigerating Your Food

At the risk of stating the obvious, to store produce at low temperatures you need to place it in a fridge (as I describe in this section) or a freezer (something I cover in the next section 'Lowering the Temperature with Freezers'). Fridges and freezers carry out different tasks in different ways. *Fridges* keep things cool but unfrozen while *freezers* turn water to solid ice (and your vegetables are at least 70 per cent water) so you need to choose the appropriate piece of equipment for your intended use. Well-maintained household appliances are sufficiently good for the average home grower's needs.

Most fridges (and some freezers) come as uprights (they're taller than they are wide) like cupboards. They usually have an adjustable door opening too – the door can open with hinges to the left or right of the main body. Consider where you're going to place your upright equipment and fit the door for easy access.

Some upright fridges are small enough to fit under a worktop; a few go on top. You can also buy larger, larder-style fridges without a freezer compartment and others that are a combination of fridge and freezer. You can have a whole separate freezer with its own set of doors or, less commonly nowadays, an ice box within the body of the fridge.

A few fridges have fancy features for cooling and dispensing drinks, but all have a cooling mechanism and pipes (usually at the back) that need an airflow to work properly, especially to allow automatic defrosting to take place. Consult your fridge's instruction manual on exactly where to place it to ensure that the cooling mechanism works most efficiently.

Regulating your fridge's temperature

Maintaining the correct inside temperature of your fridge is vital. Use the settings dial to regulate the temperature so that it stays between 1 and 4 degrees Celsius (34–40 degrees Fahrenheit). You need to do more than turning to full blast in summer and less in winter.

The following factors affect your fridge temperature:

- ✔ Where you site your fridge
- ✔ How you heat your home
- ✔ How often you open the fridge door
- ✔ The age of your fridge model

You can buy small fridge temperature gauges for a couple of pounds that hook onto a shelf and are easy to read.

Using a fridge temperature gauge is good practice; get into the habit of glancing at it each time you open the fridge door. If the temperature consistently reads above 6 degrees Celsius (43 degrees Fahrenheit), adjust it cooler. If you keep the temperature too cold, however, you use extra energy and have frozen food in the fridge.

Avoiding cross-contamination and frosting

Although most fridges have a 'salad drawer' at the bottom of the fridge, in fact this space is most likely to get dripped on by raw meat juices. To avoid cross-contamination, commercial fridge users stack their fridges with food safety in mind and make sure that they're kept clean, and so take a leaf out of the experts' book at home too.

Ideally, to avoid any risk don't keep raw meat in the fridge at all when you know that you're going to be processing your home-grown produce. (Of course, you still need to keep the fridge scrupulously clean, meat or no meat!)

If you're using a normal domestic fridge for storing your home-grown produce, remember that cross-contamination from raw meat and especially chicken is one of the most common causes of poor food safety. (Read Chapter 3 for loads more tips on storing food safely, to put your mind at rest.)

Another problem is *frosting* – when a part of the food becomes frozen, goes limp or slimy – which is caused when you place your produce next to the cooling plates behind the fridge walls. Study your fridge carefully and place produce above any raw meats but not touching the cooling plates – when the fridge is working hard, these plates show beads of ice.

Lowering the Temperature with Freezers

Freezers come in two configurations: upright and chest (as shown in Figure 7-1). Upright freezers have both merits and drawbacks. They're already in the space under a fridge, making best use of a small area, or they're freestanding, which means they take up a small area in the kitchen or garage/utility room and the top surface is useful as storage space or a dumping ground.

Using the drawer compartments in an upright freezer, for an organised person, makes finding frozen goods easy – although badly labelled frozen goods are notoriously difficult to identify whatever the freezer. In badly organised uprights, however, drawers can get jammed with rock-solid frozen foods, and because doors open from top to bottom a load of cold air tumbles out of the open door. Thus, these models can be less energy efficient. In their defence, however, they're designed with solid drawer fronts to minimise the loss of cold and efficient use keeps energy loss to a minimum.

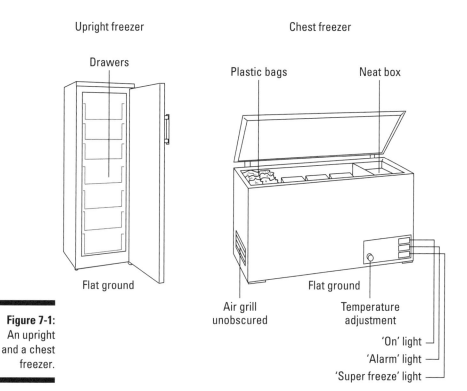

Upright freezer

Chest freezer

Drawers

Plastic bags   Neat box

Flat ground

Flat ground

Air grill
unobscured

Temperature
adjustment

'On' light
'Alarm' light
'Super freeze' light

Figure 7-1:
An upright
and a chest
freezer.

Chest freezers generally take up more space than upright freezers. They're essentially a big box. Most are wider than they are tall (you can get small chest freezers too, but they're less common) with a lid that opens upwards. On the whole, chest freezers hold more, volume for volume, than even the best-stacked upright freezer.

A well-insulated freezer may look bulky from the outside and yet in fact be quite small inside. Study both outer and inner dimensions when you're looking to buy one for your produce: the better the insulation, the wider the walls, the more efficient the freezer. Decide what makes a good freezer for you by using your own criteria.

Inside a freezer is a main chamber and a less deep, smaller chamber that contains all the workings and mechanisations; this latter chamber is the 'heavy' end, which is something to bear in mind when choosing who lifts this end while moving the freezer! Generally, a reflective layer on the inner walls reflects cold back into the freezer, and a plughole drains away the melted water when you're defrosting (see the section 'Defrosting and thawing out', later in the chapter).

Stacking and organising your chest freezer

The large open space of a chest freezer can take some organising, and so stack your own system of boxes inside to make finding what's at the bottom much easier. Sturdy cardboard boxes are fine (check out the sidebar 'Boxing clever in the freezer'); some hard plastic boxes go brittle and shatter. From time to time, go through the freezer because you'll be amazed at what lurks in the bottom (along with a few esca-peas!).

The best place for a chest freezer is away from general living spaces: a garage, outhouse or utility room is perfect and a real boon for home produce growers. You don't want to dash to the freezer with your hands full of carefully prepared produce, or to grab something for a quick meal, only to find it piled high with other people's coats and schoolbags.

Positioning your freezer: Things to consider

Place your freezer on flat ground. If you have your freezer outside or anywhere with wonky floors, 'trig' or wedge up any corners to stop wobbles that put a strain or tilt on the body of the freezer, or that stop the lid from fitting perfectly or the door from closing properly.

Freezers work most efficiently with a perfect seal around doors and lids.

To work efficiently, freezers need to be able to 'breathe', which means that air needs to circulate to keep the motor that drives the cooling mechanism working efficiently. Look at the outside of the freezer and you see a grill (usually a plastic cover) that keeps dust (and little fingers) out but allows air to pass through. The grill may have horizontal, vertical or other-shaped holes in it. Keeping some space between the grill and any obstruction or the wall is important. Although this distance varies from model to model, as a guide allow 10 centimetres (4 inches) as a minimum. Take this extra room into consideration when planning where your freezer is going to stand.

Plugging in and revving up

All freezers and fridges need an energy supply. You usually situate upright freezers in or near a living place for convenience where electricity sockets are to hand, so that plugging one straight in is a doddle. But bulky chest freezers are often (for good reasons) away from the general living space, and so you need a safe electricity supply to that location. You can use an *extension lead* – a long extra length of electricity wire usually coiled up inside a drum with sockets, single or multiple, at one end and a plug at the other – if no wired-in sockets are available.

When using an extension lead, take the following aspects into consideration:

- ✔ Check the length of the extension lead you plan to use, measuring from your most convenient socket to the freezer, making sure that you take into account the length of the lead already attached to the freezer.

- Extend all the coiled wire within an extension lead drum if the manufacture's instructions say so. Doing so is a common safety measure. Buy or use an extension lead that's close to the required length to avoid having metres and metres of extra unwound cable to deal with or trip over.

- ✔ Make sure that your extension lead is up to the job. If you're tracking electricity to an outbuilding and this tracking involves the lead going outside at any point, use a heavy-duty extension lead especially designed for outdoor use; if possible, fix it off the ground above head height. This positioning is safer and ensures that people don't trip over the wire or garrotte themselves on the way to fetch the peas for tea!

Reading the dials

Keep the temperature of your freezer at –18 degrees Celsius (–0.4 degrees Fahrenheit) or just below to ensure that most produce stores safely for six months to a year. (How you wrap the food also influences the length of this period, as I discuss in Chapter 7.)

Boxing clever in the freezer

Keeping a freezer menu is good practice: a set of cards with the contents of the freezer written on them. I've tried, honest, but I found this method totally confusing. When I wanted something out of the freezer, there was never the time, or a pencil handy to amend the list. And although to begin with the intention was to return and update, I never did. Soon the list was so hopelessly out of date that it was worse than having no list at all. I expected items to be in the freezer that weren't.

Now I use a couple of sturdy cardboard boxes that fit the space well and keep the things I use most often in them. I can lift my big boxes right out of the way when I want to have a rummage around to find any surprises. This arrangement works well for me.

Freezer manufacturers have their own designs for telling you whether the machine is working efficiently (read the instruction manual for a new freezer), but here are two common methods:

✔ An alarm light if the temperature drops; pay attention if you see it

✔ A power light to show that the freezer is on

All fridges and freezers are colder at the bottom; hot or even a bit warmer air rises.

If you're thinking of buying a new freezer, upright or chest, check the energy rating: newer freezers have an 'A' rating system whether they're the most basic designs or the all-singing, all-dancing versions. 'A' rating models have good insulation and energy efficiency. Over time, you save in energy costs the extra you pay on initial expenditure (compared, say, with buying an older model second-hand), and they're altogether more environmentally friendly.

Defrosting and thawing out

Whereas modern fridges (which I discuss in the earlier section 'Refrigerating Your Food') often have a defrosting cycle so that you never see a build-up of frost and ice on the inside, and the defrosting cycle doesn't harm the already chilled food, the situation is different with freezers. You can't just defrost a freezer with all the food still inside. Here are the steps to take in order to defrost a freezer successfully:

1. **Choose a time when the freezer is at its emptiest.** This time is probably spring, when you've eaten your way around the previous seasons and are planting and growing new crops to take the place of all the food you've eaten.

2. **Find a way to empty your freezer of produce, keeping it all together and under some form of insulation in a cool place safe from marauding children and pets – the airing cupboard isn't a good idea.** Fill any insulated cool boxes and bags. Fill the washing basket or other large containers, heaping a thick layer of covering – towels and duvets – over the produce to keep the cold in. Trust that you've done the job of insulating and don't be tempted to take a peek; you only let the warm in.

3. **Remove the freezer drawers and partitions and wash them with warm, soapy water.** Rinse and leave to dry.

4. **Pick out any stray labels from the now empty freezer, along with escaped peas and beans rattling around in the bottom.** No doubt you can see a thick layer of frost and ice attached to the inner walls.

5. **Upright freezers: Most upright freezers have a small attachment in the form of a tube that you can fit to a drainage channel low down and at the front of the appliance.** Fitting this tube allows you to collect the water that drains out when the ice is thawing. Place a dish under this outlet to catch the water. If your freezer doesn't have one of these handy tubes or you've lost it, use towels or newspaper to keep any leaking defrosting water to a minimum by mopping up frequently.

6. **Chest freezers: Remove the plug to allow the water to drain out.** Find a shallow dish to catch the water. You may be surprised at how much water comes out.

   Tuck an old towel or newspapers around the bottom of the freezer when you're defrosting, to soak up any spillages or overflows.

7. **Wait for defrosting to finish.** Defrosting time varies with each freezer and its situation, but as long as the surrounding ambient temperature isn't below freezing (0 degrees Celsius/32 degrees Fahrenheit), the process takes a maximum of 24 hours from start to finish. So that your frozen produce spends as little time out of the freezer as possible, speed up the process by placing bowls of hot water inside the freezer.

8. **Clean the freezer using a bowl of hot water (as warm as your hands can stand), liquid detergent and a soft cloth.** Wipe the interior, paying special attention to the corners, inside the lid and round the door/lid seal. Don't forget to give the outside a wipe over too.

9. **Allow your freezer to air dry.** Alternatively, wipe it dry with a clean cloth.

10. **Return the produce in an orderly manner and put the freezer onto the 'super freeze' mode for a few hours until your temperature dials show at least –18 degrees Celsius (–0.4 degrees Fahrenheit).** See the section on 'Reading the dials', earlier in this chapter.

Don't be tempted to stick a knife down behind the ice and frost to prise it off; many freezers have been punctured and ruined like that. Be patient and wait until the temperature rises a little, or use the hot water trick. The ice then comes off in satisfactory large lumps that you can chuck straight into the sink to melt.

Preparing for the Big Freeze

Deciding what you plan to do with all your frozen produce eventually gives a guide to how you need to prepare it for freezing. Some fruits and vegetables lend themselves to you pre-preparing them ready for a meal – for example, tomato, onion and courgette base – whereas storing for further processing makes better sense for some jam fruits. Keeping a cosy session of jam-making for the cold winter months to bring back memories of the warm days of harvest is one great thing that your freezer can do for you.

Some small fruits such as currants and gooseberries are better frozen with their 'tops and tails' on. Rubbing them between your fingers removes these parts when they're in a frozen state much more quickly and efficiently than while fresh, so don't waste time on that job when the freezer can do the work for you.

Here are some tips to bear in mind when freezing:

- Set your freezer to its 'super freeze' setting for a couple of hours beforehand and leave it on this setting until the new produce is frozen through. Doing so keeps the already-frozen food frozen when you add new unfrozen food that raises the overall temperature of the freezer.

- Chill your produce in the fridge first, especially if you already have a partially filled freezer.

- Add only 10 per cent of the volume of your freezer at any one point. Hold the rest of your produce in the fridge and add it when the new produce is down to –18 degrees Celsius (–0.4 degrees Fahrenheit), even though doing so may mean waiting 24 hours for a complete freeze before you add the next batch.

- Keep your freezer topped up because doing so adds to its energy efficiency. You don't have to use produce: filling empty spaces with piles of newspaper or plastic bottles of water (always leave a gap at the top for the liquid to expand into) adds to the efficient and economical running of the freezer. Just remove the appropriate amount of 'filling' when you add new food to freeze.

Blanching in brief

Blanching is a process used for vegetables only: it destroys certain enzymes and bacteria while helping to preserve the colour, texture and flavour of the food, as well as retaining more vitamin C.

Use blanching to keep your favourite foods as perfect as possible. The vegetables that you know are destined for use in stews and casseroles don't need to look as good as those you intend to serve as a vegetable in their own right. Keep blanched goods for 'cosmetic' dinners or the last that you're going to use in the freezer.

Here's how to go about blanching vegetables (see Figure 7-2):

1. **Use a large pan (with a lid if possible) and bring plenty of water (2.8 litres (6 pints) for 0.5 kilograms (1.1 pounds) of produce) to a rolling boil.** You can reuse this water and the chilled water from Step 2 until it looks cloudy.

Adding a squirt of lemon juice to the boiling water for light-coloured vegetables helps retain the colour, for example for parsnips and turnips.

2. **Have two other pans/bowls of chilled water at the ready.** Float ice cubes in the water for a rapid cooling effect.

3. **Hold the produce in a blanching basket or sieve and immerse in your large pan of water and then plunge into the chilled water.**

   Timing with a 'pinger' is essential. Blanching times vary from vegetable to vegetable (see the individual recipes throughout the book for these).

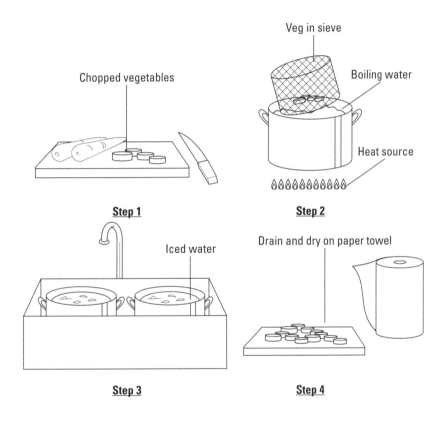

Chopped vegetables

Veg in sieve

Boiling water

Heat source

Step 1

Step 2

Iced water

Drain and dry on paper towel

Step 3

Step 4

Pack in portion sizes

Step 5

Figure 7-2:
Blanching,
at the ready.

4. **Drain and dry produce before bagging up and freezing.** The earlier section 'Preparing for the Big Freeze' gives more hints on that part of the proceedings.

Experience tells you which vegetables to blanch and when putting them straight into the freezer is just as good.

Wrapping up well

The key to useful freezer storage is in the wrapping. Use the following items:

- ✔ Clean, strong, recycled bags with no holes – excluding the air is impor- tant to avoid drying out frozen goods
- ✔ Juice cartons with a plastic bag as lining for liquids
- ✔ Plastic containers with lids – good-quality, non-brittle plastic
- ✔ Purpose-made freezer bags; cookery shops and supermarkets sell them
- ✔ Recycled yoghurt pots, well washed-out plastic milk bottles (cut down to size) and ice cream cartons

If you know that you're saving a certain vegetable or fruit for a special occa- sion more than six months hence, double wrap it as an extra precaution to keep it fresh for use. Frozen food goes rock hard and you can easily knock it about, making tiny holes in the plastic bags, which allows air into your bags and starts the drying process.

Working out portion size for meals

Consider portion size *before* you fill a bag with damp produce to the brim, thinking, mistakenly, that you're saving on packaging. The food ends up as a solid lump and no amount of thumping or sawing reduces its size.

The main thing is to make useful-sized packs for everyday meals.

Make portion sizes that are useful to you and your family. You can always use more than one portion if extra people come for a meal.

Portioning for further processing

If you're storing for more processing, check out Chapters 5 and 6, which give you the information for making jam or chutney. Find your recipe and put exact amounts into bags; doing so speeds up the next process and you're not left with silly quantities to deal with.

Packing cooked or par-cooked foods

Some produce lends itself well to being cooked or par-cooked before freezing –
for example, tomatoes, onions and courgettes are ready at the same time and
are a base for other dishes:

1. **Cook or par-cook the produce.**

2. **Allow to cool completely to room temperature.**

3. **Pack into portion sizes, label and date.**

4. **Chill to fridge temperature (4 degrees Celsius/40 degrees Fahrenheit).**

5. **Freeze in 'super freeze' mode, overnight or until solid.**

Dealing with liquids and soups

When freezing juices or soups – a super ready meal that takes up minimum
space in the freezer – remember to leave room for expansion.

Liquids expand on freezing. Leave at least 2.5 centimetres (1 inch) at the top
of plastic containers or prop up bottles carefully in the freezer while freezing
with the lid slightly open. Tighten after freezing. Line square containers with a
clean plastic bag to store liquid in; they also stack neatly in the freezer.

Remembering what's what

Label everything; write on the bag with an indelible marker or use labels suitable for freezer use. (Everyday labels ping straight off and you're left wondering what on earth your bags are full with!) Also, take a look also at the earlier
section 'Stacking and organising your chest freezer'.

As a general rule, if you haven't eaten your frozen, home-grown produce
before you harvest the next season's growth, the food's past its best and you
produced too much; plant less next year. Compost what's left in the freezer,
eat as much fresh as you can and give over the freezer space to the surplus
of the new harvest.

Preventing freezer burn

Freezing is a form of drying – freeze-dried coffee granules are common in
the shops. Water is removed in the freezing process and when your produce
is poorly packaged, or unevenly frozen, *freezer burn* occurs – scorched or
pale-looking patches on your food. The produce isn't unsafe to eat, but is no
longer at its best.

Use good-quality containers or bags. In containers, leave a 1-centimetre (half
an inch) gap at the top for your frozen food to expand into. Expel as much air
as possible from plastic bags. The plastic bag is pliable enough to expand on
freezing, so avoid crashing and bashing your frozen produce about making
tiny holes in the packaging materials.

Blanching, but not from fear!

I've spent hours blanching and find it rather tedious work. I'm happy to freeze most vegetables without blanching, especially if they're destined to be casseroled or made into soups.

I never blanch peas or broad beans and have one big bag of each that I add to over time as crops ripen. They look and taste fine to me. But all the loose frozen vegetables for sale in shops have been blanched under strictly controlled temperatures, and although yours may not look exactly the same, they taste twice as good. Picking is time-consuming too, so I plant little and often in order to 'catch' my produce just as it ripens in manageable amounts. If you're like me, gardening has to fit around a busy life.

Working with bulk packing: Open freezing

One way to store larger amounts of produce in bulk (which also helps to keep your energy cost down), while avoiding the hazard of ending up with a giant, frozen, solid lump, is to *open freeze* (also called *tray* or *loose* freezing). This approach works for both blanched and unblanched produce. Some freezers, particularly the upright design, have a special tray built in for this process:

1. **Lay out your prepared fruits or vegetables on a tray or a baking sheet so that they aren't touching.**

2. **Place the tray into the freezer and leave for a few hours depending on how big your pieces are.**

3. **Have a robust plastic bag handy, big enough to place your tray into the mouth of the bag.**

4. **Tip the pieces into the bag when frozen.**

You can repeat the process as many times as you want, as long as you keep the bag as air-free as possible and totally frozen between batches.

Place small dry fruits and vegetables – non-mushy raspberries and peas, for example – straight into your 'bulk' plastic bag; make it a robust one. Lay the bag out so that the fruit is fairly separate, and from time to time give the bag a shake to ensure that drier items don't stick together.

Freeze one or two loose citrus fruits among the produce to keep your freezer smelling fresh.

Chapter 8

Drying, Salting and Vacuum-Packing Your Produce

In This Chapter

▶ Drying food for successful storage

▶ Salting away your produce

▶ Removing the air from stored food

*H*umans have had to find ways to store their food ever since they became hunters and gatherers. Buying sun-dried tomatoes from a delicatessen may be trendy nowadays, but remove the fancy packing and you've the oldest form of storing food in the world. People have been sun-drying for thousands of years, although sometimes finding enough sun in the UK can be difficult!

In this chapter, I describe three common ways to store your home produce. As well as discussing drying food, I also examine another time-tested method – using salt – and a nifty modern way to make the most of your gardening efforts: home vacuum-packing.

Drying Up Your Food – Deliberately

Drying – that is, removing moisture from produce – is the oldest method of storing food and is what the natural world does everyday using free sunshine and wind. Enzymes, bacteria, yeasts, fungi and other nasties thrive in an environment containing water (and Chapter 3 says much more about the most common culprits). They can multiply to unacceptable and even dangerous levels in a damp environment unless you stop that happening. In this section, I cover some basic drying methods and a few that are a little more complicated.

Drying food has the following advantages:

- ✔ Intensifies flavour and sweetness
- ✔ Reduces weight, making your dried produce light to carry with you
- ✔ Removes bulk, therefore reducing storage space needed
- ✔ Removes the opportunity for growth of micro-organisms, making your food safe to eat

Dried food can be:

- ✔ Added as a dry ingredient to many dishes and soups
- ✔ Eaten dry for snacks
- ✔ Rehydrated before use

Using the sun and air to dry

To dry in the sun, clear a sunny windowsill so that you're ready when your produce is. Find or make racks that fit your space and line them with *muslin* – a loose-weave cloth often used in food preparation – if the pieces are small enough to fall through your grid. The racks need to allow air to circulate under your drying produce – wire cake-cooling racks or the grill pan are fine but remember that you need to leave them in situ while the drying process takes place.

The UK is sometimes lacking in consistent sunshine. Therefore, laying your produce out on movable racks to dry allows you to move the whole rack into a warm environment – such as an airing cupboard or cooling down oven – to hurry along the process of drying. Turn to Chapter 16 for more hints on handling herbs and leafy produce.

Delicate produce may dry out successfully in the sun but then reabsorb moisture from the atmosphere on cooling. To reduce this problem, pack the produce away in the warmth of the day while the food is at its driest.

Seed heads, long-stemmed flowers and leafy produce need a slightly different approach. Hang, heads down, in an airy place (again, consult Chapter 16 for more info). Squashes and strings of onions and garlic respond well to safe-keeping in a cool weatherproof shed or barn.

Use recycled greengrocer nets for bags of vegetables and hang them on nails out of reach of pests (flip to Chapter 3 for the lowdown on these low-lifes) – take your lead from the greengrocers, who are the experts.

Your dried goods may harbour tiny moths or the eggs from other bugs living quite comfortably in dried leafy goods – such as bundles of herbs (see Chapter 16 on drying specific herbs and a special way to wrap them). When your dried herbs are really properly dry and well packed, pop them into the freezer for 48 hours. This process kills off any tiny residents and their eggs. You can take them out and store them in airtight containers out of direct sunlight after that.

Saving seeds

Saving seeds is nature's method of conserving life itself. Although you bring your seeds indoors to protect them, nature manages to achieve this aim outdoors through all weathers. Some plants, known as annuals, produce their seeds in the first year of growing – such as beans, peas and coriander – whereas others, known as biennials, take two years – including roots such as carrots, parsnips and beetroot. Therefore, you have to leave some roots in the ground over the winter to allow them to shoot to seed the following year – to understand the process better, look in Chapter 4 for clamping solutions where you're expressly trying to stop your plants from running to seed.

You can dry seeds by removing the seed heads when they're completely ripe on the plant and upending them. Store in brown paper bags in an airy place. (Check out Chapter 16 for more on saving herb seeds.) The principle is the same whether you're saving seeds for eating raw or to add as flavouring.

Making and using solar dryers

If you want to go the extra mile with drying food, you can build a basic and simple solar dryer out of recycled materials – visit your local recycling centre or go to a window- or conservatory-making company and find out whether it has any rejected materials. Everyone makes mistakes and the company may have the perfect item for you at a reduced price. Or go upmarket with new gear to make a super-duper version for dehydrating your produce.

Here are the basic requirements of a simple solar dryer (see Figure 8-1):

- ✔ **Box or container:** Look for clean, serviceable materials. Avoid treated woods, because they may give off harmful chemicals and you're going put food right next to them.

- ✔ **Shelves, screen or racks:** These are necessary to allow an air flow. Use something that you don't mind putting your dinner on: the grill off the front of a car may look good but if you've spilt oil through it, you may add flavours you didn't bargain for – not to mention toxicity! Racks for cooling cakes or from the grill pan on the oven are food grade.

Every time you use a shiny surface in your food dryer, you reflect the heat radiation back out of the box. A sheet of stainless steel – although clean and food worthy – with small holes acts in opposition to your intentions!

✔ **Single-glazed window:** Perspex-type materials are fine, but they don't last as well as glass, tending to yellow in the sun. Double-glazing units are too heavy.

✔ **Solar collector or absorber plate:** A black matt metal sheet is ideal, but any black surface absorbs heat.

✔ **Source of warmth:** The sun! Be prepared to reposition your solar dryer from time to time; it works just as well outside on fine days.

✔ **Ventilation holes:** Or gaps built into your box. You need ventilation near the top, because hot air rises and takes the moisture with it, and near the bottom to allow new air in.

If you want the luxury version, add

✔ **Back-up heat:** For those gloomy days.

✔ **Carrying handles:** You need to move the solar dryer around to catch the best rays.

✔ **Legs:** Legs mean less bending and stooping while you're filling and emptying, and they keep produce away from pesky pests who may want to share your booty. Stand the legs in plastic cups full of water in order to deter crawling bugs.

✔ **Screens:** Place over your vent holes to keep out bugs and flies attracted by your delicious drying food.

If you catch the food-drying bug, you may want to invest in some back-up heat for your solar dryer, or want to go for more complicated designs with higher efficiency rates – in case you're in a hurry for a snack or the sun isn't showing! One of the simplest and safest ways to do get this heat is to incorporate a heating mat. You can find these in pet shops that sell reptiles; they're flat and add gentle heat, but the power source doesn't come free! Reading *The Solar Food Dryer* by Eben Fodor (New Society Publishers) takes your solar food drying to another level.

Solar drying can take place wherever you can harness the sun's rays; it works best in midsummer. Seek out south-facing situations behind glass, using a greenhouse, conservatory or window in the house or shed. Lay out your produce in a single layer without touching for the best results. Allow the sun to reach every part and the released moisture to escape.

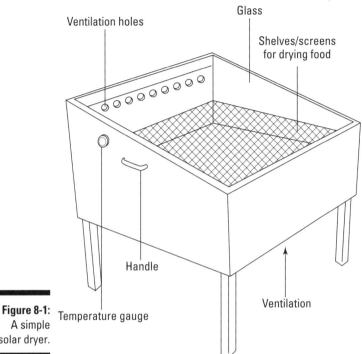

Ventilation holes

Glass

Shelves/screens
for drying food

Handle

Ventilation

Figure 8-1: Temperature gauge
A simple
solar dryer.

Pre-treating fruits and vegetables

If you don't want your apple rings or other light-coloured fruit and veg to
look brown from exposure to the air, pre-treat them as follows:

- ✔ **Dip the fruit in ascorbic acid:** You can buy this ingredient at health food
  shops or chemists.

- ✔ **Employ citrus juice:** Squeezed lemon juice stops the browning of fruits
  and vegetables.

- ✔ **Use a simple syrup:** Pre-treating prevents discoloration. Boil water and
  sugar in a 1:1 ratio (1 kilogram of sugar to 1 litre of water or 2 pounds 4
  ounces to 1¾ pints). Let it cool before using it on the fruit and protect it
  from hungry wasps and flies, who love syrup too.

If you've taken the trouble to grow chemical-free organic produce, remember
that pre-treatments are normally for cosmetic purposes: you soon get used to
the idea of brownish apples rings and they taste just as good. Eat them with
your eyes shut as a test. Try some with and some without the pre-treatments
and you can judge whether labour saving wins over cosmetic appearance.

Helping with powerful incentives

Powered dehydrators are becoming more popular as people want to take advantage of growing their own fruit and vegetables. You can buy a dehydrator in cooking and catering shops and online. They range in price from around £30 to £200, depending on the quantity they can dry at one time, the quality of materials and variations in heating. You need somewhere to plug in a dehydrator.

Some dehydrators are designed to hold pureed food so that you can make fruit leathers (Chapter 5 has more information about fruit leathers) by spreading them on special non-drip dehydrator trays and peeling the dried fruit off in strips. This excellent snack keeps for ages.

Testing for dryness

Whatever drying method you use, check for dryness by feeling the produce. Fruits – such as apple rings – should bend and tear easily; sugary fruits – such as apricots – become sticky; and leafy produce – such as herbs – should crumble between your fingers. Simply continue to dry anything that's not ready. If you're using a solar dryer, replace for a few more hours.

Extending the shelf-life with delicate things in mind

You can crystallise certain kinds of flower petals to keep them out of their season for a special occasion or to decorate a cake. When done well, such flowers make a beautiful and delicate decoration.

 Before you set your heart on a colour scheme, be aware that some petals do change colour – especially white ones – and others with stronger colours keep very well, so do some experiments first. People have used crystalline violets and rose petals in confectionery for years.

Here are the necessary ingredients for preserving flowers:

- A delicate, clean paintbrush less than 3 millimetres (eighth of an inch) wide
- A clean, dry plate
- A steady hand

✔ Fresh egg white

✔ White caster sugar

Follow these steps to keep flowers:

1. **Choose edible flowers with thin, flat petals (white petals sometimes turn brown and curled-over petals stick together).**

   Primroses, primulas, roses, violets and apple and pear blossom are all good for starters.

2. **Paint both sides of the petal with egg white or dip it in the egg white if doing so is easier. Alternatively, dissolve gum Arabic in rosewater to a consistency that allows you to paint a thin layer onto the petals. (You can buy these items from herbal suppliers and health food shops.)**

3. **Shake enough caster sugar over the coated petal for it to stick and soak in.**

4. **Leave to dry in a warm, airy place (the airing cupboard is fine).**

5. **When completely dry, the flowers fall onto a dry plate with a 'ticking' sound. Store in an airtight container until you want to use them.**

Many flowers are poisonous, especially foxgloves and laburnum flowers. Check that the petals you choose aren't dangerous; stick to roses if you're not sure because they're tried and tested. You're not allowed to pick wild flowers, and nor can you pinch flowers from other people's gardens, no matter how pretty they are!

Shrivelling with Salt: An Old-fashioned Method

Although you often hear warnings about over-consuming salt in your food, you may be pleased to hear that you can make use of its preservation properties without leaving the salt in the end result.

Salt as a natural preservative still has some uses in the modern world – mostly for bacon and hams. People used to pack vegetables purely in salt to preserve them, but modern tastes simply can't stand those levels of saltiness any more. These days, salt is most useful as part of a process for vegetables destined for the pickle jar (see Chapter 6 for information on completing the process) and as a way of keeping eggs (go to Chapter 17 to discover how to salt eggs the Chinese way).

Understanding osmosis

Vegetables consist of up to 90 per cent water, and spoilage bacteria and micro-organisms need water to survive (see Chapter 3 for more about these rogue spoilers). Although pickling in a 5 per cent (or higher) acidity vinegar solution (more in Chapter 6) changes the environment of the produce so that spoilage bacteria can't survive, your water-laden vegetables may inadvertently dilute the vinegar to a level (less than 5 per cent acidity) that allows bacteria to survive and grow without you realising. So read on to discover how to reduce the moisture content of your vegetables – using salt.

Salt uses *osmosis* (the tendency of water to move from a less dilute solution to a more concentrated one) to draw the moisture through the cell walls in the vegetable. The concentration of salt on one side of the cell wall is higher than the other and the natural physical inclination is to equalise this concentration. Water can be pulled out, but the salt doesn't enter the cell.

Working with salt

You can choose from two methods of salting: dry or as a brine. Both do the job. You can choose which salt to use too. Ordinary, everyday table salt has an anti-caking agent (sodium hexacyanoferrate) allowing it to run freely from a salt cellar, whereas sea salt is a mineral-rich product without additives that may be more expensive.

Dry-salting

Layer fruits and vegetables in dry salt to draw out the moisture. Leave to drain. The timing depends on the particular vegetable or fruit.

Salting in brine

Dissolve salt in water – usually at a concentration of about 100 grams of salt in 1 litre of water (3½ ounces in 1 and ¾ pints), but observe individual recipes for concentration and timings – and cover the prepared vegetables with the brine. Placing a plate over your bowl holds the produce under the brine.

The vegetables don't taste salty – contrary to popular belief – as long as you rinse off the salt thoroughly. (Check out the earlier section 'Understanding osmosis' if you're interested in the technicalities of this process.)

Do this job quickly to avoid re-absorption of water:

1. **Pour away the brine or knock off the remaining dry salt.**

2. **Use a colander and rinse vegetables under plenty of cold running water.**

3. **Shake off excess water.**

4. **Dry with paper towels.**

Your produce, with the excess moisture removed, is now ready for pickling. (See the relevant chapters on individual vegetables for recipes, or for further information on the pickling method check out Chapter 6.)

Trying supersaturated solutions

Chinese supermarkets sell salted eggs. This method is a way of conserving eggs in a supersaturated salt solution – made by dissolving a quantity of salt in hot water – creating a sterile environment where nothing can grow and at the same time, because egg shells are porous, drawing moisture out of the egg. (For the whole story and instructions on how to make Chinese salted eggs, read Chapter 17.)

Sucking Out the Air

Freezing your produce to store (something I discuss in Chapter 7) is of course very effective, but you can increase this effectiveness even more when you remove as much air as possible from the bags containing your food. You can certainly squeeze packed bags by hand to remove the air before freezing your produce, but vacuum-packing is the modern, technological way of storing your home-produced food. Vacuum-packers – at one time only suitable for industrial use – have shrunk in size and expense and so are now available for domestic use. Home food storers can now enjoy some of the fun that was previously the preserve of professional food processors. Vacuum-packers are still relatively expensive and have limited uses, but nonetheless the process is good fun and space-saving.

Getting help from a real sucker

Small-scale, table-top vacuum-packers are now an affordable piece of kit for the serious home grower. You get all the benefits associated with removing air from packets (see the next section 'Appreciating the advantages of vacuum-packing') and extend shelf-life too. A new vacuum sealer for home use costs around £200; look in cook or catering shops or online.

You need to use specialist bags or vacuum-sealing containers with these vacuum-packers.

Appreciating the advantages of vacuum-packing

Taking the majority of air out of food packages before storing them in a fridge or freezer makes all round good sense, whether you use a vacuum- packer or do the job by hand. In a sealed bag and stored in the fridge, fresh goods – depending what they are – last much longer than in air-filled packages: quite simply, eliminating the air increases the lifetime of your produce.

Modern, commercial packing methods often include packing in a modified atmosphere where the air is flushed out and replaced by gases high in carbon dioxide and nitrogen. Of course, you can't achieve this modified atmosphere at home – and you probably don't want to – but the fact that the professional food packers use this method indicates the undesirable effect of air while packing food.

Vacuum-packing helps you avoid the following issues that are associated with packing in a normal air atmosphere:

- ✔ **Enclosing bacteria and other micro-organisms with the air:** Some bacteria continue to multiply under refrigeration (not freezing), thus causing deterioration of your food produce.

- ✔ **Extra costs:** Vacuum-packing avoids the extra costs associated with air within packaging heating up quickly when you open fridges and freezers and of paying for the power to cool it back down again.

- ✔ **Freeze drying:** The water droplets in air form crystals in your frozen packets and the extra packed-in air draws liquid out of your produce, resulting in the item being of poorer quality than when you first packed it. Vacuum-packing avoids this problem.

- ✔ **Oxidisation:** *Oxidisation* happens when oxygen from the atmosphere combines with other substances. One visual example of oxidisation is when the cut surface of an apple goes brown.

- ✔ **Taking up valuable room:** Compressing air is a tough job, which shows how much space air takes up. Removing the air means that each pack uses the minimum space in your fridge or freezer.

You can of course remove some of the air by hand. When you have pliable packaging – such as plastic bags – you can employ a little trick to remove as much air as possible without damaging the produce in the packs. Squeezing air out manually is okay but a gentle squeeze under the arm gives a gentler force over a larger area than hands. Hold the top of the bag loosely to let the air escape.

Vacuum-packing gone mad

Vacuum-packing is fun! Have you ever seen a vacuum-packed egg? Or shoe? I have – it came as a bit of a shock and you can easily get carried away with vacuum-packing. I thought that vac-packing my dried apple rings would be a clever idea. It did reduce the size of the pack incredibly, but when I opened it I didn't have apple rings so much as a great big, solid sweetie – probably what you'd call a giant apple chew! The sugar in the apple had welded the apple rings into one large lump under pressure – perhaps I should do the same to controlled amounts of sweet, squishy, dried goods and make a business selling fruity chews!

Better still, you can collapse the packaging. Insert a drinking straw into the bag (as Figure 8-2 shows), hold it closed round the top and suck the air out until the package collapses in on itself. This method removes even more air and what the air contains.

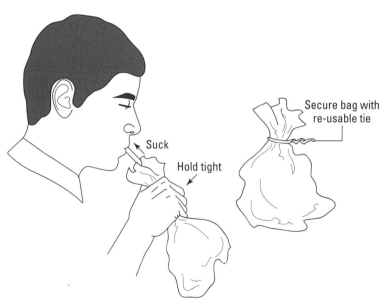

Figure 8-2:
Removing air with a straw.

Suck

Hold tight

Secure bag with re-usable tie

To seal the bag, tie a knot in the end if the bag is large enough. Otherwise, you can fasten with string, rubber bands, purpose-made clips or metal twist ties (some of which you can re-use).

Chapter 9

Drinking Up Time: Imbibing Your Own Liquid Refreshments

Cordials and home-made alcoholic drinks are another way to preserve fruity flavours in liquid form, and you can produce them using just natural ingredients. Some need heating up and some need watering down; others you can drink straight from the bottle. But they all have one thing in common: the uniqueness of enjoying home-made drinks that are available nowhere else. Producing both child- and adult-friendly home-made potions from home-grown and foraged plants is a joy, and this chapter gives you the step-by-step guides you need to do it.

Unnatural colourings and preservatives in food and drink have come in for some stick lately, and rightly so. If you don't trust the marketing hype and haven't the patience (or a strong magnifying glass!) to be able to read the labels, you can get around any potential problems by producing your own cordials. You can add fizzy water to imitate the bubbly feel of shop-bought drinks while leaving out any suspect ingredients – which puts parents back in charge of what goes into 'the mouths of babes and sucklings'. Making cordials is surprisingly easy and doesn't always involve any cooking, and the taste of home-made, sweet, fruity drinks surpasses anything jostling down a factory line.

If you fancy a cuppa right now, just pour boiling water over your fresh or dried herbs (Chapter 16 tells you how) – leave for a few minutes to infuse and drink while reading this chapter!

Being Cordial: Family-friendly Drinks

You can transform your children's experience of fizzy and still drinks by providing home-made cordials, the freshness and lightness of flavour in which surpasses anything you can buy in the shops. Just water them down in the same way as any shop-bought concentrated drink.

It doesn't matter whether you call these fruity sugary liquids cordials, syrups or squashes to make them more acceptable to any reluctant youngsters, just be prepared to cross the line of convention in a delicious manner.

Making and keeping fruit cordials

The only real problem with making cordials is choosing where to start. If you're reading this chapter in midwinter and you've fruit in the freezer, skip to the later 'Heating things up' section where I describe berry cordials. If the season is early summer and you know where your local elderflowers hang out, start with the later 'Checking out elderflower cordial' section. If growing your own is still a budding project and the season for finding freebies in the hedgerows hasn't come around yet (Chapter 18 advises on when to pick up your basket and go foraging), start with the following simple lemon squash and get the family converted before becoming more adventurous.

Basic Lemon Squash
(leading into Elderflower Cordial)

This recipe is simple, delicious on its own and a basis for flavour additions. The freshness of lemons enhances the perfume of the elderflowers if you take it to that stage. You can feel that summertime really has arrived if you sit outdoors with a cool glass of this squash and dangle your feet in the swimming pool!

Preparation time: *20 minutes*

Processing time: *Standing time 48 hours; straining and bottling 30 minutes*

Yield: *About 2 litres (3½ pints)*

2 large or 3 smaller lemons – buy organic or unwaxed lemons (the wax is for cosmetic reasons only)

1 kilogram (2 pounds, 4 ounces) granulated sugar

50 grams (2 ounces) citric acid – buy from a chemist

1.2 litres (2 pints) water

1 Pare the zest from the lemons using the smallest gradation on the grater; cut lemons in half and squeeze the juice into a large stainless steel or ceramic bowl (a large mixing bowl, for example).

2 Tip in the lemons, zest, leftover shells, sugar, citric acid and water.

3 Using a wooden spoon, stir until the sugar dissolves. Cover with a clean tea towel propped up by the spoon to stop it sagging into the bowl.

4 Leave for 48 hours – a cool spot in the kitchen is fine, but don't leave it right next to a hot oven or heater. Stir when you pass it, or at least twice daily.

5 Strain through a sieve, making sure that you tip the lemon shells over to allow any trapped cordial to run out.

Tip: *With its high acid and sugar content, this cordial keeps in a jug in the fridge for six to eight weeks and stores excellently in the freezer for much longer (up to a year). (Chapter 7 provides ideas on freezing liquids.)*

Per 100-millilitre serving: 200 calories; 0 grams protein, 50 grams carbohydrate, 0 grams fat, 0 grams saturated fat, 0 milligrams cholesterol, 0 grams fibre, 1 milligram sodium.

You can ring the changes in taste by swapping some of the lemon for other combinations of citrus fruit, such as

- Lime with lemon

- Orange with lemon

- Grapefruit with lemon – don't try this one on the children for your first experiment; it has a more adult ring to it

- Any of or all the above in combination

Checking out elderflower cordial

Leave out one of the lemons and, keeping the other quantities the same, substitute 25 freshly picked elderflower heads. Give them a gentle shake to dislodge any large debris or living creatures, but don't wash them; you want the pollen grains in the mix not down the sink. (Chapter 18 has advice on getting the best out of your countryside-picking expeditions.) Elderflower cordial stores in the fridge for up to six weeks or in the freezer for much longer.

Smoothing it out, or enjoying the rough with the smooth

You can simply sieve the basic lemon juice to remove any pips, the shells of the lemons and the parings of the zest, but if you prefer the 'lemonyness' and want a 'with bits' experience, the zesty bits soften in the sugar give a chunkier 'meal' of a drink. Sieve the mixture using the sieve like a fishing net, examining each 'catch' and removing the lemon shells, pips and any other bits you don't approve of. Return the zesty bits to enjoy with the drink.

This technique doesn't work quite so well with elderflower cordial because the flower heads turn a rather drab brown while imparting their flavour. Having said that, personal taste is what counts – I'm perfectly happy with a few floating flower petals, the odd tiny insect and a 'peck of dirt'. Depending on how pristine you like your juice, you can sieve it roughly or strain it through muslin for the purer look, perhaps adding an ice cube containing trapped elderflower blossom for effect.

You can also make a no-cook version of cordial with rhubarb (you can find this fruit stalking in the berry section in Chapter 11).

Heating things up

Some fruits need a little heat to encourage the juices to flow, such as when you're making cordial or fruit syrups from garden berries, currants (Chapter 11 is the place to look) or wild berries (Chapter 18 has the information) or a combination.

Use one of the two methods in this section as a guide and substitute your single or mixture of berry flavours. Try loganberries, raspberries, strawberries, gooseberries and the red and white currants.

Don't add water to the fruit unless the year has been exceptionally dry and the bushes are starved of moisture.

The exceptions to this rule are:

- **Blackcurrants:** Add 300 millilitres (½ pint) of water to 450 grams (1 pound) of fruit.

- **Blackberries:** Add 300 millilitres (½ pint) of water to 2.7 kilograms (6 pounds) of fruit.

Choose the following method that suits you best.

Berry Cordial (with indirect heat): Method 1

This method of making berry cordial is 'safe' because, with the safety net of water all around it from your bain-marie, your juice can't burn. So, if you're prone to daydreaming or taking long phone calls, this method may be the one for you. Just keep a good focus when the time comes to add the sugar because that can burn. See Chapter 2 for equipment descriptions.

Special tools required: *Jelly bag*

Preparation time: *10 minutes*

Processing time: *Heating approx. one hour; straining, minimum 4 hours; further cooking 15 minutes*

Yield: *Approx 2 litres (3½ pints) from 2.7 kilograms (6 pounds) fruit*

2.7 kilograms (6 pounds) of your chosen fruit (note: this amount is only a guide; smaller amounts work well too, the important thing is the proportion)

350 grams (12 ounces) granulated or caster sugar for each 600 millilitres (1 pint) of cordial

1 Put the fruit – with water if necessary – into a basin standing in a larger pan of gently boiling water (also called a *bain-marie*). This method stops the fruit overcooking.

2 Leave for about one hour for every 2.7 kilograms (6 pounds) of fruit. Crush fruit from time to time with the back of a stainless steel fork to release juices.

3 Crush again, and then strain through a scalded (cleaned with boiling water) jelly bag or muslin-lined sieve. Leave to drip for four hours or longer.

4 Measure juice.

5 Add the sugar, 350 grams (12 ounces) for each 600 millilitres (1 pint). Put juice and sugar into a large, heavy-bottomed pan – a preserving pan is ideal.

6 Heat particularly slowly, stirring all the time to dissolve the sugar.

Tip: *Don't try to speed up the process up or the sugar burns. Chapter 5 has more detailed information about using jelly bags.*

Per 100-millilitre serving: *106 calories; 0 grams protein, 24 grams carbohydrate, 0 grams fat, 0 grams saturated fat, 0 milligrams cholesterol, 0 grams fibre, 1 milligrams sodium.*

Berry Cordial (with direct heat): Method 2

With this method of making cordial, concentrate on crushing the juice out of your fruit without allowing it to burn. This method is speedier, but for the maximum amount of juice to turn into delicious cordial you still need to be patient while the jelly bag works. See Chapter 2 for equipment descriptions.

Special tools required: *Jelly bag*

Preparation time: *10 minutes*

Processing time: *Crushing 30 minutes; straining minimum 4 hours; further cooking 15 minutes*

Yield: *Approx 2 litres (3½ pints) from 2.7 kilograms (6 pounds) fruit*

2.7 kilograms (6 pounds) of your chosen fruit (note: this amount is only a guide; smaller amounts work well too, the important thing is the proportion below)

350 grams (12 ounces) granulated or caster sugar for each 600 millilitres (1 pint) of cordial

1 Place fruit – with water if necessary – into a heavy-bottomed saucepan.

2 Stand pan over as low a heat as possible and crush fruit until the juice runs freely.

3 Bring to the boil; boil rapidly for one minute and remove from heat.

4 Crush fruit again, strain through a scalded (cleaned with boiling water) jelly bag or muslin-lined sieve. Leave to drip for four hours or longer.

5 Measure juice.

6 Add the sugar, 350 grams (12 ounces) for each 600 millilitre (1 pint). Put juice and sugar into a large, heavy-bottomed pan – a preserving pan is ideal.

7 Heat particularly slowly, stirring all the time to dissolve the sugar.

Tip: *Don't try to speed up the process up or the sugar burns.*

Per 100-millilitre serving: *105 calories; 0 grams protein, 26 grams carbohydrate, 0 grams fat, 0 grams saturated fat, 0 milligrams cholesterol, 0 grams fibre, 1 milligram sodium. Analysis is approximate.*

Storing sweetness for the future

Use the following options to extend the time you've your sweet, fruity drinks available.

One option is to store them in the freezer. Ice cube squares in plastic bags are an easy pre-portioning method (visit Chapter 7 for more freezing tips). Alternatively, pour your cordial into sterilised bottles using a sterilised funnel. Leave 2.5 centimetres (1 inch) of headroom in the bottle (Chapter 3 helps with options for sterilising equipment).

Hot bottling

You can increase the ambient (that is, room temperature) storing time of bottles of cordial by heat-treating them. Chapter 5 contains a full section on the hot-bottling technique, so here I just describe a few safety issues and pieces of advice relating to storing cordials in this way:

- ✔ Use the hot-bottling method only for high-acid foods such as fruit – don't attempt to extend the shelf-life of any vegetables or juice made with vegetables this way. Insufficient acid is present for your vegetables to be safe. (If you need more convincing, read Chapter 3.)

- ✔ Don't recycle thin or flimsy bottles; use only good-quality glass bottles made especially for preserving. If you use screw-top bottles when hot bottling, make sure that they've clean, new screw tops. Tighten them and then loosen by a quarter turn to allow any steam to escape in the heating process.

- ✔ Keep the bottles from touching each other or coming into direct contact with the heated base of the pan. Wrap them in newspaper or cloth and stand them on the wrapping or on a *trivet* (a tripod-like stand).

For hot bottling cordials, you use the water-bath heat-treating method that I describe in full detail in Chapter 5, but here are some particulars:

- ✔ Fill the deep pan with water to within 2.5 centimetres (1 inch) of the tops of the bottles and bring slowly to the boil.

- ✔ Simmer gently for 20 minutes.

- ✔ Remove the bottles carefully (wear protective gloves) and stand the bottles on a non-slip surface – such as a cloth or newspaper – sealing the lids firmly. Label as soon as possible to avoid confusion later.

Hot bottling increases your cordials' storage time to one year (which is plenty of time to make a new batch), but check for deterioration occasionally and discard any leaking or discoloured produce. When opened, drink within two to three days if left at room temperature, or up to ten days in the fridge.

Chapter 5 has more ideas and other methods of heat-treating for you to consider.

Making a special champagne

Elderflower champagne is an exquisite countryside drink. The alcohol content is negligible – around 2 per cent. Children have thrived on it for centuries.

Elderflower Champagne

This Elderflower Champagne recipe is naturally fizzy with explosive tendencies and is ready to drink within two to three weeks; or keep it much longer and it carries on improving. When gathering the elderflower, choose frothy cream flowers and pick on a sunny day – not straight after rain. Avoid the temptation to wash the elderflowers before use as the wild yeast in the pollen is responsible for the fizz. See Chapter 3 for more on sterilisation.

Special tools required: *Sterile rubber-ringed lever-top bottles*

Preparation time: *10 minutes, plus picking time*

Processing time: *20 minutes and 24 hours standing time*

Yield: *4.5 litres (8 pints – 1 gallon)*

8 elderflower heads, full and open	*2 organic or unwaxed lemons*
900 grams (2 pounds) granulated sugar	*4.5 litres (8 pints – 1 gallon) cold water*
30 millilitres (2 tablespoons) white wine vinegar	

1 Pick over the elderflowers, ridding them of any undesirable bits and placing them, the sugar and the vinegar into a clean plastic bucket big enough to hold 4.5 litres (8 pints, 1 gallon). Top up with cold water.

2 Squeeze the lemons, adding the juice to the mix, stirring to dissolve the sugar. Chop and add the lemon skins. Cover and leave for 48 hours, stirring at least six times.

3 Strain the liquid and pour into sterile, rubber-ringed lever-top bottles or plastic lemonade bottles, keeping in a cool place. The champagne is ready to drink in two to three weeks.

Tip: *Large, strong plastic bottles made for fizzy drinks are fine as long as they're perfectly clean. (Check out Chapter 3, which has tips on cleaning and sterilising awkwardly shaped bottles.) When the pressure builds up in a plastic bottle, it 'domes' out and wobbles, making it clear that you need to release some of the pressure before the bottle explodes!*

Per 100-millilitre serving: 80 calories; 0 grams protein, 20 grams carbohydrate, 0 grams fat, 0 grams saturated fat, 0 milligrams cholesterol, 0 grams fibre, 1 milligram sodium. Analysis is approximate.

Check your bottles regularly and release some pressure from bottles that are over-pressured.

Being sweet with children

You can use your home-made, flowing, fruity liquids in other ways too; for example, adding vitamin goodness in a flavoursome way:

- Add zip to a fruit smoothie with a splash of cordial.

- Cheer up a party jelly for a bit of variety – only use a dash, though, because reducing the recommended water amount means that your jelly refuses to set well.

- Pour into a glass of cold milk and stir vigorously, or blast in a blender for a milkshake with home-produced attitude.

- Dress up a drab dish by drizzling over plain ice cream, or into a plain yoghurt or custard pudding.

Adding cordials to adult drinks

Although a dash of blackcurrant in stout isn't to everybody's taste, a slurp of blackcurrant syrup in cider – known as 'cider and black' – is a longstanding tradition in the hayfield. And replacing a lemonade top on a refreshing cool lager with elderflower keeps the light, summery feel.

If you enjoy a stronger alcoholic drink, experiment using your home-made cordials as mixers. The white spirits, vodka and gin, easily handle a dash of red syrup: plop a strawberry and a refreshing herby ice cube (see Chapter 16 for lots of herbal wisdom) in the top to take your drink to another level. Invent your own cocktail – after all, a special occasion deserves a new combination of flavours.

Weave your way to the later section 'Getting Delightfully Tipsy on Home-made Hooch' for more tips on tipples.

Juicing: Getting Straight to the Point

Orchard fruits, especially apples and pears, lend themselves to pure fruit juices without any additional sugar (see Chapter 10 for lots more about the treetop fruits and about juicing in large quantities). Apple varieties have their own levels of sweetness from cloying to sharp and all stages in between, depending on which of the thousands of varieties you've access to.

Mix more than one fruit variety if you're in the luxurious position to do so, or press what you have. Mechanical and manual juicers are available on the market: good seed catalogues and fruit tree sellers stock these items too.

If you've plenty of apples and a local apple juice manufacturer in the area, you can sometimes do a deal whereby they press and process your apples to a high commercial standard and you pay for your apple juice by returning some of your own juice to them. Look out at your local farmers' market and farm shops for someone near you.

To do the pressing in any quantity yourself – by which I mean wheelbarrow loads rather than a basketful – you need some basic equipment.

The preliminary stage of cider-making is extracting the juice from apples; just make sure that the quality of apples is good enough to drink on its own (flip to Chapter 10 for more on making cider).

Apple Juice (small amounts only)

This method is ideal if you're planning on making just one or two litres at a time. Forget the manufactured stuff; this method of making juice can take you back to generations when apple juice tasted of the real fruit. Swap it for milk on your muesli for a lactose-free start to the day. See Chapter 3 for more on sterilisation.

Special tools required: *Jelly bag (or muslin cloth), sterilised bottles*

Preparation time: *10 minutes*

Processing time: *30 minutes – more if hot bottling*

Yield: *1 litre (1¾ pints)*

2 kilograms apples (4 pounds, 8 ounces) –   *425 millilitres (¾ pint) cold water*
eating apples are sweetest

1 Chop the apples roughly – don't peel or core. Place into a large pan with the cold water. Bring to the boil and reduce the heat immediately, allowing the fruit to simmer gently for about 20–30 minutes or until the apples are really squishy.

2 Put the whole mixture into a scalded jelly bag (I give more jelly bag info in Chapter 5) – or strain through two thicknesses of muslin cloth; leave overnight. Squeeze the bag to hurry the process if you're not patient, but the juice is cloudier that way.

3 Bring the juice back to the boil and pour into sterilised bottles using a sterilised funnel. Cool and refrigerate. The apple juice lasts for one week.

Tip: *For longer keeping, freeze (Chapter 7 has information about freezing liquids); or preserve your juice by using the hot-bottling method that I touch on in the earlier section 'Hot bottling' and describe in detail in Chapter 5.*

Per 100-millilitre serving: *97 calories; 0 grams protein, 25 grams carbohydrate, 0 grams fat, 0 grams saturated fat, 0 milligrams cholesterol, 0 grams fibre, 0 milligrams sodium.*

Getting Delightfully Tipsy on Home-made Hooch

No chapter on producing home-made drinks is complete without covering the alcoholic drinks you can make at home. After all, alcoholic drink must be one of the most traditional uses for your garden produce or wild countryside finds.

In this section, I introduce you to the basics of wine-making, explain some of the jargon and equipment used, and run through the process. When you understand the home-made wine-making process, you can make almost anything into wine. Only your imagination and the amount of equipment and space you give over to this hobby stop you making beverages with the ability to get you and your friends rolling in the aisles.

If you're going in for home-made wine-making, understanding the appropriate jargon and lingo is worthwhile before following a recipe. But don't get bogged down in the details if you don't want to: home-made wines have been bubbling and fermenting in people's homes forever, just start making wine anyway!

The basic wine-making jargon you're likely to come across when reading recipes includes the following:

- ✔ **Must:** The liquid containing the flavouring for wine-making.
- ✔ **Fermentation:** The action of yeast on a must is a two-stage process: with oxygen (*aerobic*), the fast and furious stage; and without oxygen (*anaerobic*), a slower, longer stage.

  Different recipes call for different times for adding the yeast. The yeast – a tiny living cell that needs an acid environment, warmth and food to reproduce – feeds on sugars, and converts them into alcohol and carbon dioxide in roughly equal parts. Bubbling during fermentation is the escaping gas. A demijohn fermentation jar with an airlock excludes air as well as unwanted organisms, but fermentation continues until the alcohol content reaches around 15 per cent, when the yeast dies, floating to the bottom. If all the sugar is used up at this point, the wine is dry; any unconverted sugar gives a sweet to syrupy flavour to the wine.
- ✔ **Lees:** The sediment formed at the bottom of cleared wine.
- ✔ **Racking:** Siphoning off the clear wine.

Wading into the world of wine

A whole wine industry is available if you need it, complete with products (chemical and natural) for sterilising, starting and stopping fermentation, feeding yeasts, clearing wines and blending flavours. If you want to obtain a deeper understanding and firmer control on the subject, find the acclaimed *First Steps in Wine-making* by C.J.J. Berry (Argus Books); the author's enthusiasm is infectious.

Equipping yourself for wine-making

No doubt you've some of the following items in the house, but wine-making does need some specialist equipment – specialist home brew/wine-making shops exist or you can buy online. At the very least, you need the following:

- ✔ **A large, clean bucket or pan that easily holds 4.5 litres (8 pints – 1 gallon):** Specialist fermenting bins have lids but a light-coloured food-grade plastic bucket is serviceable if you've a way of closing the top, such as polythene kept in place with a secure elastic band or a clean cloth draped over the top with some means of preventing it sagging.

- ✔ **A large, heavy-bottomed pan:** A stainless steel preserving pan is ideal – but don't use any metal that reacts with acid, so steer clear of iron, copper, zinc, chipped enamel or aluminium.

- ✔ **A nylon fine sieve and a smaller jug or bowl:** These items are useful when removing your original taste-making items and mixing up yeasts.

- ✔ **A jelly bag or muslin cloth:** You need enough muslin to make a double layer. Chapter 5 has information on jelly bag improvisation.

- ✔ **A wine-maker's thermometer:** Or simply use your little finger to test for heat for starters (if you decide to go further with wine-making, extra equipment soon seems irresistible).

- ✔ **A funnel:** It needs to have a top about 12.5 centimetres (5 inches) in diameter – not the one used to put petrol in the lawnmower, though!

- ✔ **Polythene tubing for siphoning:** You need about 1.5 metres (5 feet) in length with a 5-millimetre (¼ inch) diameter.

✔ **A glass u-bend:** If you've shaky hands (and even if you don't), this nifty little tool is a 'must-have' item – a neat little u-bend of glass tubing that fits neatly over your plastic siphon tube. When attached, you place the u-bend in the wine, resting the curve of the 'U' gently on the bottom of the demijohn, doing your best not to disturb the *lees* (or sediment). With the u-bend in place, you can safely siphon off the clear part of your wine. The siphon stops working as soon as air enters the tube.

✔ **A demijohn:** A fermentation jar that holds 4.5 litres. You definitely need one, which you can clean and use again, but preferably two for an easier life.

✔ **An airlock and bung fitting your demijohn:** You can get these items at specialist wine-making shops or online.

✔ **Bottles and tops, dark glass if possible, corks, lever tops, plastic stoppers or screw tops:** You need something in which to store all that lovely wine in, after all.

✔ **A bottle brush with a long handle:** Cleaning demijohns is much easier with one of these brushes.

All this equipment must be scrupulously clean. Read Chapter 3 for methods of sterilisation and ways to clean awkwardly shaped bottles.

Good year, bad year

The first demijohn of home-made dandelion wine I ever made used a recipe by a lovely old country couple, Freda and Vick. I followed the recipe to the letter, and was a bit shocked at just how long it took to clear. After four months, I'd given up on it when suddenly in about 24 hours the mixture was clear as a bell. I siphoned it off, stored for a little while – I couldn't wait long – and drank it: delicious!

After the upheaval of a house move, I fished out the recipe again and made another lot. This time I was ready to wait four months and in its own time the wine cleared. My family called it Dandelion Hooch. It was thicker, more like a liqueur, but still delicious.

The following year, disaster struck. Although I followed the recipe to the letter and the used yeast that was in similar packaging to the first time, on checking I found that the all-important little qualifying sentence on the packet, 'suitable for home wine-making', was missing! The wine didn't clear, and it didn't smell nice either. But there you go: try, try and try again. When the wine's nice, it's very, very nice and when it's bad, it's horrid. I'm keeping my fingers crossed for this year's batch.

Fermenting fruits and flowers

When making wine, the ingredients you choose impart the flavour. You can make almost anything into wine, but some ingredients have a reputation for producing delicious flavours. Grape comes out on top (unsurprisingly) and new vineyards are springing up in the UK. You can also buy wine-making kits with concentrated grape juice to get you started, but you don't need to own a grapevine to produce good home-made wines.

Here are a few sensible rules to follow when you gather ingredients for wine-making:

- ✔ **Use fresh ingredients for the best results.** Picking flowers in the middle of the day after the dew's gone and the sweet nectar is in full flow is best; wet produce is more likely to harbour moulds. You can use frozen fruit; picking fruit a little under-ripe and freezing is preferable to using old over-ripe produce.

  Find out whether the ingredients you're picking were recently sprayed. For this reason, your home-grown produce is safest because you know its history. Some plants or parts of plants, both garden and wild, are poisonous, so stick to the ones you know or have recipes for and leave anything else (however pretty or sweet smelling) if you're at all uncertain.

- ✔ **Consider which water to use.** Using potable – that is, drinking – water needs consideration (breweries have made a name for themselves because of the water used in their ingredients). If your tap water smells strongly of chlorine, draw enough for your wine-making 12 hours beforehand and allow it to stand. The chlorine taint diminishes on standing. Or you can use bottled water if you're feeling fussy.

- ✔ **Take note of which sugar your recipe requires.** Most recipes expect you to use white refined granulated sugar, whereas some traditional recipes require a darker sugar, such as Demerara, to give colour and impart flavour. Unrefined sugar gives a slightly deeper colour to a light wine; the sugar still does the job of feeding the yeast and a hint of syrup in the aroma (or bouquet) doesn't detract from the overall effect.

- ✔ **Use the right type of yeast.** Yeasts are the fermenting agents in wine- and beer-making. They come in several shapes and sizes, and not all yeasts are suitable for wine-making; reading the packaging is worthwhile. Natural yeast on fruit is sometimes the only source of fermentation in a recipe.

Whole shops dedicated to wine-making and home-brewing exist, as well as online sites ready to sell you yeast in tablet, powder or granulated form. Brewer's yeast is available in health food shops too – sold as a vitamin B supplement. You need to mix some yeasts with a little warm liquid before mixing into the main body of the liquid and others you sprinkle directly into the demi-john; your recipe tells you which method to use.

Making wine: The basic formula

Although each recipe has its own peculiarities, wine-making features a basic formula:

1. **Extracting the flavour:** Place the raw materials in a bowl or bucket, pour on cold (for delicate flowers) or boiling water (for fruits) and break up the materials with a wooden spoon or vegetable masher (the recipe gives the method and timing). You may have to boil vegetables to extract their juice and flavour. Keeping this liquid for wine closely covered while standing keeps out spoilage bacteria and other nasties. You strain this liquid – the *must* – and discard the flavourings.

2. **Adding the sugar:** Depending on the advice of your recipe, you add sugar to the strained liquid, or *must*, as dry sugar or as a syrup, stirring all the time to dissolve the sugar. Some recipes require heating at this stage too.

3. **Adding the yeast:** A living organism *starts* (reproduces) best at a temperature of 21 degrees Celsius (70 degrees Fahrenheit), so allow your heated (or boiled, if your recipe requires) liquid to cool down. Sometimes you mix the yeast with a little must and distribute it by stirring into the wine, or you may sprinkle it onto the top of the liquid when the wine's already in the fermentation jar. The recipe tells you which approach is best for each particular wine.

4. **Fermentation:** This stage is rapid to begin with when the yeast (a tiny living cell) is reproducing, producing a bubbly layer of carbon dioxide that protects the liquid from spoilage bacteria. After about seven to ten days, when the rapid fermentation slows, you siphon your wine into a fermentation jar (*demijohn*) – excluding any more oxygen, wild yeasts, vinegar flies or other spoilage organisms – with an airlock topped up with clean water. This airlock (or *glugger*, as it's affectionately known; you can hear the wine glug, glug, glugging gently as the yeast is working, a homely sound) allows gas to escape from your wine but nothing to enter. This second stage fermentation – without oxygen – works best at temperatures between 16–18 degrees Celsius (60–65 degrees Fahrenheit) and can take months; lower temperatures slow it down further.

5. **Racking:** The yeast sinking to the bottom of the fermentation jar and forming a sediment is a signal that fermentation has slowed down – the wine begins to clear. Wine benefits from being *racked* – or siphoned – off into a clean fermentation jar for another round of clearing. Some wine-makers take this process to the extreme by racking off two or three more times; others bottle

it straightaway, taking the chance that further fermentation in the bottle may blow the top off. Wine bottles have a ridge round the rim so that you can tie the cork in with strong string or florists' wire, leaving it slightly loose to allow the swelling gas pressure to be relieved so that the bottles don't explode.

Slow fermentation continues for a long time; moving your wine to a warmer spot and seeing it begin to bubble again – about 21 degrees Celsius (70 degrees Fahrenheit) – shows that fermentation isn't complete.

6. **Storing and maturing:** After fermentation stops, the wine is as strong alcoholically as it ever gets but the flavour may continue to improve with time. Most wines are best left for 6–12 months before drinking. Fill to within 2.5 centimetres (1 inch) of the top, allowing head space below the cork or stopper. Store screw-top and plastic-stoppered wine bottles upright, but place corked bottles – unless the corks are tied down – on their sides to keep the cork base moist and swollen, checking occasionally that all tops are secure.

Enjoying alcoholic recipes

Recipes with more and less alcohol content are dotted throughout this book. I look at cider-making in Chapter 10, so if you're inundated with apples and pears pop there now. Turn to Chapter 13 for how to transform your root vegetables into delicious tipples (despite their earthy feel), and look at Chapter 18 for how to make flower wines.

Wines

As well as the other great wine recipes in this book, here's a fantastic one for potato wine.

Potato Wine

Using Demerara sugar, this recipe transforms the humble potato into something from another sphere – although Irish in origin, don't mistake it for the famous illegal drink 'poteen'.

Special tools required: Demijohn

Preparation time: 15 minutes

Processing time: 45 minutes cooking; about 4 months fermentation; 6 months storage

Yield: About 4.5 litres (8 pints – 1 gallon)

1.8 kilograms (4 pounds) old potatoes

6.8 litres (12 pints) cold water

1.3 kilograms (3 pounds) Demerara sugar

1 lemon sliced

1 orange sliced

2.5 centimetres (1 inch) root ginger, smashed with a rolling pin to release the flavour

25 grams (1 ounce) wine yeast – buy from a specialist wine-making shop or online

1 Wash but don't peel the potatoes. Cut into small pieces and put them into a large pan, adding the cold water next. Bring this mixture to the boil, and continue boiling until the potatoes are cooked but not mushy (about 15 minutes depending on your potato variety).

2 Strain off the liquid into a 6.7-litre (12 pint – 1½ gallon) bowl, adding the sugar, lemon, orange and ginger, and stir until the sugar dissolves. Return to the pan and simmer gently for 30 minutes.

3 Allow the liquid to cool to 21 degrees Celsius (70 degrees Fahrenheit), and then strain again and pour into a *demijohn* (a 4.5-litre (8 pint – 1 gallon) fermentation jar). When the jar is about three quarters full, sprinkle in the yeast. Stopper the demijohn with a fermentation airlock and leave until all bubbling ceases – siphoning as necessary before bottling and storing for six months or longer before drinking.

Tip: *To discover how this process works, see the earlier section 'Making wine: The basic formula'.*

Per 100-millilitre serving: *147 calories; 1 gram protein, 36 grams carbohydrate, 0 grams fat, 0 grams saturated fat, 0 milligrams cholesterol, 0 grams fibre, 3 milligrams sodium. Analysis is approximate.*

Here are a few wine recipes you can find elsewhere in the book:

✔ **Beetroot Wine:** Chapter 13

✔ **Peapod Wine:** Chapter 14

✔ **Coltsfoot Wine:** Chapter 18

✔ **Dandelion Wine:** Chapter 18

Other alcoholic recipes

Here are a couple of recipes for some other great alcoholic drinks.

Nettle Beer

Use only fresh, young, tender leaves cut at the base of the stalk. You only get the right quality in early spring. (Check out Chapter 18 for hints on picking plants that fight back.) With a reputation for high vitamin content and tonic properties, nettle beer is a short-time brew, ready in seven days, with a low alcohol content. Watch it, this beer can be quite lively!

Special tools required: *Rubber-sealed clamp-type lever bottle tops or plastic 'fizzy pop' bottles*

Preparation time: *20 minutes*

Processing time: *Boiling 15 minutes; standing time three days*

Yield: *3.6–4.5 litres (6–8 pints)*

2 unwaxed lemons scrubbed

900 grams (2 pounds) young, fresh nettle tops

4.5 litres (8 pints, 1 gallon) water

450 grams (1 pound) Demerara sugar

25 grams (1 pound) cream of tartar – buy from a chemist

15 grams (½ ounces) wine or brewer's yeast

1 Place the nettles in a large saucepan, adding the water and boiling steadily for 15 minutes; top up to 4.5 litres (8 pints – 1 gallon).

2 Pare the lemon rind thinly and squeeze the juice, placing these items with the sugar and cream of tartar in a large bowl or clean food grade plastic bucket. Strain in the boiling nettle water, stirring briskly. Leave to cool to 21 degrees Celsius (70 degrees Fahrenheit).

3 Using a small amount of the warm liquid, cream the yeast, and then stir it into the main bulk. Cover with a clean cloth or polythene lid and leave for three days.

4 Strain the liquid and using a funnel pour straight into strong bottles, using rubber-sealed clamp-type lever bottle tops or plastic 'fizzy pop' bottles.

5 Store in a cool place, allowing a little gas to escape from the bottles if the fermentation is vigorous. The nettle beer is ready to drink after one week and best finished off within two or three months.

Tip: *You can make this beer at other times of the year using dried nettles picked in early spring. Chapter 18 has hints on how to do so – just substitute half the weight of fresh nettles for dry and carry on with the recipe.*

Per 100-millilitre serving: *65 calories; 1 gram protein, 15 grams carbohydrate, 0 grams fat, 0 grams saturated fat, 0 milligrams cholesterol, 0 grams fibre, 20 milligrams sodium. Analysis is approximate.*

Rumtopf

Germans use special earthenware pots decorated with fruits to hold their rumtopf (meaning 'rum pot'), but you can make this boozy fruit mix in any sterilised 3-litre or bigger preserving jar. After making the first batch, you can top up with soft fruits, sugar and the rum of your choice. Just keep the whole thing going, dipping into the pot whenever you feel like it. Drizzle the liqueur onto desserts or enjoy a tipple in midwinter to remind you of summer days. The smell is heavenly and can convert a non-rum quaffer into one easily! Prost!

Preparation time: 15 minutes

Processing time: 1 hour

Yield: About 3 litres (5 pints) depending on size of pot used, but ongoing

900 grams (2 pounds) soft fruits, such as blackcurrants, strawberries, redcurrants, peaches, cherries and plums; apples and pears if you like

450 grams (1 pound) sugar

1 litre (1 ¾ pints) rum

1 Wash and then dry the fruit and prepare according to type: for example, top and tail currants, leave cooking cherries whole, de-stone and half or quarter larger fruits.

2 Place fruit and sugar into a glass or ceramic dish and leave for one hour while the sugar draws juice from the fruit. Put fruit and any remaining sugar into the preserving jar.

3 Cover with the rum of your choice, holding the fruit under the liquid with a plate placed on the top of your container or a lid. Use as you like, topping up with further fruit and sugar in similar proportions as it comes into season. Always keep the rum covering the fruits by 1 centimetre (½ inch).

Vary it! If you're struggling to find enough fruits through the lean times of year, cheat and add something exotic such as a fresh pineapple, or use defrosted frozen soft fruit.

Per 100-millilitre serving: 140 calories; 0 grams protein, 17 grams carbohydrate, 0 grams fat, 0 grams saturated fat, 0 milligrams cholesterol, 1 gram fibre, 1 milligram sodium.

Here are a few more recipes for other alcoholic drinks that I've peppered throughout the book:

- ✔ **Lovage Cordial:** Chapter 16
- ✔ **Sloe Gin:** Chapter 18
- ✔ **Cider:** Chapter 10

Part III
Working with Home-Grown Fruits

'Well, at least the neighbours
aren't complaining.'

In this part . . .

This part travels high up into the orchard boughs and low down into drooping, heavily laden bushes dripping with summertime currants. Whether you grow in your garden or allotment, in a polytunnel or greenhouse, on your sunniest windowsill or in pots and containers on your patio, balcony or decking, this part lets you into the secret of keeping your ripening harvest of fruits. You can enjoy your apples and redcurrants, exotic aubergines and tomatoes, not just for their brief fresh window but all through the year. With the knowledge and recipes in Chapters 10, 11 and 12, you can start choosing varieties to grow for your favourite jams, jellies, chutneys and sauces, or launch straight in with the basketfuls of fruitfulness you've just harvested yourself.

Chapter 10

Enjoying Outstanding Orchard Offerings

In This Chapter

▶ Understanding roots and fruits

▶ Matching up and combining tastes

▶ Storing, preserving and using orchard fruits

Recipes in This Chapter

🍲 Three-Fruit Autumn Jam

🍲 Apple, Date and Walnut Chutney

🍲 Apple Cider

🍲 Apricot and Brandy Conserve

🍲 Damson Cheese

🍲 Medlar Cheese

🍲 Seville Marmalade

🍲 Mulled Pears

🍲 Savoury Plum Sauce

🍲 Quince Jelly

Hanging from the boughs of orchard trees in autumn is the most amazing bounty. These sweet treats have grown from a flurry of springtime blossom, magically kissed by the bees (I'm coming over all poetic!) and other pollinating insects to 'set' the fruits and provide the power to swell and grow into the juicy fruits you know and love.

Whether you own a whole orchard, belong to a community orchard scheme or grow a few small fruit trees and magic has happened, this chapter helps you to preserve and use the resulting fruits. I discuss how orchard fruits come about and how to handle their contents, and I suggest some common recipe combinations (for example, apples are a good background flavour and contain properties that are helpful in jam-making).

This chapter also lists the most common orchard trees and their fruits – plus some, such as apricots and oranges, that you have to buy (I just can't leave them out!) – and advises on which varieties store effectively.

Getting to Grips with Tree Roots and Top Fruits

As the name suggests, picking top fruits is taking the fruit from the high branches; you may even need a ladder to get up to the highest delights. If your plan is to go straight off to the juicer with your harvest (Chapter 9 has this juicy story), shaking the trees to bring the apples down to the ground for easier picking is fine because a few bruises don't matter. If you intend to store the fruit for longer, however, take extreme care in the picking (see the later section called 'Tricking and picking'): bruised fruit's keeping qualities diminish, leaving you with an empty dry store or apple loft (I cover apple storage in Chapter 4).

Although reaching up high seems to be the main activity for picking top fruit, what's going on under the soil with the tree roots governs just how high you have to reach. Therefore, in this section I examine a few practicalities of the tops and roots of orchard trees, describing grafting (adding one or more varieties to an already-growing root system) methods and how to pick and handle these delicate fruits.

Grafting isn't always hard graft

Each fruit tree, except ancient established old orchard trees, is grafted –that is, part of one living plant is joined to another – onto a rootstock, whose characteristics are identified by a code or name, such as M9, M26 and so on (see Table 10-1).

A sweet little apple tree that you easily carry back from the garden centre may be destined to grow into a 10-metre-high (33-feet high) monster, blocking your view and disrupting the drainage around the house, unless you check which rootstock the tree is on.

Table 10-1	Rootstocks and Their Uses	
Rootstock Name	*Size Range and Maximum Mature Height*	*Common Uses*
M27	Very dwarfing (2 metres/6 feet)	Uncommon, possibly for pots; requires support
M9	Dwarfing (2.5 metres/8 feet)	Small low-growing structures called cordons; requires support
M26	Semi-dwarfing (3.5 metres/ 10 feet)	For bushes; requires support
MM106	Semi-vigorous (4 metres/ 12 feet)	All purpose; useful and needs no support when established
M25	Vigorous (6–7 metres/20 feet)	Commonly used for cider apple trees and commercial growing; requires harvesting machinery but needs no support when established

Different grafting methods do different jobs:

- ✔ **Grafting *scions* – small whippy branches – onto rootstocks:** Essentially, making a new type of tree, with the bonus of knowing how big your tree is going to grow.

- ✔ **Grafting scions onto existing trees:** Adding variations on the type of fruit that a tree bears. One tree may be grafted with several different varieties; this technique is worth noting if your growing space is small or you're not keen on the fruit variety you already have.

- ✔ **Budding:** Adding buds of a different type to a rootstock. The bud establishes itself over time and is growing well when you can remove the rootstock top and the new bud grows to produce a tree with fruit relating to the bud.

If you're thinking of extending an orchard, planting a few trees in the garden or even making a container orchard (keeping your trees in large pots that you can move around), you really need to understand a little about rootstocks so that you choose wisely.

The rootstock governs the height and spread of the tree and the grafted part determines the variety of the particular fruit that's going to grow.

Perfecting your picking techniques

If your orchard or where you pick your fruit is recently planted and well maintained – possibly a well-trained peach tree fanned across a south-facing wall – you probably can stand on the ground while reaching the fruit. Older orchards and one-off trees growing in cottage gardens, however, may be of larger varieties and require climbing to gather those tempting fruits.

Tricking and picking

The stalk (the little stick poking out of the top of the fruit) joins the fruit to the tree branches and all the goodness and liquid to swell the fruit has tracked through that point (fruit is 75–90 per cent water!). The tree uses the tastiness of the fruit to trick you – or a bird or wild animal – into moving the fruit containing the seeds (pips in the case of apples and pears, hard stones in the plum and cherry types of fruit) to another location in the hope that a new tree grows from these tree seeds. When you spit out an unpalatable pip, or discard a hard cherry stone, you're doing exactly what the tree desires. As with animals that eat the fruit and then deposit it in their own private dollop of manure, you're making it more likely that a new tree is going to grow.

This approach works well for low-hanging fruits, but what about those high up in the branches? Fewer animals – the ones without wings, climbing ability or ladders – have the opportunity to eat the flesh of these fruits and therefore move the seeds to a new location. Getting these fruits onto the ground maximises the chances of the tree's seeds being transported to pastures new, which requires the tree to perform another trick. The perfectly ripe fruit no longer needs goodness from the mother tree, so the stalk and adjoining branch throttle off communication channels and produce a little band of cork, causing a deliberately weak point and making the fruit's grasp to the tree tenuous.

This moment is the exact time for picking, before high winds cause the ripest fruits to become windfalls and fall to the ground naturally. Windfalls have uses (for example, juice or cider if you work quickly – more about juice and cider in the later section 'Apples'), but catching the fruit before it falls with a bump to the ground gives you more options for using it.

Only the best fruits survive dry storage – Chapter 4 takes you to the heights of apple loft storage.

Of course, you need to get to these top fruits in the high branches to pick them. When doing so, make sure that you:

- ✔ Check out your ladder for safety and height.

- ✔ Lean your ladder only against the strongest boughs (large branches), preferably the tree trunk.

- ✔ Take a stout rope with you and lash the top of the ladder to a firm part of the tree. This confidence-giving move allows you to reach for an awkwardly positioned fruit without fear.

- ✔ Have a helper for steadying the ladder – especially if the ladder is a freestanding one – and taking heavy baskets or containers of fruit from you before you climb down. Alternatively, organise helpers to catch the individual apples as you throw them down – don't ask a butterfingers or your fruit gets bruised!

- ✔ Work out what's the easiest container to hold while up the tree: a canvas bag with a shoulder strap may be easier than a basket, because it leaves both your hands free for holding on and picking, or design yourself an apron with a huge 'picker's pocket' to fill.

- ✔ Look at websites and in garden centres for long-arm fruit-picking tools; some people like working with them.

Handling fruit carefully

The storing possibilities for the fruits depend entirely on how you pick them. The most common varieties in shops are bred to travel well, and chosen for their tough skins to protect their looks and avoid bruising. Your own trees yield much tastier fruits that may have tender skin, prone to bruising with any rough handling.

For this reason:

- Handle each fruit as if your stern auntie's precious china!

- Use the whole of the palm of your hand to enclose each fruit (or pick from the long stalk with cherries), lifting the fruit to take the weight and twisting slightly. If the dividing cork barrier (which I describe in the preceding section) is mature, the fruit breaks away easily. If you're choosing to pick less ripe fruit (for example, for jam- and jelly-making), twisting with a sharp tug dislodges the fruit.

- Place every fruit in your container – a quick glance sorts out any obvious poor-quality or insect-damaged fruits, which you can put to one side for immediate eating.

Preserving the most pristine, undamaged fruits gives the best results.

Swapping Fruity Tips and Tastes

When mixed together, fruits can work for or against each other. If you find that your fruits are low in pectin – the setting agent released by simmering and acid – combine these (preferably under-ripe) fruits with ones of high pectin content for an easy set, or add extra acid in the form of lemon juice if your fruit is ripe. (Chapter 5 bulks this information out and shows you how to do pectin testing.)

When you've a bit of jam-making experience under your belt, you can create your own jam concoction according to what's in season on your patch. (Use Table 10-2 to help you decide which combination to make.)

Table 10-2	What's What with Pectin and Acid Content	
Fruit	**Pectin Content**	**Acidity**
Apricots	Medium	Medium
Cherries (cooking)	Medium	Medium
Cherries (sweet)	Low	Low
Cooking apples	High/medium	High/medium
Crab apples	High	Medium
Grapes (unripe)	Medium	Medium
Figs	Low	Low
Medlars	Medium	Low

(continued)

Table 10-2 *(continued)*

Fruit	Pectin Content	Acidity
Pears	Low	Low
Plums (unripe and damsons)	High	High
Quinces	High	High/medium

High pectin means an easier set, especially if a high acid content is also present. Stones and pips contain pectin too, so boiling them along with the fruit keeps the pectin levels up (just fish them out at the end).

The following combinations are all tried and tested. Some are squishy and some lumpy, but all are delicious in their own way:

- ✔ Apple, Date and Walnut Chutney – I provide this recipe later in the 'Apples' section

- ✔ Apple with chilli

- ✔ Crab Apple Jelly – see Chapter 18

- ✔ Apple, pear and plum – see the Three-Fruit Autumn Jam recipe in the later section 'Trying Out Some Treetop Treats'

- ✔ Apricot and Brandy Conserve – approach the 'Apricots' section later in this chapter for details

- ✔ Damson and marrow

- ✔ Pear and pomegranate

- ✔ Pear and walnut

- ✔ Pear in red wine

- ✔ Quince and lemon – flip to the Quince Jelly recipe in the later 'Quinces' section

- ✔ Swede, tomato and apple – check out the Year Round Chutney recipe in Chapter 13

If I include appropriate recipes in this book, I note this fact in the preceding list, but otherwise borrow books from friends, neighbours and the library or search online for recipe ideas.

Trying Out Some Treetop Treats

This section runs through the orchard favourites. By all means, adapt the recipes in this section to your own selection of fruits. Be creative – if a combination feels right, it's right, and you can invent new preserves along the way.

One of the joys of having a glut of a particular fruit is that you can afford to experiment – and the compost heap awaits if family and friends fail to appreciate your newfound flavour combinations!

In this section, I organise the fruits alphabetically, but to begin have a go at the following mixed-fruit jam recipe.

Three-Fruit Autumn Jam

Autumn brings its own orchard rewards with this jam (picking fruit slightly under-ripe gives the best results). The flavour of this jam is excellent and firmer fruits hold the differing textures – plum skins 'candify' in the jam, pears have their own grainy feel and apples generally soften to a surrounding 'jamminess'. The result is autumn flavours released in every bite. Chapter 2 has information on jam-making equipment. See Chapter 3 for more on sterilisation.

Special tools required: *Muslin bag, sugar thermometer, sterilised jars*

Preparation time: *45 minutes*

Processing time: *1 hour*

Yield: *4.5 kilograms (10 pounds)*

1.3 kilograms (3 pounds) cooking apples	*3 kilograms (6 pounds, 12 ounces) sugar*
1 kilogram (2 pounds, 4 ounces) pears	*300 millilitres (6 pounds, 12 ounces) water*
1 kilogram (2 pounds, 4 ounces) plums	

1 Preparing the fruit is a little time consuming, but worth the effort. Peel, core and roughly chop the apples and pears in 2.5–5-centimetre (1–2 inch) pieces. When coring pears after peeling them, cut them in half lengthways, and use a teaspoon to scoop the core and stringy bits out. Keep the peel, pips and stones, tie them up in a muslin bag and simmer with the fruit. Place apples and pears into a heavy-bottomed pan – a jam pan is ideal – with the water. Halve and stone the plums and add to the pan – leave the plum skins on to add to the texture.

2 Apply gentle heat until the fruit is simmering. Simmer gently for about 10–25 minutes or until the fruit is softened but still mainly in chunks.

3 Remove from heat, squeezing out and discarding the muslin bag, and add the sugar, stirring until it totally dissolves.

4 Returning the saucepan to the heat, bring the mixture to the boil, boiling rapidly until the mixture reaches the setting point – use a sugar thermometer or use one of the set-testing methods that I outline in Chapter 5.

5 Remove the pan immediately when you reach the setting point. Allow the jam to settle for a few minutes, giving a final stir to distribute the fruit. Pour into warmed, sterilised jars.

6 Seal, label and store. Leave for two to three weeks before eating, allowing the textures to develop.

Vary it! *Chop and change with different varieties of apples and any of the plums, including greengages and damsons.*

Per 100-gram serving: 296 calories; 0 grams protein, 76 grams carbohydrate, 0 grams fat, 0 grams saturated fat, 0 milligrams cholesterol, 1 grams fibre, 1 milligrams sodium.

Apples

The old adage 'An apple a day keeps the doctor away' proves to be a sensible strategy. Fresh apples – and 'stored', uncooked apples count as fresh – are full of antioxidants and are key in a healthy diet; definitely part of the feted 'five-a-day' strategy.

Five main, and to be honest, pretty boring varieties of apples adorn the supermarket shelves, all within 5 millimetres in size of each other. Life's not like that when you meet the real deal in nature. Apple trees (and apples themselves) come in all shapes and sizes, and jams, jellies, chutneys and relishes often have apple as a main ingredient; this tree is really worth making space for.

If you're choosing one tree or even a whole orchard-full, read the earlier section on 'Getting to Grips with Tree Roots and Top Fruits', which helps you get apple trees and their possibilities into perspective. Ask about local varieties too and perhaps even consider having more than one type of apple on a tree (check out the earlier 'Grafting isn't always hard graft' section).

Bringing 'flower power' back

Using an apple jelly as a clear background medium can create a beautiful preserve as follows:

✔ Rose petal suspended in apple jelly, with a splash of rose water for added flavour

✔ Star anise suspended in apple jelly

✔ Borage flowers suspended in apple jelly

The most common varieties of apples in the supermarkets – Golden Delicious, Braeburn and Gala – often aren't suited for the UK climate and need a lot of specialist looking after. You get a better choice of names from the older, evocatively named varieties: Slack Ma Girdle, Pig's Snout, Queenies, Egremont Russet and Ashmead's Kernel conjure up a much more interesting image, and no doubt taste better too.

Apples fall roughly into four categories, with some in-betweeners:

- ✔ **Eating:** The sweetest of apples with early and late varieties. The later the variety, the better the apple keeps and the sweeter it tastes. Eat Katy and Discovery varieties soon after picking, and nutty little Russets and Ashmead Kernels store well.

- ✔ **Cooking:** The trusty Bramley is the best known of the sharper, more acidic, cooking apples – also referred to as cookers – but many others are also available. Use cooking apples for jam (see Chapter 5) and chutneys (see Chapter 6) and watch out for a wide variation in texture as well as flavour – some cookers reduce to a froth as soon you heat them and others hold their shape well. Bake batches of apple pie and freeze.

    Buy a stack of tin foil pie cases for batch baking – when frozen, you can stack these cases neatly. Chapter 7 gives you cold hard advice on freezing.

- ✔ **Cider:** If your apple tree yields sharp, astringent, bullet-like, inedible apples – don't despair. Simply jolly yourself up with a tankard of home-made cider (check out the later section 'Cider-making: Transforming apples into a tipple).

- ✔ **Crab apple:** The ancestor of the orchard apple (see Chapter 18 for more on this wild relative). Because crab apples are a useful addition in the kitchen, people domestically cultivate some, such as John Downie.

Thousands of varieties of apples (and, to a lesser extent, pears) exist. Your local soil type and climate dictate what's best for you. Find out the necessary info from a local tree nursery or at an Apple Day (see the nearby sidebar 'An apple a day and an Apple Day!').

Drying apples

Dried apple rings are a healthy and delicious snack and you can use them in sweet and savoury dishes. Both eating and cooking apples respond well to drying:

1. **Peel and core your apples.** Leave the peel on if you're a fibre lover.

2. **Slice thinly.** Some people like to pre-treat their apples to stop discoloration (Chapter 8 has for hints on pre-treatment). Alternatively, just accept a brown but equally delicious apple ring.

An apple a day and an Apple Day!

Apples are accessible almost all year round, and always were, even before the days of mass chilling and irradiation of food. When you understand your own varieties, you find lots of varieties specific to your own area.

If you move house and discover a tree or even an old orchard and want to know the varieties, keep a record of the flowers and the ripe fruit (usually late August to October). Just take pictures, find an Apple Day in your area and take along your images and a few samples of your fruit. (You need to take several samples, and sometimes the number is stipulated, in case a single fruit happens to be unusual for its type – remember that home-grown also means unique.) If you find a different fruit than you expect and aren't sure about it, still go to the Apple Day, which is where your local experts hang out.

To find out where you're nearest Apple Day takes place, ask at your local farmers' market (or the library, if you still have one). Apple Days are often a feature of a farmers' market in autumn, or search out your local allotment society, which usually knows what's going on in and around the growing scene.

---

3. **Lay out singly and without touching on a baking sheet or drying rack.**
   Place in a cool oven (110 degrees Celsius (225 degrees Fahrenheit; Gas Mark ¼) for 3–4 hours (or longer if your apple isn't yet dry to the touch, bendy and easy to tear) or a purpose-made dehydrator – again, flip to Chapter 8 for dehydrator gen.

If you're thinking of making your own sausages at home, use dried apples rather than fresh in pork sausages. Not only do the flavours marry perfectly – pork and apple is a traditional combination, as demonstrated by all those old paintings of a boar's head with an apple stuffed into its mouth – but also the dried apple stops the sausage from becoming overly wet in the making.

Creating jams and chutneys

Using apple as an extra ingredient to top-up pectin and acid levels (the stuff that helps with setting) is common practice. For example, Chapter 18's Crab Apple Jelly recipe is ripe for adapting: simply substitute your own cooking apples and blackberries for a combination recipe. Apple makes up the squishy part of the All Year Round Chutney recipe in Chapter 13.

Apple, Date and Walnut Chutney

This recipe uses apples for the squish, onions to add the flavour, dates for an exotic sweetness and walnuts for a nutty bite. This chutney is delicious with savoury and cold meat dishes, stirred into a winter soup to liven it up or as part of a hearty Ploughman's lunch. See Chapter 6 for more about chutneys, Chapter 2 for more on equipment and Chapter 3 for info on sterilisation.

Special tools required: *Sterilised preserving containers, non-corrosive/plastic-lined lids*

Preparation time: *About 50 minutes*

Processing time: *1½–2 hours*

Yield: *1.8 kilograms (4 pounds)*

450 grams (1 pound) onions	*225 grams (8 ounces) sugar*
900 grams (2 pounds) cooking apples	*5 millilitres (1 teaspoon) salt*
675 grams (1 pound, 8 ounces) pitted dates	*5 millilitres (1 teaspoon) ground ginger*
75 grams (3 ounces) chopped walnuts	*5 millilitres (1 teaspoon) cayenne pepper*
600 millilitres (1 pint) malt vinegar	

1 Prepare the onions by peeling and chopping. Choose the size you prefer because they retain some of their form: large chunky pieces or fine slices. Peel, core and slice the apples and check your dates for any leftover stones (pits).

2 Using a heavy-bottomed pan, and splashing in enough water to stop the onions from burning, simmer until soft. Add the apples and continue cooking gently for a further 20 minutes, after which add the dates, walnuts, salt, spices and half the vinegar. Continue cooking until the mixture thickens – add the remaining vinegar and sugar last. Remove from the heat while you stir the sugar to dissolve it.

3 Return to a gentle simmer until the chutney is really thick and drawing a wooden spoon across the base of the pan leaves a line behind revealing the base of the pan.

4 Pot into sterilised jars with non-corrosive or plastic-lined lids when still warm.

Per 30-gram serving: *67 calories; 1 grams protein, 16 grams carbohydrate,1 grams fat, 0 grams saturated fat, 0 milligrams cholesterol, 1 grams fibre, 42 milligrams sodium.*

Juicing up your apples

Making juice is an excellent way to use your apples but you need help to extract (press) the liquid. The first four steps of the later 'Cider-making: Transforming apples into a tipple' section are the same for extracting apple juice; just choose better-quality fruit in the first place for juice, because bruised and bashed fruits are already fermenting naturally.

Freezing (Chapter 7) and pasteurising – the commercial type of hot bottling (see Chapter 5) – add shelf-life to homemade apple juice (don't even try to compare this nectar to commercial homogenised apple juice, you can't!).

Different methods of apple pressing need different equipment:

- ✔ **Fruit press:** This design is a basic wooden barrel with a framework holding in place a plunger on a screw thread. You place the bashed up apples into the barrel and apply the screw. Your apple juice trickles out at the bottom: catch it and taste it straightaway – even in the fridge it doesn't last more than a couple of days in this delicious form.

- ✔ **Electric juicer:** Nothing's better than a fresh jug of apple juice for breakfast. Grab a couple or three and whiz through the electric juicer for an instant treat. For larger quantities – this juice lasts only a couple of days in the fridge – pop some into containers in the freezer for added shelf-life (check out Chapter 7 for more on freezing liquids).

- ✔ **Simple straining:** See the recipe for juicing small quantities in Chapter 9.

You're going to have apple pulp and mush left from your pressings. If you haven't got a handy pig to feed this treat to before it starts to ferment, compost it and waste nothing from your harvest.

Cider-making: Transforming apples into a tipple

Why stop at the juice stage when cider's just ahead?

Apple Cider

For this recipe, choose over-ripe and bruised apples including windfalls (the apples on the ground under the trees) that you can't store in any other way. Some will have started to ferment naturally anyway. Use any mixture of varieties, including cider apple varieties – you may have Dabinett, Morgan's Sweet, Somerset Redstreak or any of many other varieties on your patch – that are usually hard and sometimes bitter and astringent to taste. You can jolly them up by turning them into cider. Chapter 3 has more on sterilisation of equipment.

Special tools required: Fruit press, demijohn, fermentation lock

Preparation time: 30 minutes with a hose

Processing time: 2–3 hours and several months fermentation time

Yield: About 4.5 litres (8 pints, 1 gallon) for each 4.5 kilograms (10 pounds) of apples

4.5 kilograms (10 pounds) of apples, or more if you have them	*40 grams (1½ ounces) brewer's yeast for each 4.5 litres (8 pints, 1 gallon) of juice*

1 Hose the apples off to wash, allowing the dirty water and debris to drain away.

2 Put your washed chopped apples in a stout plastic bucket and pound them with a heavy – but clean – wooden post, crushing them to a lumpy pulp. Alternatively, use a purpose-built crusher (some come as an attachment for electric drills).

3 Place all the pulp into a fruit press (see the preceding section), applying pressure to extract the juice.

4 Using a little of the juice and a small jug, mix up 40 grams (1½ ounces) of brewer's yeast – you can buy this yeast in health food shops – for each demijohn (a demijohn holds a gallon, which is 4.5 litres).

5 Pour the juice into the sterilised demijohn – see Chapter 3 for methods of sterilisation.

6 Fit a fermentation lock to exclude any air-containing undesirable micro-organisms (see Chapter 9 for further explanation). Leave in a warm place to ferment, such as a warm kitchen or airing cupboard. This step is when you hear a gentle 'glug glug glug' as the yeasts go to work and gases escape through the fermentation lock. This stage may take several weeks.

7 Siphon off into a clean vessel, perhaps another demijohn, leaving the sediment behind (or put into a sterile holding vessel while you clean out the original demijohn). Return for further fermentation; you may have to go through this stage two or three times until the cider is clear.

8 When the fermentation stops – no more bubbles blobbing through the fermentation lock – siphon off the cider into sterilised bottles with firmly fitting lids and store in a cool, dark place. If you make the cider in October, wait until Christmas before drinking it; it improves with further aging, if you can bear to leave it alone.

Vary it! *You can make pear cider (called perry) in the same way. This cider is especially good for using up hard, inedible pears.*

Per 100-millilitre serving: *54 calories; 0 grams protein, 13 grams carbohydrate, 0 grams fat, 0 grams saturated fat, 0 milligrams cholesterol, 0 grams fibre, 12 milligrams sodium.*

 If you're making more than 4 or 5 litres (7 or 9 pints) of apple juice for cider using your poor little electric juicer, it may well feel the strain and burn out. If you're itching for homemade cider in larger quantities, invest in heavy-duty equipment and get friends in to help.

Going well with everything

The apple harvest is the mainstay of preserving. Check out these recipes in other sections and chapters:

> ✔ **Apricot and Brandy Conserve:** For this recipe in the next section, you need apples too. Also, look at the list in the earlier section 'Swapping Fruity Tips and Tastes' too.

✔ **Blackberry and Apple Jam:** Find this jam in Chapter 18 (where the wild fruits are).

✔ **Crab Apple Jelly:** This recipe (in Chapter 18) leaves the field wide open for all sorts of imaginative variations, and for using your cooking apples.

Apricots

Soft, lightly furred skins, delicately flavoured and blushingly coloured, you don't commonly find apricot trees in the UK, and they aren't easy to grow. But if you're lucky enough to have access to ripe apricots, they may well be a variety called Moorpark or perhaps Tomcot, which freeze well as a puree (Chapter 7 has more chilling news) or poached in a light syrup. Alternatively, try something with a bit of an adult twist such as the following recipe.

If growing your own is out of the question, buying up a quantity of in-season apricots from a market stall gives you the opportunity to make high-class preserves at a fraction of the cost in a fancy delicatessen. See the later section on peaches to swap ideas between the two fruits.

Apricot and Brandy Conserve

A splash of apricot brandy is the icing on the cake. Scooping some of this special conserve onto a warm croissant hints at the continental, or save it for a special birthday breakfast with a kick. Chapter 2 gives you information on jam-making equipment. Chapter 3 has more on sterilisation.

Special tools required: *Sterilised jars*

Preparation time: *15 minutes*

Processing time: *About 2 hours, less if you use a food mill*

Yield: *About 3.5 kilograms (7 pounds)*

900 grams (2 pounds) cooking apples

600 millilitres (1 pint) water

1.8 kilograms (4 pounds) fresh apricots

1.8 kilograms (2 pounds) granulated sugar

90 millilitres (6 tablespoons) apricot brandy (or normal brandy)

1 Chop the whole apples roughly without peeling or coring (apples have a high pectin content, which helps with the set – Chapter 5 gives more information on what makes a good set). Place into a large, heavy-bottomed pan such as a jam pan with the water, heating gently until simmering. Cook for about an hour, stirring occasionally – until the fruit is soft. During this cooking time, halve and stone the apricots.

2 Strain the cooked apples through a nylon sieve, pushing the pulp through with the back of a wooden spoon. Alternatively, use a food mill if you have one (see Chapter 2 for information). Keep the juice and pulp, discarding the peel and pip bits left in the sieve or food mill. Using the heavy-bottomed pan again, cook the apricots in the apple juice until they're really soft –for about 30–40 minutes. Remove from heat.

3 Add the sugar and stir, returning the pan to the heat when all the sugar dissolves. Bring rapidly to the boil until you get a soft set; test frequently with a sugar thermometer (or another method from Chapter 5).

4 Remove from the heat as soon as you reach the required set, and allow the conserve to settle for a few minutes. The final task is to pour in the brandy, stirring to distribute the fruit and amalgamate the brandy. Pot up while still hot into warm, sterilised preserving jars, seal, label and store out of bright light.

Vary it! *Substitute ordinary brandy if the apricot variety is too hard (or too expensive) to buy.*

Per 100-gram serving: 45 calories; 0 grams protein, 8 grams carbohydrate, 1 grams fat, 0 grams saturated fat, 0 milligrams cholesterol, 1 grams fibre, 0 milligrams sodium.

Cherries

Who doesn't love dangling cherries, even if you just annoy your children by hanging them over their ears as bright jewel earrings! If you're buying a cherry tree, the good news is that growers are developing better and better domestic varieties all the time: try Sunburst or Stella for full, plump fruit with fantastic ruby colour.

Breeders are experimenting with old varieties, grafted – that is, joining one living piece of tree wood to another – onto small dwarfing rootstocks, which makes cherry picking a doddle (you no longer need a cherry picker ladder, as those tall concertina-like lifting platforms are called). These smaller trees also make netting your cherry trees against the hungry birds easier.

If you inherit cherry trees, some varieties are acidic and suited to cooking and making jams, or bottle them in a syrup – Chapter 5 gives plenty of encouragement for preserving sweetly. If you feel ready for an experiment, adapt the Apricot and Brandy Conserve recipe from the preceding section.

Stone cherries by cutting them in half with a sharp knife and prising out the stone before open freezing (check Chapter 7 more information on freezing). Roll them in a little caster sugar to soak up the juices.

Crab apples

Eating, cooking and cider apple varieties all originate from this wild fellow. Sometimes you can see one or two still growing in cultivated orchards, often of the John Downie variety, because of their use as a high-pectin and acid source – helpful for setting jams and jellies, as I describe in Chapter 5. More often, you find crab apple trees in woodlands and as a hedgerow tree (flick to Chapter 18 for all about collecting and using fruits from the wild version).

Damsons

Dark purple damsons have a delicious strong plummy taste. Making a preserve with a method that incorporates removing the stones is easiest; proportionally, they've little fruit to the stone, but they do set well. Try Farleigh damsons, or spread into the world of Merryweather damsons for a plumper, 'plummier' variety.

Damson Cheese

When this cheese is mature, remove the lid of the pot, dunk up to the rim in scalding water to melt the outer edges of the cheese and then up-end onto a plate. You can cut the damson cheese like cheese and the cheese is equally delicious as a dessert with chopped nuts and cream, on scones with cream or as an accompaniment to cold meats and poultry (duck and home-made damson cheese is yummy!). Chapter 2 has more information on equipment and Chapter 3 has the info on sterilisation.

Special tools required: *Sterilised jars*

Preparation time: *30 minutes*

Processing time: *1¼ hours*

Yield: *1.3–1.8 kilograms (3–4 pounds)*

2.7 kilograms (6 pounds) whole damsons

300 millilitres (½ pint) water

Granulated sugar – the amount depends on fruit yielded: 450 grams (1 pound) to each 450 grams (1 pound) fruit

1 Wash whole damsons and place in a pan with the water. Bring to the boil, cover and simmer particularly gently for about 30 minutes until the fruit is tender.

2 Push the fruit through a fine nylon sieve with the back of a wooden spoon and discard the stones, or use a food mill if you have one. Weigh the pulp. Return the weighed pulp to a clean, heavy-bottomed saucepan, adding an equal amount of sugar to each amount of pulped fruit.

3 Heat gently until all the sugar dissolves, and then cook gently for 45–60 minutes, stirring frequently to avoid burning or sticking. When you can draw a wooden spoon across the base of the pan leaving a clean line behind, the cheese is ready to pot up into sterilised jars. Seal immediately and allow to mature for two months before using.

Tip: See the later section 'Plums' for another plummy recipe.

Vary it! Use this method for blackberries (see Chapter 18 for protective picking hints), plums and greengages as well.

Per 100-gram serving: 230 calories; 0 grams protein, 59 grams carbohydrate, 0 grams fat, 0 grams saturated fat, 0 milligrams cholesterol, 1 grams fibre, 1 milligrams sodium.

Figs

The fresh fruit – green or purple on the outside with a rich red flesh when ripe – of this biblically acclaimed tree start as budding fruits in the autumn. These autumn fruits don't thrive as well as the spring developing ones, so remove the autumn fruits and concentrate on the spring ones for a better, healthier crop of figs.

Fig trees grow best in large greenhouses or up against a south-facing wall. If you've one of these trees, you probably inherited it. Fig trees are pretty rare, but choosing varieties to suit your size of garden is possible. For example, the Bavarian Fig Violetta is a tree with large juicy fruits but the Jerusalem Fig comes as a miniature – ideal for smaller spaces. Whichever your variety, don't try to save picked fruit in the fruit bowl; figs have a short shelf-life. Instead, eat them straight from the tree and appreciate the exotic luxury. If bottling in syrup or making fig jam, turn to Chapter 5 for more instructions.

You can dry your figs by cutting them in half and sprinkling over a little caster sugar before laying them on a rack and placing in a cooling oven, homemade dryer or food dehydrator (see Chapter 8 for more about drying). When you can't press the juice out of the fruit, they're ready to seal in an airtight jar and be used as snacking material; or rehydrate them in a little water to add to other dishes.

Wasps like ripe figs so beware when picking. Wasps may enter the fruit through a small hole and eat it from the inside, leaving you with a shell – make sure that you get there first.

Grapes

Grapes do grow in the cooler climes of the UK. Boskoop Glory, for example, is a garden variety that produces sweet black grapes, and Black Hamburg does best in the greenhouse. In a good cropping year, they hang in luscious large bunches – a delightful sight. If you're planting grapes, take advice from your supplier, depending on whether you want red, pink or white, seedless or not.

If you've luscious bunches of grapes festooning a sunny wall or greenhouse, use scissors to snip the bunches (and cut a short portion of branch too). Place the branch in a jar of water in a cool, dark place and your grapes keep for a further six to eight weeks.

Dry the seedless varieties for homemade raisins – see Chapter 8 for ideas on drying – or use for chutneys and jellies. If you've plenty of grapes, press them for juice just as for apples (see the earlier section 'Juicing up your apples' and go to Chapter 9 for other drinking options).

Greengages

Queen of all the plums, a bountiful harvest of glorious pale green, almost translucent in the sunshine – you can't beat greengages. Old Greengage Tree is the original sweet variety, but modern rootstocks (see Table 10-1 to understand how rootstocks affect your tree) make many varieties available. Cambridge Gage Tree, for example, comes in all sorts of sizes to fit into your growing space.

Check out the section 'Plums' later in the chapter, and swap or mix in greengages for a sweeter more aromatic version of the Savoury Plum Sauce recipe. You can also find a Three-Fruit Autumn Jam recipe earlier in this chapter (in the 'Trying Out Some Treetop Treats' section), which nicely uses up a glut of harvest fruits.

If time is pressing, simply pop the clean, dry fruit into a bag and freeze – Chapter 7 has chilling information – until your ideal jam-making time comes round.

Medlars

Medlar fruit – an unappetising-looking brown fruit with a five-spiked calyx at the top – has to be bletted (that is, allowed to soften) before you can use it.

Choose a smaller tree in the Royal Medlar variety or, if space isn't an issue, go for the Nottingham Medlar Tree, but take your supplier's advice before parting with any cash because these trees originate from warm sunny climes.

After picking in early November, put to one side in a cool spot and leave for a few weeks. Check the medlar to see whether the fruit is ready – that is, softened up. Consume fresh, follow the Medlar cheese recipe below or make into a jelly (check out Chapter 5 before attempting this jelly – you need to do a pectin test first).

Medlar Cheese

Old-fashioned flavours such as the ones in this recipe go well with the cheese board and with cold meats and game. Find small, upright, open-topped jars and bottle in small amounts; dunking a pot in hot water for a couple of minutes and up-ending onto a clean board makes an attractive cheese ready for slicing. Alternatively, use as a sweet with a dollop of cream or yoghurt. See Chapter 2 for more about suitable equipment and Chapter 3 for more on sterilisation.

Special tools required: *Sterilised jars, waxed discs and lids*

Preparation time: *15 minutes*

Processing time: *40–60 minutes*

Yield: *About 1.8 kilograms (4 pounds)*

1 kilogram (2 pounds, 4 ounces) bletted medlars

300 millilitres (½ pint) water

2 unwaxed lemons

Granulated sugar – matched weight for weight with sieved fruit

1 Chop up the medlars and lemons into small pieces, and place the fruit and water together into a heavy-bottomed pan.

2 Bring to the boil and simmer gently until the fruit is soft.

3 Push the mixture through a nylon sieve using the back of a wooden spoon. Return this pulp to the pan and cook slowly until thick, and then weigh.

4 Add the same weight of sugar as pulped fruit. Stir together over a low heat until the sugar dissolves. Boil until the mixture reaches a thick consistency.

5 Pot into sterilised jars, and top with waxed discs and lids before labelling and storing.

Per 100-gram serving: 233 calories; 0 grams protein, 60 grams carbohydrate, 0 grams fat, 0 grams saturated fat, 0 milligrams cholesterol, 1 gram fibre, 1 milligram sodium.

Nuts (cultivated)

If you haven't heard of forest gardens yet, you soon will. Cultivating nuts is the way forward for low-carbon protein production. If you're going to plant trees, consider nuts; they may not be so great for making jam, but most store well in a dry place – away from squirrels!

For a treat and to prevent nuts from shrivelling up, shell them and toast them spread out on a baking tray in a cool oven (120 degrees Celsius; Gas Mark ½) for an hour or two, depending how big the nuts are. Sprinkle with salt and store in an airtight container.

Keep a look out for new varieties of nuts (and I don't mean on TV talent shows!) and new ways to manage productive trees. Many are in development right now and include sweet chestnut, hazel and walnut if you've room. A whole book could be devoted to the subject of nut varieties, so I don't recommend any here. Chapter 21 has for more ideas at the cutting edge of growing food and how you can join in.

Oranges

Okay, as I hint in this chapter's introduction, I'm cheating here by including oranges with these other orchard favourites! To be honest, the chances of you having your own orangery are pretty unlikely (if you do, you're one of the few people to live in a stately home, where they used to be a common feature). But that's no reason for everyone else to miss out; most people who are into their preserves simply buy special oranges to make marmalade.

I love using the bitter, thick, rough-skinned Seville variety for marmalade (see the recipe in this section), and January is the season for Seville oranges.

Buy your Seville oranges as soon as you see them in the shops; the season is short and so any fruit lingering quickly loses freshness.

If you can't spare time to make your marmalade as soon as you buy the fruit, or you want to stagger your marmalade-making sessions throughout the year, let your freezer help you out (I provide tips about freezing, and uses for, fruits in Chapter 7). Just glance at your recipe to see the quantities of fruit you need to make one batch and freeze accordingly. Simply scrub well and dry before popping the correct number of oranges, and a lemon (usually part of a marmalade recipe) into a stout plastic bag and into the freezer – you're going to boil your saved fruits so freezing first does no harm.

Pippin' good!

A friend of mine heard that citrus pips were 'good for you', and so rather than tying the pips up, boiling them with the fruit and then removing them from the end product, she ground the pips up and added them as part of the marmalade. It worked – at least, she looks well on it! – so perhaps there's something in the idea!

Freezing the cooked pulp of the oranges is fine too; you simply add another eighth to the weight of fruit in order to offset the pectin (the setting agent) lost through freezing. For example, if you're following the Seville Marmalade recipe in this section, go through Steps 1 to 4 and add 125 grams (4½ ounces) to the stated 1 kilogram (2 pounds, 4 ounces) of Seville oranges.

If you're already growing in a chemical-free manner in your garden or allotment, extend your attitude to your buying habits too. Organic citrus fruit isn't sprayed and is without an added wax layer – which only makes fruits look unnaturally shiny.

Seville Marmalade

This bitter-sweet Seville orange marmalade recipe provides you with lashings of marmalade for putting on your toast for breakfast. Or you can find a recipe for a marmalade cake and use it for that too.

The traditional English breakfast marmalade has a strong, tangy flavour with large, chucky pieces of rind. Make a texture of your choice by cutting the fruit as chunkily or finely as you want. Chapter 2 gives more details on the necessary preserving equipment and Chapter 3 has more on sterilisation.

Special tools required: *Muslin, sugar thermometer, sterilised jars*

Preparation time: *1–1½ hours*

Processing time: *About 2½ hours cooking time*

Yield: *about 2.7 kilograms (6 pounds)*

1 kilogram (2 pounds, 4 ounces) Seville oranges – preferably organically grown – scrubbed clean and free from any stalks

1 large organic lemon

1 kilogram (2 pounds, 4 ounces) granulated sugar

1.8 litres (3 pints) water

1 Cut the oranges and lemons in half, squeeze the juice into a jug and store temporarily in the fridge. Place the pips, and any loose pith, into a square of muslin – a clean, disposable dishcloth does the job too – gather in the top and tie with string to make a little bag.

2 Using a large preserving pan or a heavy-bottomed large saucepan, place the fruit and your little bag of goodies into the water. Bring to the boil, cover lightly and simmer gently for one to two hours. Check the consistency of the citrus peel shells from time to time – soft is good – and test with a knife that they cut easily and cleanly. Don't let them go mushy.

3 Tip into a large colander or sieve, collecting all the liquid, and making sure that the shells aren't holding pools of liquor.

4 Clean the shells by scooping out any stringy pithy or mushy bits (a light scraping with a spoon does the job); discard the mush and your bag of pips. Choose your preferred texture now, cutting the cooked skins as fine or chunky as you desire.

5 Pour the liquid, prepared peel and the fruit juice you reserved in the fridge as well as the sugar into the saucepan. Heat gently, stirring all the while, until the sugar dissolves. Then turn the heat up high and boil rapidly until you reach setting point (test in one of the ways that I describe in Chapter 5 or play safe and use your sugar thermometer as I describe in Chapter 2).

6 Skim off any surface scum and allow the marmalade to settle for a few minutes. When you see a skin forming, give the marmalade a last stir to redistribute the peel. Ladle into sterilised jars, seal and label. Store in a cool, dark place until breakfast beckons.

Vary it! *If you prefer something less bitter sweet, swap the Seville oranges with the same total weight of a grapefruit and sweet oranges mix. Also swap the lemon for four limes and cut the peel fine. If you're a whisky fan, wait until the last stirring in Step 6 and add 125 millilitres (4 fluid ounces) of whisky.*

Per 100-gram serving: *161 calories; 0 grams protein, 42 grams carbohydrate, 0 grams fat, 0 grams saturated fat, 0 milligrams cholesterol, 1 grams fibre, 0 milligrams sodium.*

Peaches

Peach trees need special requirements to produce a good crop in the UK. The variety Peregrine has a good reputation; a good tree nursery can supply you with the necessary information. Consult the earlier section 'Apricots' because peach trees have the same joys and problems.

Enjoy the fruits if you inherit a productive peach tree: they're versatile. Eat the best straight from the tree, freeze (Chapter 7 helps you out with methods) or make sweet preserves as I discuss in Chapters 5 and 6.

If you love peaches but can't grow them, bulk-buy when you see them in season in the greengrocer's; you can use peaches (or nectarines – a non-fuzzy, peach-like fruit) in similar quantities to replace apricots in recipes.

Pears

The Conference pear is the king of pears and probably stores best. The later a pear naturally ripens, the better it stores, so look for late-maturing varieties, especially if you're planting up your own orchard with preserving in mind. Look out for forgotten varieties from your locality too: Apple Days, which are becoming a common autumn event (ask at farmers' markets and farm shops as well checking local advertising boards), also extend to local pear identification.

Sweet yellow pears are prone to bruising and turning mushy quickly – catch them as they become ripe and turn the softer varieties into juice. (See the recipe in Chapter 9 for small quantities of apple juice, and just substitute pears.) Chutneys preserve pears the best.

If you come across a tree with hard, sour, inedible pears, use them to make perry (pear cider – see the earlier section 'Cider-making: Transforming apples into a tipple' and use pears instead).

Pears have a tendency to discolour when you expose the flesh to air; recipes staining the pear, with red wine or raspberry vinegar, for example, enhance the attractiveness.

Mulled Pears – a Christmas treat

Pears dyed red from wine retain the flavour but lose the alcohol in the heating. Opening a jar of these pears releases the aroma of Christmas complete with spicy, citrusy decorations.

Special tools required: *Sterilised purpose-made preserving jars with rubber ring seals*

Preparation time: *30–40 minutes*

Processing time: *3½–4 hours*

Yield! *About 1.3 kilograms (3 pounds)*

1.8 kilograms (4 pounds) small firm pears

1 unwaxed organic orange – thin rind parings

1 unwaxed organic lemon – thin rind parings

2 cinnamon sticks

10–12 cloves

5-centimetre (2-inch) piece of root ginger – peeled and thinly sliced

350 grams (12 ounces) granulated sugar

1 bottle of light fruity wine – Beaujolais, for example

1 Preheat the oven to 130 degrees Celsius (250 degrees Fahrenheit; Gas Mark ½).

2 Peel the pears, leaving the stalks in place. Using sterilised preserving jars, pack the raw pears into the jars; arrange the citrus parings and spices decoratively in the jars.

3 Make the wine syrup by combining the wine and sugar in a large, heavy-bottomed pan, stirring over a low heat until the sugar dissolves. Bring to the boil for five minutes.

4 Pour the hot wine syrup over the pears, covering them completely and tapping the jars to dislodge any air pockets.

5 Cover with lids but don't fasten the seal. Place in the oven on a baking sheet and cook for two and a half to three hours.

Be particularly careful when using the oven hot-bottling method here, for two reasons. Firstly, you're dealing with sugar, which boils at a higher temperature than water, and burns naked skin. Secondly, any minute chips or cracks not visible to the naked eye are put under extreme pressure and your jars may crack. If you're at all doubtful about your jars or your ability to lift and carry hot objects, use the water bath method, which places less strain on the jars at the boiling point of water. The end result is just as good. (See Chapter 5 for hot-bottling options and Chapter 3 for more about risk-free preserving.)

6 Using protective gloves, remove from the oven (or water bath if you choose that method) onto a slip-free surface – a dry tea towel, for example. Allow to cool slightly, then seal the clamp-top jars. With screw tops, shut and then loosen them by one quarter turn. Allow to cool completely. Test the vacuum seal by loosening the lever clip or outer screw lid – if the vacuum takes the weight of the jar, re-seal and store in a cool, dark place.

Warning: *Use up preserves in jars not achieving a strong enough suction to take their own weight straightaway.*

Per 100-gram serving: *147 calories; 0 grams protein, 37 grams carbohydrate, 0 grams fat, 0 grams saturated fat, 0 milligrams cholesterol, 2 grams fibre, 3 milligrams sodium.*

Plums

If you decide to make plum jam, you're in for a treat! Plum jam (apart from being the hardest thing to say when you've a bad cold), left for a little while to mature in the jar, transforms the plum skins into caramelised slivers of delight.

Victoria plum is well known for abundant harvests of red plums, and Opal makes a good choice if your space is restricted, but chat to a fruit tree supplier to find out more about varieties before stocking up an orchard. Every situation is different.

Savoury Plum Sauce

Fruity and thick, you can use this sauce with any cold meat and poultry; the sauce is especially good to cut the richness of roast duck or Christmas goose. Chapter 3 gives you several sterilising options and Chapter 6 expands on preserving with vinegar.

Special tools required: *Sterilised preserving containers*

Preparation time: *15 minutes*

Processing time: *70 minutes*

Yield: *850 millilitres (1½ pints)*

*900 grams (2 pounds) plums – use a mixture
and include damsons if you wish*

225 grams (8 ounces) granulated sugar

600 millilitres (1 pint) malt vinegar

5 millilitres (1 teaspoon) salt

5 millilitres (1 teaspoon) ground ginger

2.5 millilitres (½ teaspoon) cayenne pepper

8 cloves

1 Wash and dry the plums, putting them (stones and all) into a large, heavy-bottomed pan; add in the rest of the ingredients. Keep stirring over a gentle heat until all the sugar dissolves, and then bring the mixture to the boil.

2 Reduce the heat and simmer until for 30 minutes, stirring occasionally. Remove from the heat and strain your mixture through a nylon sieve, pressing it through with the back of your wooden spoon. Clean the pan and return the fruit puree. Simmer until the mixture reaches the consistency of thick but pourable sauce.

3 Bottle into sterilised containers. Seal – using non-corrosive or plastic-lined lids – and store for at least a month before using.

Per 100-gram serving: 188 calories; 1 grams protein, 47 grams carbohydrate, 1 grams fat, 0 grams saturated fat, 0 milligrams cholesterol, 0 grams fibre, 295 milligrams sodium.

Quinces

With a fragrance in a class of their own, quince fruits need to ripen on the bush – their yellowy, pear-shaped fruit stores well. Varieties like Meech's Prolific and Serbian Gold serve you well.

Chapter 4 has ideas on how to keep your stored fruits safe from pests who easily sniff out aromatic options such as quinces. You need to keep a place aside for quinces where they don't impart their smell. Quinces make great jellies, the exotic forerunner of the well-beloved marmalade; naturally high in pectin, quinces set well.

Quince Jelly

This recipe combines the freshness of lemon with the exotic heady scent of quince. Step things up a level and leave the apple sauce behind, using quince as an accompaniment to your next roast pork dinner or with any savoury dish. See Chapter 2 for information on jam-making equipment.

Special tools required: *Jelly bag; sugar thermometer; sterilised jars*

Preparation time: *20 minutes*

Processing time: *Cooking 2–3 hours; straining about 4 hours*

Yield: *1.8–2.2 kilograms (4–5 pounds)*

1.8 kilograms (4 pounds) quinces

Granulated sugar – 450 grams (1 pound) for every 600 millilitres (1 pint)

Juice of two lemons

1 Begin by washing the quinces and chopping them roughly, placing them in a heavy-bottomed pan – a jam pan is ideal. Use just enough water to cover. Bring to the boil and simmer, covered, for one to one and a half hours or until the fruit is soft. Ladle into a scalded jelly bag and leave for a minimum of four hours.

2 Heat the oven to 110 degrees Celsius (225 degrees Fahrenheit, Gas Mark ¼), warming the sugar in an ovenproof dish for 10–15 minutes. Measure the strained liquid and add 450 grams (1 pound) sugar for every 600 millilitres (1 pint) of liquid.

3 Gently warm the strained quince liquid, adding the lemon juice and then stirring in the warmed sugar until it all dissolves. Bring the jelly to a rapid boil and cook rapidly – on average 10–15 minutes – until the mixture reaches the setting point (use a sugar thermometer or one of the methods I provide in Chapter 5 to test the setting point).

4 Remove any scum by skimming and pot into warm, sterilised jars (Chapter 3 gives sterilising options), seal and store.

Tip: *Squeezing the jelly bag to hurry along the straining of your jelly is a big no no! If you do, the jelly loses clarity.*

Per 100-gram serving: *146 calories; 0 grams protein, 38 grams carbohydrate, 0 grams fat, 0 grams saturated fat, 0 milligrams cholesterol, 1 grams fibre, 3 milligrams sodium.*

Chapter 11

Making the Most of Your Berry, Berry Good Soft-Fruit Harvest

In This Chapter

▶ Ensuring a great fruit harvest

▶ Creating classic soft-fruit combinations

▶ Going soft on soft-fruit recipes

*T*raditionally, your soft fruits – squishy berries and currants (both juicy little round fruits without stones) – are low bushes or even ground-hugging plants such as strawberries, as opposed to the higher-off-the-ground orchard or top fruits – the apples, pears and so on that I discuss in Chapter 10. Of course, exceptions exist in the form of rhubarb, which goes soft when cooked and definitely has a fruity taste, though the part you cook originates from a surprising non-fruit part of the plant.

This chapter gives you classic tried-and-tested ideas for dealing with your soft-fruit crops in style: jams, jellies and syrups all feature. I suggest ways to keep your harvest safe and gather in the yield effectively, and I encourage you to make up your own combinations and use common sense to substitute similar fruits in different preserves.

Protecting and Picking Your Soft Fruits

Before you can enjoy the fruits of your fruits, so to speak, you need to raise healthy, productive plants. To keep your home-grown soft fruits safe from perils, I suggest growing them under fruit netting. A netted-off area of the garden can foil the ravaging attempts of pests that can strip the plant bare.

You can buy fruit netting from garden centres or via seed catalogues. If you don't manage to net the fruit in (and the raiding parties out) effectively, you need to keep a constant eye on your fruit bushes.

Just a few creatures who happily tuck into soft fruits are:

- ✔ **Deer:** Can cause damage to the whole bush and graze on strawberry beds.
- ✔ **Mice:** Your fruit net probably can't keep mice out, so a patrolling cat is more effective.
- ✔ **Squirrels:** Can strip a bush bare in hours when they put their mind to it.
- ✔ **Wasps:** Generally, wasps like ripe fruit so pick early to avoid major damage, and beware of grabbing an unsuspecting wasp when picking fruit.

  If you do suffer a wasp sting, apply vinegar to the site straight away; it helps to neutralise the poison.
- ✔ **Wild birds:** Fruit lovers include blackbirds and sparrows.

For loads more information on combating pests as well as encouraging helpful animal guests, check out Chapters 3 and 4.

By keeping your harvest safe, you help to ensure that you've a healthy yield to gather. For the best soft-fruit results, pick dry just-ripe fruit, preferably in the middle of the day when all danger of dew is past and the pectin content is at its optimum – Chapter 5 explains the vital role of pectin in jam- and jelly-making and contains many more fruity insights as well. Instead of allowing your fruits to become over-ripe or suffer the battering of a rainstorm, select slightly under-ripe yet full, colourful fruits and open freeze them (as I describe in Chapter 7). You can then process them further at a later stage.

Mixing and Matching with Berries

The soft-fruit season starts with the gooseberries, which are early fruiting and just right for combining with wild flavours blossoming in the spring; try the Gooseberry and Elderflower Jam combination that I provide in the later section 'Writing the Alpha-berry of Soft Fruits and their Currant Friends'.

Raspberries ripen early in spring, or later with the autumn cropping varieties, and the warmest months yield a ripening currant harvest for your best ever summer pudding. When your garden is flowing with berries, you can mix and match flavours. Save some early fruit in the freezer for adding to preserves later in the season, or use your orchard fruits (Chapter 10 has you hanging from the branches) to bulk up a meagre harvest.

Here are a couple of recipes using mixtures of soft fruit. You can change the mix to suit what's growing on your patch – just keep to the basic bulk quantities.

The majority of recipes in this chapter call for you to use a heavy-bottomed preserving pan (check out Chapter 2 on getting properly tooled-up and for all equipment-related issues) and sterilised jars (which I discuss in Chapter 3).

Summer Pudding in Suspense

Classically, this recipe is a summer dish for the days when your fruit bushes are bursting full, and is especially good when you're all 'jammed out' and the fruit's a little on the ripe side. Make Summer Pudding to eat the next day, because you can easily find the bread part at any time of year, and sort out a quick fix for your over-ripening fruit by freezing measured quantities of mixed fruits for fillings later in the year. This dish certainly brightens up a dull winter day. Freeze raw fruit and start the recipe from the beginning or partially cook the fruits until the juices are running and save in a plastic container in the freezer, just waiting for the right occasion to present itself.

Combine raspberries, stoned cherries, blackberries, blackcurrants, redcurrants and so on. Use a minimum combination of three for a classic look and taste, but go light on the blackberries and blackcurrants, which like to dominate. Keeping it light and fruity and a scarlet red is most authentic.

To speed up what can be a fiddly process, pick sprays of currants and use a wide-toothed fork to remove the berries, running the fork down the stalk.

Although this recipe is a great quick fix when your berry and currant bushes are overwhelming you, after thawing you do need an eight-hour standing time to produce perfect results, so this recipe isn't a last minute pudding. Refer to Chapter 2 for a full explanation of equipment.

Preparation time: *30 minutes*

Processing time: *10–15 minutes cooking time and 8 hours standing time*

Serves: *6*

7–8 day-old slices from a white loaf, with the crusts cut off

900 grams (2 pounds) mixed soft fruit (open freeze at this stage if you like – Chapter 7 has all the freezing details)

110 grams (4 ounces) caster sugar

1 Top and tail the currants, picking over the berries and stoning cherries to remove any debris, stalks or stray caterpillars, and place them in a heavy-bottomed saucepan – a preserving pan is ideal. Wash the fruit only if you really must.

2 Add the sugar and cook over a low heat to dissolve the sugar and encourage the fruit juices to flow. If you want to, stop here and allow to cool to fridge temperature, ready for freezing. You've done half the work: when you're ready to make the pudding, just allow the fruit mixture to thaw at room temperature and continue with the recipe.

3 Line the base and sides of an 850-millilitre (1½ pint) pudding bowl with the slices of bread, overlapping and leaving no gaps; use about two thirds of the bread. Pack in the sweetened fruity mix – freshly cooked or thawed – using a slotted spoon. Sprinkle a little of the juice to soak without saturating the bread (to avoid your pudding collapsing – not so impressive!) and cover with the remaining slices. Save the rest of the juice for later.

4 Find a saucer or plate that fits over the pudding bowl, curved side down, neatly pressing the pudding and weigh it down with something heavy – a 450-gram (1 pound) tin or jar does the job nicely. Leave to stand in the refrigerator overnight or for at least eight hours.

5 To turn the pudding out successfully, remove your weight and saucer. Carefully ease around the side of the pudding with a broad, blunt-bladed knife – a palette knife is perfect. Place your flat serving plate over the top of the pudding dish, invert both plate and pudding dish, giving a sharp few knocks on the base and sides. Carefully lift the pudding bowl off the top and – 'ta-da!' – your pudding stands alone.

6 Serve with single cream and the remaining fruit-sugar juices and bringing a little bit of summer into a wintery gloom.

Tip: Frozen currants are really easy to top and tail: just rub the little bits off with your fingers (wear clean rubber gloves if your fingers are sensitive to the cold). This approach is much less fiddly than when they're fresh.

Per serving: *219 calories; 4 grams protein, 48 grams carbohydrate, 2 grams fat, 0 grams saturated fat, 0 milligrams cholesterol, 4 grams fibre, 205 milligrams sodium.*

Five-Fruit Jelly

If your home-grown fruit efforts yield a wide enough variety to make this jelly, congratulate yourself heartily. Use it sparingly, savouring every mouthful on freshly baked scones or in tiny jam tarts for special occasions. Buy preserving sugar – Chapter 5 has some sweet advice on sugar types – to ensure a good set and add sparkle to your jelly.

Prepare yourself by reading about methods for testing the set in Chapter 5 before you get underway, as a reminder if you're not totally confident and definitely if this recipe is your first ever jam. Your favourite testing method becomes second nature after a while.

Don't try to make more than 4.5 kilograms (10 pounds) of this jelly in one batch in a domestic situation. A standard-sized jam pan is designed to hold this amount or less (see Chatper 2 for more on equipment). These pans enable evaporation – an essential part of the cooking process – to take place, allow moisture to escape and the pan contents to reduce. The reduced amount of moisture means less chance of a home for spoilage bacteria (Chapter 3 spills the beans on their idea of mouldy fun). The flavours then concentrate and even boiling takes place for a good set. Chapter 3 shows methods for sterilising jars.

Special tools required: *Jelly bag*

Preparation time: *15 minutes*

Processing time: *40 minutes cooking and 3–4 hours straining time*

Yield: *About 900 grams (2 pounds)*

225 grams (8 ounces) strawberries

225 grams (8 ounces) raspberries

225 grams (8 ounces) cherries

225 grams (8 ounces) redcurrants

225 grams (8 ounces) gooseberries

450 grams (1 pound) preserving sugar per 600 millilitres (1 pint) of liquid

1 Wash the fruit, leaving any hulls, stones and stalks and removing any debris and the green tops from the strawberries. Put all the fruit in a heavy-bottomed preserving pan with enough water to cover it.

2 Bring to the boil and simmer over a gentle heat for about 30–40 minutes until the fruit is totally soft; squeeze the fruit with the back of a wooden spoon from time to time to release the juices.

3 Strain the fruit and juices through a scalded jelly bag (Chapter 5 has the low-down on jelly bag practices). Leave for at least four hours or even overnight to strain, avoiding the temptation to hurry the process along by squeezing the bag.

4 Preheat your oven to 110 degrees Celsius (225 degrees Fahrenheit, Gas Mark ¼), placing the sugar in an ovenproof bowl in the centre of the oven for 10–15 minutes to heat it gently through.

5 Measure the strained liquid and add the necessary amount of preserving sugar. Return the juice to the clean pan and heat gently on the top of the stove, adding the warm sugar and stirring until the sugar dissolves. Turn up the heat to a rapid boil for 10–15 minutes, using your favourite method test for set. Pot into warm, sterile jars – and label when cool.

Tip: *Don't squeeze the jelly bag; it makes your jelly cloudy.*

Per 100-gram serving: *225 calories; 1 grams protein, 57 grams carbohydrate, 0 grams fat, 0 grams saturated fat, 0 milligrams cholesterol, 0 grams fibre, 1 milligrams sodium.*

Writing the Alpha-berry of Soft Fruits and their Currant Friends

This section is the one for jam and jelly lovers, with loads of great recipes and hints on varieties to get your soft-fruit bushes off to a firm start and a ripe future. For even more jammy advice, don't forget to check out Chapter 5.

Blackberries

The best blackberries are wild – pop along to Chapter 18 for recipes and pick-your-own good sense because the wild variety has jolly prickly stems. If you love blackberries and hate prickles, you can find varieties of easy-to-grow-and-pick cultivated blackberries with large fruits and thornless stems, such as Chester and Waldo.

Blackberries generally need help with pectin levels, so they pair well with high-pectin cooking or crab apples and in other combinations: try the Blackberry and Apple Jam recipe in Chapter 18 or use the Blackcurrant Syrup recipe (in the following 'Blackcurrants' section) and substitute blackcurrants with blackberries.

Blackcurrants

Blackcurrants are the jam-maker's dream fruit, perhaps a bit fiddly to pick but certainly worth the hassle; a new giant comb tool is on the market to hurry the process up and you may spot it in a seed catalogue (the earlier Summer Pudding in Suspense recipe has more on safe picking). Just enjoying losing yourself in concentration, searching out the drooping heavy sprays of berries hidden in among the leaves on a warm summer day is a grounding, recuperative occupation; the tasty jams, fruit syrups and cordials are the reward.

Use the just ripe fruit for jams and jellies and the riper, less perfect fruits in cordials or syrups.

If you're thinking of planting blackcurrants, consider the Ben Sarek variety for the smaller garden or, if space isn't an issue, Ben Connan. Most garden centres and catalogues have a good range; speak to a salesperson for a variety that suits your needs.

Juicing with an electric juicing machine produces a drink needing dilution – maybe in lager on a hot sunny day for adults and in apple juice or water for children – but this juice ferments after a couple of days in the fridge and needs freezing for longer storage (Chapter 7 has hints on freezing liquids). Freeze the whole blackcurrants loose, stewed or as a puree. Although freezing affects the pectin level, blackcurrants are high in this substance so it isn't a problem.

The Summer Pudding in Suspense recipe earlier in this chapter contains hints on the fiddly topping-and-tailing process.

Blackcurrant Jam

Blackcurrant jam has everything going for it, especially the taste. The high pectin levels mean that you get plenty of jam for your fruit (making it economical) and blackcurrant is one of the best home-made jams to start with if your confidence is a bit low. Add it to the list for a plate of jam tarts, giving exceptional taste as well as the darkest colour on the platter. See Chapter 2 for more on equipment.

Special tools required: *Jam funnel, waxed paper discs*

Preparation time: *45 minutes*

Processing time: *45 minutes*

Yield: *4.5 kilograms (10 pounds)*

1.8 kilograms (4 pounds) blackcurrants

1.8 litres (3 pints) water

2.7 kilograms (6 pounds) granulated sugar

1 Wash the blackcurrants removing 'tops and tails', leaves and any other debris. Place in a large, heavy-bottomed preserving pan. Add the water to cover the fruit.

2 Bring to the boil and simmer for 30–35 minutes, until the fruit is tender and soft, stirring occasionally as the pulp thickens. Meanwhile, place the sugar in an ovenproof dish in the centre of a preheated oven at 110 degrees Celsius (225 degrees Fahrenheit, Gas Mark ¼) for ten minutes to warm through.

3 Remove the pan from the heat, stirring in the warmed sugar to dissolve it. Bring to a rapid boil for a further 15 minutes, testing for set using one of the methods that I outline in Chapter 5.

4 Allow to cool for a couple of minutes, skimming any scum off with a slotted spoon if necessary. Using a jam funnel (the easy method, but a steady hand works well too), spoon into warm, sterilised jars. Cover with waxed paper discs and seal. Label when cool and store in a cool, dark place.

Per 100-gram serving: 258 calories; 1 grams protein, 66 grams carbohydrate, 0 grams fat, 0 grams saturated fat, 0 milligrams cholesterol, 0 grams fibre, 1 milligrams sodium.

Blackcurrant Syrup

One commercial company makes millions of pounds from this plant syrup, and yet your homemade drink (whether you call it syrup, juice or cordial) tastes superior to anything you buy in a shop. The much vaunted Vitamin C content is just as valuable in your home-made version and an added bonus is that you can use up your over-ripe fruit because pectin levels and setting don't come into the equation.

If your fruit's really ripe and squishy, reduce or even leave out the water, and if you're harvesting in bucket loads just multiply all the ingredients up to make a larger quantity of juice.

Special tools required: *Jelly bag*

Preparation time: *10 minutes*

Processing time: *25 minutes and straining time*

Yield: *500 millilitres (18 fluid ounces)*

450 grams (1 pound) ripe blackcurrants

150 millilitres (¼ pint) water

5 millilitres (1 teaspoon) citric acid (optional): buy from a chemist

350 grams (12 ounces) sugar per 600 millilitres (1 pint) juice

1 Wash the fruit, if necessary removing any leaves and debris, and place it in a heat-proof glass, ceramic or stainless steel bowl over a larger pan of hot (but not boiling) water (in other words, you improvise a *baine-marie*). Crush the fruit with a vegetable masher or the back of a wooden spoon to allow the juices to flow.

2 Strain the fruit into a measuring jug through a sieve lined with scalded muslin or a scalded jelly bag for a clearer juice – I explain jelly-bag wisdom in Chapter 5. Add the sugar and stir to dissolve it without reheating the juice.

3 Use a funnel to pour into bottles (clasp-top lemonade bottles are good, and store in a fridge for up to six weeks, or use the hot-bottling technique in Chapter 5). Remember that heat processing removes some natural goodness. Alternatively, freeze in sealed pots, allowing enough head space for expansion.

Tip: *Using gentle heat retains more of the natural goodness in your syrup that fierce heat destroys. Also, using caster sugar speeds up the process. You can make your own caster sugar by putting your ordinary granulated sugar in a food processor and blitzing it a few times.*

Vary it! *Adapt this recipe for any sound, ripe fruit berries: blackberries, chokeberries, jostaberries, loganberries, raspberries, tayberries or similar. Use your judgement as to whether you need to add water; tough-skinned and under-ripe fruit benefit from a small amount.*

Per 100-millilitre serving: *328 calories; 1 grams protein, 84 grams carbohydrate, 0 grams fat, 0 grams saturated fat, 0 milligrams cholesterol, 0 grams fibre, 3 milligrams sodium.*

Chokeberries

Chokeberries come from a commercial fruiting bush that produces fruits that look like large blackcurrants; use them in any recipe in place of blackcurrants or freeze whole, stewed or as a puree. In fact, you can convert any of the currant and berry recipes in this chapter to make use of chokeberries.

Gooseberries

If you don't already know whether you have the cooking or dessert gooseberry variety, use your taste buds:

- ✔ **Cooking variety:** A tart, under-ripe gooseberry (*goose-gog* as they're affectionately known) such as the high-yielding cooking variety Invicta gives a sharp green jam.

- ✔ **Dessert variety:** The red (Pax, with large juicy fruit) or yellowy dessert gooseberry yields something sweeter.

Ensure that the sweet dessert variety isn't over-ripe or your jam setting and keeping qualities won't be up to muster.

You have to brave the prickles on most gooseberry bushes, but their early cropping makes them irresistible; just watch out for stray babies traditionally left under these bushes!

Gooseberry and Elderflower Jam

Nature made a heavenly marriage of flavours and you find them coming into their prime at exactly the same time – one in your fruit patch and the other in the wild hedgerows and along grassy tracks – just in time for a healthy late spring walk. This recipe is just right for kicking off the fresh fruit jam-making season. Keep your eyes peeled for your favourite elderberry bush (Chapter 18 gives you a clue if you're not sure what you're looking for). Choose white open blossoms, picking at midday in the warmth of the sun for maximum fragrance. Chapter 3 has more on sterilisation.

Special tools required: *Muslin bag, sterilised jars, waxed paper discs*

Preparation time: *45 minutes (plus the walk!)*

Processing time: *45 minutes*

Yield: *4.5 kilograms (10 pounds)*

2 kilograms (4 pounds, 8 ounces) gooseberries	*8–12 heads of elderflowers*
850 millilitres (1½ pints) water	*2.7 kilograms (6 pounds) granulated sugar*

1 Wash (if necessary) the gooseberries and top and tail them, placing them in a heavy-bottomed preserving pan with the water and the elderflower heads tied up in a muslin bag. Bring this lot to a boil and simmer for about 30 minutes, stirring from time to time.

2 While the fruit is simmering, preheat your oven to 110 degrees Celsius (225 degrees Fahrenheit, Gas Mark ¼), placing the sugar in an ovenproof bowl in the centre of the oven for 10–15 minutes to heat through.

3 Remove the pan from the heat when the fruit is soft and pulpy – leave some fruits whole if you like the texture; remove and squeeze the muslin bag to extract the last drop of flavour and liquid, and discard. Add the warmed sugar next, stirring to dissolve it completely. Return to a low heat to help the process along if you need to.

4 Turn the heat up, bringing to a rolling boil, and cook rapidly for about 15 minutes. Test for set using one of the methods in Chapter 5.

5 Allow to cool for a couple of minutes, skimming any scum off with a slotted spoon if necessary. Using a funnel, spoon into warm, sterilised jars. Cover with waxed paper discs and seal. Label when cool and store in a cool, dark place.

Vary it! *Make plain gooseberry jam with this recipe too; just leave out the elderflowers.*

Per 100-gram serving: : *252 calories; 0 grams protein, 65 grams carbohydrate, 0 grams fat, 0 grams saturated fat, 0 milligrams cholesterol, 2 grams fibre, 1 milligrams sodium.*

Gooseberry Butter

With this recipe, you can make something spreadable as a change from jam, or use gooseberries that are just too ripe for jam-making. Chapter 2 explains more about equipment and Chapter 3 has more on sterilisation.

Special tools required: *Sterilised jars, waxed paper discs*

Preparation time: *10 minutes*

Processing time: *1½–2 hours*

Yield: *About 1 kilogram (2 pounds, 4 ounces)*

2 kilograms (4 pounds, 8 ounces) gooseberries

600 millilitres (1 pint) water

750 grams (1 pound, 10 ounces) granulated sugar for every 1 kilogram (2 pounds, 4 ounces) of fruit

5 millilitres (1 teaspoon) ground cinnamon

5 millilitres (1 teaspoon) ground cloves

1 Wash the gooseberries and place in a heavy-bottomed preserving pan with the water. Bring the fruit to the boil, simmering until the fruit is soft (about 20 minutes).

2 Push through a sieve using the back of a spoon or use a food mill, reducing the gooseberries to a pulp. Return the pulp to the clean pan, cooking for a further few minutes until the mixture is a thick, soft consistency. Do so carefully, without burning the pulp.

3 Weigh the pulp, adding three quarters of the weight of sugar to that of the fruit. Sprinkle in the ground spices, stirring slowly over a gentle heat while the sugar dissolves.

4 Increase the heat slightly, stirring all the time and boiling until thick: the butter solidifies a little on cooling. Pot up into warm, sterilised jars (see Chapter 3 for more on sterilising), covering the butter with waxed discs; seal and label when cool and store in a cool, dark place.

Tip: *Weighing the pulp is easy if you record the weight of the pan you're using. Just take the total weight of pan and fruit pulp, and then subtract the weight of the pan; much easier and quicker than trying to remove the pulp to weigh it.*

Per 100-gram serving: 153 calories; 0 grams protein, 39 grams carbohydrate, 0 grams fat, 0 grams saturated fat, 0 milligrams cholesterol, 2 grams fibre, 1 milligrams sodium.

Ground cherries

This shrubby little bush with round yellow-orange berries (about the size of cherry tomatoes) shielded in tiny crinkly bonnets is also called *physalis* and *husk tomato*. The fruits stay clean, the bonnet giving protection from soiling even when you pick them off the ground. The flavour is fantastic, somewhere between a tomato and a pineapple or mango. Just peel off the bonnet and pop straight into the freezer in a bag, although they also last for weeks sitting on a dry shelf.

Aunt Molly is a good variety of ground cherry to buy but, better still, if you find ground cherries growing in a neighbour's garden, just ask for a handful of seeds and scatter them in the greenhouse or polytunnel to get your own crop.

You need a polytunnel or greenhouse to grow ground cherries. For an exotic twist to your soft-fruit harvest, go off the beaten track to www.bangorsorganic. co.uk for your first seedlings; after that you have them forever because they readily self-seed.

Ground Cherry and Blackberry Jam

On its own, ground cherry flavour can be a little heady and overpowering, but combine just a little blackberry tartness from the hedgerow and the balancing act is amazing, bringing this jam back down to earth in a heavenly manner.

Special tools required: *Sterilised jars, waxed paper discs*

Preparation time: *20 minutes*

Processing time: *25–35 minutes*

Yield: *2.2 kilograms (5 pounds)*

1.3 kilograms (3 pounds) ground cherries

1 double handful of hedgerow blackberries

1.3 kilograms (3 pounds) granulated sugar

1 Prepare the fruits by removing any stems, stalks or 'bonnets', and rinse. Place all the fruit in a large, heavy-bottomed preserving pan. Bring gently to the boil, allowing the juices to flow.

2 Boil for about 10–15 minutes until the fruit is soft. Meanwhile place the sugar in an over-proof dish in the centre of a preheated oven (110 degrees Celsius/225 degrees Fahrenheit, Gas Mark ¼) for ten minutes to warm through. Remove the cooking fruit from the heat while you add the sugar and stir until the sugar totally dissolves.

3 Bring back to a rapid boil for about 10–15 minutes, testing for set with a method from Chapter 5.

4 Allow to cool for a couple of minutes, skimming any scum off with a slotted spoon if necessary. Spoon into warm, sterilised jars (see Chapter 3 for more on sterilisation). Cover with waxed paper discs and seal. Label when cool and store in a cool, dark place.

Per 100-gram serving: *285 calories; 1 grams protein, 72 grams carbohydrate, 1 grams fat, 0 grams saturated fat, 0 milligrams cholesterol, 2 grams fibre,1 milligrams sodium.*

Jostaberries

If you're choosing soft-fruit bushes for your garden and you don't like thorns, consider the jostaberry, a blackcurrant/gooseberry hybrid producing large, sharp-flavoured fruits. Use them, weight for weight, in any of the berry or currant recipes or mixtures in this chapter, but be aware that they need space to spread; if your growing area is tiny, you may prefer to find a different plant.

Loganberries

This hybrid between a raspberry and the American blackberry mixes well with rhubarb or stands alone and freezes well. Add it into your Summer Pudding in Suspense mixture from the earlier 'Mixing and Matching with Berries' section.

As the loganberry is a hybrid, expect compromise; varieties are limited to the Thornless. If you're choosing new soft fruit bushes, although the loganberry may beguile you with large beautifully coloured fruits, you may prefer to go for the humbler, smaller raspberry, which offers a fuller, more delicate flavour.

 Have a go at adapting the Raspberry Jam recipe from the later 'Raspberries' section to create Loganberry Jam, adding 500 milliliters (18 fluid ounces) of water to each 1.5 kilograms (3 pounds, 5 ounces) of loganberries. They need this little bit of extra help to get the juices flowing.

Mulberries

Perhaps the traditional song should go 'Here we go round the mulberry *tree*', because (as the exception in this soft-fruit chapter) mulberries grow on medium-sized trees; the fruits look much like a slightly larger version of a loganberry. You get dark fruits from the slower-growing Black Mulberry variety and sweeter paler fruits from the faster-growing White Mulberry.

The same rules for all berry-picking apply to mulberries: dry, just ripe fruit performs best in jams and jellies. You can adapt the Raspberry Jam recipe from the next section for mulberries, but add a tiny amount – 30 millilitres (2 tablespoons) – of water to encourage the juices to flow. Freeze loose or stewed, or, for a puree, try the following Mulberry Cheese recipe.

Mulberry Cheese

You can use this fruity cheese as a condiment, with cold meat or vegetarian dishes, or in its own right on warm, buttered toast or scones. Chapter 2 has more about specialist equipment. Chapter 3 has the info on sterilisation.

Special tools required: *Food mill, sterilised jars, waxed paper discs*

Preparation time: *10 minutes*

Processing time: *1½–2 hours*

Yield: *500 grams (1 pound, 2 ounces)*

1 kilogram (2 pounds, 4 ounces) mulberries	*Sugar – amount equal to weight of puree*
30 millilitres (2 tablespoons) water	

1 Place the mulberries and water in your heavy-bottomed pan and simmer until the fruit is soft and breaks up (about 10–15 minutes). Push through a sieve or a food mill, leaving the pips and skin behind to discard.

2 Weigh the puree and return it to the clean pan with an equal weight of sugar. Heat slowly while the sugar dissolves and then boil to a stiff consistency, stirring to stop the mixture sticking. Consider it ready when a spoon drawn across the base of the pan leaves a line and no traces of liquid.

3 Pot up into small, straight-sided, warm, sterilised jars. Seal the top of the cheese with waxed paper discs, seal and label when cool. Store in a cool, dark place.

4 To use the cheese, open it and loosen the sides with a blunt knife before turning out onto a plate.

Tip: Smear the inside of your pots with glycerine from a chemist's shop so that the cheese turns out easily (vegetarians watch out for animal-based glycerine). Find small moulds, such as jelly moulds, to add interesting shapes to your fruit cheese creations.

Per 100-gram serving: 215 calories; 1 grams protein, 55 grams carbohydrate, 0 grams fat, 0 grams saturated fat, 0 milligrams cholesterol, 1 grams fibre, 6 milligrams sodium.

Raspberries

Your raspberry crop comes in late spring or early summer with heavy crops from a variety such as Malling Jewel, or up until frosts halt production with the autumn-fruiting varieties such as Autumn Bliss. But then again, why not have both varieties on your plot! Whatever your harvesting time, your best use for the under-ripe and just ripe fruits is in jams, jellies and preserves where a good set is important. Freeze or hot bottle in syrup as alternative preserving methods – Chapters 7 and 5, respectively, take you through these options.

If you miss the mark, or your crop is just too prolific to keep up with and your soft fruits are going soft, don't despair; steeping raspberries in vinegar makes fantastic use of their flavour and colour (see Chapter 6 for a Raspberry Vinegar recipe – with suggestions for alternative uses too).

Raspberry Jam

To be sure to keep the bright red colour and sharp but aromatic quality of this fresh fruit jam, avoid overcooking (or a sticky brown concoction results); expect a soft set and use the jam up quickly when opened. Swiss rolls and sponge sandwich cakes traditionally use raspberry jam to hold them together. The 'post box' red raspberries in a colourful platter of jam tarts (fit for a knave to steal) are a delicious flavour too. Chapter 3 has more on sterilisation.

Special tools required: *Sterilised jars, waxed paper discs*

Preparation time: *30 minutes*

Processing time: *20–25 minutes*

Yield: *4.5 kilograms (10 pounds)*

2.7 kilograms (6 pounds) raspberries   *2.7 kilograms (6 pounds) granulated sugar*

1 Your own freshly picked, 'just ripe' raspberries don't need to be washed: just pick them over carefully to remove any cone-like middles left inside the fruit, stems or stray leaves. Wash the fruit only if you feel you really have to. Place in a heavy-bottomed pre-serving pan and bring slowly to a simmer (heating slowly releases the natural juices). Stir gently to distribute the heat, allowing to simmer for five to ten minutes, depending on the juiciness of your particular fruit.

2 Preheat your oven to 110 degrees Celsius (225 degrees Fahrenheit, Gas Mark ¼), placing the sugar in an ovenproof bowl in the centre of the oven for 10–15 minutes to heat through. Add the warmed sugar; take your pan off the heat for this operation, stirring and returning to a low heat to help the process along if the sugar isn't completely dis-solved after five minutes. Turn the heat up, bringing to a rolling boil and cook rapidly for five minutes; test for set using one of the methods from Chapter 5.

3 Allow to cool for a couple of minutes, removing scum with a slotted spoon if necessary. Use a funnel to spoon into warm, sterilised jars nearly to the brim. Cover with waxed paper discs and seal. Label when cool and store in a cool, dark place. Refrigerate when opened and use within a month.

Per 100-gram serving: *262 calories; 1 grams protein, 67 grams carbohydrate, 0 grams fat, 0 grams saturated fat, 0 milligrams cholesterol, 4 grams fibre, 1 milligrams sodium.*

Pickled Pink Pears with Raspberry Vinegar

You may like to change this recipe to Pickled Pink Parsnips, or Apples or Peaches, but whatever fruit you use you can be sure that the colour will be glorious without any fear of browning as long as all the fruit remains totally submerged in the special syrup made with your own raspberry vinegar (see Chapter 6 for this recipe). Keep any left-over syrup for topping up the jars as the fruit may absorb it over the period of a few days. Leave stems where possible, and slightly undercook the fruit so it holds together well. The hot pickling method continues the cooking process in the jar.

Special tools required: *Sharp-edged teaspoon or melon baller*

Preparation time: *20–30 minutes*

Processing time: *35 minutes*

Yield: *1.3 kilograms (3 pounds)*

1 small unwaxed lemon	*8 centimetres (3 inches) cinnamon stick*
900 grams (2 pounds) firm pears	*4–6 cloves*
450 millilitres (16 fluid ounces) raspberry vinegar (see Chapter 6)	*150 millilitres (¼ pint) water*
450 grams (1 pound) granulated sugar	

1 Pare off a couple of thin strips of lemon rind and squeeze 30 millilitres (2 tablespoons) of juice; put both into a pan. Add the sugar, raspberry vinegar, spices and water to the pan and over a low heat dissolve the sugar, stirring all the time. Slowly bring to the boil.

2 Peel the pears (if the pears are particularly small, leave them whole, peeling alternate strips of skin for a stripy effect), cut in halves or quarters, depending on the size of your pears, removing the seeds but leaving the pear stalks. A sharp-edged teaspoon or melon baller gouges out the seedy area neatly and efficiently.

3 Cook the pears in the pink syrup, simmering gently for about 20 minutes or less. Remove your fruit with a slotted spoon, arranging pieces neatly in a warm sterilised jar with the lemon rind and spices before turning up the heat and boiling the syrup for a further five minutes, reducing it slightly. Skim any scum, and ladle the syrup over the pears covering them completely, before sealing. Label when cool and store in a cool dark place, topping up the syrup in the next few days if necessary and storing for at least one month to allow the flavours to mature before using.

Per serving: 149 calories; 0 grams protein, 38 grams carbohydrate, 0 grams fat, 0 grams saturated fat, 0 milligrams cholesterol, 1 gram fibre, 2 milligrams sodium.

Redcurrants

Try the Jonkeer Van Tets variety if you're planting new soft-fruit bushes; they give a good all-round quality and yield. Or go modern with Rovada, whose currants are large and prolific (white currants do the same job but without such a luscious colour). Add any of these berries to the earlier Summer Pudding in Suspense mix from the 'Mixing and Matching with Berries' section.

Open freeze (See Chapter 7) redcurrants for later without hours of preparation (currants are fiddly to pick and prepare). You can use them as a pectin stock too, as I describe in Chapter 5.

Redcurrant Jelly (with Savoury Herbs)

Here's a sexy red number for you. Eat this redcurrant jelly as a side helping (with or without savoury herby flavours) with game, turkey and other hot or cold meats. The sharpness lifts savoury dishes and cuts the amount of fat. Use straight redcurrant jelly on scones, in tartlets or any other sweet way you think up: this jelly is an incredibly versatile preserve. Chapter 3 has more on sterilisation.

Special tools required: *Jelly bag, sterilised jars*

Preparation time: *About 10 minutes*

Processing time: *30 minutes cooking and 2 hours straining time*

Yield: *1.3 kilograms (3 pounds)*

1.8 kilograms (4 pounds) redcurrants

600 millilitres (1 pint) water

450 grams (1 pound) sugar for every 600 millilitres (1 pint) strained redcurrant liquor

1 Wash the currants: you don't need to be too pernickety, just remove any debris but leave attached stalks. Place into a heavy-bottomed preserving pan with the water. Simmer for 30 minutes, using a wooden spoon to break the fruit up and stirring from time to time until the fruit softens.

2 Strain through a scalded jelly bag (go to Chapter 2 for jelly-bag talk) for at least two hours; four is better. Heat the oven to 110 degrees Celsius (225 degrees Fahrenheit, Gas Mark ¼). Put the sugar into an ovenproof dish and warm through in the centre of the oven for about 10–15 minutes. Measure the strained redcurrant liquor and add appropriate amounts of sugar.

3 Return the juice to the clean pan, and over a low heat add the sugar, stirring until it dissolves completely. Bring to a rapid boil for 10–15 minutes, testing for set as you prefer (Chapter 5 gives you various options). Skim if necessary and pot up into warm, sterilised jars, then seal and label when cool.

Tip: Add flavour to redcurrant jelly for use with savoury meals by scalding a couple of sprigs of rosemary or another herb that you're fond of. Break the sprigs up (I write more about herbs in Chapter 16), stirring the leaves into the jelly to distribute them before the potting-up stage. Don't squeeze the jelly bag; it makes your jelly cloudy.

Per 100-gram serving: 240 calories; 1 gram protein, 60 grams carbohydrate, 0 grams fat, 0 grams saturated fat, 0 milligrams cholesterol, 0 grams fibre, 1 milligrams sodium.

Rhubarb

Watch your rhubarb grow early in the season. Established plants yield for many years; they enjoy an annual generous helping of well-made compost – preserving the abundance in your garden is really important and heavy croppers such as rhubarb repay you well with care and attention. Pile on the well-rotted manure or compost in autumn to keep the rhubarb's growing tips insulated against the freezing winter temperatures and to add feed value to varieties such as Glaskin's Perpetual and the tasty pink-skinned Victoria.

The edible part of rhubarb is the stem; trim off the leafy tops and white bottoms. Rhubarb leaves are poisonous: don't ever eat them or include them in your recipes.

Rhubarb and Ginger Jam

This jam recipe 'cooks' the rhubarb overnight in the sugar before heating. Rhubarb and ginger complement each other perfectly and this recipe gives options for the avid ginger lover as well as the gentle ginger lover. Use this combination as a cordial too by leaving the rhubarb, bruised ginger and sugar 'cooking' for an extra 24 hours, and then straining and bottling. The resulting cordial keeps in the fridge for six weeks and is a refreshingly unique cold drink. Make cordial with less-than-perfect rhubarb stalks because you need to discard these stalks anyway. Chapter 2 has more on equipment and Chapter 3 has the info on sterilisation.

Special tools required: *Sterilised jars, waxed paper discs*

Preparation time: *15 minutes*

Processing time: *Overnight standing plus 20 minutes cooking time*

Yield: *4.5 kilograms (10 pounds)*

2.7 kilograms (6 pounds) rhubarb

2.7 kilograms (6 pounds) granulated sugar

Juice of 6 lemons

50 grams (2 ounces) root ginger

50 grams (2 ounces) crystallised ginger (optional)

1 Cut the rhubarb into chunks, placing in a noncorrosive, ceramic, glass or stainless steel dish; sprinkle the sugar over the fruit and add the lemon juice. Cover and leave to stand overnight to draw the juices. (Add the bashed ginger at this stage for cordial or if you're an avid ginger lover.)

2 The following day, transfer the rhubarb sugar mix into a large, heavy-bottomed preserving pan. (For a gentler flavour, add the ginger now, but bash it first with a rolling pin and tie it in a muslin bag.)

3 Heat slowly while the sugar dissolves completely and then raise the heat to a rapid boil for 15–20 minutes or until you reach setting point (test for set – Chapter 5 gives you various options). Remove the bashed ginger in its bag (and add in the crystallised ginger if you like, stirring to distribute well). Using a funnel, pour the liquid into warm, sterilised jars, cover with waxed discs, seal, label when cool and store in a cool, dark place.

Per 100-gram serving: 245 calories; 0 grams protein, 62 grams carbohydrate, 0 grams fat, 0 grams saturated fat, 0 milligrams cholesterol, 1 gram fibre, 3 milligrams sodium.

Strawberries

Clever strawberry growers plant varieties with different cropping times to make the most of this queen of the soft-fruit patch: Honeoye, for early picking; Pegasus for mid-season and excellent disease resistance; and Symphony to take you to the end of the season with bright red fruits. And you've an even larger range of options if you look in plant catalogues, plant sales and garden centres.

This ground-covering creeping plant needs net protection from birds, which justifiably enjoy strawberries too. Strawberries freeze (see Chapter 7), bottle and preserve (check out Chapter 5) well and are just the fruit to dry for a healthy, home-grown snack. Or just go ahead and follow the three recipes below for a tasty preserving session.

No better excuse exists to seek out that old scone recipe than strawberry jam!

Strawberry Jam

This jam has a reputation for being difficult, but if you follow this recipe, which is from my mother's personal handwritten cookbook, written in capital letters is 'THIS JAM WILL NOT FAIL TO SET', so take heart. Don't expect a really firm set from strawberry jam; this jam is better slightly on the runny side than overcooked. See Chapter 3 for more on sterilisation.

Special tools required: *Sterilised jars*

Preparation time: *20 minutes*

Processing time: *30–40 minutes*

Yield: *4.5 kilograms (10 pounds)*

2.7 kilograms (6 pounds) strawberries   *3.5 kilograms (7 pounds) granulated sugar*

1 Clean strawberries by wiping on a damp cloth, if necessary. Don't wash them but do pinch out the green leafy tops and discard them. Place all the strawberries and half the sugar into your heavy-bottomed preserving pan. Dissolve the sugar over a gentle heat and then bring to the boil for 20 minutes.

2 Place the remaining sugar in an ovenproof bowl in a preheated oven at 110 degrees Celsius (225 degrees Fahrenheit, Gas Mark ¼) for 10–15 minutes until warmed through. Add the warm sugar to the pan, stirring until it dissolves, and then boil rapidly, checking for set in your chosen manner from Chapter 5.

3 Skim off any scum with a slotted spoon, stir once to redistribute the fruit and pot up into warm, sterilised jars. Seal and label when cool. Store in a cool, dark place.

Remember: *This jam never fails to set!*

Per 100-gram serving: *318 calories; 0 grams protein, 81 grams carbohydrate, 0 grams fat, 0 grams saturated fat, 0 milligrams cholesterol, 1 grams fibre, 1 milligrams sodium.*

Strawberry Conserve

Keep to similar, medium-sized fruits for this conserve. The slightly runnier, syrupy, soft-set consistency around the whole fruit is just right for spooning onto scones with cream or for filling tarts, and also for transforming plain rice or custard dishes into something really special. Don't expect this conserve to be ready in a hurry, but the wait is worth it. Chapter 3 has the info on sterilisation.

Special tools required: Sterilised jars

Preparation time: 20 minutes

Processing time: 3 days standing plus 20 minutes cooking time

Yield: 2.7 kilograms (6 pounds)

1.8 kilograms (4 pounds) strawberries   *1.8 kilograms (4 pounds) granulated sugar*

1 Place layers of strawberries and sugar in a large ceramic bowl (use two bowls if you need to), covering with a clean cloth and leaving to stand for 24 hours in a cool place.

2 Tip the whole lot into a preserving pan. Heat gently until all the sugar dissolves; bring to the boil and boil for five minutes. Remove from the heat and return the mixture to the bowl(s). Cover and allow to stand in a cool place for a further 48 hours.

3 Return to the preserving pan and bring to a rapid boil for about 10–15 minutes; check for set using one of the methods in Chapter 5.

4 Allow to cool until a skin begins to form, stir once to redistribute the fruit and pot up into warm, sterilised jars. Seal, label when cool and store in a cool, dark place.

Per 100-gram serving: 277 calories; 0 grams protein, 70 grams carbohydrate, 0 grams fat, 0 grams saturated fat, 0 milligrams cholesterol, 1 gram fibre, 1 milligram sodium.

Strawberry Freezer Jam

This uncooked jam has a fresh coolness. The strawberries keep their bright colour, but make plans to eat it up within six months because the keeping qualities are limited.

Preparation time: 20 minutes

Processing time: 24–48 hours standing time

Yield: 1.3 kilograms (3 pounds)

800 grams (1 pound, 12 ounces) strawberries

900 grams (2 pounds) caster sugar

30 millilitres (2 tablespoons) lemon juice

125 millilitres (4 fluid ounces) commercial liquid pectin such as Certo (buy from a supermarket, health food shop or cook's shop)

1 Use strawberries straight from the garden, wiping clean and avoiding washing if you can to keep the fruit as dry as possible (if you have to wash the strawberries, for example if they've a lot of soil on them, pat them dry on paper towels). Prepare by removing the green stems and any hard bits, and then quartering. Place all the cut-up strawberries in a bowl with the caster sugar. Using a fork, lightly mash the fruit, releasing the juices but leaving a lumpy texture rather than a totally mashed puree.

2 Cover, leaving to stand at room temperature for about one hour while the sugar 'draws' the juices out. Stir once or twice. Combine the lemon juice and commercial pectin with the fruit/sugar mixture, stirring thoroughly for four minutes.

3 Fill scrupulously clean freezer-proof pots, leaving head room for expansion – Chapter 7 gives helpful chilly hints for successful freezing. Cover and leave to stand for around four hours.

4 Chill the jam in your refrigerator for 24–48 hours until it sets and then place in the freezer. Use straight away or within six months.

5 Before use, thaw for a minimum of one hour or until defrosted and keep any leftovers in the fridge; use up within a few days.

Per 100-gram serving: 287 calories; 0 grams protein, 74 grams carbohydrate, 0 grams fat, 0 grams saturated fat, 0 milligrams cholesterol, 2 grams fibre, 2 milligrams sodium.

Tayberries

This commercial blackberry/raspberry hybrid produces enormous berries, resembling loganberries, without thorns or prickles. Plant up the Buckingham variety to use for freezing or jam-making in the same way as you do for raspberries or blackberries.

Chapter 12

Storing and Enjoying Fruiting Vegetables

*W*hether you've an elaborate polytunnel overflowing with tomatoes, courgettes and aubergines, or a modest balcony with tubs and hanging baskets, you need ways to preserve the delights of your fruiting vegetables. (*Fruits* generally refer to the seed-producing parts of a bush, tree or vegetable plant (such as currants and apples) and its tasty fleshy part (such as tomatoes). Do expect some blurring of the lines though, as nature doesn't fit easily into neat boxes.)

The varieties you grow at home are seldom available in the shops where consistency of size and toughness of skin (or 'travelability') rank higher than flavour. Experiencing the difference in taste puts you into an altogether higher produce league. Use the tips and recipes in this chapter to preserve your produce and stretch your home-grown flavours and goodness around the year.

Turning on to Tastes from the Mediterranean (and Beyond)

Travelling broadens the mind and brings with it tasty reminders of heady holidays in the sun. British diets are blossoming and your home growing reflects this reality: seed catalogues each year add more exotic produce as the world 'shrinks'.

Discovering perfect veg combos

Some fruiting vegetable combinations form natural partnerships. Here are a few to try:

- Aubergine and garlic

- Aubergine and lemon

- Aubergine with Indian spices

- Chilli with everything – a little or a lot

- Fennel and toasted sesame seeds

- Gherkins with dill

- Pickle fennel with crisp seasonal vegetables

- Roast pepper mixture

- Tomato and basil

- Tomato with any mix of garden herbs

Despite the unpredictable British summer and the fact that few people have unlimited undercover polytunnel or greenhouse space and unlimited time for growing the plants from sunnier regions, don't be put off attempting some of the more tender exotic plants. Breeders have been successfully adapting plants so that they perform well in a wider climatic range.

Always read the seed catalogue to understand how your chosen plant can perform best for you: your soil and outlook is unique.

Go to local fetes and plant sales to buy interesting one-off plants to grow. Usually, they're extras from green-fingered neighbours, and cost the same as a packet of exotic seeds.

Alongside the everyday fruits and vegetables, allotments and gardens are bursting with more exotic produce. For instance, growing garlic in your back garden, unheard of in the UK just 40 years ago, is now common: garlic is easy to grow and totally tolerant of the capricious UK weather. (You find ways of making your home-grown garlic last all year round in recipes throughout the later section 'Preserving Fruiting Vegetables: From Aubergines to Tomatoes'.)

Usefully, some cucumber varieties prefer to live outdoors, withstanding wet summers and performing with remarkable abundance even outside a greenhouse. Courgettes are unstoppable when they take off: plant them straight onto your compost heap and watch them go, go, go! In addition, you can grow peppers and chillis anyway, even if your undercover space is limited. Clear a window ledge in the house or conservatory, and one prolific chilli plant provides enough dried chilli hotness for a family for a year. See the later 'Chillies', 'Cucumbers' and 'Peppers' sections for more on these vegetables.

Partnering up the exotics

Fruiting vegetables are wonderful on their own, but combined with other produce they make delicacies fit for royalty and hearty staples to keep working peasants productive in the fields (or garden)!

Combining vegetables is a great help when you need to cope speedily with a seasonal tomato, onion and/or courgette glut (the latter are quite daunting when in season). Use the following ploy to capture the garden goodness of these prolific plants at their best:

1. **Make a quick, basic mix of chopped seasonal vegetables.**

   Cut up the tomatoes, courgettes and roughly chopped onion, along with any fresh and in-season garden herbs (check out Chapter 16 for more on herbs). Use in whatever quantities you have without worrying about proportions.

2. **Cook this mixture up in a large pan for 15 minutes (thus bypassing any fiddly blanching).**

   Don't add any salt to this mixture: you may want to reduce the volume later, which leaves an over-salty taste. Always adjust seasonings at the last stage of cooking.

3. **Allow to cool to fridge temperature and freeze in quantities useful to your household**. (Chapter 7 has more on freezers.)

   Label the container with comments such as 'add more onion' or 'mostly toms' as a reminder to balance the ingredients in the final dish. This truly versatile mixture can form the basis for a Bolognese sauce; or add to stews and soups or reduce to a pulp for a pizza topping.

Grab a bag out of the freezer in the morning, allowing it to defrost slowly during the day: in or out of the fridge, you've all day to decide how to finish the dish. Or cook a bag of semi-prepared vegetables from frozen by adding a little water to the base of the pan, covering and heating (stir often to free up the frozen clump). You're now halfway towards a filling dinner for the hard-working people in your household.

Mediterranean Mixture Chutney

You've plenty of scope to partner up home-grown vegetables with herbs and spices from warm Mediterranean lands. With this recipe, feel free to chop and change with the type of vegetable to suit your unique home-grown successes, but keep the basic quantities the same.

Special tools required: *Noncorrosive pan, sterilised jars, jam funnel*

Preparation time: *30 minutes*

Processing time: *2 hours 15 minutes*

Yield: *Approximately 1.8 kilograms (4 pounds)*

450 grams (1 pound) mixed peppers, prepared weight

450 grams (1 pound) courgettes (small ones are best)

450 grams (1 pound) aubergines

450 grams (1 pound) tomatoes

1 red onion

600 millilitres (1 pint) cider vinegar

450 grams (1 pint) soft brown sugar

5 millilitres (1 teaspoon) coriander seeds

5 millilitres (1 teaspoon) dried mixed herbs or four times as much mixed fresh garden herbs (include thyme, rosemary, sage, bay, parsley and dill, together or to your taste)

1 Dice the aubergine and courgette into similar-sized pieces. De-seed and chop the pepper and roughly chop the tomatoes. Cut the onion into fine pieces, putting all these vegetables into a heavy-bottomed, noncorrosive pan.

2 Next pour in the vinegar and sugar, mixing it all together. Add the spices and herbs and heat gently, stirring until the sugar dissolves. Increase the heat to boiling point, simmering for about one and half to two hours or until the mixture thickens, taking care to avoid burning the mixture towards the end of cooking time.

3 Using your jam funnel (or a steady hand), spoon into warm, sterilised jars, pat down to remove any air pockets, seal and label when cool.

4 Store in a cool, dark place for at least one month for the flavour to mature or leave for up to a year. Refrigerate after opening.

Per 30-gram serving: 43 calories; 0 grams protein, 12 grams carbohydrate, 0 grams fat, 0 grams saturated fat, 0 milligrams cholesterol, 1 gram fibre, 5 milligrams sodium.

Using oil as a preserving tool

You can now match the exciting dishes you see in modern delicatessens by using a good-quality oil: olive or sunflower from your larder or, if you want to keep things local, rapeseed oil from the UK.

Preserving at a basic level means excluding air, halting oxidisation and preventing micro-organisms from growing (Chapter 3 gives more information about this subject). Oil floats on water and so has the power to exclude air, making it a useful short-term preserving tool.

Make sure that the oil totally covers the produce and remove all air bubbles under the oil. You can keep food preserved in oil in the fridge for up to ten days only; leave long-term storage in this manner to the professionals.

Depending on the produce you intend to preserve in oil, you need to perform a veg-appropriate preliminary step:

- **Acidify:** Entails briefly cooking in vinegar, sometimes with a portion of salt and sugar to lift the taste; suitable for all vegetables including fennel, garlic, courgettes and mushrooms.

- **Cook:** Renders food edible and destroys spoiling enzymes; use for any vegetables, especially roast peppers.

- **Salt:** Helps remove the water content: wash and pat dry beforehand and use for aubergines, okra and cucumbers.

- **Sun-dry or dehydrate in a purpose-built dryer:** Lessens the water content and is perfect for tomatoes (especially an Italian paste variety) peppers and chillis.

Layer your prepared vegetables with other similarly prepared herbs or mixtures, placing them loosely into jars. Pour on oil to completely cover, and use an implement (a wooden skewer is good) to poke around in the produce to dislodge any air pockets, before sealing and storing in the fridge. Leave for 1 week to mature and use up within 10 days of maturing.

Keep some extra oil handy; if your vegetables soak up the oil and the level drops, simply top up again.

Process all vegetables – even a sprig of herb, dunk it in clean, boiling water and then dry – before using this method. Read all about food safety in Chapter 3.

Heating things up

The Scoville Scale is a measurement of the hotness of chilli peppers to help you judge what you want to grow and harvest. Normal bell peppers start the Scoville Scale at zero and the Scotch Bonnet, a well-known 'hotty', kicks in with around 200,000! As a guide, the jalapeño peppers that you come across in restaurant dishes measure around 3,500–8,000. The Scoville number refers to the number of times a measured portion has to be diluted before you can't discern the heat.

Don't be fooled into thinking that you can only grow the hot chillies in hot, overseas climates: the Dorset Naga (a tremendously hot variety first grown by chilli plant breeders in Dorset) proves that theory wrong.

Firing up the senses

Put a spark in your life (or a positive fire!) by adding home-grown chillis to your preserves. You can make chilli vinegar by steeping chillis in a bottle of vinegar, and shaking the bottle from time to time. Dried chillis keep well in a dry, airtight jar (or make the Moroccan Harissa Paste recipe in the later 'Chillis' section).

Chilli seeds are often the hottest part, so control the heat by de-seeding. Always test out quantities when using your home-grown chillis; how little you need may surprise you.

Other flavourings to keep handy to spice up your preserving life are cardamom, cloves, juniper berries and peppercorns, as well as mustard, coriander, ginger and caraway seeds. Whole spices keep their flavour for much longer than ground spices, so use your pestle and mortar or spice grinder with your favourites.

Preserving Fruiting Vegetables: From Aubergines to Tomatoes

In this section, I provide hints on preserving some of the more exotic fruiting vegetables varieties, or choose a variety recommended by a friend or from saved seeds. A seed catalogue can also give you loads more info. I also give you recipes, from speedy no-cook pickles to more time-consuming chutneys and ketchup. Whatever you choose to grow or preserve, enjoy!

Many of the recipes in this section require the use of a noncorrosive pan (I discuss tools in Chapter 2) and sterilised jars (something I cover in Chapter 3).

Aubergines

Also known as *eggplant*, you can give an exotic look to any growing area with the dark glossy Black Beauty variety, which has a long and noble tradition. But long, pointed aubergines come in loads of heritage varieties and many colours from almost black to light pink. Your growing area takes on a magical quality if you're successful with aubergines; their swelling fruits are almost unreal in their perfection.

If you miss the boat with starting off aubergine seeds, check out village fetes and market stalls. People sell off their extra seedlings, which is a great way to get a variety of different plants in small quantities.

Scrutinise any small plants you buy before making your final decision. Look out for tiny aphids or signs of disease; you don't want to unwittingly infect your clean greenhouse or polytunnel.

Freeze aubergines chopped in chunks: toss briefly in lemon juice to preserve the colour. Blanch for four minutes or sprinkle the chunks with salt and leave for half an hour to draw out some of the moisture before rinsing well and patting dry on paper towels. Fry in oil for five to ten minutes, before laying out and freezing singly and packing in bags or containers. Use these chunks straight from frozen in chutneys, or moussaka and ratatouille, or allow them to thaw before use.

Chillies

Chillies, the hot part of the pepper family (if you're looking for sweet peppers, turn to that later section), are perfect for drying to preserve. Just lay them on a warm sunny windowsill, turning them from time to time, or tie them up in small bunches along the length of a string in an airy place. When you can snap the pods, they're dry. Transfer them to an airtight container, and store them whole or cut up in a dark place. Experiment with whatever variety you grow to find out the heat you can tolerate; you need only a tiny quantity, often much less than a teaspoon, to blow your socks off!

Aubergine and Garlic Chutney

Aubergine supplies the bulk and smoothness to this chutney and whole garlic cloves give the rich flavour. You can change the flavour subtly by substituting your favourite spices. Using your large aubergines speeds the preparation process up, especially if the garlic cloves are on the small size and fiddly to peel. Chapter 3 has more on sterilisation.

Special tools required: Jam funnel, sterilised jars

Preparation time: 45 minutes to 1 hour depending on garlic cloves

Processing time: Salting time plus 1½ hours cooking time

Yield: 1.5–1.8 kilograms (3–4 pounds)

1 kilogram (2 pounds, 4 ounces) aubergines

30 millilitres (2 tablespoons) salt

15 millilitres (1 tablespoon) nigella seeds (or substitute cardamon seeds)

45 millilitres (3 tablespoons) olive oil or sesame oil

45 millilitres (3 tablespoons) sesame seeds

4 or 5 whole bulbs of garlic

250 grams (9 ounces) shallots (or onion)

2–3 dried chillis, de-seeded

700 millilitres (1¼ pints) white wine vinegar or cider vinegar

150 grams (5 ounces) soft brown sugar

15 millilitres (3 teaspoons) sweet red paprika

1 Cut off and discard the aubergine's green collar (mind your fingers because some aubergines have nasty sharp spines). Cut into 2.5-centimetre (1-inch) cubes. Sprinkle half the salt onto the aubergine pieces and leave to drain for an hour. Rinse under running cold water and dry on paper towels straight away.

2 Heat up the oil in a preserving pan and fry up your spices and the sesame seeds for about three to four minutes to release the flavour and the sesame seeds begin to pop. Add in the dry aubergine, shallots, whole garlic cloves and chillies, frying and turning frequently for a further five minutes.

3 Pour in the vinegar and bring to the boil; simmer for 15 minutes until the aubergine is soft and the shallots are going clear. Add the rest of the ingredients, sugar, paprika and salt, stirring over a low heat until thoroughly mixed and the sugar dissolves.

4 Raise the temperature a bit to a simmer, stirring the mixture frequently until all the liquid absorbs or evaporates – about 45 minutes to 1 hour – and a spoon drawn across the base of the pan leaves a clean line.

5 Using a jam funnel, pot into sterilised warm jars, patting down to release air pockets, seal and allow to cool. Label when cold and leave for one month or longer to mature and use up within the year. Refrigerate after opening.

Tip: Pull apart the garlic heads and steep the cloves in lukewarm water while you prepare the other vegetables: soaking makes the garlic skins easier to remove. Dry after peeling.

Per 30-gram serving: 35 calories; 1 gram protein, 6 grams carbohydrate, 1 gram fat, 0 grams saturated fat, 0 milligrams cholesterol, 1 gram fibre, 173 milligrams sodium.

Harissa Paste

Mediate the fiery hotness of this hot chilli paste from Morocco by mixing it with tomato puree. If your harvest is small, simply half or quarter all the quantities.

Special tools required: *Small sterilised jars*

Preparation time: *10 minutes*

Processing time: *30 minutes*

Yield: *About 500 grams (1 pound, 2 ounces)*

450 grams (1 pound) dried red chillies, de-seeded

125 millilitres water (4 fluid ounces; saved from soaking chillies)

150 millilitres (¼ pint) olive oil (keep a little handy for topping up)

30 millilitres (2 tablespoons) sea salt

1 Place the dried, de-seeded chillies into a bowl, cover with hot water; allow to stand for 15–20 minutes until soft. Drain the chillies, saving 125 millilitres (4 fluid ounces) of the soaking water.

2 Using a food processor, blast the chillies to a paste, adding in the saved chilli-soaking water, and stir in the salt and oil. Pack into small sterilised jars.

3 Cover the paste with a thin layer of oil, seal and store in the refrigerator. You can use straight away or keep for up to four months.

Per 100-gram serving: 534 calories; 10 grams protein, 62 grams carbohydrate, 33 grams fat, 4 grams saturated fat, 0 milligrams cholesterol, 26 grams fibre, 2,884 milligrams sodium.

If you like a colour scheme to your hotness, grow Early Jalapeño for the green and Barak for a red variety. If you're reckless with hot stuff, have a blast with Numex Bailey – not for the faint hearted.

Eyes and other sensitive body parts are vulnerable when handling chillies – wash your hands thoroughly.

Cucumbers

Home-grown cucumbers don't stick to the rules (hooray!): depending on the variety, they're just as likely to be curly, twisted, ridged and a bit prickly as straight. Leave the breeding to the experts because cucumbers pack a bitter punch unless you stick to the F1 varieties. All F1 hybrids come as female fruits, whereas male cucumbers are bitter. For the classic, short, pickling gherkin, go for Stimora F1 and grow indoors or out. You pick them when they're tiny, but if you miss that stage the quality stays good enough for the salad bowl. If you're an indoor gardener, try Picolino for high yields of mini cucumbers.

Pickled Gherkins

This no-cook recipe is easy and quick: just prepare in advance to get the salting stage underway, to ensure that your pickles are firm and crunchy. Chapter 3 has more on sterilised jars.

Special tools required: *Sterilised jars*

Preparation time: *10 minutes*

Processing time: *15 minutes and 24 hours salting time*

Yield: *About 1 kilogram (2 pounds, 4 ounces)*

500 grams (1 pound, 2 ounces) pickling gherkins	*2 or 3 dried chillies (optional)*
125 grams (4½ ounces) sea salt	*2.5 millilitres (½ teaspoon) dried whole pickling spices*
3 or 4 shallots (or equivalent onion)	*Sprig of dill and/or tarragon*
1 or 2 garlic cloves (optional)	*700 millilitres (1¼ pint) white wine vinegar*

1 Wash your gherkins and trim off any flower ends. Quarter or half the gherkins unless your jars are large enough to fit them in whole.

2 Lay the prepared gherkins in a bowl, and layer with salt. Leave to stand at room temperature for 24 hours. Wash briskly to remove all salt, patting dry as you go on paper towels.

3 Cut the shallots into thin slices, filling the clean, sterile jars: alternate gherkin with the other vegetables and flavourings in an attractive manner.

4 Pour in the white wine vinegar to cover the gherkins. Store in the refrigerator for one month before eating or use up within a year.

Per 100-gram serving: *35 calories; 1 gram protein, 8 grams carbohydrate, 0 grams fat, 0 grams saturated fat, 0 milligrams cholesterol, 1 gram fibre, 528 milligrams sodium.*

Fennel (bulb)

Two kinds of fennel exist. One's a herb (Chapter 16 concentrates on herbs) and one's a vegetable: both have an aniseed flavour. Florence fennel is the vegetable, which with its feathery fronds and bulbous fruit grows happily outdoors. Pick early and marvel at the delicacy of the aniseed taste. You need to catch these plants when the bulbs are small, maximum 8–10 centimetres wide at the base, before they bolt to seed. Try Finale and Romanesco varieties for bolt resistance – you can still use the feathery fronds for flavouring. Save for up to two weeks in a plastic bag in the fridge or in cool, dry storage for several weeks.

Cut fennel up before blanching (Chapter 7 shows you how) for two minutes and lay out and freeze singly. Add to stews straight from frozen or use alone as a vegetable.

Garlic

Garlic goes well with everything and has fantastic health-giving properties. The humble garlic is a blood cooler, wormer and midge repellent, and keeps you safe from vampires. It grows by the acre in Brittany, France, and does well in most UK gardens. The Thermidrome variety has an excellent flavour and Printanors are small cloves that store well.

Garlic is the back to front crop: it likes to be planted in the cold winter months and is ready to harvest by June: pull and allow to dry.

Tie your garlic up in bunches to store (about ten bulbs in a bunch allows the air to circulate and keeps mould at bay) or use a simple stringing method (as I describe in Chapter 13). Smaller bulbs store longer than large ones, and if you find a variety that grows and stores well in your area, save some cloves to plant the following winter.

Don't be tempted to hang strings or bunches of garlic in the kitchen, no matter how fantastic they look. Instead, bring the strings or bunches inside one at a time from a cool, airy place as you use them, because the warmth and humidity of the kitchen accelerates their demise.

Well-stored garlic keeps you going to December, after which the bulbs begin to shrivel. Pickle some to use for any dish until early spring, when the garden garlic is ready again for picking as 'wet garlic'. Garlic all year round . . . nice!

Pickled Garlic

This recipe gives you pungent preserved cloves and stores easily for many months. Pickle whole garlic bulbs in their skins: even the tiniest cloves are easy to peel after this treatment, jumping out of their skins into the cooking pot at the merest touch. Create a garlicky snack by mashing a few cloves onto delicious bread, drizzling with olive oil. Chapter 3 has more on sterilisation.

Special tools required: *Sterilised jars*

Preparation time: *30–40 minutes depending on quality and size of garlic bulbs*

Processing time: *15 minutes*

Yield: *About 1 kilogram (2 pounds, 4 ounces)*

10–20 whole garlic bulbs (according to size of bulbs)

1 litre (1¾ pint) vinegar

15 millilitres (1 tablespoon) honey

1 Remove the main stalks. Place garlic into a bowl of lukewarm water, allowing to soak for a few minutes before cutting back the root end to a clean flat plane and peeling as many layers of papery skin to leave the garlic clean. No need to peel the cloves any further.

2 Pour the vinegar into a heavy-bottomed, noncorrosive pan, adding the honey and stirring to dissolve. Add the whole garlic bulbs: toss any loose cloves in too. Bring to the boil and simmer for five minutes.

3 Using a slotted spoon, fill sterilized, warm jars with bulbs, pouring in the vinegar to completely cover. Seal, allow to cool and label; leave for one month before using and eat up within the year.

Tip: *Use freshly picked garlic or cloves that have been dried but before they show any signs of deterioration.*

Vary it! *The Okra Pickle recipe later in this chapter helps to brighten up your preserving jars.*

Per 100-gram serving: *61 calories; 3 grams protein, 14 grams carbohydrate, 0 grams fat, 0 grams saturated fat, 0 milligrams cholesterol, 1 gram fibre, 16 milligrams sodium.*

Melons

Although they usually grow in a greenhouse or polytunnel, you can produce melons if you've a sunny, warm spot in the garden. They keep well for several weeks at normal room temperatures. Go for the early-maturing Hale's Best Jumbo variety if you're growing outdoors, or a popular variety such as Sweetheart, which has a reputation for easy growing. If you're aiming to make melon jam, the Pastèque à Confiture variety is the one for you.

Melon Jam

This jam brings fond memories of foreign holidays to mind; making it from your home-grown melons proves that you needn't stray far from home for an exotic experience.

Use a heavy-bottomed preserving pan (check out Chapter 2 on getting properly tooled-up) and sterilised jars (which I discuss in Chapter 3).

Special tools required: *Sterilised jars*

Preparation time: *10 minutes*

Processing time: *Standing time plus 20 minutes*

Yield: *1.8 kilograms (4 pounds)*

1 kilogram (2 pounds, 4 ounces) melon	*50 grams (2 ounces) crystallised ginger*
1 kilogram (2 pounds, 4 ounces) granulated sugar	*Juice of 4 lemons*

1 Dice up the melon flesh and place in bowl with sugar and ginger. Mix well, leaving overnight to 'cook' in a heavy-bottomed preserving pan.

2 The next day, simmer the mixture until soft and then add the lemon. Boil rapidly, checking for set in your chosen manner from the options in Chapter 5.

3 Pot up into warm, sterilised jars, seal and label when cool. Store in a cool, dark place.

Per 100-gram serving: 246 calories; 1 grams protein, 63 grams carbohydrate, 0 grams fat, 0 grams saturated fat, 0 milligrams cholesterol, 1 grams fibre, 7 milligrams sodium.

Okra

This exotic beauty, also called 'lady fingers', is often seen in Indian dishes: grow it under cover or in a garden sun-trap. Try the Mammoth or Clemsons Spineless varieties. Pick the pods when young and bright in colour (5–8 centimetres long), and freeze after two minutes of blanching, or pickle.

Okra Pickle

Okra pods benefit from being pricked all over before applying the salt, allowing any excess liquid to flow: makes an attractive picture with contrasting colours in the pickle jar. Chapter 2 has more on equipment, Chapter 3 has the info on sterilisation.

Special tools required: *Sterilised jars, noncorrosive pan*

Preparation time: *25 minutes*

Processing time: *1½ hours*

Yield: *About 1 kilogram (2 pounds, 4 ounces)*

675 grams (1½ pound) young fresh okra	*Small handful of mint*
15 millilitres (1 tablespoon) salt (for brining)	*1 litre (1¾ pint) cider vinegar*
250 grams (9 ounces) carrots	*60 millilitres (4 tablespoons) honey*
6 cloves of garlic	*15 millilitres (1 tablespoon) salt*
3–4 chillies (optional)	*10 millilitres (2 teaspoons) ground turmeric*

1 Trim any dark bits of stalk without removing the ends of the okra. Prick all over with a cocktail stick and lay out before sprinkling with the brining salt; leave for one hour for juices to flow. Rinse well and pat dry on paper towels.

2 Cut the carrots into thin strips and blanch for two minutes. Slice and de-seed the garlic cloves, then slice the chillies and tear up the mint.

3 Arrange the produce attractively and evenly, but not tightly, in warm, large, sterilised jars.

4 Place the vinegar, honey and salt in a noncorrosive pan and bring to the boil, skimming any scum off with a slotted spoon. Add the turmeric and return to the boil for three to five minutes. Fill the jars to the top, making sure that all the vegetables are covered and no air bubbles are lodged in the layers of vegetables. Seal and leave for a minimum of two weeks, preferably longer, before eating and use up within a year. Store in the fridge after opening.

Warning: Don't be dismayed if your okra pickle turns a little cloudy; okra has a naturally glutinous texture, you love it or hate it.

Tip: Keep a few long wooden skewers around – sterilise in boiling water – to poke among the veg to dislodge any trapped air.

Per 100-gram serving: 82 calories; 2 grams protein, 22 grams carbohydrate, 0 grams fat, 0 grams saturated fat, 0 milligrams cholesterol, 3 grams fibre, 797 milligrams sodium.

Peppers

With the sweet varieties of pepper, the F1 varieties generally perform best, and so don't save seeds: F1s are professionally grown hybrids and the seeds are expensive. Allocate a windowsill, conservatory or covered spot for peppers because they do need protection: Bendigo F1 is suitable for cold greenhouses. Create a colour scheme by choosing Gilboa, which ripens from green to orange, sweetening with the colour changes. Corno Di Toro Rosso has attractive, long, curvy, pointed fruits and Bell Boy gives a high yield of deep green fruits. Hungarian Wax is another well-respected variety.

If you struggle for space or are late with planting, look out for *transplants* (small seedlings ready for potting on) in plant sales and open garden sales. Buying transplants is a cost-effective way of accumulating a range of varieties.

Keep your ripe peppers fresh in the fridge for several weeks, or freeze to use at a later date, but don't attempt to blanche them. Roast them in oil (look at the 'Using Oil as a Preserving Tool' section earlier in this chapter for more delicious hints) before laying out to freeze singly then bag up in quantity, or try one of the following recipes.

Whole Pepper Pickle

Small peppers are best for this pickle. Tiny tomato peppers (the name gives away their shape) are ideal, but by all means substitute any small colourful range (stick to lighter, brighter colours for best effect because green peppers tend to lose their colour soonest). The quantities of water, vinegar, sugar and salt you use depend upon the jar size and density of peppers in the jar. Proportions of the main ingredients are the most important thing; keep a little spare for topping up. Chapter 3 has more on sterilised jars.

Special tools required: *Sterilised jars, noncorrosive pan, muslin cloth*

Preparation time: *10 minutes*

Processing time: *20 minutes*

Yield: *About 1 kilogram (2 pounds, 4 ounces)*

1 kilogram (2 pounds, 4 ounces) small red or yellow sweet peppers

2 small dried chillies

2 bay leaves

White wine vinegar (jar size determines quantity)

30 millilitres sugar (2 tablespoons) per 1 litre (1¾ pint) liquid

30 millilitres salt (2 tablespoons) per 1 litre (1¾ pint) liquid

A spice bag: 10 millilitres (2 teaspoons) black peppercorns, 5 millilitres (1 teaspoon) juniper berries, 2 bay leaves; wrap in muslin

1 Wash the peppers, leaving a portion of the stalk on each. Arrange attractively in warm, sterilised jars with the chillies and bay leaves.

2 To gauge how much pickle liquid to make, fill the jars containing the peppers and so on with water, and then drain the water into a measuring jug. Pour half the water away, replacing it with white wine vinegar. Prepare salt and sugar amounts.

3 Using a noncorrosive pan, pour in the contents of the measuring jug, adding the spice bag and stirring to dissolve the salt and sugar. Heat the liquid to boiling point, simmering for ten minutes. Remove the spice bag, and allow the liquid to cool slightly.

4 Pour the liquid into your sterilised jar to cover the peppers and other ingredients, and seal. Revisit after a few days and top up if necessary with your saved liquid. The peppers are ready to eat in two weeks, use them up within six months.

Tip: *Make a little extra pickle to these proportions: you may need to top up the jars after a few days when the pepper cavities suck some liquid in.*

Per 100-gram serving: *37 calories; 1 gram protein, 9 grams carbohydrate, 0 grams fat, 0 grams saturated fat, 0 milligrams cholesterol, 2 grams fibre, 1,418 milligrams sodium.*

Sweet Pepper Ketchup

As an alternative to the ubiquitous tomato ketchup, try this fruity sweet pepper ketchup. The pepper preparation gives a slightly smoky flavour. Chapter 3 has more on sterilisation.

Special tools required: *Sterilised jars, muslin cloth*

Preparation time: *50 minutes (less with a food processor)*

Processing time: *3–3½ hours (less with a food mill)*

Yield: *About 1 litre (1 ¾ pints)*

2 kilograms (4 pounds, 8 ounces) sweet peppers (red ones give the best colour, but use what you've grown)

500 grams (1 pound, 2 ounces) onions or shallots

250 grams (9 ounces) prepared weight, cooking apples

2–3 fresh chillies, de-seeded (optional)

1.5 litres (2½ pints) water

700 millilitres (1¼ pints) red wine vinegar or cider vinegar

150 grams (5 ounces) light soft brown sugar

15 millilitres (1 tablespoon) salt

15 millilitres (1 tablespoon) cornflour

A herb bundle: sprigs of tarragon, parsley, mint, thyme and sage with a strip of lemon rind; tie with string

A spice bag: 15 millilitres (1 tablespoon) coriander seeds, 15 millilitres (1 tablespoon) black peppercorns, 5 millilitres (1 teaspoon) cloves; wrap in muslin

1 Roast the peppers by grilling until the skin blackens and blisters or by applying direct heat (blowtorch or gas flame). Put into a plastic bag for five minutes (the skin peels off easier afterwards), run under a cold tap and rub off the blackened skin. De-seed, wash again and chop the pepper finely along with the onions or shallots. Peel and core the cooking apples and chop finely as well.

2 Place all the chopped ingredients into a large, wide-mouthed, heavy-bottomed preserving pan with the water. Add the herb bundle and spice bag and bring to the boil. Reduce the heat to a gentle simmer, cooking until the onions are soft (about 25 minutes). Discard the herbs and spices and allow to cool.

3 Push this mixture through a sieve with the back of a spoon, or use a food mill (much easier and quicker!). Clean the preserving pan and return the pureed vegetables to it, adding the vinegar, sugar and salt. Bring to the boil, stirring to dissolve the sugar and salt. Simmer for one to one and a half hours or until the mixture loses half its volume.

4 Make a paste of the cornflour with a little vinegar; stir into the ketchup, boiling for two or three minutes. Pour into warm, sterilised bottles or jars, seal and label. For long-term keeping, heat-treatment (hot bottling; see Chapter 5) is necessary or keep in the fridge for up to three months.

Tip: *When chopping large quantities finely, a food processor speeds the task up. Preserving pans often have a calibration on the inside wall; jot down the measurement when you first return the puree to the pan to judge when the sauce is half its original volume.*

Per 100-gram serving: *170 calories; 3 grams protein, 42 grams carbohydrate, 0 grams fat, 0 grams saturated fat, 0 milligrams cholesterol, 2 grams fibre, 713 milligrams sodium.*

Storing sweetcorn out of the freezer

If your freezer is already full, leave your cobs on the plant until they naturally start to dry. Remove the whole cobs from the plant and hang indoors until the sweetcorn kernels are totally dry, hard and shrivelled (speed the process up in a warm kitchen). Strip the kernels from the cob, pushing them off with your thumbs, and keep in dry, air-tight jars. Re-hydrate when you want to use by soaking overnight in water. Add to soups and stews, or if completely dry, try popping some for a homemade popcorn feast, sprinkled with salt or drizzled with honey.

Sweetcorn

When using sweetcorn, pick what you're going to use straight away before the sweetness turns to starch. The Golden Bantam variety works well as a garden crop, or try the heirloom variety True Gold. Planting sweetcorn in a block gives the best results: patchy cobs are the result of poor pollination.

Freeze whole cobs by blanching for six minutes (the blanching process is explained in Chapter 7) or cut the kernels from the cob with a sharp knife and blanch for two minutes. Lay out and freeze singly.

To remove the kernels, hold the cob vertically and run a sharp knife down the side of the cob; discard the core.

Remove your dried sweetcorn kernels whole from the cob (don't cut off with a knife) and they can double up as next year's seeds, or make sweetcorn relishes.

Sweetcorn and Cabbage Relish

You can mix this relish into a potato salad or use as a filler for sandwiches and wraps. It also works fabulously well at barbeque time and for dips. Chapter 3 has more on sterilisation.

Special tools required: *Sterilised jars*

Preparation time: *25 minutes*

Processing time: *25 minutes*

Yield: *About 1.8 kilograms (4 pounds)*

5 ripe corn cobs

1 small red or white cabbage, about 675 grams (1 pound, 4 ounces)

2 medium onions

600 millilitres (1 pint) white vinegar

110 grams (4 ounces) sugar

10 millilitres (2 teaspoons) salt

15 millilitres (1 tablespoon) dry mustard

5 millilitres (1 teaspoon) turmeric

1 Remove your home-grown sweetcorn's silky outer layer and tassels, peeling back to a clean cob. Boil the whole cob for five minutes. Using a sharp knife and holding the corn vertically, strip the corn, discarding the central core. Remove the outer leaves and thick core from the cabbage; shred the leaves finely. Peel and chop the onions finely.

2 Put the vinegar, sugar, salt and spices in a large, heavy-bottomed pan. Over a low heat, dissolve the sugar and then bring the mixture to a boil and add all the prepared vegetables. Simmer for about ten minutes or until the vegetables are cooked, but still crunchy.

3 Pot into warm, sterilised jars, seal and allow to cool before labelling. Leave for 6–8 weeks to mature, then use up within a year. Store in a fridge after opening.

Per 30-gram serving: 18 calories; 0 grams protein, 4 grams carbohydrate, 0 grams fat, 0 grams saturated fat, 0 milligrams cholesterol, 0 grams fibre, 81 milligrams sodium.

Tomatoes

Tomatoes have their own place in people's hearts and stomachs, and come in many shapes and sizes. They're the most versatile of the fruiting vegetables and the base for most Mediterranean dishes. If you choose a recipe that involves thorough cooking, you can use frozen veg and still return the finished dish to the freezer quite safely. Or you can preserve with vinegar and sugar for a moderate term in the fridge, or heat-treat (see Chapter 5) to preserve for the long haul at ambient temperatures.

If you get a good growing season, tomatoes just keep coming, leaving you with some tomatoes that haven't had time to ripen. You can keep these green tomatoes on a sunny windowsill, or put the unripe toms into a dark drawer or box: just remember to look inside regularly for a pleasantly ripe surprise. You can store 'fresh' tomatoes right round to Christmas in this way (removing any that go brown or crinkly). Speed up the ripening by putting a banana in a bag with your toms.

If pesky slugs and snails are a problem in your garden, grow your tomatoes in tubs and hanging baskets up off the ground.

Whole tomatoes freeze well (Chapter 7 has more freezing details): just give a cursory glance to ensure that they're basically clean and edible. Don't bother to remove stalks or skin; as long as they're whole and dry just keep adding to a bag in the freezer: give an occasional shake to keep the fruits separate. Do keep varieties separate, though, and label well if you can't easily recognise them.

Cut tomatoes with a portion of stalk, also called 'on the truss', if you aren't using them immediately, for better keeping.

Unsurprisingly, breeders have developed the ever-popular tomato into different varieties for different needs. Here are a few:

- **Gardener's Delight, tall type:** A long time favourite, sweet, small tomato for home producers with good yield and taste.

- **Golden Queen, tall type:** Yellow tomatoes (like this one) are less acidy than red tomatoes, if that worries you. This heirloom variety is popular and high-yielding, and brings a lovely flavour as well as colour to your dishes.

- **Koralik, bush type:** If you live in a damp area, or have local knowledge of a blight problem (a common tomato disease associated with damp and humidity), try this early bush tomato. You get a surprisingly high yield of sweet, bright red tomatoes with an excellent tolerance to blight.

- **Principe Borghese, bush type:** If you fancy sun-dried tomatoes, bottling and home-made puree, choose this variety, the king of the Italian paste tomato.

- **San Marzano, tall type:** Produces heavy crops of plum-type tomatoes that are excellent for bottling, sauces and purees: grows best under cover.

If you need to remove the skins from frozen tomatoes, drop briefly into a pan of boiling water. Fish them out one at a time with a slotted spoon and squeeze the skin to rip your tomatoes out of their skins. You don't burn yourself because the bulk of the tomato is still frozen.

Tomato Ketchup

This recipe makes a delicious ketchup, especially if you go for the handmade version by pushing the mixture through a sieve. Make the job easier and quicker by cooking the veggies until properly soft. A food mill makes lighter work of pureeing and a liquidiser even less time, but with slightly different results. Chapter 3 has more on sterilisation.

Special tools required: *Sterilised bottles or jars*

Preparation time: *25 minutes*

Processing time: *3 hours (less with food processing equipment)*

Yield: *About 600 millilitres (1 pint) (more using a food processor)*

900 grams (2 pounds) tomatoes ('pulpy' tomatoes are best)

225 grams (8 ounces) shallots (or onions)

2 medium garlic cloves

2 centimetres (¾ inch) piece of fresh root ginger

150 millilitres (¼ pint) cider vinegar

40 grams (1½ ounces) soft brown sugar

5 millilitres (1 teaspoon) paprika

5 millilitres (1 teaspoon) salt

1 Prepare the vegetables by peeling both the garlic and ginger and then chopping all veg into small pieces to aid thorough cooking.

2 Putting all the vegetables into a heavy-bottomed pan, bring them slowly to the boil, stirring to encourage the juices to run. Reduce the heat, cover and simmer for about 20 minutes, stirring from time to time until the shallots (or onions) are soft.

3 Push the mixture through a sieve with the back of a spoon, or use a food mill or food liquidiser to puree the cooked mixture, pouring it into a clean pan.

4 Heat this puree up, bringing it to the boil (uncovered this time), reducing the mix to around half the original volume: measure by eye or use 45 minutes as a guide.

5 Remove from the heat to add the vinegar, sugar, salt and paprika, stirring to dissolve the sugar. Return to the heat and simmer for another 30 minutes, reducing the mix until it thickens to the right pouring consistency (it continues to thicken on cooling).

6 Seal into sterilised bottles or jars and heat-treat to extend the shelf-life to up to one year (Chapter 5 deals with hot bottling). Or jar as normal and keep in the fridge for up to two months.

Per 100-gram serving: 84 calories; 4 grams protein, 20 grams carbohydrate, 0 grams fat, 0 grams saturated fat, 0 milligrams cholesterol, 2 grams fibre, 515 milligrams sodium.

Green Tomato Chutney

Use your unripe tomatoes to good effect with this traditional chutney. Eat it with cold meats or cheese or as an accompaniment to an Indian meal. Chapter 3 has more on sterilisation.

Special tools required: *Sterilised jars, muslin cloth*

Preparation time: *30 minutes*

Processing time: *2 hours*

Yield: *2.7–3.5 kilograms (6–7 pounds)*

1.8 kilograms (4 pounds) green tomatoes

675 grams (1½ pounds) shallots or onions

450 grams (1 pound) (when peeled and cored) cooking apples

600 millilitres (1 pint) vinegar

8 red chillis

2.5-centimetre (1-inch) piece of root ginger

225 grams (8 ounces) seedless raisins (or chopped dates)

10 millilitres (2 teaspoons) salt

450 grams (1 pound) sugar

1 Chop the tomatoes, onions and apples and place in a heavy-bottomed pan with half the vinegar. Bring to the boil and simmer gently for 30 minutes until tender.

2 Tie the chillies and ginger into a square of muslin, and bash with a hammer or rolling pin to bruise (releasing the flavours). Add to the pan with the raisins (or chopped dates) and cook, stirring to redistribute the mixture for about one hour, or until thickening occurs. Add the salt and sugar (remove or lower heat while stirring to dissolve the sugar) and press the bag of flavourings from time to time.

3 Continue cooking until the mixture is thick and drawing a spoon across the base of the pan leaves a distinct trail. Remove the muslin bag before potting up into sterilised warm jars, patting down well to remove any air pockets. Leave to mature for a minimum of one month before using and use up within a year. After opening, store in the fridge.

Vary it! Chutneys don't require your best produce; just use up any glut of ripe red tomatoes in place of the combined weight of the green tomatoes and raisins. Just remember to simmer the mixture a little longer if your tomatoes are juicy. Try replacing the root ginger with 1 millilitre (¼ teaspoon) cayenne pepper and 10 millilitres (2 teaspoons) paprika, to ring the 'taste' changes.

Per 30-gram serving: 32 calories; 0 grams protein, 8 grams carbohydrate, 0 grams fat, 0 grams saturated fat, 0 milligrams cholesterol, 0 grams fibre, 56 milligrams sodium.

Tomato and Carrot Soup

Easy to prepare and handy for freezing, soups are so versatile. Use this recipe for hearty lunches or in smaller quantities as the starter to a special evening dinner. The robust tomato taste has a hint of sweetness from the apple and carrot. When prepared, just grab from the freezer and freshen up with a swirl of cream or natural yoghurt and a garnish of fresh parsley or chives; leaving you time for socialising as well as feeding your guests beautifully.

Preparation time: *15 minutes*

Processing time: *1¼ hours*

Serves: *4*

15 grams (½ ounce) butter	*175 grams (6 ounces) carrots*
10 millilitres (2 teaspoons) olive oil	*1 eating apple*
1 onion	*1 bouquet garni (as I describe in Chapter 16)*
2 garlic cloves	*1.2 litres (2 pints) chicken or vegetable stock*
450 grams (1 pound) tomatoes	*Salt and freshly ground black pepper*

1 Skin the tomatoes, and roughly chop. Peel the carrot if necessary and chop finely; do the same for the onion. Peel, core and chop the apple and garlic.

2 Heat the butter and oil in a heavy-bottomed saucepan. Cook the garlic and onion first over a low heat until they're soft and transparent. Add the carrot and continue cooking until the carrot softens. Add in the tomatoes, apple, bouquet garni and stock; season lightly with salt and pepper, and bring to the boil.

3 Cover and simmer for 45 minutes.

4 Remove from the heat and allow to cool slightly before pushing through a sieve by hand (or use a food mill, hand-held blender or liquidiser). Eat straight away or pour into suitable freezer containers (Chapter 7 gives you ideas); adjust the seasoning at the final heating stage.

*Per **100-millilitre serving:** 174 calories; 4 gram protein, 18 grams carbohydrate, 11 grams fat, 4 grams saturated fat, 15 milligrams cholesterol, 4 grams fibre, 1,521 milligrams sodium. Based on 4 servings.*

Part IV
Keeping and Eating Garden Vegetables

'So _this_ is why you've not brought me
any fresh vegetables home all year!'

In this part . . .

You can find all the information you need for keeping your home-grown garden vegetables in a kind of suspended animation to enjoy throughout the year in these three chapters. Some, particularly the root veg in Chapter 13, have a built-in natural storage function of their own: switch it on by giving root veg the correct conditions while keeping them safe from unwanted hungry mouths. Other normally mundane vegetables (for example, beans in Chapter 14 and cabbage in Chapter 15) may amaze you with their versatility when you look into the possibilities for preserving them with well-tried methods and a handful of other ingredients. Many of the recipes in this part use the same type of food your ancestors ate and drank, giving your new-found preserving skills a place in history as well as your cupboards.

Chapter 13

Going Underground: Rootin' Around with Root Vegetables

In This Chapter

▶ Perusing root vegetables for storing and recipe ideas

▶ Providing hints for individual veg varieties

▶ Combining foods for storage

Root vegetables are a real homely blessing during the cold winter months. For example, a good hearty frost brings out the sugars in parsnips and swedes, so leave these veggies until after a spell of cold, preferably frosty, weather before using straight from the garden or from a clamp or store.

This chapter provides loads of great ideas for storing and using root vegetables, including some that work well as combinations. The cold weather is the time for warming winter soups and stews to keep away the seasonal blues; a frozen stew pack all prepared and ready for the pot adds speed to cooking. Don't forget the baby new crops too: tiny onions, beetroot and baby carrots are the root's tasty gift to you in the summer months, just right to be stored in the pickle and chutney jar along with other summer goodies.

Considering an A–Z of Roots (Don't Cry . . . The Onion Family's Here Too!)

In this section, I include plants whose roots are edible: carrots, potatoes with their bulbous growing ends; onions, shallots and their swollen stems; swedes, turnips and so on. You commonly bring these root veg together in the 'root' bed within the garden *rotation* – growing different types of plants in different areas of the plot each year to avoid the build-up of pests and diseases and to use soil nutrients evenly – and I bring them together in this chapter too, along with some recipes.

I also include hints on varieties suitable for storing, in case you're flummoxed by the options in the seed catalogues or on the seed stands. If you've already planted and grown other varieties, you may find that yours store just as well.

Beetroot

This stalwart of the vegetable patch is easy to grow and people have stored it in various ways for years. Beetroot is a fun vegetable, whose brilliant red colouring forms the basis for natural red food dyes, especially since awareness of allergies and sensitivities to chemical dyes have come to light.

Eat enough beetroot and you can 'wee red', a condition called *beet urea*. The condition is completely harmless but a fine incentive for encouraging less adventurous children to give beetroot a go. Other golden and striped beetroots are available too.

Choosing varieties with purpose

Gardeners have tested all varieties of beetroot seeds on sale, so they grow well for you under the right conditions. But if you're reading this book sitting by a winter fire choosing from a bewildering number of seeds in a catalogue, the varieties I mention here are renowned for their particular storing and preserving properties.

Alvro Mono is an early season variety, just right when picked young, with the smooth, small baby beets perfect for pickling. Storuman is a uniform, smooth, tasty root that stores well – the name gives a hint! Alternatively, if you're after a good flavoursome beetroot, go for the large main crop Bolivar, noted for its excellent storing qualities.

For storing in clamps or boxes of sand, roots with smooth skins are easier to examine for blemishes and bugs. Craggy skins can easily harbour moisture too, which starts up rot spots.

Clamping and storing

Beetroot responds well to clamping, storing in dark root cellars away from light or pulling (picking) and re-burying in boxes of sand or compost. See Chapter 4 for detailed information on these storage methods.

Pickling

When you're preparing beetroot for any kind of cooking, be careful not to damage the skins – cooking whole with 'rooty' bits and leaving five centimetres of leaf stalk on while cooking avoids *bleeding*, which reduces the vibrancy of the colour.

Pick your beetroots before they get too big – up to the size of a tennis ball – and before they take too long to cook or go woody inside. After you cook the beetroots, run them briefly under a cold tap until you can hold them without burning yourself and the skin pops off in an easy and highly pleasing manner.

Pickled Beetroot

Pickled beetroot is something you can eat on its own or with just about any kind of salad. Chapter 2 has info on equipment and Chapter 3 outlines several methods for sterilising your jars.

Special tools required: Sterilised jars with noncorrosive tops

Preparation time: 10 minutes

Processing time: 1–2 hours, depending on how large the beets are and the size of jars used

Yield: 1.3 kilograms (3 pounds)

900 grams (2 pounds) uncooked fresh beetroot

Brine made from 50 grams (2 ounces) salt dissolved in 600 millilitres (1 pint) water (see Chapter 6 for more on why you use salt)

600 millilitres (1 pint) malt vinegar (Chapter 6 tells you more about vinegars and pickling)

Sugar or honey, if you prefer a milder taste

1 Place the washed, trimmed (see the tip in the previous section 'Pickling' about avoiding damage to the skins) whole beetroots into a large pan, and cover with the brine. Bring to the boil and simmer until tender. Baby beets take about 10–15 minutes and large beetroots up to one hour. Cook without piercing to keep the colour.

2 Drain and peel the beetroots. Leave baby beets whole, and slice or cube larger ones before packing into your sterilised jars using noncorrosive – plastic-coated or glass – lids.

3 Cover with cold vinegar, seal and store for two to four weeks before use.

4 Add just 5 millilitres (1 teaspoon) of sugar or honey the first time. You may like a sweeter version next time, so record what you've done if your memory isn't that great.

Vary it! A grating of zest and a squeeze of orange juice with a dusting of warm toasted sunflower and pumpkin seeds - just dry fry them for five minutes to bring out the nutty flavour – elevates your pickled beetroot to dinner party standard. And if you need a hearty meal with the kids, make creamy mashed potatoes with pickled beet as a side dish, dribbling a little of the pickle liquor onto the mash for some crazy colourful fun – all without 'E' numbers!

Per 100-gram serving: 30 calories; 1 gram protein, 7 grams carbohydrate, 0 grams fat, 0 grams saturated fat, 0 milligrams cholesterol, 1 gram fibre, 220 milligrams sodium.

Beetroot Wine

You can thank your ancestors for trying out many unusual hedgerow fruit and garden vegetables in wine. Sometimes, as with beetroot, the end result is something quite elegant and subtle, and believe me – beetroot wine tastes much better than it sounds (hic!). Ask your friends to guess the humble origins of this wine, the truth may surprise them.

Special tools required: Demijohn or fermentation jar, siphon, airlock (see Chapter 9 for the full array)

Preparation time: 15 minutes

Processing time: Several days for first fermentation and four months plus for second fermentation. After bottling, a wait of 6 months minimum is recommended.

Yield: Approx 4.5 litres (1 gallon)

1.5 kilograms (3 pounds, 5 ounces) uncooked beetroot

6.8 litres (12 pints) cold water

1.5 kilograms (3 pounds, 5 ounces) granulated sugar

6 cloves

3 unpeeled oranges, scrubbed and sliced

15 grams (½ ounce) wine or brewer's yeast

1 Wash the beetroot well but don't peel it.

2 Cut the beetroot into thin slices and place into a large saucepan. Add the water and bring to the boil.

3 Simmer until the beetroot is just tender; about 30–40 minutes.

4 Strain off the liquid – use cheesecloth lining a stainless steel sieve if you've still got some gritty bits in the water – into a large bowl and discard the beetroot.

5 Put the liquid back into the saucepan and add the sugar, cloves and oranges. Heat gently, stirring to dissolve the sugar, and then boil gently for 15 minutes.

6 Strain the liquid back into the bowl and let it cool to 21 degrees Celsius (70 degrees Fahrenheit).

7 Add the yeast to some of the warm liquid – an easy amount to deal with in a handy jug or bowl – and mix until any lumps are gone. Return the mixture to the bulk of the warm liquid. Stir in gently to amalgamate.

8 Cover the bowl with a clean tea towel.

9 Leave for a few days while rapid fermentation takes place – as a guide, 3–5 days, depending on factors such as the ambient temperature.

10 Once the fierce bubbling ceases, strain the liquid into a demijohn fermentation jar of 4.5 litres (8 pints, 1 gallon), filling it to the bottom of the neck.

11 Fit an airlock – remembering to top it up with water – and leave until fermentation ceases after a few months and the wine clears. Each batch differs depending on many factors: for example, the quality of the beetroots and other ingredients; how warm the wine storage room is.

12 Rack off! No, I'm not being rude; rack off is the wine-maker's term for siphoning the liquid. Use a plastic tube to transfer the clear liquid to another vessel while leaving the murky bits (*lees*) in the bottom of the jar. You may have to rack off more than once to achieve clear wine; some wine-makers rack off up to four times.

13 When clear, bottle and store for six months or longer before drinking.

Per 100-millilitre serving: 140 calories; 1 gram protein, 36 grams carbohydrate, 0 grams fat, 0 grams saturated fat, 0 milligrams cholesterol, 0 grams fibre,18 milligrams sodium. Analysis is approximate.

You can find more tips on tipples and wine-making instructions in Chapter 9.

Preserving beetroot seed for another year's sowing

If you find a beetroot variety that grows well in your plot and you like its flavour and colour, you may want to keep seeds from it for another year. Here's how.

Leave one or two beetroots in the ground, and you may get seeds the same year as you planted the beetroot. If you planted late in the growing season – August/September – leave in the ground over the winter.

Most beetroots shoot up strong, colourful leaves and stems, as tall as 1 metre, and beetroot flowers form. Leave the plant to do its stuff. Support with a stake if necessary, and when the flowers have turned to mature seed heads, chop the stem down and up-end it into a paper sack or bag, leaving it hanging up to dry (Chapter 16 has more information on the seed-saving skill). The seeds come loose and you can use them for another year's crop: plenty for you and probably enough to share with gardening friends as well.

Carrots

If you can see well in the dark, carrots must be a part of your diet – or so the old saying goes, but ancient wisdom often holds a grain of truth. One thing's for sure: you can eat carrots all year round with a bit of planning.

With the first baby carrot thinnings straight from the garden in June, you can make Summer Vegetable Pickle (see the later section 'Coming Together Beautifully: Effective Food Combinations'). Or you can use the older, tastier hardies that you've stored safely in a clamp – see Chapter 4 for building a clamp and other cool storage – for the rest of the year, or as part of a frozen stew pack (Chapter 7 helps to keep your options open with freezer knowledge). The later 'Florence Fennel' section contains a handy tip on maintaining carrot quality.

If the storing quality of the carrot is important to you, avoid the F1 hybrid varieties, easily spotted because F1 is always mentioned alongside the name. F1s are newer varieties bred especially for commercial growers who need to produce uniform, neat and tidy vegetables for the supermarket, all ready to harvest at the same time. You can't save seeds from F1 varieties either, so be sure to start with the older varieties (such as the ones I mention in the next paragraph) if seed-saving is part of your plan.

As a home grower, you've the opportunity to go for the tastiest varieties with a reputation for storing well. With a bewildering number of varieties to choose from, try Autumn King, a really popular variety: this carrot is high-yielding, has excellent flavour and stores the really easy way by staying in the soil until a real freeze sets in. Choosing late-maturing varieties means a shorter storing time: Rodelika is a late crop with large, blunt-ended roots, just right for clamping or re-burying in sand boxes.

If you're a fan of carrot juice, the late main cropper Rothild is the one for you, with an intense red colour and super 'carroty' taste.

Juicing your carrots

Juice your carrots at any stage, straight from the garden, or after storage in a clamp or sand box. You can freeze the juice if you fancy a juicing session or have borrowed a juicing machine and need to return it. Freezing liquids requires a little forethought; see Chapter 7 for more.

Drink carrot juice on its own, with a dash of piquant sauce or with a combination of other vegetables for a healthy, refreshing drink or as part of a calorie-controlled diet.

Clamping and storing

Carrots are made for storing. Smooth, even-sized roots are best, but all late main crop carrots of a non-F1 variety store in sand or compost in boxes, or if you've grown loads, in a clamp (Chapter 4 gives more details).

Celeriac

This knobbly fellow is a good friend to the vegetable grower who shuns the use of chemicals in the garden. It has a fantastic taste; like the name suggests, similar to celery. Celeriac is the king of savoury dishes and well worth growing.

Storing smooth varieties

Celeriac is a round vegetable with a tangled mass of rooty bits near the base. Growers are now developing celeriac plants that are smoother in shape. This smoothness adds to the keeping quality of all vegetables, with less nooks and crannies for wet, disease and bugs to hide. Choose any celeriac variety for picking and eating straight from the garden, but if your aim is storing in a root cellar, clamping or re-burying (Chapter 4 shows you how), the Ibis variety is noted for fast growth, smooth roots, good disease tolerance and storing qualities. Prinz, which has excellent flavour, also stores well.

Keeping celeriac in other ways

If you run out of celery for a freezer stew pack, substitute diced celeriac. Celeriac is an excellent ingredient for hearty winter soups and broths; make them ahead of time and freeze them too. Chapter 7 has the information you need, or take a look at the Year Round Chutney recipe in the later 'Swede' section; substitute celeriac instead of swede for a different flavour while keeping the texture of the chutney.

Florence Fennel

What a beauty this plant is, with its feathery fronds, bulbous root end and aniseedy aroma. Grow and early crop with the Finale or Fino varieties and finish the season with a late-cropping Romanesco, with its heavy large bulbs. Florence fennel has a tendency to *bolt* (run to seed). If bolting happens to any of your plants, you can just use them as a frondy backdrop in your flower displays, just as professional florists do. The pretty leaves and seed heads last for ages, as long as you keep the vase topped up with water.

You can keep the wicked little carrot fly (a bug that lays eggs on the carrot and causes internal damage) off the scent by placing a handful of crushed fennel fronds – or any other highly scented plant that you've grown, such as sage, lovage and onion tops – onto the disturbed soil around freshly picked carrots. Doing so keeps the carrots unharmed and therefore enhances their keeping quality.

Keeping Florence Fennel

Cut and lightly trim the bulbs and they keep in a cool, dark dry place for several weeks. Chapter 4 gives more details.

Freezing Florence Fennel

Trimming and cutting to short lengths before freezing keeps fennel at its best. This plant benefits from blanching for three minutes, and some pre-treatment to preserve its colour (Chapter 7 contains more freezer tips including blanching information).

Garlic

Take garlic with everything. The fantastic unknown and unfathomable health-giving properties are worth benefiting from: blood cooler, wormer and anti-midge bite, it even keeps you safe from vampires. Garlic's grown by the hectare over the English Channel in Brittany, and does well in most UK gardens too.

Garlic is the 'back to front' crop: it likes to be planted in the cold winter months and is ready to harvest by June.

Pull and allow to dry. Professional garlic growers plait their garlic into neat ropes. Tie yours up in bunches; about ten bulbs in a bunch still lets the air circulate and keep the moulds at bay, or use a simple stringing method (the later section 'Onions' contains a step-by-step guide. Smaller bulbs store longer than large ones, and if you find a variety that grows and stores well in your area, save cloves to plant the following year. Don't be tempted to hang your lovely strings of garlic in the kitchen, no matter how fantastic they look. Bring the strings or bunches inside one at a time as you use them, because the warmth and humidity of the kitchen accelerates their demise.

The Thermidrome variety has an excellent flavour and Printanor's small cloves store well. Work it out right and your saved garlic carries you round to spring when you can pick and use the garlic in your garden as 'wet garlic'. Nothing's better than home-grown garlic all year round.

Jerusalem artichoke

With their knobbly roots, you can use Jerusalem artichokes as an alternative to potatoes. Choosing the variety called Fuseau gives the smoothest, easiest-to-peel results. Dig straight from the ground until really hard frosts set in, and then store them throughout the rest of the winter in sand boxes or bags in a root cellar (Chapter 4 has more on this type of storage). Alternatively, scrub them clean and keep in a plastic bag in the fridge for a week or so.

Boil and mash into a puree before freezing to use as a bulking agent in winter soups and stews. Chapter 7 has plenty of tips on freezing.

If you've got a scatological side to your sense of humour and can find a good rhyme for the beginning of artichoke, you may find that they live up to the rhyme!

Kohlrabi

Kholrabi are an unusual vegetable and at their best when picked small – the size of a tennis ball as a maximum. If you like this vegetable, picking young and storing with a tuft of greenery on the top by burying it in sand boxes keeps it at its best. The Azur Star variety has an attractive purple tinge, or choose Superschmeltz for the more traditional pale-green bulbs.

Mash kohlrabi into a puree or cut it into chunks and freeze loose before packing; Chapter 7 goes into detail on freezing.

Swede, kohlrabi and turnips are really swollen stem plants; they're in the root chapter because people often referred to them as roots.

Onions

You've plenty of options when storing onions. They're a main ingredient in chutneys and pickled onions are a legendary accompaniment to a good Ploughman's lunch.

Fresh onions store well, but although the traditional string of onions is pleasant to see and stores well when hanging up in a cool, dry, airy shed, don't use the kitchen; the room is too warm and the onions begin to shoot, the green tops beginning to grow.

Choose spring-sown onions, whether as seeds or as *sets* (partially grown tiny onions for planting out into the ground). Eat or use the autumn-sown varieties early in the year – and use them for pickles and chutneys by all means.

Varieties such as Sturon and Stuttgart Giant are golden bulbs and store well. If you grow red onions, use them up first because they don't store as well as the golden varieties.

Stringing onions

Stringing up onions (not as violent as it sounds!) keeps them neat and packed up so that you can store them out of the way (see Figure 13-1).

You can choose from several different stringing methods, some more complicated than others, but I favour this simple approach. Most importantly, make sure that you start with a really well-dried onion, with several layers of papery skin over the bulb before you get to the fleshy part, and leathery and strong stems at the neck end at least 10 centimetres (4 inches) long:

1. **Take four onions and tie the stems together with strong garden twine or similar string.**

2. **Tie another string, about 75 centimetres (2 feet 6 inches) long, to the bunch and make a loop that you can hang from a convenient nail in a shed.** The original onions weigh the string down and form a 'stop' at the bottom of the string.

3. **Use the dried stems of your onions to loop round the string and tie off.** Add them one at a time, arranging them neatly around the string. Start a new string when the first is about 45–60 centimetres (18 inches–2 feet) long or too heavy for you to lift comfortably.

4. **Hang your strings of onions in a cool, airy shed.**

Onions can impart their flavour to other items, so keep them apart from delicate dried goods.

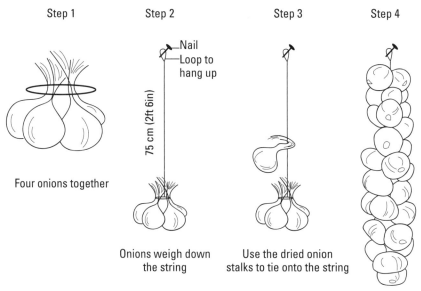

Step 1 — Four onions together

Step 2 — Nail / Loop to hang up / 75 cm (2ft 6in) / Onions weigh down the string

Step 3 — Use the dried onion stalks to tie onto the string

Step 4 — Hang onions in a cool, airy shed

Figure 13-1:
Stringing onions the easy way.

Pickled Onions: The basic recipe

For pickling, choose small onions such as the white Paris Silverskin or a red-skinned Purplette – see the later section 'Shallots' if you're looking for a crop for pickled onions early in the year. One thing to mention is that pickled onions are pretty potent. If you eat pickled onions near someone who doesn't, you may find that the non-onion eater keeps their distance! Chapter 3 gives you options on sterilising jars.

Special tools required: Sterilised jars, noncorrosive lids

Preparation time: 40 minutes

Processing time: 24 hours soaking time plus 2–3 months waiting

Yield: Approx 2.2 kilograms

1.8 kilograms (4 pounds) pickling onions (Chapter 6 has more pickling tips)

1.2 litres (2 pints) vinegar

225 grams (8 ounces) salt

2.3 litres (4 pints) water to make brine

1 Peel the onions and place in a large dish.

2 Dissolve the salt in 2.3 litres (4 pints) of water.

3 Pour over the onions to completely cover – use a plate to hold them under the brine.

4 Leave for 24 hours (check out Chapter 8 for more salty information and to find out why you use salt).

5 Drain and rinse thoroughly and quickly under cold, running water.

6 Pat dry on kitchen/paper towels.

7 Pack into sterilised jars.

8 Cover with cold vinegar.

9 Seal with noncorrosive lids – vinegar attacks some metals so use plastic-coated or glass lids.

10 Label and store for two to three months before using; they're ready just in time for Christmas.

Tip: For step 2, soaking in warm water makes onions easier to peel. If your eyes run, peel the onions under the water. If this trick fails, try wearing swimming goggles – they do help!

Tip: Take care when cutting to leave the base of each onion intact – doing so holds them together and stops them separating.

Per 100-gram serving: 68 calories; 1 gram protein, 17 grams carbohydrate, 0 grams fat, 0 grams saturated fat, 0 milligrams cholesterol, 0 grams fibre, 419 milligrams sodium.

Creating your own speciality pickled onions

Using your favourite spices, ginger, peppercorns or mustard seeds, or sprigs of herbs, rosemary, bay leaves or thyme, wash well, scalding sprigs of herbs under a stream of boiling water, and add before the vinegar.

Sweet-toothed picklers may like to dissolve up to 110 grams (4 ounces) of sugar or honey in the vinegar to reduce the sharpness.

Parsnips

All parsnips store well and improve in sweetness because the starch in a parsnip turns to sugar with a good hard frost. Leave them in the ground for as long as you can, just keep an eye out for freezing conditions coming up when they're likely to become frozen solid in the ground – many a home grower has broken a garden fork trying to lever out deep-rooting parsnips from rock-hard frozen ground.

Using unblemished specimens, free from most of the soil they were dug up with, make a clamp, re-bury in sand boxes or bag up in hessian or paper sacks – that is, of breathable material – and keep cool and dark (Chapter 4 gives the low-down on storing and clamping).

Some well-tried parsnip varieties are Harblange White and Tender and True.

If you go for the freezing option, parsnips look better for being blanched. Trim and peel young parsnips and cut into strips before pre-treating with one of the methods I give in Chapter 7; doing so helps to keep their pale flesh colour from browning. Blanch for two minutes.

If you don't mind the browning and the parsnips are to go straight from the freezer to the stew pot, by all means skip the blanching stage. Better still, make them into one of the winter warmer favourite soups.

Spicy Parsnip Soup

Sweet and spicy, this delicious soup is the perfect dish to greet you after a frosty winter walk. Just remember to take enough out of the freezer before you go out to exercise because you're sure to want seconds. The added croutons give a crunchy texture to complement the creaminess of the parsnips.

Preparation time: *10 minutes*

Cooking time: *35 minutes*

Serves: *4–6 servings*

50 grams (2 ounces) butter

1 clove of garlic, crushed

375 grams (13 ounces) parsnips, peeled and chopped

30 millilitres (1 tablespoon) flour

5 millilitres (1 teaspoon) curry powder

1.2 litres (2 pints) vegetable or chicken stock, warmed

150 millilitres (¼ pint) creamy milk (optional when serving)

Garnish: chopped chives or parsley and/or crispy croutons

1 Melt butter in a large, heavy-bottomed saucepan.

2 Add the vegetable ingredients and stir to cover with melted butter.

3 Cover the pan with a lid and allow to cook at a low heat until softening; about 10–15 minutes.

4 Stir in flour and curry powder and cook for a further two minutes.

5 Incorporate the warm stock gradually. Simmer until the parsnip is completely cooked through and soft.

6 Allow to cool a little before liquidising or pushing through a sieve.

7 Cool to below 4 degrees Celsius (40 degrees Fahrenheit) before freezing (Chapter 7 has tips on freezing soups).

Tip: Add a swirl of creamy milk and garnish to each bowl before serving.

Per 100-gram serving: *139 calories; 3 grams protein, 17 grams carbohydrate, 8 grams fat, 4 grams saturated fat, 18 milligrams cholesterol, 3 grams fibre, 853 milligrams sodium. (Based on 6 servings)*

Parsnips have a reputation for poor germination – you need to buy seeds each year even if you've got some left from previous years to get good germination results. However, if you've the room to leave a healthy parsnip specimen in the ground all winter, then for the next year's growing period you may be rewarded with a 'parsnip tree' around 1–1.5 metres high, which sets umbrella-like fronds of seeds.

When the seeds have matured on the plant, cut stems, seed heads and all, place upside down in a bag and keep in a dry place. (Chapter 16 explains the process for drying herb seed, and the process is the same for parsnips.) Making this a habit every year ensures a regular supply of new seeds and maximum germination.

Leave vegetable seed-saving to those with spacious gardens and plots. If you've only a pocket handkerchief-sized plot, buy new seeds. Some plants grow large before flowering and then setting seed.

Potatoes

Chipped, mashed, roasted, sautéed, as toppings for pies or to bulk up soups and stews, potatoes are the nation's favourite bulky, starchy meal filler. With sound storage methods and the right varieties you can eat your own potatoes all year round – depending, of course, on how much growing space you've access to.

New potatoes don't store, and so relish them when they're young and fresh – look at Chapter 21 for ideas and community incentives in your area allowing you to join in with a potato-growing project by offering help in the potato field. Maybe you want to start your own initiative and get permission to dig up a forgotten corner of the local park to grow spuds for the community!

Throw out any green potatoes even if they look unblemished in other ways; these have been exposed to the light when growing and are poisonous.

Potatoes are easy to clamp and store in a root cellar or in sacks and bags – Chapter 4 expands on these methods.

Potato varieties are divided up according to when during the season they mature: first and second early potatoes mature enough to harvest and eat in the summer months but don't store well, whereas main crop potatoes give good storage results. Main crop potatoes are ready to harvest in autumn. Of all the potatoes, these have the most robust 'set' skins (you have to use a knife or special peeling implement to peel potatoes with set skins compared to new potatoes whose skins just rub or scrape off easily).

Choose main crop varieties when planning on storing your potatoes.

Using main crop varieties – so you don't come a-cropper!

Some well-known main crop potato varieties are:

- ✔ **Arran Victory:** A gourmet potato with beautiful bright-purple skin; late maturing but with no *blight* (the most common potato disease) resistance – probably the best roasting potato ever!

- ✔ **Cara:** Popular pink-eyed potato, high yielding and with some blight resistance; a big baking and roasting spud, but excellent for all other uses too.

- ✔ **Desiree:** Another tried and tested potato with pink skin and yellow flesh; excellent for baking and roasting but doesn't do so well in sandy soils.

- ✔ **Sante:** Professional organic growers use this variety a lot, so take your lead from them if you're growing without chemicals. They've some built-in disease resistance, and fine-tasting yellow-fleshed tubers – a good all-round potato.

- ✔ **Valor:** Good disease resistance including some blight resistance. They've oval tubers with tasty white flesh; a consistent performer in the potato plot.

Potatoes are prone to disease, and by far the most common one is blight – the leaves begin to brown and 'melt'. In a small garden, if your crop succumbs, cut off all the blighty *haulms* – potato stems and greenery – and burn them. This approach is impossible, however, with a larger crop – most non-organic, commercially grown crops are liberally sprayed against blight.

Blight reduces the yield of the crop, and blighty potatoes in storage can turn to a revolting smelly mush – but all is not lost. Blight is worse in low-lying, damp areas or in wet, muggy years. If you've a good windy spot to grow your potatoes, blight is less likely to take hold of your crop. Don't despair even if you get blight: grit your teeth and wait until the greenery has died away – or remove it yourself and dig up some potatoes; you may still be pleasantly surprised.

Sort through your crops in storage from time to time, removing any bad or mushy tubers. If you know from local knowledge that blight is prevalent in your area, choose a newly developed, blight-resistant variety.

Checking out blight-resistant varieties

Crop failure due to blight has always been a problem. You can take advantage of years of research into blight resistance, however, by choosing these main crop varieties.

- ✔ **Sarpo Mira:** A red floury-fleshed potato that's good for roasting and baking
- ✔ **Sarpo Axona:** Floury but with uniform tubers; good for roasting and baking

Looking at the new and the old – the best of both worlds

Watch out for new blight-resistant potato varieties coming onto the scene – the research is ongoing; with the advantage of disease resistance comes the disadvantage of a less flavoursome spud than some of the older varieties, but perhaps plant breeders can overcome this problem in time.

Mix and match in your patch to get the best of both worlds. The season may turn out to be perfect for growing, with bumper yields and no blight-inducing, muggy, damp weather, or your potato growing venture may be 'blighted' from the start – it's a grower's gamble!

Radish

People usually treat radish as a fast-growing summer salad crop, but if you love the taste of radish or want to be able to add interest and colour to your winter dishes, you can pack them into boxes of sand or compost, trimming off the bulk of the foliage first, and keep them in a cool, dark place. (Chapter 4 gives further advice on this cool way to keep yourself in interesting radishes throughout the winter months.) For storing, choose varieties that crop best later in the season.

For autumn and winter use, choose varieties such as China Rose – long rose-pink roots with pure white flesh ready to be harvested in autumn – or Black Spanish Round, a black-skinned round root with white flesh.

Radishes respond well to being stored in a clamp too (see Chapter 4 again) but unless you've an army to feed you're unlikely to find this method necessary.

Winter radishes may surprise you with their size, if you're only used to the marble-sized summer varieties.

Radish Pickle

If creating interesting winter salads is on your 'to do' list, add this little number to your armoury. As a vegetable on its own, the radish is probably a bit too acidic for most people's tastes so mix into *coleslaw* – shredded cabbage salad – with some crushed nuts. There, it lifts the flavour and adds interest with a splash of colour too, if you choose the right variety. Check out Chapter 3 for options on sterilising containers.

Special tools required: *Sterilised jars with noncorrosive glass or plastic-coated lids*

Preparation time: *20 minutes*

Processing time: *24-hour soaking*

Yield: *1 kilogram*

1 kilogram (2 pounds, 4 ounces) radishes of an autumn/winter variety

Dry salt to cover or brine made with 50 grams (2 ounces) salt dissolved in 600 millilitres (1 pint) water

600 millilitres (1 pint) vinegar

1 Scrub the skins clean.

2 Slice radishes into ½-centimetre- (¼ inch) thick rounds.

3 Layer with salt between or cover with made-up brine – make more brine to the same strength if you need to (find out more about brine in Chapter 6). Make sure that all the radish slices are under the liquid by holding them down with a plate.

4 Leave for 24 hours.

5 Rinse quickly and thoroughly. Pat dry with a paper towel and pack into sterile labelled jars.

6 Top up with vinegar covering all the radish slices.

7 Store for one month before use.

Per 100-gram serving: *18 calories; 0 grams protein, 4 grams carbohydrate, 0 grams fat, 0 grams saturated fat, 0 milligrams cholesterol, 1 gram fibre, 118 milligrams sodium.*

Salsify

If you like a change from the norm and appreciate delicate flavours, grow salsify (also called the oyster plant), boil and then serve with a knob of butter to bring out the best of flavours.

Sandwich Island is a variety with long, smooth, tapering roots and light-coloured skin that happily stays in the ground over the winter – the easiest way to store your roots until you want to eat them. If you can't leave the salsify crop over winter outside in the ground, dig up the long roots carefully, avoiding any damage for best results and choose the smoothest roots to store – they harbour fewest potential substances or creatures that may begin spoilage – then re-bury in boxes of sand or compost and keep in a cool dark place. Chapter 4 gives you the low-down on this type of storage.

Scorzonera

Scorzonera is a similar root to salsify but with black skin (see the preceding section on salsify for advice on storing scorzonera). This easy-to-grow vegetable has a variety called Long Black with excellent flavour and a good resistance to *bolting* (running to seed when you don't want it to).

Shallots

Shallots traditionally complete the year-round onion cycle. When the last of your beautifully stored golden onions are failing you by beginning to sprout in their sacks or on the strings – but before the overwintering red onion varieties are mature enough to use – the shallots are ready to pull.

Shallots are easy to grow. When choosing varieties, the French grow an elongated bulb called Longor, or you may prefer a rounder bulb called Red Sun. Keep a few of your favourite variety in frost-free conditions. Break off the bulbs and plant them the following year for another round of these versatile plants.

Use them like onions in everyday cooking and for pickling – use straight from the ground or allow to dry in the warm summer air for a day or two before stringing. (The earlier section 'Onions' gives instructions for a simple method of onion stringing and a pickling recipe that you can also use for shallots.)

Swede

Swede is a staple of the winter months, a round, bulbous root (actually a swollen stem, not a true root), often with a purple tinge to the top and yellow flesh. Choose the variety Joan if you like an early crop and pull them small. For a later crop to store, use a variety such as Wilhelmsburger; with its firm yellow flesh, it grows well in a chemical-free garden.

If your gardening plot is large enough, leave it in the growing spot until you want to use it, or if you have to make room for other crops pull the swede, twist off the majority of the green foliage and store in boxes of sand or compost. Larger quantities of swede also store well in a clamp (I describe building clamps in Chapter 4). If you like your vegetables sweet, leave swedes outdoors until after a good hard frost, which converts the starches to sugar.

Freeze chunks of washed and trimmed swede, and blanch for three minutes (Chapter 7 covers storing in the freezer). Swede is one of the best vegetables to add that special 'bite' to a chutney because it doesn't easily disintegrate during cooking.

Year Round Chutney

The 'waste not, want not' of chutneys, Year Round Chutney puts you totally in charge. Follow the basic recipe to get the proportions right and then experiment with the spiciness, or simply use it to mop up what's bountiful in your garden. Every variation has its special virtue. See Chapter 3 for ways to sterilise your jars. See Chapter 6 for more on making chutneys.

Special tools required: *Sterilised jars, muslin, noncorrosive lids*

Preparation time: *15 minutes*

Processing time: *1–2 hours cooking*

Yields: *2.5 kilograms*

600 millilitres (1 pint) pickling malt vinegar or vinegar of your choice

900 grams (2 pounds) skinned tomatoes or another 'mushy' fruit, such as marrow or gooseberry

2 medium onions (or equivalent), roughly chopped

450 grams (1 pound) cooking apples, peeled, cored and sliced

450 grams (1 pound) swede, trimmed, peeled and cut into 1-centimetre cubes

225 grams (8 ounces) raisins

225 grams (8 ounces) sugar, soft brown or another of your choice

5 millilitres (1 teaspoon) salt

Spice bag – a collection of tasty goodies to impart flavour only, with 4–6 whole peppercorns, 6–12 coriander seeds, 2–3 bay leaves, and 3–6 cloves or any other spice or flavouring of your choice

1 Clean the fruit and veg of any bruised parts. Top and tail gooseberries and scoop the seeds out of the marrow. Chop everything into chunks – 2.5-centimetre dices or less – or mince roughly for a smoother chutney.

2 Tie up your flavouring ingredients in a piece of muslin to make the spice bag and add to the cooking mixture. Taste your chutney from time to time during cooking and remove the spice bag when the right depth of flavour for you has been imparted – usually between 20 and 40 minutes.

3 Place all your ingredients in a large, heavy-bottomed saucepan and bring gently to the boil.

4 Allow to simmer, stirring now and again, for one to two hours or until the mixture is thick and pulpy with no 'spare' liquid lying on the top. The swede retains its shape while all the other ingredients reduce to a similar consistency.

5 The chutney is ready to spoon into sterilised jars and cap with glass or plastic-coated lids – avoiding reactions between the acid of the chutney and the metal in the lid.

6 Label and store for a minimum of two weeks, preferably one month, before using.

Tip: *Towards the end of cooking when the chutney is getting to the correct consistency, draw the wooden spoon through the chutney to part it, revealing the base of the pan.*

Per 30-gram serving: *26 calories; 0 grams protein, 6 grams carbohydrate, 0 grams fat, 0 grams saturated fat, 0 milligrams cholesterol, 0 grams fibre, 41 milligrams sodium.*

Swede are grown in the fields for sale as both human and animal food – you can see flocks of sheep nibbling on a crop of swede still growing in the fields, particularly in the dead of winter, proving that the hardy swede withstands staying in its growing position whatever the weather.

Some good country folk reckon that swedes fare better as a field crop, so if you've disappointing results in the garden keep your eyes open for nets of swedes being sold at farm gates, farmers' markets and farm shops. Buy a net of swedes – usually about 15–20 kilograms – and store them as if you've grown them yourself.

Hollering out at Hallowe'en

Where I come from in Scotland, people hollow out swedes ('neeps') to make Hallowe'en lanterns (using pumpkins is an American idea). Scraping out the insides with a spoon takes hours of hard work before the fun part: cutting out scary features and placing a candle inside. The lanterns last for at least a couple of weeks before collapsing in a shrivelled mess. I can still remember the smell of toasting swede and candle wax when the candle burned low and singed the flesh.

Turnip

Turnips have a peppery taste and are another of the swollen-stemmed, so-called roots. Golden Ball, a yellow-fleshed turnip, has the best storing qualities when re-burying in sand or compost to keep – Chapter 4 tells you more about this type of storage. Purple Top Milan is a commonly grown quick cropper you can use in the same way as swede in chutneys where it holds its texture – adapt the Year Round Chutney recipe from the preceding 'Swede' section by substituting turnips for swedes.

Coming Together Beautifully: Effective Food Combinations

Vegetables (and fruits) that are ready to be picked and preserved at the same time often make perfect combinations.

Onions, whose sweetness and flavour enhances chutneys and relishes, also boil down to an excellent consistency for spreading; or whiz them through a blender with a little more liquid to make a pourable sauce or ketchup. (Turn to Chapter 6 for more on the chutneys, relishes, sauces and ketchups.)

Root vegetables such as turnip and swede (as well as carrot) give bite to a preserve by retaining their shape and texture with cooking, even when you use young plants. Without doubt, the root family is a really important and versatile ingredient in many preserving mixes.

Summer Vegetable Pickle

Use this pickle right away or keep it – out of bright sunlight – as a winter treat to remind you of the early days of summer. The pickle is a good way to use carrot *thinnings* – plants removed from a growing row to create optimal spacing for the other plants to flourish. Chapter 3 has more on sterilisation.

Special tools required: *Sterilised jars*

Preparation time: *20 minutes*

Processing time: *15 minutes*

Yield: *1.3 kilograms (3 pounds)*

110 grams (4 ounces) celery, cut into bite-size pieces

110 grams (4 ounces) baby carrots, trimmed and cut lengthways

1 red onion, sliced into rings

110 grams (4 ounces) green beans, trimmed

110 grams (4 ounces) button mushrooms

225 grams (8 ounces) cherry tomatoes

110 grams (4 ounces) baby sweetcorn

600 millilitres (1 pint) distilled malt vinegar

150 grams (5 ounces) caster sugar

2 bay leaves

Salt and black pepper

30 millilitres (2 tablespoons) fresh dill, chopped – optional

90 millilitres (6 tablespoons) walnut oil

1 Place all the vegetables, except the tomatoes, in a large saucepan along with the vinegar, sugar and bay leaves.

2 Season with salt and pepper, bring to the boil and gently simmer for five minutes, and then remove from the heat.

3 Stir in the remaining ingredients carefully, trying not to break the cherry tomatoes.

4 Pack into warm, sterilised jars – seal, label and store.

Tip: *You can substitute with your own home-grown summer vegetables, the younger the better, up to 800 grams.*

Per 100-gram serving: *144 calories; 1 gram protein, 22 grams carbohydrate, 0 grams fat, 0 grams saturated fat, 0 milligrams cholesterol, 1 gram fibre, 73 milligrams sodium.*

Getting in a stew pack

Look in any freezer compartment for vegetables in the supermarket and you can see 'ready packs' of frozen vegetables just right for winter stews and soups. You can make these packs at home, adding your favourite vegetables. Of course, your home-grown vegetables are far superior to the pallid, over-packaged offerings from the shops, and you can make up your own delicious combinations.

Do a mass blanching – Chapter 7 shows you the steps to successful blanching and loose freezing. Pack up some individual root vegetables for special occasions and tumble together a mixture of carrot, swede, celeriac and onion for stew and soup packs. Just tip them into tasty stock with a handful of lentils for a quickly prepared winter meal.

The Big Three for a savoury meal are celery (substitute celeriac if you have it), carrot and onion. This mix goes with everything or even as a vegetable accompaniment in its own right. Pour a sauce – parsley, mustard or perhaps cheese – over *parboiled* (a quick 10–15 minute blast in water) veg, then bake in the oven in a heatproof dish until the vegetables are soft and the sauce is bubbling.

Unless you love parsnip with everything, make a few separate packs containing parsnip and label them well; its flavour can overpower the other vegetables.

Spicing up your life

Some combinations of root vegetables with spices, herbs or other staples go really well together. Try the following:

- **Carrot and coriander:** Together in the vegetable tureen or combined as a soup, is a perfect pairing. Use fresh coriander (the leaves stalks and stems all impart flavour) when available straight from the garden or from your stash in the freezer.

    Discover how to store your herbs, both leaf and seed, in Chapter 16 – or grind coriander seeds for a subtly different version of the same dish in winter.

- **Cheese, onion and potato:** These three go hand in hand in hand to make an inexpensive warming and filling meal, in pasties, pies, quiches or bakes.

- **Parsnip with curry flavours:** Check out the later section 'Parsnips' for a delicious spicy soup recipe.

- **Swede, potato, celeriac and carrot:** Mashed together and seasoned with salt and black pepper, these veg complement each other in both taste and colour as dishes to serve at the table.

Chapter 14

Making Room for Legumes: The Bean Harvest

*B*eans and peas are *legumes* – flowering plants with the fruit in the form of a pod – and, as far as children are concerned, among the most fun of vegetables. Peas act as great ammo for traditional pea-shooters or for finger-flicking across the dinner table towards Dad's startled face, and beans . . . well, the less said about the potential after-effects of eating (particularly baked) beans, the better (I promise no breaking wind puns in this chapter!).

In addition to their undoubted humorous possibilities, legumes have a secret natural property (that I describe in the later section 'Preserving something magical for future use'), which means that as well as preserving the fruits of beans and peas for feeding friends and family, you should also keep the roots of these plants after their growing season to preserve another kind of natural harvest, the kind that keeps you growing and growing. Read on to find out how.

Walking Through the Season with Legumes

Beans and peas need to have a plot of their own and are particularly useful in the context of your garden's crop rotation system (for the reasons I describe in the later section 'Preserving something magical for future use'). When you avoid the use of unnatural substances and compounds on your growing patch or allotment, and are doing your best to stay chemical-free in your food supply, a rotation helps the soil to stay fresh and disease-free. Moving the different types of plants from plot to plot in an organised manner gives the soil time to recover from feeding one plant and replaces the nutrients taken.

Such a rotation system helps enormously with the health and general wellbeing of your crops – and healthy crops store and preserve best – but you still need to feed your soil by spreading compost or animal or *green* manure (the latter is where certain growing plants add nutrients and are eventually incorporated into the soil or left on an empty patch to stop goodness leaching away in wet weather).

Different types of beans and peas have a natural progression through the growing season. If you have protected cropping areas, you can hurry things along for an early crop and extend the season well into autumn and cooler darker days, but for most gardeners growing on an outdoor plot a typical bean and pea calendar is as follows:

- ✔ **Broad beans, tall or dwarf, modern and heirloom (the later 'Broad beans' section describes some varieties):** Harvest these in May to July, or later if you plan to dry the beans for eating in stews and soups or save them as seed for further harvests. Harvest the edible podded varieties of peas or eat the young forming pods of any peas while they're tender and sweet.

- ✔ **French beans, climbing and dwarf (for varieties, flip to the later 'French beans' section):** Ready in June through to autumn with staggered sowings; leave beans on the stem for drying and seed-saving. The first peapods swell and ripen, producing delicious sweet, tiny peas.

- ✔ **Runner beans (for varieties, see the later 'Runner beans' section):** Ready in early August until frosts appear in late autumn. Leave beans on the stem for drying and seed-saving. Successional sowings of peas continue until adverse weather conditions cause mildew and rotting.

You can, of course, have all these varieties running side by side with careful sowing, as long as the weather's on your side. Late frosts and early droughts slow up the early crops and high winds can easily tear your wigwam of climbers out of the ground.

Cover your bases by doing a little of everything and *guying* (securing with twine) your tall crops down well.

Some people like to plant pots of beans and individual peas really early in the season under cover or on windowsills in the house (keeping them safe from frosts and marauding slugs) and then planting them out as seedlings after a little toughening up. Staggering plantings of peas and beans makes life less fraught in the picking season, which can extend from early June and into September depending on the variety you choose.

Making the most of freshness

Surely one of the most fantastic treats for any gardener is your first boiling of tender young broad beans in spring: don't try to preserve these, just get on and enjoy them fresh. The same applies to the first of the French and runner beans as well as your first pea of the summer (sorry about that, but I only promised no breaking-wind puns!): eat fresh or add some of your tiny tender beans into a Summer Vegetable Pickle (you can find the recipe in Chapter 13).

After the first thrill is over and the beans just keep coming – regular picking encourages new flowers, which in turn produce more beans – considering how you keep the rest of the harvest to enjoy throughout the coming year is the next challenge (the subject of the later section 'Creating a Scene with Peas and Beans').

Preserving something magical for future use

Something special applies to your bean and pea harvest that you need to consider. Beans and peas are nitrogen-fixing plants: in conjunction with other natural organisms – study a root and you spot tiny white bobbles that house friendly working bacteria – they take nitrogen from the air and convert it into a usable plant food. This combination of legume and bacteria-making nitrogen is a different kind of harvest from the edible one, and is well worth preserving; after all, you have to feed your growing plot somehow. Instead of spending money at a garden centre buying an expensive bag of chemically prepared nitrogen fertiliser, though, try feeding your hungry soil for free.

To do so, when picking your last bean and pea fruit and clearing your plot, cut the stems off near the ground and leave the roots in the earth to decompose naturally, thus providing a free feed of nitrogen to the next set of plants in your garden rotation.

Creating a Scene with Peas and Beans

Salting-down beans (I cover preserving with salt in Chapter 8) used to be common practice and certainly preserves your harvest, but the taste is rather harsh for modern tastes. Modern freezers do a better job (check out Chapter 7 for more). Try fast-freezing dry, whole broad beans and peas, or blanching (for two minutes) prepared French and runner beans.

Salting is useful as part of the pickling process. A few hours in salt – reducing the water content and the possibility of diluting the pickling vinegar to unsafe levels – and then into a jar of vinegar makes good sense if you want to preserve beans for your winter stews and curries. Chapter 6 gives hints on preserving with vinegar.

If you do want to give salting beans a go and experience what your ancestors ate, use French or runner beans and 1 kilogram (2 pounds, 4 ounces) of salt for every 3 kilograms (6 pounds, 12 ounces) of beans:

1. **Wash your beans, and leave whole.**

2. **Pack into a glass or ceramic jar, starting with a layer of salt and then beans, finishing with salt and a weight of some sort on top of a plate to hold the beans down.**

3. **Check your salted beans after a few days, topping up with more beans and salt.**

The resulting strong brine preserves your beans for up to a year, by which time you should have a new crop anyway. Remove the beans you need at any time and soak for an hour in warm water before preparing as you like and simmering them in unsalted water until tender. You may find that salted beans are to your taste, and one great advantage applies: the process involves no electricity, whereas freezer food is vulnerable to breakdown and power failure.

Broad beans

Start off with a late autumn sowing for the earliest broad beans the following spring: choose Super Aquadulce or Supersimonia varieties, saving some seeds for spring sowings too, extending your broad bean harvest into July. Even if your growing space is small, you needn't miss out on broad beans: Sutton is a dwarf variety especially for you. Heirloom varieties of broad beans may not be as sweet as modern varieties for eating fresh but, staying small in the pod, they're excellent for drying and rehydrating in stews or as a meal in themselves (see the later 'Heirloom varieties' section for more info).

You can eat the whole pod of any bean type with the bean inside when tiny and nip the tops off the growing plant, using it as a fresh green vegetable. Alternatively, wait until the beans have swollen in the pods – you see the shape of the bean from the outside of the pod – and open the thick, padded outer pod to reveal the squat or 'broad' bean.

To be taken with a pinch of salt

A traditional folklore remedy says that if you rub the pithy inside of a broad-bean pod onto a wart, and then hide the piece you use in a secret place (allowing no one else to see it), your wart disappears as the broad bean skin rots away. A useful tip for all witches who prefer to stay anonymous!

Storing broad beans

Broad beans are the basis for some great vegetarian meals. You can have a protein-packed and filling meal ready in no time from frozen beans: simply blanch for one to two minutes and open freeze (Chapter 7 outlines blanching and open freezing for you) and you can then keep the beans frozen for more than six months.

The less time between picking and freezing, the better, otherwise starches begin to form, changing the sweet flavour. For a quick no-blanching method, just pop dry, freshly picked broad beans into a bag in a good freezer at –18 degrees Celsius. As long as the broad beans are dry when frozen, they don't stick together; rattle the bag once or twice to keep them separate.

Broad beans respond particularly well to drying (a cost-effective method of storage that involves no electricity) when dry and bagged up (as long as you keep them out of bright sunlight and away from nibbling pests – Chapter 8 has plenty of suggestions for successful drying and Chapter 3 helps with pesky pest-spotting).

Pick your beans while young and tender (the beans, that is, not you!) or, if you want to dry some for seed-saving. Yes, you needn't buy bean seeds ever again, just leave a few plants standing while the bean pods mature. When the plant begins to die back naturally, pick the pods and dry them. You can remove the beans from the shrivelled-up pods at a later stage. Rehydrate the beans in water overnight before using in the dish of your choice.

Snacking on broad beans

Among the snack packs available to buy, you can find a broad-bean treat. Make your own version of this Spanish-snacking treat by drying and lightly roasting your home-grown broad beans. With your fingers, crumble off the outer shell, breaking each bean into two perfect pieces. Sprinkle with salt (and tasty spices for a posher version) and you've your very own Habas Fritas.

Broad Bean Hummus

Ideally, you pick your broad beans when they're young and tender, but sometimes you can't keep up with the growth and the beans grow large and the skins or shells become tough and unpalatable. This recipe makes use of those overgrown beans in a delicious way with a hummus-style spread for tasty dips (or if you prefer to keep it more solid, call it Broad Bean Pâté) for spreading on crusty bread. Keep the result plain or add your favourite garlic and herby flavours. Beans are high in protein, making this recipe a valuably nutritious part of a vegetarian meal.

Preparation time: *15 minutes*

Processing time: *15–20 minutes with use of a food processor; longer by hand*

Yield: *450 grams (1 pound)*

450 grams (1 pound) large, overgrown broad beans	*2–3 Garlic cloves, up to 30 millilitres (2 tablespoons) dried mint, rosemary and/or flavours of your choice*
Lemon juice to taste	
Coarse sea salt	*Olive oil (to your preferred consistency) 15–30 millilitres (2–3 tablespoons) for thick, 60–90 millilitres (4–6 tablespoons) for runny*

1 Boil the broad beans for five to six minutes or until the outer shell splits. Allow to cool to an easy handling temperature. Pop them out of their shells, discarding the skins.

2 Place the beans into a food processor, with a squeeze (or more) of lemon juice and a grinding of sea salt, adding any more flavours – garlic, herbs and so on – that you like. Pulse in the food processor, trickling in a fine line of olive oil. When you reach the consistency, as stiff or runny as you like, taste and adjust the seasoning.

3 Press or pour into ramekins or small containers to freeze (but see the warning at the end of the recipe). Eat straight away or store in the fridge for up to four to five days. If you don't have a food processor, use a vegetable masher or push the mixture through a sieve; it takes a bit longer but you end up with the same result while working up an appetite!

Warning: *Using frozen broad beans is fine – label the overgrown ones as such in the freezer so that you know which to defrost – but don't refreeze your homemade hummus or pâté because the cooking time is too short. Store in the fridge and use up within four or five days. See Chapter 7 for more on freezing.*

Vary it! *Adapt this recipe by substituting your own home-dried beans. Soak them overnight and simmer until soft and the skins are beginning to split when you remove them from the water and blow on them (sometimes this process takes as long as 40 minutes).*

Per 30-gram serving: *31 calories; 2 grams protein, 4 grams carbohydrate, 1 grams fat, 0 grams saturated fat, 0 milligrams cholesterol, 2 grams fibre,53 milligrams sodium.*

French beans

French beans present you with a choice, depending on your gardening space: you can make frames or 'wigwams' from beanpoles or bamboo canes and grow the climbing varieties of French beans upwards. Try the Barlotto di Fuoco variety, which picks well as a young tender bean or leave it to mature for drying beans and seed-saving (Chapter 8 contains helpful drying tips). Alternatively, plant a more compact dwarf variety if space is in short supply: the stringless Tendergreen's reputation aligns with its name, and is probably best for freezing; or go for colour with Helios for a yellow bean or the climbing Blauhilde for a purple pod.

For two more options for preserving your French bean harvest, nip along to the later 'Runner beans' section for a bean chutney recipe or read about old-fashioned salting in the introduction to this section.

Freeze French beans whole or cut up, whichever you prefer, but do blanch them for the best results (you can find the blanching method explained in Chapter 7). Blanch for two minutes and cook from frozen for five minutes or until they've the 'bite' you enjoy.

Leaving the plants to mature for drying beans works with all French beans.

Baked Beans

Use your own dried French beans or any others you like (try the classic Cannellino variety) for your own unique version of the classic accompaniment to your bangers, or on its own as a high-protein dish (to use straight away or freeze in family meal- size portions). In fact, you don't bake the beans at all. This recipe is one of many for baked beans: experiment until you find the version you most enjoy.

Preparation time: *Soaking time and 15 minutes*

Processing time: *1½ hours*

Yield: *500 grams (1 pound, 2 ounces)*

400 grams (14 ounces) home-dried beans

30 millilitres (2 tablespoons) olive oil

1 large onion

2 stalks of celery

1–2 garlic cloves

150 millilitres (¼ pint) white wine vinegar or water

1 red pepper

400 grams (14 ounces – a tin) of tomatoes or equivalent home-grown, skinned

Herb bundle: thyme, sage, a couple of sprigs and 2 or 3 bay leaves

Seasoning to taste

1 Soak the beans in cold water overnight. Drain and refresh the water, simmering for 45 minutes; drain again.

2 While the beans are simmering, heat the oil in a heavy-bottomed pan and fry the finely chopped onion, celery, pepper and crushed garlic for five to ten minutes until translucent. Add the remaining ingredients except the beans and simmer uncovered for 45 minutes to reduce.

3 Add the beans for a last 15 minutes of cooking. Remove the herb bundle and discard. Eat straight away or freeze in meal-sized portions (see Chapter 7 for freezing info) and use up within a year. On thawing, heat thoroughly until piping hot before eating.

Tip: *If you like a smooth sauce, allow to cool slightly and liquidise before adding in the beans, and then cook for a further 15 minutes.*

Per 100-gram serving: *355 calories; 19 grams protein, 58 grams carbohydrate, 7 grams fat, 1 gram saturated fat, 0 milligrams cholesterol, 22 grams fibre, 41 milligrams sodium.*

Heirloom varieties

As a gardener, you've the power to keep unusual varieties alive and kicking. Plant varieties are in just as much danger of going extinct as animal species. Seed companies always go for the safe option – their business depends on it – but human ancestors grew a much wider range of plants, especially beans and peas, some as stunning for their flowers as the edible part. Old-fashioned gardeners always saved seeds, and you can too; after all, the plant is willing its offspring to last another season and helps out as much as it can.

Heirloom varieties are usually easy to dry, given the right conditions, and are an excellent form of protein (they arose before freezers or meat-eating were everyday luxuries). Add them to stews and soups or make *cassoulets* (meat and bean mix casseroles).

You aren't going to find many heirloom varieties in a normal seed catalogue. Instead, seek them out at local plant sales, gardening clubs and seed swaps to help keep your heritage alive. Here are a few varieties to look out for, but loads more are available:

- ✔ **Cocoa Bicolour:** This French climbing bean needs a good summer but is an excellent drying bean. It has a great taste (and is attractive to look at) and makes a good hummus (see the recipe in the earlier 'Broad beans' section).

- ✔ **Czar:** This runner bean is good for drying and eating green; this bean is hardy and prolific even in wetter summers.

✔ **Hunter:** This French climbing bean is nice as a green bean but excellent as a dried *haricot* type too – that's the type you may recognise from a tin of baked beans.

✔ **Martock:** This broad bean is a medieval drying variety, which grows up to 1.7 metres (5 feet) tall and usually needs support while growing.

Mangetout peas: Edible podded peas

With mangetout, you eat the whole pod including the immature pea. Mangetout are best eaten fresh with a little butter but also freeze well: blanch for one minute. Add into the Summer Vegetable Pickle or Year Round Chutney recipes in Chapter 13.

Sugar Snap is probably the best-known variety, producing podding peas if left to grow; but do have a go at eating any immature peapod; most are delicious. To save seeds, leave the pods to grow on to maturity before drying (Chapter 8 has all about preserving through drying).

Peas

One of the UK's favourite veggies: people eat more frozen peas than any other frozen vegetable, hence the number of varieties available. The sweetness of a pea deteriorates from the moment you pick it, so plan your picking carefully. If you want to preserve the peas, get on with the whole job quickly: picking, podding and preserving within an hour or two. Blanching is an option but not necessary. Dry peas don't stick together so keep a sturdy bag in the freezer and top it up with freshly picked and podded peas.

Pickle peas and beans by salting for an hour before washing, drying and adding vinegar. Although perhaps not suitable as a standalone vegetable, you can easily add the result to winter soups and stews. Check the saltiness of any dishes using these as ingredients *before* adding extra salt.

Pea varieties for an early crop include Kelvedon Wonder (a wrinkle- seeded pea) and Progress No 9. Maincrop varieties worth noting are Greenshaft (a heavy cropper), Onward (a popular pea), Petit Pois (small and sweet, and an excellent freezing pea) and Rondo (which matures late but grows a heavy crop of long, dark-green pods with excellent taste). Sow in successional batches (in other words, leave two weeks between each planting) to keep the harvesting under control.

Peas with wrinkled seeds are sweetest, so check out that attribute if sweetness is high on your list of priorities. A good catalogue differentiates between wrinkle and round-seeded varieties, and can advise you when you order.

Peapod Wine

You need waste nothing from your pea harvest: use peas for eating, the roots of the plant for producing fertility and the peapods for wine with this recipe. Don't worry if your peapods turn yellow in the *must* (the flavoured liquid making the wine's taste) before you discard them. The wine develops a good flavour in six months or keeps much longer (turn to Chapter 9 for an explanation of wine-making terms and equipment in this recipe).

 Wine-making is an art rather than an exact science, and so all the preparation and processing times for this recipe are necessarily approximate and you need to be flexible. *Home Winemaking For Dummies* by Tim Patterson (Wiley) gives loads more information. See Chapter 3 for more on sterilisation.

Specialist tools required: *Demijohn, sterile bottles*

Preparation time: *1 hour plus 24 hours soaking time and fermenting time and so on*

Processing time: *Fermentation until clear and racking*

Yield: *Approximately 4.5 litres (8 pints –1 gallon)*

2 kilograms (4 pounds, 8 ounces) peapods (use the peas elsewhere)

250 grams (9 ounces) raisins

Juice of 2 lemons

1.25 kilograms (2 pounds, 12 ounces) granulated sugar

1 sachet of wine yeast (from a brewing shop)

1 Chop up the fresh peapods and place in a large, clean container, adding in 3.4 litres (6 pints) of boiling water, the raisins, the lemon juice and sugar. Stir to dissolve the sugar and leave to cool.

2 Top up to 4.5 litres (8 pints – 1 gallon), leaving to stand for 24 hours. Add the yeast, following the instructions on the packet, leaving the must (the basic wine flavouring) to ferment for approximately one week or until rapid fermentation slows.

3 Strain into a *demijohn* (a special glass fermentation vessel) and cork with a fermentation lock. This enables gasses to escape without letting anything back into the demijohn. When *fermentation* (creating alcohol and carbon dioxide) ceases and the wine clears – be patient, because this clearing may take as long as four months – *rack* (that is, siphon) into sterile bottles, seal, label and store in a cool, dark place for six months to mature before drinking, or leave for up to two years.

Per 100-millilitre serving: 361 calories; 4 grams protein, 88 grams carbohydrate, 0 grams fat, 0 grams saturated fat, 0 milligrams cholesterol, 0 grams fibre, 9 milligrams sodium. Analysis is approximate.

Runner beans

Runner beans, originally grown only for their flowers, are the last in the season to start producing long bean pods for eating, giving you a wonderful show of flowers along the way. Picking the pods at a young and tender stage encourages further growth and a heavier crop; some runner beans go stringy at a later stage although plant breeders are reducing this trait all the time.

Buy seeds to start you off, leaving some bean pods maturing on the plant for seed-saving, which is a really easy, thrifty way to perpetuate your home-grown produce.

When the leaves of the plant begin to die back, take your now swollen pods into a dry environment and let the whole pod dry out and shrivel up. The bean inside retains its shiny outer cover, ranging in colour and size according to the variety, from a large pink-grey mottled affair to a slimmer white seed.

Freeze after slicing and blanch for two minutes, or try old-fashioned salting as I describe at the beginning of this section.

If you're still deciding which runner beans to plant, choose the Enorma variety for heavy cropping: it comes with a good reputation from commercial and home growers. Or go for a traditional white variety in White Emergo. For small areas and containers, the dwarf variety Hestia does the trick (it needs no support). Whatever you choose, think about seed-swapping at a Seedy Sunday celebration (Chapter 21 lets you into the secret of getting your hands on a huge range of free seeds, many of which you never see in a catalogue).

Runner Bean (or French Bean) Chutney

If your runner beans are productive, you really know it! Pick them before they get too old and pass handfuls around to friends and family, but make sure that you keep enough to make this sweet, yellow chutney. The recipe uses turmeric and dry English mustard powder for the straightforward version; or swap the mustard for more adventurous spices when you're feeling more confident with your chutney-making (see Chapter 3 for more on sterilisation and Chapter 6 for more on making chutneys). Go on, spice up your life!

Special tools required: *Sterilised jars*

Preparation time: *30–40 minutes*

Processing time: *45 minutes*

Yield: *2.7 kilograms (6 pounds)*

1.8 kilograms (4 pounds) beans prepared	*25 millilitres (1½ tablespoons) turmeric*
4 or 5 large onions	*25 millilitres (1½ tablespoons) mustard powder*
Pinch of salt	*30 millilitres (2 tablespoons) cornflour*
675 grams (1½ pounds) Demerara sugar	*850 millilitres (1½ pints) malt vinegar*

1 Prepare the beans as you prefer, topping and tailing and removing any stringy bits. Mince the beans for a pulpier chutney and chop them up for a chunkier version. Chop the onions finely if you're mincing the beans.

2 Put the beans and onions into a large pan, cover with water, add a pinch of salt and boil for around 15 minutes or until the beans and onions are soft. Strain through a colander, discarding the water, and transfer the beans to a large, heavy-bottomed preserving pan.

3 Add in the sugar and most of the vinegar, retaining about 150 millilitres (¼ pint) vinegar in a bowl or jug. Stir the bean mixture over a gentle heat until all the sugar dissolves, and then increase the heat to simmering point. Simmer for 15 minutes. Meanwhile add the turmeric, mustard powder and cornflour to the remaining vinegar, mixing to a smooth paste.

4 Add your paste into the boiling mix, stirring heartily to amalgamate. Continue to stir until the mixture thickens and a wooden spoon drawn across the base of the pan leaves a clear line. Pot up into warm, sterile jars, seal and label when cool. Store in a cool, dark place leaving for at least one month for the flavours to mellow before using up within a year.

Tip: *This recipe is also good for French beans. The chutney is meant to be sweet, but can stand reducing the sugar by one third for less sweet teeth.*

Vary it! *At Step 3, you may prefer to leave out the mustard powder and produce a livelier sort of chutney as follows: using a pestle and mortar, grind 5 millilitres (1 teaspoon) Fenugreek and 5 millilitres (1 teaspoon) mace blades together adding in 5 millilitres (1 teaspoon) asafoetida (smell it first before committing; asafoetida is a unique flavour), 5 millilitres (1 teaspoon) paprika and the tip of a teaspoon of cayenne pepper. Just mix this assortment into your paste in the same way.*

Per 30-gram serving: *45 calories; 1 gram protein, 11 grams carbohydrate, 0 grams fat, 0 grams saturated fat, 0 milligrams cholesterol, 1 gram fibre, 10 milligrams sodium.*

Chapter 15

Harvesting the Best of the Rest

In This Chapter

▶ Maxing out with marrows and squashes

▶ Going with the green stuff

▶ Returning again and again to the same plot

Although I cover orchard fruits, berries, fruiting vegetables, roots and beans in their own chapters (check out Chapters 10–14 respectively), plenty of plants you can grow in your garden or allotment simply refuse to play ball and fit into neat categories. So this chapter scoops up the best of the rest into one convenient chapter.

Perhaps you've a glut of fantastic oddball squashes to contend with, or you're hankering after vitamin-rich cabbage every day all year round, or you need help with controlling the perennials that keep coming back each year. If so, read through this chapter: marrow, leeks, cabbages and asparagus are just a page or two away.

Squashing in Your Vegetables

Generally speaking, squashes divide into summer (soft skins) and winter (tougher skins) varieties, although some crossover applies where the boundary is vague. Be aware that all squash types, especially winter ones, take up a lot of space on your plot and like a good, compost-rich soil to thrive.

Planting two or three squash plants on the compost heap, thus keeping them out of the vegetable plot, is common practice.

Carrying on with courgettes

Courgettes now come in shapes from the traditional, long, green gherkin copycat variety, Nero di Milan, to tiny round tennis balls, Rondo di Nizza, and all shades of green and yellow, and in stripes. Patty Pan squashes (a flying saucer shape) come in cream, Custard White variety, yellow and green. Pick these squashes when small and tender with soft, edible skin, and use them straight away (although some scope for pickling exists – see Chapter 12 for the Pickled Gherkin recipe with or without the addition of onions or incorporate crisp-fleshed baby squashes in the Summer Vegetable Pickle recipe in Chapter 13).

Allow your courgettes to grow to full size, because you then have a marrow and (as with the Patty Pan types) unblemished specimens, with careful frost-free storage, last well into the new year – almost rivalling the true winter squash.

Making the most of marrows

Your marrow harvest starts with a few delicate, tiny courgettes, but turn your back for a day or two and a secret spurt of growth turns that courgette to a marrow easily reaching 4 kilograms (9 pounds) or more. Fortunately, you've loads of options for this bulky vegetable (turn to Chapter 13 for the Year Round Chutney Recipe or try one of the following preserves).

Several recipes in this chapter require the use of preserving pans (I discuss equipment in Chapter 2) and sterilised jars (I cover sterilising in Chapter 3). And don't forget that Chapter 7 has loads more information on all aspects of freezing.

Marrow and Ginger Jam

If the quantity of marrow you produce daunts you, this recipe chomps its way through some of that marrow bulk, leaving you with a delicious jam in its wake. The ginger and lemon add a zingy flavour to what can otherwise be a dull affair. See Chapter 3 for more on sterilisation.

Special tools required: *Sterilised jars*

Preparation time: *45 minutes*

Processing time: *About 1 hour*

Yield: *4.5 kilograms (10 pounds)*

2.7 kilograms (6 pounds) diced marrow flesh

Juice and grated zest of 4 lemons (preferably unwaxed)

350 grams (12 ounces) crystallised ginger for a chunky version or 25 grams (1 ounce) ground

dried ginger for the taste without the lumpy bits

2.7 kilograms (6 pounds) granulated sugar

1 Peel, de-seed and dice your marrow, placing it in a large, heavy-bottomed preserving pan; pour on a little cold water (just enough to stop the marrow sticking). Bring to the boil, simmering for about 20 minutes or until tender.

2 Drain thoroughly through a colander, returning it to the pan to mash the flesh, adding the juice and grated zest of lemons and the chopped crystallised (or ground) ginger. Re-heat until boiling, remove from the heat, add the sugar and stir until the sugar dissolves.

3 Place the pan on the heat again, boiling until the jam reaches the setting point – Chapter 5 gives options for testing for set. Pot into warm, sterilised jars: seal, label when cool and store in a cool, dark place.

Tip: *If you prefer, steam the diced marrow until tender as a first stage.*

Per 100-gram serving: *270 calories; 1 gram protein, 69 grams carbohydrate, 0 grams fat, 0 grams saturated fat, 0 milligrams cholesterol, 1 gram fibre, 5 milligrams sodium.*

Wondering at the variety of squashes

Commonly, winter squashes are grown especially for their brilliant storage qualities, which is where the Halloween pumpkin (just one of the many varieties of squash) fits in. Leave these varieties on the plant until you fear a frost is coming and then bring them inside.

Winter squash skins harden up, protecting the edible flesh inside. Take this feature to the extreme and you have ornamental gourds, no good for eating but great for making a drum or an unusual vegetable display that lasts forever.

Keep all your squashes in frost-free conditions; they store well as follows:

✔ Hung up in nets in airy sheds

✔ Placed in a cool, dry larder in the house

✔ Sitting on a high shelf

✔ Stored in the garage away from strong-smelling products

You can choose from plenty of pumpkin varieties if you feel adventurous. Look out for transplants (well-grown seedlings) at plant sales or garden centres and ring the changes with a variety or plan with friends to share packets of seeds around (you don't need ten of the same plant unless you plan to feed an army!). Here are just three really tasty pumpkin varieties:

- ✔ **Big Max:** If you're of a competitive nature, try winning a giant pumpkin competition with this smooth-skinned beast. Fruits grow up to 50 kilograms (110 pounds). Even if you don't win, eating the tasty result isn't a problem; just ask friends to help you out.

- ✔ **Jack Be Little:** At the other end of the size scale is this small fruit (tennis-ball-sized when mature); eat them whole, roasted and stuffed.

- ✔ **Jack O' Lantern:** This pumpkin is the perfect Halloween pumpkin; medium-sized and just right for carving into scary faces.

If pumpkins aren't your thing try:

- ✔ **Cobnut:** A really tasty, early maturing butternut type squash.

- ✔ **Green Hokkaido:** A dry, nutty flavour, storing very well through to February from a September harvest.

- ✔ **Fictor F1:** Shaped like an orange onion, Fictor F1 is high yielding and easy to grow and store.

- ✔ **Turk's Turban:** Produces striking fruits matching the exotic name; fantastic to look at but also delicious to eat.

- ✔ **Vegetable Spaghetti:** A true gluten-free spaghetti; boil or bake and fork out the flesh (it comes away in long, spaghetti-like strings).

At any time during your storage period, deal with these squashes simply by de-seeding and slicing into sections that look just like a cheerful 'smile', drizzling with a generous helping of olive oil, crushed garlic and seasoning. Roast for about 30–40 minutes, or until tender, uncovered in a moderate oven at 180 degrees Celsius (350 degrees Fahrenheit/Gas Mark 4) to bring out the sweetness. Cook extra and use this sweet caramelised roast squash in soups and chutneys (see the Year Round Chutney recipe in Chapter 13) or open-freeze the roast flesh cut from the skin (Chapter 7 has the low-down on freezing).

Squash plants can grow enormous, snaking their way through your plot. Some like to climb too, so plant them where you have room or can control them before they invade your neighbours' properties.

Don't save those squash seeds

All squashes pollinate with each other, whatever the variety, so leave seed saving to the professional plant breeders. They know exactly how to produce a consistent variety.

F1 varieties (where the *F* stands for 'filial' and *1* for a first cross) are a cross between two distinct parent strains giving exceptional hybrid vigour. Don't bother saving seeds to regrow from any F1 variety, because they won't reproduce truly.

Snacking on seeds

Every time you cut open a winter squash, you de-seed it before using the flesh; but don't waste this precious seedy harvest – simply spread the seeds out in a warm, dry place. The *kernel* (inside the seed) is edible and high in natural oils.

Although peeling the seeds can be a bit fiddly, a handful makes a tasty snack that occupies children for hours. (If you grow sunflowers, add them into your snack pack too.) If you're patient enough to peel a sufficient quantity, fry them briefly in a dry frying pan to bring out a really toasty, nutty flavour.

Don't try to save the seeds for next year or to give away at a Seedy Sunday event (which I describe in Chapter 21) because you won't be successful. (If you're curious why, see the sidebar 'Don't save those squash seeds'.)

If the fiddly seed-peeling is too much for you, simply fill a wild bird feeder and give the birds a tasty meal. Birds are more than happy to crack open the outer casing of the seed with their purpose-built beaks.

Going Green in Your Cabbage Patch

Every gardener needs a cabbage patch or, to be more accurate, a brassica bed full of exciting plants that are good for your health in their *crop rotation* (a way of enhancing crop health and vigour by growing different plants in different areas; Chapter 1 has more details on how to rotate your crops). Vitamins and iron supplies are plentiful in all dark green crops (Popeye's reputation goes before him).

Our ancestors and their domestic farm animals ate cabbage throughout the winters, and the veg has been the staple diet of millions of dreary dinners down the ages; but modern greenery is different. Years of work by plant breeders has resulted in a huge range of varieties and different tastes, textures and qualities. The dark greens have had a total makeover out of the dreary into the spectacular. Your winter dinners need never be dull again with this section's variations on a theme.

Keep most of these plants in the ground all through the winter months; if space is an issue (or you simply need your vegetables closer to hand), keep some in the root cellar (something I describe in Chapter 4) or freeze to store (check out Chapter 7). Pickle- and relish-making options throughout this section give you even more preserving ideas.

Broccoli and calabrese

Broccoli and calabrese are often confused, so it seems sensible to bring them together here – what's in a name when the taste stays the same and is just as delicious! The Purple Sprouting Broccoli variety is true to its name and one of the first spring plants in the garden (it deserves all the accolades traditionally attributed to asparagus; see the later 'Asparagus' section). Harvest early, from March onwards to summer, to enjoy a fresh, succulent crop that can be a pretty addition to your Summer Vegetable Pickle (find the recipe in Chapter 13). Choose a White Sprouting variety for an even earlier crop.

The broccoli that looks like the miniature green trees that children draw is in fact calabrese. The Green Sprouting variety gives a long cropping period from August onwards, and the more you pick, the more the plant produces – regular picking extends the cropping period considerably. A really popular and fascinating-looking calabrese variety is Romanesco, forming spiralling, pyramid-shaped, yellow-green heads with a pattern that repeats itself in a smaller and larger versions; this geometric beauty doesn't detract from its superb flavour at all. Use this variety (or any other sturdy, crisp calabrese you grow) wherever you normally use cauliflower and definitely as part of an exotic version of piccalilli (see the recipe in the section 'Cauliflower', later in this chapter).

Freeze by blanching for one to three minutes, depending on the thickness of the stalks you harvest, and then open-freeze (Chapter 7 has all the necessary info on these techniques).

Stirring up some sprouts

Apart from eating Brussels sprouts as a vegetable in its own right, particularly at Christmas, I hadn't much use for them until a friend came to stay and picked sprouts fresh from the garden and made a simple stir-fry with bacon and the sprouts chopped into quarters. The result really changed my mind about sprouts, which have a tangy, nutty taste cooked in this manner. Now sprouts go into all my stir-frys!

Brussels sprouts

A new fashion for selling fresh Brussels sprouts is to harvest them still attached to the stalk. This approach works well for the newer F1 hybrids where all the sprouts mature at once (such as Nautic F1 for an early season variety or Doric F1 for Christmas lunch), but traditional varieties (such as Darkmar or Evesham Special) produce their 'buttons' over a period of time so need a different harvesting approach. Pick as soon as they produce tight buttons of Brussels sprouts, working your way up the stem, and soon more buttons mature on the same plant – don't forget to nip out the top when you get there and eat that too.

Look out for a red variety such as Rubine for adding dots of colour to a Brussels sprout dish.

To freeze, picking when small and removing any looser outer leaves gives the best results. Blanche for two minutes before cooling and open-freeze (flip to Chapter 7 for the freezing low-down).

Your F1s are likely to have mature sprouts at the same time as your traditional varieties. If freezing them all isn't your bag, uproot the whole plant and hang it in a frost-free shed; you can then continue to pick 'fresh' Brussels sprouts for several weeks.

Cabbages

Cabbages come in a wide selection of varieties with differing characteristics and tastes. If you've the space in your growing plot and can keep the hungry caterpillars away, careful selection of cabbage plants provides fresh cabbage all year round. (Kale, which I describe in the later 'Kale' section, gives a similar eating and goodness experience.)

Cabbages require room to grow and flourish as well as being a hungry plant needing plenty of good compost or well-rotted manure to give you the best crop. Growing cabbages from seed is one possibility, but sometimes finding *seedlings* – small plants ready to transplant into their permanent growing spot – from garden centres, plant and garden sales and enthusiast groups or fellow gardeners is just as cost effective, especially if taking advantage of a wide variety of cabbage plants is your aim. If your growing space is limited and you need to remove plants to make space, cabbages do lend themselves to certain kinds of useful storage.

The information in your seed catalogue or on the back of the seed packet helps you to choose which cabbage varieties take you round the seasons. If you need a little help working out where to start, consult Table 15-1 for ideas, bearing in mind that the list is by no means exhaustive. Look carefully at the harvesting times, taking into consideration whether you can leave your crops in the ground, need to find another place to store them or want to pickle some.

The harder and tighter the cabbage leaves wrap up, the longer the cabbage keeps when cut; harvest on a dry day if possible, removing the outer and damaged leaves. Store cut cabbage heads in a root cellar (see Chapter 4 for more information) and snuggle the cabbages in a cool, dry place nestled in dry straw or in shredded paper in crates with an insulating but breathable covering. (Tight-headed cabbages keep throughout the winter in this way.)

When you uncover your cabbage, don't despair if a furry mould has grown over it – a natural protective fungal growth. Just chop off a portion of the stem, unfurling the scruffy outer leaves to reveal a perfectly usable cabbage inside.

Table 15-1	Cabbage Varieties to Take You Around the Seasons	
Variety	*Harvest*	*Storage Information*
Hispi F1: Excellent variety with pointed heads; sow all year round	All year round	Stands and stores well
Minicole F1: Ideal for small gardens; regular, small oval heads	June–November	Stores in good conditions
Marner Laagerweiss: Large, strong growing white cabbage	July–October	Stands and stores well
Drago F1: High-quality, 1-kilogram ball-head cabbage	September–October	Stores in good conditions

Variety	Harvest	Storage Information
Impala F1: White, professional-quality cabbage	Up to late November	Stands and stores well
Dottenfelder: Large, firm, white winter cabbage; excellent for coleslaw	Up to mid-October	Stores very well
Holland Late Winter: White cabbage excellent for coleslaw and sauerkraut	Hardy winter	Stands and stores well
January King: Solid head with red tinge on outer leaves; very tasty winter cabbage	Hardy winter	Stands well
Marner Grufewi: Very frost- hardy, savoy- type cabbage with crinkly green leaves	Late autumn and winter	Stands well
Marner Lagerrot Red Cabbage: Medium-sized solid heads; good for Pickled Red Cabbage (see later recipe)	Up to autumn	Stores well, remove large outer leaves

Cabbage F1 varieties, like any other F1 varieties, aren't suitable for home seed-saving. (See why by looking at the earlier 'Don't save those squash seeds' sidebar.)

Red Pickled Cabbage

Use a tightly furled red variety of cabbage for the most traditional pickle, although the recipe is adaptable for any amount of cabbage, large or small, so feel free to experiment with white cabbage if you prefer. You lose the crunchiness after about three months so use up beforehand. Chapter 3 has more on sterilisation.

Special tools required: *Sterilised jars*

Preparation time: *20 minutes*

Processing time: *24 hours standing time*

Yield: *1 kilogram (2 pounds, 4 ounces)*

1 kilogram (2 pounds, 4 ounces) red (or white or a mixture) cabbage from a tight-headed variety

Fine ground sea salt – (keep at least 1 kilogram (2 pounds 4 ounces) handy but use only as much as you need to cover all cut surfaces)

Pickling vinegar

1 Shred the cabbage finely and, using a ceramic or glass bowl, sprinkle liberally in between layers with salt, leaving to stand.

2 After 24 hours, rinse under copious running water and pat dry with a clean cloth or paper towels (or see the tip after this recipe).

3 Pack your dry cabbage into sterilised jars, filling to the brim with cold pickling vinegar to cover (an excellent excuse for using your own home-made pickling vinegar or buy ready-made – Chapter 6 covers pickling vinegars). Label and store in a cool, dark place, using after one week and within three months.

Tip: *To rid your shredded cabbage of unwanted water quickly, place the salted, freshly rinsed cabbage in a clean tea towel and gather up the corners. Find a spot (preferably outside) where spattering water doesn't matter and rotate your arm in a 'windmill' motion. Or you can use a salad spinner.*

Per 30-gram serving: *9 calories; 0 grams protein, 2 grams carbohydrate, 0 grams fat, 0 grams saturated fat, 0 milligrams cholesterol, 1 gram fibre, 1,179 milligrams sodium.*

Cauliflower

As with cabbages, the cauliflower has many different varieties bred to mature throughout the growing season. All-year-round crops from July to late autumn and over-wintering varieties such as Medallion and Chester provide until spring arrives. Most are white but watch out for other fancy colours too; new developments are taking place all the time.

The cauliflower *curds* (the florets in the middle) should be tight and hard – keep your eye on a maturing cauliflower, picking just too soon rather than too late. Cut plants store for a week or so in a cool place or break up the curd into florets and freeze. (Blanche for two minutes before cooling and open-freezing, as I describe in Chapter 7.) Add a generous squeeze of lemon to the blanching water to prevent discoloration.

Piccalilli

This recipe makes use of end-of-season vegetables: bright yellow, chunky piccalilli goes well with cold meats, but of all the vegetables you expect to see in piccalilli, cauliflower is the one. Use equal amounts of vegetables to make up the total for the recipe, and be inventive from your home-grown plot. Chapter 3 has more on sterilisaton.

Special tools required: *Sterilised jars*

Preparation time: *45 minutes*

Processing time: *24 hours standing time plus 15–20 minutes cooking*

Yield: *2.7 kilograms (6 pounds)*

2.7 kilograms (6 pounds) prepared vegetables (cauliflower florets, firm marrow, cucumber or gherkin in 2-centimetre (¾ inch) cubes; green beans prepared and cut into 2.5-centimetre (1-inch) pieces; tiny onions, peeled; small green tomatoes, sliced; or any other home-grown produce you feel is suitable)

450 grams (1 pound) salt

15 grams (½ ounce) turmeric

25 grams (1 ounce) dry mustard powder

25 grams (1 ounce) ground ginger

175 grams (6 ounces) granulated sugar

1.2 litres (2 pints) white vinegar

40 grams (1½ ounces) cornflour

1 Spread the vegetables on a large glass or ceramic plate and sprinkle on the salt. Place a similar plate on top and add a weight, leaving to stand for 24 hours.

2 The next day, thoroughly wash and drain the vegetables; pat dry with a paper towel or a clean tea towel.

3 With a wooden spoon, stir the spices, sugar and most of the vinegar (retain a little (about 3 tablespoons) to mix with the cornflour later) in a large, heavy-bottomed preserving pan until the sugar dissolves.

4 Add the prepared vegetables, simmering gently for 10–15 minutes until you approach the texture you like: crunchy or more cooked, but never mushy or mashed for piccalilli. Use the remaining vinegar blended with the cornflour and stir carefully to thicken the mix. Simmer for two to three minutes. Pot up into warm, sterilised jars, seal and allow to cool. Label and store out of bright sunlight. Allow to mature for one month before using.

Tip: *Use distilled malt vinegar or white wine vinegar to preserve the vivid colour of your piccalilli.*

Per 30-gram serving: *20 calories; 1 gram protein, 4 grams carbohydrate, 0 grams fat, 0 grams saturated fat, 0 milligrams cholesterol, 1 gram fibre, 205 milligrams sodium.*

Celery

Leave celery in the ground until you need it, because it withstands most weathers and temperatures. Celery is the flavoursome crown of all savoury dishes and stocks. Solid White variety is an old favourite for winter picking, and Daybreak matures early for summer cropping. Use in chutneys (for example, Year Round Chutney) or add baby celery stalks into Summer Vegetable Pickle (both recipes are in Chapter 13).

Bloody Mary Relish

With a dash of vodka and the heat of Tabasco® sauce, you may want to keep this relish as an 'adult's only' treat for special occasions and a seafood platter. Store for up to three months or eat after only one week. Chapter 3 has the info on sterilisation. Chapter 6 has more on relishes.

Special tools required: *Sterilised jars*

Preparation time: *40 minutes*

Processing time: *Overnight salting and 40 minutes*

Yield: *1.3 kilograms (3 pounds)*

1.3 kilograms (3 pounds) ripe-but-firm, flavoursome tomatoes	*175 millilitres (6 fluid ounces) white wine vinegar*
1 medium cucumber	*15 millilitres (1 tablespoon) granulated sugar*
15 millilitres (1 tablespoon) fine sea salt	*60 millilitres (4 tablespoons) vodka*
3 celery sticks, finely chopped	*5 millilitres (1 teaspoon) Tabasco® sauce*
Bunch of fresh parsley, finely chopped	*10 millilitres (2 teaspoons) Worcestershire sauce*
2–3 garlic cloves, crushed	

1 Skin and chop the tomatoes. Peel, de-seed and chop the cucumber flesh. Using a stainless steel colander, layer the vegetables with sprinklings of salt; cover and refrigerate overnight, catching any moisture in a bowl.

2 The following day, rinse the salted vegetables under running water, and drain well. Place into a heavy-bottomed preserving pan the finely chopped celery and parsley, the peeled and crushed garlic, and the vinegar and sugar.

3 Stir over a gentle heat until the sugar dissolves, and then bring to the boil, lower the heat and simmer uncovered for about 30 minutes, stirring from time to time until the vegetables are soft and most of the liquid has evaporated. Remove from the heat; allow the mixture to cool for five to ten minutes before adding the vodka, Tabasco® and

Worcestershire sauces. Stir well to amalgamate before potting up into warm, sterilised jars, sealing and labelling when cool. Store out of direct sunlight for one week or up to three months before use and keep refrigerated when open.

Remember: *Vegetarians be warned: traditional Worcestershire sauce contains anchovies so isn't vegetarian.*

Per 100-millilitre serving: *43 calories; 1 gram protein, 7 grams carbohydrate, 0 grams fat, 0 grams saturated fat, 0 milligrams cholesterol, 2 grams fibre, 572 milligrams sodium.*

Kale

Kale is a hardy plant, taking you all the way through the winter months. The dark green leaves give a clue to the high iron content. Grow the Dwarf Green variety, curled for a late autumn to spring supply straight from the garden, or Red Russian Kale for an attractive alternative (or choose from many varieties in your seed catalogue).

Pick young shoots to freeze after blanching for one minute; make sure that you freeze in quantities you like to use because they tend to stick together. Chapter 7 has the low-down on freezer fun.

Leeks

Leeks have their own built-in 'antifreeze', so are truly frost-hardy. Planting three different varieties that mature at slightly different times throughout the year allows you to eat leeks from September all the way to May. Examine your seed packets to find out when your choice of leek matures.

Alternatively, choose the Axima variety for early leeks (ready to eat at the end of summer), harvest the popular main crop of Mussleburgh throughout the winter months and lead on to Bandit, which is still good to eat straight from the ground well into spring.

If leaving your leek crop standing in the ground isn't an option for you, freezing can work. Top and tail the leeks and wash well, making sure that no soil is left between the layers. Slice into 5-centimetre (2-inch) lengths, blanch for three minutes and bag up into suitable portions or open-freeze (Chapter 7 tells you more details).

Or make one of the most popular and tasty winter soups in batches to freeze down (see the Leek and Potato recipe coming up next) and you've a hearty meal ready quickly whenever you need it. If you're in a big hurry for a bite to eat, just pour a little water into the bottom of a sturdy pan and add the frozen soup. Stir frequently while defrosting takes place, making sure that you heat it to a piping hot temperature before adding cream or yoghurt and chopped parsley or chives.

You can make a more substantial meal by cooking up a chunky cheese on toast while the soup defrosts and floating mega chunks on the top of the piping hot soup. For microwave owners, the defrosting scenario is much quicker.

Leek and Potato Soup

This recipe is a real winter favourite – warming, comforting, tasty and economical to boot. A swirl of double cream and a sprinkle of chopped parsley transforms this humble farmhouse kitchen luncheon dish into a dinner party treat.

Preparation time: *20–30 minutes*

Processing time: *45 minutes*

Yield: *2.3 litres (4 pints)*

4–6 leeks

4–6 potatoes (about equal weight as the leeks)

1 litre stock (2 pints)

50 millilitres (3 tablespoons) sunflower or olive oil

Salt and pepper

Double cream and a garnish of chopped parsley (optional when eating)

1 Wash and chop leeks, and scrub and chop the potatoes into smallish pieces – maximum 2-centimetre (¾ inch) cubes (leave the skin on the potatoes for a fuller potato taste and healthy roughage). *Sweat* in the oil – cooking at a low heat with the lid on your pan for 10–15 minutes.

2 Add the stock, bring to the boil and simmer gently until the vegetables are tender, stirring occasionally, for about 20–30 minutes.

3 Season to taste as you cook. Add a swirl of double cream (or plain yogurt or crème fraiche, if you prefer) and a sprinkle of chopped parsley as a garnish to lighten up the dish.

Vary it! *Choose your texture: leave lumpy like a vegetable stew, mash roughly with a vegetable masher or cool enough to use an electric whisk or food processor to reduce it to a creamy smoothness, before freezing in suitable amounts.*

Per 100-gram serving: *47 calories; 1 gram protein, 5 grams carbohydrate, 3 grams fat, 0 grams saturated fat, 1 milligram cholesterol, 1 gram fibre, 213 milligrams sodium.*

Salad leaves

For home-grown salad varieties (including Chicory and Endive) – from quick-growing summer ones to those withstanding the cold weather (or at least giving you some green leaf choice from a polytunnel or greenhouse) – check out your seed catalogue for picking times. They're much more interesting than bought salad and easy and quick to grow – use your windowsill space in winter for extra leaves; in addition, you can trust yourself to know how your salad is washed (you probably won't use a mild bleach like commercial processors do). Long-term preserving is impossible with very delicate leaves – they just don't withstand freezing – but cleaned and dried (spin or simply shake about in a colander and bag up into a plastic bag or container) salad leaves keep for a week or longer.

Place your salad carefully in the fridge away from the cooling plates – the areas in your fridge where the cooling elements are – which can cause frosting and so reduce the keeping time.

Spinach

With careful sowing, you can be picking spinach for most of the year, making preserving in other ways unnecessary. Sow the Giant Winter variety for late winter use, or Spinach Beet, for a year-round crop producing greens in winter and on into the following year.

If your crop overwhelms you or you haven't the space for successional crops, cut, wash and blanch: just dunk the spinach briefly (less than one minute) before squeezing out excess moisture and freezing into portions suitable for family use or to add to vegetable lasagnes and other dishes.

Dealing with Perennials: Vegetables That Don't Go Away

Perennials are plants that may die away so that you no longer see the growing tops, but the roots stay viable, just waiting for the seasons to turn when they reappear refreshed from their period of dormancy.

Asparagus

Delicate asparagus is a highly prized vegetable: its aphrodisiac properties are legendary, but I leave you to decide for yourself whether this reputation is true!

To harvest, cut the spears when they show 15 centimetres (6 inches) above the ground. Using a long knife, cut under the surface of the soil about 5–8 centimetres (2–3 inches). Best eaten fresh, asparagus quality declines speedily after cutting but you can freeze the veg after washing and blanching for two to four minutes, depending on the thickness of the stem. Open-freeze for convenience, freezing singly but packing in bulk. A well-established asparagus bed produces many spears, often at the same time, so a great idea is to make soup to freeze.

When asparagus is past its best for eating, the stalk soon turns woody and the plant produces feathery green fronds and, eventually, seeds. You can use the tall, stick-like stems and their delicate array of leaves as a backdrop in flower arrangements (as professional florists do). When cut, they last a long time in a vase if you refresh the water from time to time.

Asparagus Soup

When your asparagus crop gets out of hand and the spears are still tasty (not too woody but not perfect enough to eat singly), make this silky green soup and freeze it in portions for another day. Add a swirl of cream, yoghurt or crème fresh, and a sprinkle of fresh parsley as garnish to make this soup fit for the most impressive of dinner table feasts.

Preparation time: *20 minutes*

Processing time: *30 minutes*

Yield: *1.2 litres*

25 grams (1 ounce) butter

1 onion, chopped

1 garlic clove, crushed

450 grams (1 pound) asparagus spears, after woody parts are discarded

850 millilitres (1½ pints) vegetable stock

Mixed herbs (dried or fresh) to taste

Juice of one small lemon

Seasoning – salt and pepper to taste

1 Using a heavy-bottomed pan, melt the butter adding in the chopped onion and crushed garlic. Fry gently until the onions are transparent (about five minutes).

2 Cut the clean asparagus spears into approximately 2.5-centimetre (1-inch) pieces or smaller adding them to the pan; stir and fry gently for a further five to ten minutes with the lid on the pan: shake the pan around to stop any sticking.

3 Add the stock and herbs, stirring well. Bring to the boil, cover and simmer for ten minutes or until the asparagus is very soft. Allow to cool before processing in a liquidiser/food processor or with a hand-held bender until you've a silky-smooth texture.

4 Add lemon juice, salt and pepper to taste, stirring well in.

5 Freeze in sensible amounts for your needs (Chapter 7 has more on freezing). Reheat until piping hot before using.

Per 100-gram serving: 39 calories; 1 grams protein, 5 grams carbohydrate, 2 grams fat, 1 grams saturated fat, 5 milligrams cholesterol, 1 grams fibre, 142 milligrams sodium.

Globe Artichokes

These great big plants, resembling giant thistles, hold an edible pad at the base of the outer scales on the flower head (the artichoke heart) and some finger-food edible 'bites' at the base of some of the mature leaves.

The Green Globe variety produces the traditional green head and Arad is an attractive purple-headed variety. Harvest the whole head before it flowers: further, smaller heads form for a later, bite-sized harvest. Preserve initially, if you need to, by leaving a portion of stalk attached (about 10 centimetres (4 inches)) and standing the cut flower heads in water. Changing the water daily allows you to keep it for up to week.

Preparing your artichoke for eating, or freezing, is a fiddly job. Use this step-by-step guide to help you:

1. **Trim the stalk off.**

   Make it level with the base of the head.

2. **Cut off any damaged outer scales (also called *bracts*).**

   Use scissors to trim the points from any remaining hard scales before slicing off the top of the head.

3. **Wash the artichoke at this stage, if necessary, turning it upside down to drain.**

   Rub the cut surfaces with lemon as you go to prevent discoloration.

4 **Spread the remaining scales apart to reveal *the choke*, a hairy throat-tickling bundle within the plant.**

   Remove this by scraping with a teaspoon (or a grapefruit spoon), leaving the edible heart as a chunk of flesh and lower parts of the larger bracts as finger food.

If you're using very young baby artichokes, the choke is still tender and edible so don't bother to remove it.

To freeze, blanche for six minutes, cool and freeze; open-freeze for convenience, freezing singly (see Chapter 7 for more on freezing).

Preserved Artichokes

Use baby artichokes for this recipe for the best results. The whole or halved prepared hearts in oil soak up the rich, salty, herby, lemony taste of the marinade and, with the warmth of the oil, are a Mediterranean treat. Eat as they are or as part of a pasta dish. Keep the jar in the fridge and consume within ten days. Chapter 3 has more info on sterilisation. See Chapter 12 for more on preserving in oil.

Special tools required: *Sterilised jars*

Preparation time: *30 minutes*

Processing time: *30–40 minutes*

Yield: *1.5 kilograms*

2 large lemons, preferably unwaxed

25 millilitres (1½ tablespoons) salt

A few sprigs of fresh thyme

1.3 kilograms (3 pounds) baby globe artichokes

500 millilitres (18 fluid ounces) good-quality olive or rapeseed oil

1 Grate the zest from one lemon, and combine this, the juice of both lemons and the salt in a glass or ceramic bowl mix until the salt dissolves. Keep the lemon shells for later use.

2 Wash and scald the thyme by pouring boiling water over it; pat dry on kitchen towel. Chop the scalded thyme, adding it to the lemon/salt mixture; stir well because this mixture is your marinade.

3 Trim the globe artichokes, following the instructions earlier in this section, rubbing the cut parts with the lemon shells as you go and halving or quartering any larger pieces. Coat the artichoke hearts on all sides, turning them in the marinade immediately when prepared. After the last artichoke is ready, leaving it to stand for 30 minutes allows the marinade to penetrate the artichoke flesh.

4 Pack the marinated artichokes into wide-topped, sterilised jars. Using a hand-whisk or blender, whisk the oil into the remaining marinade and top up the jar, making sure that you cover all the flesh. Store in the fridge and shake the jar daily to mix the ingredients. Use up within 10 days.

Per 100-gram serving: 312 calories; 3 grams protein, 10 grams carbohydrate, 31 grams fat, 4 grams saturated fat, 0 milligrams cholesterol, 5 grams fibre, 315 milligrams sodium.

Home preserving in oil is a short-term storage solution, up to ten days only, so keep your home-made produce in the fridge. Long-term storage in oil needs a professional approach to keep the food safe – check out Chapter 3 on food safety if you want to know more.

Horseradish

You can buy bundles of horseradish roots to plant in your garden, or if a friend grows horseradish, ask for a little root to plant in the spring – small roots take two years to establish themselves although you can harvest large roots later in the same year.

Horseradish also grows wild in field boundaries and railway embankments where you can pick up a portion of root to start you off. Make sure that you know exactly what you're looking for, though: check it out in a good wild plant book or online, or you may just relocate a common dock into your garden (it looks a bit similar to horseradish and has a very long, strong root too – visit Chapter 18 before going foraging for tips on the Country Code).

Be careful when you're dealing with horseradish. If it likes your growing space, it can soon become the bully boy of the garden roots, pushing its way in where you don't want it. Horseradish is very difficult to eradicate when established, so choose your spot carefully, preferably in a hedge bank or the very edge of your plot. Use the fresh, young leaves in salads for their hot, tangy bite; only the root has preserving uses.

Harvest horseradish in the autumn. You can't dig the whole root out, so dig down a spade's depth and break off what you need – horseradish has a tap-root that penetrates deep underground, making it impossible to pull up. The useful part of the root is the first 25.5–30 centimetres (10–12 inches) under the ground, which has a 2.5-centimetre (1 inch) diameter approximately. Store some of these roots in boxes of damp sand in a frost-free place to use at a later date. Replant the following spring, or give away to friends for a spring sowing (see Chapter 4 for more straightforward storage options).

Horseradish is pungent and stings more potently than onion. One old-fashioned remedy is to hold a piece of bread in your mouth while peeling and grating, claiming that 'the tears still fall but not so copiously'. Better still, wear swimming goggles (I'm not joking!) and protective plastic gloves, wash, clean and peel quickly with a sharp vegetable peeler or knife (with a piece of bread in your mouth for luck!) and put the whole root through the shredder attachment on a food processor, standing well back until the job is done.

Use the resulting grated horseradish immediately in your dishes because its pungent flavour dissipates quickly.

Pickled Horseradish

This useful ingredient can be an ingredient in the following Horseradish Sauce recipe, or add to stews and casseroles in small quantities – about 30 millilitres (2 tablespoons) at a time in a dish for four depending on taste – for an interesting tasty twist (horseradish loses some of its potency on cooking). Chapter 3 has more on sterilisation.

Special tools required: *Sterilised jars, non-corrosive lids*

Preparation time: *20 minutes*

Processing time: *24 hours (plus 1 week) standing time*

Yield: *350 grams (12 ounces)*

350 grams (12 ounces) of horseradish root (perhaps two 25-centimetre (1- inch) roots or equivalent in smaller roots)

Approx. 110 grams (4 ounces) fine sea salt

Vinegar to cover

1 Peel and grate the horseradish root – see the Warning earlier in the section and have a piece of bread (and goggles!) handy! – layer with salt and stand for 24 hours. Rinse well and dry, packing into sterilised jars.

2 Cover with vinegar and seal using a non-corrosive lid. Allow to stand for one week before use (keeps for up to three months).

Per 30-gram serving: 18 calories; 1 gram protein, 4 grams carbohydrate, 0 grams fat, 0 grams saturated fat, 0 milligrams cholesterol, 0 grams fibre, 386 milligrams sodium.

Horseradish Sauce

Horseradish sauce is the traditional accompaniment to beef, but goes well with fish and cheese dishes too; adding a dollop to stews and vegetable bakes gives a novel tang. You can keep it simple, or make it creamy. Your home-grown, freshly prepared horseradish sauce is much more pungent than the shop-bought variety, so be prepared to have your sinuses cleared! (Check out the Warning icon at the beginning of this section if you're handling fresh horseradish.)

Preparation time: *20 minutes if starting with fresh horseradish, less with Pickled Horseradish – see previous recipe*

Processing time: *15 minutes*

Yield: *400 grams (14 ounces)*

250 grams (9 ounces) fresh horseradish root (or the equivalent Pickled Horseradish – see previous recipe)

30 millilitres (2 tablespoons) vinegar with fresh horseradish (or 15 millilitres (1 tablespoon) vinegar with Pickled Horseradish)

5 millilitres (1 teaspoon) sugar

5 millilitres (1 teaspoon) mustard

175 millilitres (6 fluid ounces) double cream (optional)

Seasoning to taste

1 Finely grate the horseradish (or use a food processor); the Pickled Horseradish is already grated.

2 Mix the vinegar, sugar and mustard to a smooth paste. Blitz this part of the mixture in a food blender for a smoother feel if you prefer.

3 Add the cream when you achieve the texture you like, whisking to a smooth and creamy finish.

Tip: *Leave out the cream and this sauce keeps for several weeks in the fridge; with cream, it keeps for only a few days.*

Per 30-gram serving: *14 calories; 1 gram protein, 2 grams carbohydrate, 0 grams fat, 0 grams saturated fat, 0 milligrams cholesterol, 0 grams fibre, 12 milligrams sodium.*

Jerusalem Artichokes

You can use knobbly Jerusalem Artichokes to replace potatoes in loads of ways: mash, boil or roast.

Jerusalem Artichokes happily stay in the ground even in freezing conditions, when you may find them hard to dig up. If you know that severe weather is coming, bring some close to the house, covering them with a layer of soil or a mat of straw for easy access. Or pack the tubers into boxes of sand, storing them in a frost-free area away from strong smells. Cleaned and placed in a plastic bag, they keep for several weeks in the fridge.

Cook, mash or puree, and freeze in family-sized portions to add to soups, vegetable bakes and stews.

Jerusalem Artichokes are notoriously difficult to remove completely from your garden; they pop up year after year and are definitely one of the serious returners.

People with delicate digestive systems or a tendency to flatulence may care to temper their intake (in quantity or frequency) of Jerusalem Artichokes (or plan an outdoor day away from fellow humans after consumption). Their childish nickname of 'Fartichokes' didn't arise by accident!

Part V
Preserving and Using Herbs, Eggs and Wild Extras

'Well how was I to know you'd stored all the eggs at the back of the garage?'

In this part . . .

This part brings a little eccentricity and civilised madness to the art of produce preserving. The herb garden, Chapter 16's focus, gives opportunities for some gentle beauty treatment as well as tasty treats, and if you have a henhouse at the bottom of the garden and don't like the idea of buying eggs from battery hens, Chapter 17 gives you information about smoothing out the seasonal flow of eggs. If the confines of garden and allotments are too restricting for your adventurous spirit, walk out into the countryside and discover a wealth of free goodies. Chapter 18 leads you to a wild time and keeps your feet on the ground (without trespassing). With your picking pots full, some unusual preserves are all yours for the taking and making.

Chapter 16

Parsley, Sage, Rosemary and Thyme: Enjoying Glorious Garden Herbs

In This Chapter

▶ Drying herbs for perfect preserving

▶ Discovering more using and preserving methods

▶ Choosing and using herbs for preserving

*H*erbs and aromatic plants are imported from all over the world and are used for their exotic properties, pungent aromas and health benefits. Some herbs, however, quite happily grow all year round in the UK climate and you can use these herbs straight from the plant. With other herbs, the plant is only available for part of the year, dying back in the cold winter months. Sometimes two versions of the same type of plant exist, and between them they span the seasons.

Herb growing is extremely popular and most gardeners give over a bit of space to their herb garden. Traditionally, the herbs were just outside the kitchen door so that the cook was able to nip out and pick a fresh herb to brighten up a dull dish.

This herbaceous chapter shows you how to enjoy your home-grown herbs all year round, explaining which ones are best for preserving and various ways to achieve that goal. Kilo for kilo herbs are an expensive commodity to buy, so keeping your own supply saves you money while brightening up your meals. I include several simple herb-based recipes and a few other ideas too.

Drying Herbs for the Future

Of all the ways to preserve your herbs, drying is by far the most common. Drying is simple, efficient and safe, and nearly everyone has somewhere handy in the home to make this process work without spending out on any expensive equipment. With a few strands of cotton or wool for tying and an airy spot in the home – hey presto! – you can have dried herbs on tap.

For those more awkward, hard-to-dry herbs, 'Hey pesto!' saves the day (look for the Basil Pesto recipe in the later section 'Finding and Using Favourites from the Herb Garden').

Ensuring that you choose herbs that dry well

Herbs with hard, resinous-feeling leaves are the easiest to dry with good results, so choose rosemary, lavender or bay for your first experiments. Leave the wetter, floppier-leaved plants with juicy stems until you're more confident in your drying methods.

The volatile oil in the plant is what gives the flavour or aroma to herbs, and although drying removes the moisture, it concentrates the oils. The harder-leaved herbs such as lavender, rosemary and bay give off their fragrances more readily than watery leaves and juicy stems like basil and chives.

Some herbs just don't dry well at all; even experts have problems with basil and chives without using specialist equipment (I provide hints of other ways to preserve these herbs in the later section 'Getting to Grips with Other Herb Use and Preserve Options').

Picking perfectly

When drying leafy herbs, the first step is to pick your chosen herbs at their optimum before they flower. On a dry day, in late morning to early afternoon when the dew has gone and the plant is looking fresh and bright, pick the freshest undamaged herbs.

Pick and then dry small amounts again and again throughout the season, as the plant produces new fresh greenery.

When you're picking herbs to dry, cut a long enough stem to have something to work with, especially if you plan to hang bunches (check out the next section 'Hanging herbs around'). That way you avoid damaging and bruising the leaves, and you can discard any woody or tough parts later.

To wash or not to wash

Two schools of thought exist on washing herbs:

✔ Some people dunk their bunches of leaves in boiling water to blanch them or give them a rinse in clean cold water, shaking off any excess moisture and then laying them on absorbent paper before the next stage. The claim is that the herbs keep a better colour that way.

✔ Most people don't wash the plant at all. They pick it at its driest, just brushing off any obvious dirt. I go with this option: if you're trying to achieve dryness, dunking the herb in water first seems like a backward step!

Seed heads are best left on the plant to mature fully before picking and drying indoors.

Hanging herbs around

If you've a warm kitchen with a handy beam (into which you can knock a row of nails) out of bright sunlight but with air circulating freely, you're really lucky. This kind of room is exactly the spot to store small bunches of herbs. Hang them upside down by the stems.

Use a natural material for tying bunches of herbs: natural garden twine, cotton, hemp or even wool. Allow the tied stems to breathe, thus reducing any risk of harbouring pockets of moisture where micro-organisms can grow.

Bunches of hanging herbs look and smell gorgeous. (If you've enough, you can leave bunches of herbs to hang just for their look, although they do lose some of their potency and begin to gather dust.) The closer you can get to the picture of an idyllic cottage kitchen scenario, the easier drying your herbs is (see Figure 16-1). A dry airy outhouse or garage is a good substitute as long as no strong petrol or oil fumes interfere with the herbal aromas you're trying to preserve. Even a spell in the airing cupboard with the door open can start off the drying process.

Sometimes you want to preserve the herb seeds and need to hang up a bunch of seed heads or even a single one. If so, place a sheet or bowl under the plant or invest in brown paper bags and place seed heads in them; leave the ends of the stems poking out of the bag and tie the whole thing upside down. Some people cut holes in the bag to aid air circulation, but that depends on the size of plant's seeds; no use cutting holes in the bags if your dried seeds simply fall all over the floor!

Figure 16-1:
Simple
methods
for drying
herbs.

Brown paper bags are the herb dryer's best friend. They're cheap and cheerful, stop drying herbs from gathering dust or fly droppings, and catch any loose bits of herbs and seeds. Gather up a stock throughout the year.

Racking up: An alternative to hanging

If you've nowhere convenient to hang bunches of herbs, a sunny windowsill, airing cupboard or a cooling or low oven at about 32 degrees Centigrade (90 degrees Fahrenheit) does the job. Avoid any fierce heat when drying your herbs: it may seem like common sense to frazzle them in the oven but that scorches the oils, spoiling the tastes and smells.

Place the herbs to be dried in single layers on a rack that allows air to circulate under the plants. If the leaves and stems are of varying thicknesses, turn them occasionally to be sure that all parts get some exposure to the warmth and air. Sunlight helps the drying process but can also bleach the colour from the plants, so use a brown paper bag (the herb dryer's best friend): lay lightly over the herbs to shade them from the direct strength of the sun.

Going professional

You can buy efficient food dehydrators. They cost in the region of £100 and have instructions and timings for all the different herbs as well as being able to dry other kinds of foods. If you want to sell packed dried herbs commercially, a dehydrator is a must-have. They also have accurate meters for measuring humidity levels in food and checking out the water activity.

Water activity (a_w) is the amount of water that's available to micro-organisms. When using a food dehydrator, note that many micro-organisms prefer an a_w of 0.99 and most need one higher than 0.91 to grow, so keep the measurements below these readings. Relative humidity and a_w are related: a_w refers to the availability of water in a food or beverage; relative humidity refers to the availability of water in the atmosphere around the food or beverage.

Using a room dehumidifier helps to speed up the herb-drying process if a long run of damp and dour weather occurs just when you're trying to set in your winter herb store. Take a look at Chapter 8 for more hints on food drying, including guidance on building your own basic solar food dryer.

Testing and storing after home drying

To check whether your herbs are ready, rub the dried herb between the palms of your hands: it should crumble easily, releasing the aroma. To speed up the crumbling process, use a rolling pin to crush the brittle leaves, removing any stalks and stems as you go. If the leaves are still holding too much moisture, they bend and roll up: give them more drying time.

Shops commonly pack dried herbs in cellophane, glass and plastic containers for sale, and they mechanically test the moisture content of these products. If you want your own dried herbs to last a long time, wrap them loosely in brown paper before placing them into a sealed container away from light, decanting a little at a time into a smaller jar for easy use. If any residual moisture is still present, the brown paper takes it up and, consequently, your herbs store for longer. Some people put a few grains of rice alongside the herbs in the hope that the rice will absorb any residual moisture. Whether this method actually works is a moot point, but it certainly won't break the bank if you want to give it a go. (Chapter 8 has more information on testing for dryness.)

Avoid using plastic bags at any stage in the drying process to prolong the useful life of your herbs.

When cooking with your own dried herbs, don't shake them out of the jar directly into a cooking pot where steam and heat may get trapped in your container. Doing so encourages moulds to form; instead, sprinkle by hand.

Sorting out problems with dried herbs

If you start with undamaged clean herbs and continue to remove moisture at a fairly constant rate, you shouldn't have any problems. But things don't always go smoothly and any pockets of stale, moisture-laden air, thicker pieces of stem, hidden damage, contamination, bruising or areas where several layers of leaves have stuck together can become a perfect patch for moulds and yeasts to grow.

Check your produce over carefully and discard any rotting or mouldy parts. If the rest smells fresh and 'herby', keep it. If all the plant is affected, look again at your drying system and ask:

✔ Did you start with the best possible produce in the best possible condition?

✔ Is the drying area warm enough for the damp air to rise, taking moisture with it?

✔ Are you allowing enough air circulation?

When drying leaves, if they're attached to a thick stalk moisture from the stalk can track into the leaves. With juicy or thick-stemmed plants, remove the leaves to dry individually.

Getting to Grips with Other Herb Use and Preserve Options

Some herbs just don't lend themselves to drying: they may be too delicate and disintegrate into dust or too juicy and have a tendency to mould before they dry. But don't despair, you have other ways to use and preserve your herby harvest:

✔ **Freezing:** Freezing small quantities of a freshly picked herb, packed loosely in a plastic bag, is quick and easy. If herbs stored in this way go straight from frozen into the cooking pot, you don't even need to *blanch* (briefly boil; check out Chapter 7 for more on blanching). Just use scissors to snip off the required amount. By working quickly, you can get your remaining frozen herbs safely back into the freezer to use another day.

✔ **Puree-ing the leaves:** Mush them up in a food processor or grind with a pestle and mortar before freezing them in usable quantities, (ice cube trays are the perfect size: see Chapter 7 for more freezing cold tips).

✔ **Making watery ice cubes:** Include herbs and add directly to soft or alcoholic drinks.

✔ **Concocting pestos:** Mix the herbs with oils and other tasty ingredients (see the Basil Pesto recipe in the later section 'Finding and Using Favourites from the Herb Garden').

✔ **Combining in butter:** In this way, you can extend the shelf-life of fresh herbs to keep in the fridge for several weeks (check the date of the butter you're using before you start in order to ensure the best shelf-life), or alternatively freeze for up to a year. (Take a look at the Fennel and Parsley Butter recipes in the later section 'Finding and Using Favourites from the Herb Garden'.)

You can make butters with any of the herbs that you enjoy, not just the tender ones. Use them to make an unusual garlic bread alternative, or add a knob of flavoured butter to steamed vegetables or sauces.

✔ **Incorporating herbs into other preserves:** Try making mint or herb jellies (see the Crab Apple section in Chapter 18 for an example).

All these approaches help your glorious garden herbs to last well beyond the growing season. I list the ideal treatment for specific herbs later in 'Finding and Using Favourites from the Herb Garden', but you can use any of the methods in the previous bulleted list with any herb if it works for you. If you've grown loads, be experimental and try several methods for one type of herb.

Making the most of aromatic herbs

Our ancestors preserved herbs and other aromatic plants to make their lives a little more fragrant. They strewed aromatic herbs on the floors in their houses: walking on them bruised and crushed the leaves and seeds, releasing aromas that people hoped would mask some of the more unpleasant smells around.

Without fridges, food deteriorated quickly and herbs were used to disguise the off-ish tastes and probably helped with digestion too! Compared to some of the artificial air freshener sprays on sale today, dried herbs are more subtle and delicate and possibly better for your health.

Mmm . . . smelling gorgeous!

Leaving bowls of homemade potpourri around adds a delicate fragrance to the air. Lavender flowers with lemon thyme and sage for a lower note make a good combination, but any of the fragrant herbs and their seeds work well. Or you can simply brush sprigs of dried herbs with your hand as you pass them, or crush a few seeds to release the volatile oils and their lovely smells.

Hang home-made lavender bags in the linen cupboard or make some of the old-fashioned lavender liquid potions I mention in the later section 'Finding and Using Favourites from the Herb Garden'. Giving gifts of homemade potpourri for Christmas and birthdays shows enterprise while saving you money.

Yum . . . tasting delicious!

Single- or multiple-flavoured herb teas or infusions (known as *tisanes*) are a delicious, calorie-free drink. Adding just-off-the-boil water and allowing your tea to cool to a drinkable temperature is worth the wait. Stir and blow on the surface to speed cooling if you must, but don't spoil the delicate flavour by adding cold water.

Drinking iced teas during the hot summer months is a cool way to relax without racking up the calories. In addition, using leftover herb teas to make flavoured ice cubes to add a zing to your drinks without watering them down adds thrift to the virtue.

Here's another thought . . . try making a *bouquet garnis*: a little bundle of herbs whose flavours blend well and add aroma and flavour to your cooking, without appearing in the meal itself (you remove it before serving). Doing so is really easy. Tie stems of dried parsley, thyme and bay together for the most basic garni and then hang it in your cooking pot, leaving a long tail attached to the pot handle for easy removal.

If your herbs are already crumbled, you can get the same effect by tying loose herbs in a muslin bag and suspending it in the desired dish. Be as adventurous as you want, and add grated zest of citrus to your herby bag for extra zing. Soups, stews and sauces all benefit from this herby addition, but you can also use them to add subtle flavouring to preserves at the initial cooking stage.

Add herbs to a bag of dried rice to infuse it with subtle flavours before cooking.

Using herbs for comfort and health

A whole wealth of knowledge is available on how to use herbs to help prevent and alleviate disease. Find a professionally trained herbalist if you want to know more, but people have used the following tried-and-tested gentle remedies safely for years:

- ✔ Chamomile tea as a relaxing bedtime nightcap
- ✔ Lavender as a gentle freshener to sooth a fevered brow and relieve symptoms of stress
- ✔ Mint and fennel as digestive soothers
- ✔ Sage teas for throat problems

If you want to find out more about medicinal herbal remedies, choosing a qualified practitioner from a reliable register is important, for example:

✔ International Register of Consultant Herblists (www.irch.org)

✔ National Institute of Medical Herbalists (www.nimh.org.uk)

✔ Unified Register of Herbal Practitioners (www.urhp.com)

Practitioners have completed extensive training (theory and practical) and are insured to treat members of the public. Many organisations and qualified herbalists offer short courses for personal interest.

Matching and mixing herbs with your food

Here are some of the classic partners for using herbs in your cooking:

✔ Basil and tomatoes

✔ Bay leaves, cloves and ham

✔ Beef and lovage

✔ Carrot and coriander

✔ Fish and dill

✔ Lamb and mint sauce

✔ Lamb and rosemary

✔ Parsley and eggs

✔ Parsley sauce with boiled ham

✔ Pizza and oregano

✔ Pork, sage and onion

And don't forget to create your own combos too!

Finding and Using Favourites from the Herb Garden

In this section, I provide information on some of the herbs you're most likely to grow at home. These herbs are the more common ones and you can find seeds for them at all garden centres and in seed catalogues.

Study the packets carefully because herbs range in size from a floppy few leaves (for example, basil) to enormous trees (bay), and although annuals die off every year (such as coriander), others perennials (lovage) return again and again and can be overwhelming in a small plot.

You can still enjoy all the herbs by confining them to pots rather than allowing them to take over your garden or allotment while you decide which tastes you like enough to be worth preserving. Ending up with invasive mint taking over your small garden when you make lamb sauce only once a year is disappointing and pointless!

Basil

Basil is a difficult plant to dry. Instead, pick a few sprigs and place loosely into a plastic bag, store in the freezer and use as much or as little as you need. Basil retains its taste in cooked dishes even if it appears droopy and dark, as if it has given up the ghost. Make yourself some aromatic vinegar by steeping sprigs in vinegar, which impart a herby flavour. Better still, make Basil Pesto using the following recipe, which is by far the best way to keep your home-grown basil round the year.

Because basil is such a well-loved herb, many varieties have been developed. Sweet Basil, with its fine flavour, is the common culinary type, but look out for tall and small, and lemony and red, varieties in seed catalogues.

Basil Pesto

You can use fresh basil leaves to make great pesto, which is the mainstay for any pasta dish, and to dollop into Bolognese. To make great Pesto you need great olive oil, so splash out on a little of the best to really bring out the flavour and warmth of this sauce. The Italians have been doing it for years, and basil pesto belongs in any dish that contains tomatoes and garlic.

Special tools: *Food processor*

Preparation time: *20 minutes*

Yield: *225 grams (8 ounces)*

110 grams (4 ounces) fresh basil leaves

30 grams (1¼ ounces) freshly grated Parmesan-Reggiano or Romano cheese

50 millilitres (2 fluid ounces) extra virgin olive oil

50 grams (1¾ ounces) pine nuts or walnuts

2 or 3 medium-sized garlic cloves

Salt and freshly ground black pepper to taste

1 Combine the basil with the pine nuts and pulse a few times in a food processor. (If you're using walnuts instead of pine nuts and they aren't already chopped, pulse them a few times first, before adding the basil.) Add the garlic, and pulse a few times more.

2 Slowly add the olive oil in a constant stream while the food processor is on (the lid has a hole for this purpose). Stop to scrape down the sides of the food processor with a rubber spatula. Add the grated cheese and pulse again until blended. Add a pinch of salt and freshly ground black pepper to taste.

3 Keep in a jar in the fridge for a few weeks or freeze in small portions to keep over the winter.

Tip: Vegetarians, remember that Parmesan and Romano cheeses traditionally contain animal rennet and aren't vegetarian. Look out for vegetarian 'Italian-Style Hard Cheese' as an alternative (the producers aren't allowed to call it 'Parmesan').

***Vary it!** You can make this recipe without the cheese if you want to freeze it and don't like the texture of frozen cheese. You can then add grated cheese to the defrosted mixture, mixing in well, or add without the cheese to cooking dishes.*

Per 30-gram serving: *119 calories; 4 grams protein, 3 grams carbohydrate, 11 grams fat, 2 grams saturated fat, 3 milligrams cholesterol, 2 grams fibre, 154 milligrams sodium.*

Bay

If you're lucky enough to own or have access to a bay tree, you need do no more than pick a few leaves at a time all year round, or pick a sprig of bay and keep it in the kitchen. The taste subtly changes on drying, and, usefully, bay is one of the easiest of leaves to dry: the leaves start out dry, shiny and tough so little can go wrong.

Use bay leaves in any meaty dish and when boiling hams, or as part of the traditional bouquet garni (which I describe in the earlier section 'Yum . . . tasting delicious!').

Bay trees are the perfect evergreen plant for making Christmas wreaths and decking the halls alongside traditional holly and ivy.

Don't confuse bay with laurel, whose leaves are similar but poisonous to eat. To tell the difference, crush a few of the plant leaves and smell them first: bay leaves have a pungent aroma and laurel leaves are practically odourless.

Chamomile

Chamomile dries well. Use the flowers only in a traditional tea for soothing fractious babies or as a relaxing nightcap. You can buy special food-grade material from cook's shops and catering outlets for making your own tea bags, some of which handily come ready-made for you to fill up. Stuff these bags with your home-dried flowers (see the previous section 'Hanging herbs around' for drying tips). Packing a few camomile teabags in a creative way – by decorating a little box or bag, for example – makes an unusual gift. Home-made gifts touch the heart of the receiver. Imagine their serene smile and their kindly thoughts towards you as they sip their calming infusion, thanks to your creative efforts.

Chives

Chives are at their yummiest when freshly cut before they flower. When it comes to storing and preserving them, these slim, hollow leaves are awkward customers to dry, and so I advise leaving drying chives to the professionals. Freezing into ice cubes is an option but the oniony taste isn't everyone's favourite addition to a cold drink!

If you grow chives, and they're among your favourite tastes, I suggest popping across to Chapter 17 to find out how use the information on preserving eggs to your advantage. Chives go well in quiches and other egg dishes, and you can store and preserve them together. Even if you don't own your own hens, you can use the tips in Chapter 17 with shop-bought eggs.

With this combination in mind, a great way to store chives for future use is by chopping your fresh chives up small and whisking them into raw egg. Freeze this mixture in little pots (Chapter 7 deals with this cold subject in detail) – individual yoghurt pots are ideal – and you preserve the chive taste too. Even at half a pot of chives to half a pot of egg, this mixture freezes well for up to six months. Defrost a pot, add however many extra fresh eggs you need for your savoury dish, whisk up the fresh and defrosted eggy mixture and you've an out-of-season chive dish – magic!

You can use this ploy with any of the leafy herbs you grow – such as parsley, chervil and basil – as long as they go with eggs!

If cheese is in your final dish, leave it out of your mix until you come to make it. Cheese doesn't freeze well – it goes crumbly. Whereas eggs are watery, and your herbs contain water and freeze well, cheese contains a lot of fat, which reacts differently when frozen.

If combining chives with egg doesn't grab you, just pop a handful of chive leaves – don't chop them up at this stage – into a plastic container and pop them straight into the freezer. When you need to retrieve them, use scissors to cut the frozen leaves straight into a hot savoury dish.

Comfrey

Comfrey isn't a culinary herb but is really useful as a home-grown organic fertiliser for tomatoes and greenhouse plants. So forget the expensive 'liquid tomato feed' on the garden centre shelves (if the feed claims to be 'natural', check the label and you may be surprised to see that the feed is made of comfrey anyway!). Making your own couldn't be easier (see the sidebar 'Making liquid fertiliser').

You don't want to eat comfrey at all, but growing it in your garden attracts bees, and bees in turn pollinate your other plants. In fact, one third of the food we eat has been pollinated by bees and other flying insects. Bees help to create good harvests, which, in turn, mean plenty of lovely produce to make into jams, jellies and chutneys!

Coriander

If you've previously grown coriander yourself, you may already have 'volunteers' in the garden where the plant self-seeded; in other words, the plant has essentially saved its own seeds outdoors through rain and snow and freezing conditions. This tendency makes coriander a really good first choice for preserving.

Making liquid fertiliser

Stuff a watertight plastic dustbin or similar container full of comfrey leaves and top up with water. Leave alone to 'brew' for a few weeks and use the liquid: the sodden leaves can go onto your compost heap.

The result smells really strong, so don't leave it near the neighbour's patio! Water down the mixture to at least quarter of its strength before using. The mixture retains its potency for at least a year and saves money on expensive tomato feed preparations.

You can use coriander whole as a pickling spice as well as ground. Usually, people dry coriander seeds, and the process is quite easy (see the previous section 'Hanging herbs around' for how to dry herb seeds). If you're careful to store them in dry, airtight conditions, coriander seeds last for several years.

For an easy way to add freshly ground seeds to any dish, fill a pepper grinder with your home-dried coriander seeds and keep it to hand. Over time, the flavour of the seeds matures, so expect a more intensely spicy flavour from older seeds.

You can dry coriander leaves carefully, freeze them or make them into a type of pesto: try adapting the Basil Pesto recipe in the earlier 'Basil' section.

Carrot and coriander have long been partners, but a less-known tasty vegetable combination is a grinding of fresh coriander seeds on cooked cabbage tossed in a little butter.

Dill

You can easily dry dill leaves and seeds. Use the seeds in food: roast them gently to release the flavours or add them into a cooking dish, but save some to sow for next year's gardening too. Tetra is a dill variety often used in pickles. See Chapter 12 for a Pickled Gherkin recipe and try it out for yourself.

Yoghurt Cucumber Sauce with Dill

In winter, use your dried dill leaves to make this healthy low-fat sauce (in summer, just use fresh leaves instead). Pile it onto crackers or fresh bread as a quick healthy snack or use it as a dipping sauce with finely sliced vegetables. This tasty sauce comes into its own as a light side dish with spicy food or fish, too.

Preparation time: *15 minutes*

Processing time: *Practically none*

Yield: *420 grams (15 ounces) (approx.)*

360 grams (13 ounces) plain yogurt

½ cucumber

2 cloves garlic

Juice of half a lemon

15 millilitres (3 teaspoons) of dried dill leaves

A pinch of cayenne pepper

1 Peel and grate the cucumber, peel and crush the garlic cloves.

2 Combine all the ingredients and stir well.

3 Serve chilled.

> *Per 100-gram serving: 65 calories; 5 grams protein, 9 grams carbohydrate, 1 gram fat, 1 gram saturated fat, 5 milligrams cholesterol, 1 gram fibre, 62 milligrams sodium.*

Fennel

You can dry fennel seed heads fine, but the leaves are feathery fronds and lose flavour on drying. If you love the fennel taste, your best bet is to make butters and store them that way.

This exquisitely beautiful plant picks well and people often use it as a green backdrop to colourful flower arrangements. Use just the frondy leaves or wait until it seeds for an interesting variation; keeping the water in your vase topped up extends the life of your arrangement. Traditionally, people use the seeds as a 'digestif' for adults and in babies' gripe water to ease colic pains.

Although similarities exist, don't confuse the herby fennel with Florence Fennel, which is an edible bulb vegetable. Chapter 13 gives you the lowdown on the Florence type.

Fennel Butter

This recipe is perfect for fish dishes, smeared directly onto the top of your fish or dotted onto the top of a fish pie with the herby butter. The slightly aniseed flavour makes a delicate accompaniment. Alternatively, instead of making the usual garlic bread – which is simply garlic mashed into softened butter, spread onto bread and baked in the oven – try making a fennel version by substituting fennel butter. This meal isn't for slimmers, though you can eat it with a fish dish to salve your conscience!

Preparation time: *Time to soften butter and then 5 minutes*

Yield: *150 grams (5 ounces) (approx.)*

30 millilitres (approx. 2 tablespoons) fresh chopped fennel fronds

150 grams (5 ounces) fresh butter

1 Take the butter out of the fridge and allow to soften at room temperature for a couple of hours. If you've neither the time nor the patience, just get straight on with the job of mashing up the butter with a fork – a slightly more arduous job but it works off the calories.

2 Chop the fennel leaves finely and combine with softened butter.

3 Store in the fridge for several weeks. Alternatively, you can portion it up into individual pieces or roll it into a log and freeze (see Chapter 7 for more on freezing), and use it up within six months. The fats and oils don't actually freeze but any bacterial growth is inhibited. You can cut portions from the frozen log as needed.

Per 30-gram serving: 215 calories; 0 grams protein, 0 grams carbohydrate, 24 grams fat, 15 grams saturated fat, 65 milligrams cholesterol, 0 grams fibre, 4 milligrams sodium.

Lavender

Bunches of lavender, picked when in flower on the stem, are just the thing to have hanging from a beam in the kitchen. Also, you can use the dried flowers to scent drawers and cupboards and keep moths at bay. Lavender is an old-fashioned scent because people have successfully preserved and used it down the ages.

Lavender's a brilliant herb to get children into herb-growing and preserving with because the storing is almost bound to succeed.

I present three lavender 'recipes' in this section that aren't for consumption (even though the preserving agent in two of them is alcohol!). The alcohol inhibits spoilage and its evaporating effects, when used sparingly to dab or spray onto the skin, add a cooling effect.

Light lavender water

Use this delightful lavender water as a gentle scent or to spray on linen.

1. **Using the same cup size as a measure, place one cup of lavender flower buds, one cup of distilled (or boiled and then cooled) water and an eighth of a cup of vodka into a container.**

2. **Close the lid and shake well.**

3. **Leave the mixture on a sunny windowsill for two weeks, shaking from time to time.**

4. **Strain the lavender water into a pretty bottle and use as desired.**

If the scent is too light, simply add a few drops of lavender essential oil at any stage.

Old-fashioned lavender toilet water

The name of this toilet water can raise a smile, but it refers to attending to one's *toilette*: the act of washing and primping in which this delicate scented water comes into its own. The other term is *aromatic water*, which because the meaning of the word *toilet* has changed over the years is probably more appropriate. Use it after bathing or shaving and to cool a fevered brow in times of stress or illness.

1. **Steep handfuls of lavender flowers in white wine vinegar.**

2. **Store the jar in a warm place (on the back of the stove, for example) for three days, after which you can strain and bottle.**

Lavender bath water

Use this lavender water to take the strain out of a stressful day:

1. **Pour two cups of boiling water over two large handfuls of dried lavender flowers.**

2. **Steep until cool and strain into your bath water.**

Lemon Balm

This prolific plant gives off its 'citrussy' scent most pungently when fresh, but dry lemon balm retains its aromatic properties too (see the earlier section 'Hanging herbs around' for how to dry herb seeds). You can use dried lemon balm as a refreshing *tisane* (where herbs are infused in hot water as a drink), traditionally done to relive headaches and fatigue, or in the pot pourri bowl to add a fresh aroma. Alternatively, you may try taking a leaf from our medieval ancestors' book by strewing the dried herbs on the ground and crushing them underfoot to release the aroma. You can then let loose on the dance floor and boogie on down to the Lemon Balm Blues!

Lemon balm is just right for preserving in ice cubes, making an unusual cooling and refreshing way to enliven a cool lager or white wine spritzer on a summer evening.

Lovage

Preserve lovage leaves by drying or freezing. You can then use them to complement beefy stew and root dishes, the flavour giving a savoury depth unlike any other. Add it cautiously to start with, though – just a half teaspoon at a time until you establish the correct amount for your taste buds.

In English pubs, you always find a bottle of lovage wine behind the counter. You can make fresh wine (see Chapter 9 for home wine-making methods) or the following alcoholic cordial.

Lovage Cordial

This delicious adult cordial is not for the faint hearted. Use it as a toast for special occasions or as an aperitif, especially when the main dish contains beef – lovage and beef complement each other well. But don't overdo things. Lovage Cordial may indeed be a cordial, but this drink is as strong as any other vodka.

Preparation time: *20 minutes*

Yield: *1.4 litres (2¼ pints)*

30 grams (2 tablespoons) fresh lovage seeds

1.2 litres (2 pints) vodka

100 grams (3½ ounces) sugar

5 grams (1 teaspoon) coarsely ground black pepper

1 Bruise and crush the lovage seeds.

2 Using a container big enough to hold 1.4 litres (2¼ pints) without slopping over the sides when you stir, add all the ingredients.

3 Stir until all the sugar dissolves.

4 Seal and store away in a cool, dark place for one month before straining and rebottling.

Tip: Drink with a few ice cubes that contain lovage leaves.

Per 100 millilitre serving: 223 calories; 0 grams protein, 9 grams carbohydrate, 0 grams fat, 0 grams saturated fat, 0 milligrams cholesterol, 0 grams fibre, 3 milligrams sodium.

Marjoram

People most commonly dry Sweet Marjoram because it has an unusual property where the flavour strengthens when you do so, but you can keep a pot alive on a kitchen windowsill all winter too. For its more bitter near relative, see the later section on 'Oregano'. Substitute Marjoram anywhere Oregano is mentioned in meaty, cheesy, vegetable dishes for a slightly milder, more refined version of the dish.

Dry some of the leaves (see the section on 'Hanging Herbs Around' for tips) and make a *pot pourri* – a dish of dried aromatic herbs – to scent a room. Mix Sweet Marjoram and Lavender and add cinnamon quills (you won't be able to grow these quills, but they give a musky edge to the aroma).

Mint

Mint has wild counterparts in the UK and its smell is immediately recognisable. Mint is clean, strong and distinctive, but many subtle variations on the theme exist. Keep your eyes (and nose) open when you visit friends' gardens and try out any mints you see (or smell). Because it regrows quickly, your friends won't mind if you pull up a handful to transplant in your garden (so make sure that you have some robust roots too), but be careful – mint has brutish tendencies when established so confine it to a pot if space is an issue.

The common garden mint is traditionally used for the following Simple Mint Sauce recipe, but you may prefer Apple Mint, Ginger Mint or Lemon Mint. Use whichever takes your fancy. This herb is ideal for combining with Crab Apple Jelly (see Chapter 18 for the recipe). If crab apples are hard to come by, just substitute any tart cooking apples, resulting in your very own Apple Mint Jelly.

You can store fresh mint over the winter as follows:

1. **Dig up a clump of mint.**

2. **Remove a few sprigs carefully, with the roots attached.**

3. **Lay the sprigs in a box and bury in enough compost (Chapter 4 explains how to make this compost) to keep your mint in the dark.**

4. **Keep in a cool, frost-free place and you have fresh mint available throughout winter.**

Lots of mints dry well but spearmint (the toothpaste-tasting one) and peppermint (the sweetie-tasting one) are the best known.

Simple Mint Sauce

This simple, traditional mint sauce tastes delicious as an accompaniment to lamb. Use common garden mint or choose the variety you like best. Use it without straining, and eat the leaves as well. It stores well in the fridge for up to two weeks.

Preparation time: 10 minutes

Yield: 100 millilitres (3½ fluid ounces)

One handful of common garden mint (or another variety of your choice)

50 millilitres (2 fluid ounces) hot water

50 millilitres (2 fluid ounces) vinegar

A sprinkle of sugar

1 Chop the handful of mint finely and bruise with a rolling pin to release the flavour.

2 Place in a container and add just enough water to cover half the mint. Add a sprinkle of sugar and stir to dissolve.

3 Add vinegar to cover the mint generously, mix well and taste. Add more sugar or vinegar to taste and make up required quantity. See Chapter 6 for more on vinegars.

Tip: *Drinking tea from fresh or dried mint leaves has long been known to aid digestion after a heavy meal.*

Per 100-millilitre serving: *24 calories; 1 gram protein, 5 grams carbohydrate, 0 grams fat, 0 grams saturated fat, 0 milligrams cholesterol, 3 grams fibre, 14 milligrams sodium.*

Oregano

Oregano is the bitter brother of marjoram (check out the earlier section on 'Marjoram') and its gutsy taste has travelled around the world, cropping up in many ethnic dishes in Mexican, Italian, Greek and French cooking, and many others besides. Oregano dries well with an increasing pungency of flavour (see the previous section 'Hanging herbs around' for tips), and you can use the fresh and dried versions in any dish with tomatoes and garlic.

Stand a sprig or two in your favourite wine vinegar to infuse. It looks good and imparts flavour, but do remember the Sweet Marjoram, (also in this chapter) – Oregano's less pushy brother. You may interchange these herbs from time to time in the same type of dishes to experience a refinement of flavours.

Parsley

You can dry parsley, but also keep it indoors in a pot over the winter, because the taste is fuller when fresh. Substituting fresh parsley for basil in Basil Pesto (see the earlier 'Basil' section) works well.

Parsley is one of the basics for a bouquet garni (see the earlier section 'Yum . . . tasting delicious!'): use as dried sprigs or crumble alongside bay and thyme and wrap loosely in muslin.

Parsley Butter

Parsley Butter is a great item to keep handy for various situations. Toss knobs of it into drained boiled vegetables or onto grilled fish. Smear generous portions of parsley butter into a French stick (cut lengthways, add the butter and a clove or two of crushed garlic if you fancy it, wrap in foil and place in the oven at 150 degrees Celsius (300 degrees Fahrenheit, Gas Mark 2) for twenty minutes) for a variation on the usual garlic bread. This delicious butter stores for several weeks in the fridge or longer in the freezer.

Preparation time: *15 minutes*

Yield: *180 grams (6 ounces)*

30 grams (2 tablespoons) fresh parsley   *150 grams (5 ounces) butter*

1 Chop the fresh parsley leaves finely, discarding the stalks, and combine with softened butter.

2 Make into tiny pats or create a herb butter log.

Tip: *For best results, keep in the freezer (see Chapter 7 for more on freezing) and use unsalted butter.*

Per 30-gram serving: *181 calories; 0 grams protein, 0 grams carbohydrate, 20 grams fat, 13 grams saturated fat, 55 milligrams cholesterol, 0 grams fibre, 6 milligrams sodium.*

Rosemary

Having your own rosemary plant means that you can harvest fresh leaves all year round; otherwise, try to collect prunings from someone else's rosemary, which dry easily or pop some into a plastic bag in the freezer taking a little whenever you need. Rosemary has many folklore attachments one being 'Rosemary is for Remembrance' with a place at the wedding and at the graveside.

Rosemary hair rinse

Rosemary promotes good health for hair, so you never need to have another 'bad hair' day again!

Take a good handful of rosemary, pour boiling water over and allow to it cool. Strain and use in the last hair wash rinse for squeaky-clean hair with a healthy shine.

The taste of rosemary is distinctive and besides the name, not at all 'girly' taste-wise. Toss it in among roasting vegetables or lamb dishes to enhance the dish or use it as a beauty treatment.

Sage

You can keep sprigs of fresh Sage for up to a week in a pot of water by changing the water daily and keeping the plant out of direct sunlight. To dry the leaves, pick them young – before the plant flowers – to ensure a better flavour for your dried sage. Sage leaves have a thickness and a textured look, and they dry well (see the previous section 'Hanging herbs around' for tips). Dried, *rubbed* (broken up) Sage should be grey and woolly with a greenish tinge and have the characteristic balsamic aroma and savoury taste of fresh Sage.

Store dried sage in airtight packaging, keep it in a cool, dark place and bring it out to use with fatty foods like pork, duck and goose or use it in herby dumplings and stuffings to round off a wintery meal.

Tarragon

Drying tarragon doesn't give the best results. Instead, pick young growth only and preserve using a different method: for example, steeping in vinegar to impart the flavour works really well. Making herb butter (by adapting the earlier Parsley Butter recipe) and placing freshly picked sprigs straight into the freezer are other options.

Tarragon's 'aniseedy' flavour turns bitter if you overcook it, so add it to stews and soups in the last 15 minutes of cooking. It complements fish, chicken, egg and tomato dishes extremely well, but watch out because it has a tendency to overpower more delicate herby flavours.

Thyme

Common and lemon thyme are brilliant kitchen companions. Place it in water, or even in the fridge without water, and its robustness may surprise you. Thyme has a long fresh growing season but drying is easy too: just hang it up in an airy place. With its slightly resinous leaves, thyme keeps well after being picked.

With flavours that concentrate on drying, Thyme has a place in almost any dish and is a mainstay of the bouquet garni (the earlier section 'Yum . . . tasting delicious!' describes how to make this herby flavouring bag).

Chapter 17

Enjoying Eggs All Year Round

In This Chapter

▶ Understanding the seasonal nature of hens

▶ Calculating egg numbers

▶ Developing a hen routine

▶ Preserving, storing and using eggs

*I*f you keep hens, you know that their egg production varies during the year, peaking around Easter. People painted eggs and rolled hard-boiled ones down hills only because of this seasonal bounty, and the huge number of chocolate eggs at Easter is simply copying what nature provides in a less fattening way!

This seasonal variation means that at certain times of the year you've too many eggs and at other times not enough. Just when you reach out for some of your own eggs to bake a cake, your egg-producing girls seem to have gone on strike. Unlike at the supermarket, your own eggs simply aren't readily available all year round. However, after you taste a fresh egg, store-bought varieties may no longer cut the mustard. Therefore, you need to store your eggs, which is where this chapter comes in.

All this eggy information is for those adventurous people who keep chickens at the bottom of the garden or are thinking of doing so. I provide a variety of information, from understanding why fluctuations in egg production happen to ensuring a continuous, all-year-round supply of home-produced eggs with some recipes for storage. And I discuss storing your precious eggs when the nest boxes are overflowing and preserving at least part of the egg for future use.

If you want more hen-keeping information, check out *Keeping Chickens For Dummies* by Pammy Riggs (yes, me!), Kimberley Willis and Rob Ludlow (Wiley).

Keeping Hens for Eggs

To make the best use of your own egg harvest – for example, to ensure that you can use your eggs in the Christmas cake – you need to understand hens and their egg-producing ways. This section describes how to get more eggs by buying the right breeds and using their natural seasonal tendencies to your advantage.

The modern-day hybrid breeds of hen have been carefully bred to produce a lot of eggs. They need one whole day to make an egg and produce continuously throughout the year. Things used to be different: wild jungle fowl, the ancestor of the modern hen, produce only enough eggs to fill a nest and make a nice little clutch of chicks. Procreation is the name of the game for these wild birds. Keeping out of the hungry jaws of predators and finding enough food to feed this little family flock takes up the rest of the year.

Any sensible bird takes on this task of looking after a hungry brood of chicks when plenty of food is in the larder and the days are longer and warmer to complete this task. So the chicken evolved to produce the most eggs in preparation for spring by responding to the increasing day length that heralds the coming of spring and summer.

Those of you who've had 'granny hens' living with you for a few years know that although they may have given up laying eggs for most of the year, even they manage to squeeze a few out at Easter time.

Eggs-tending your harvest by breed

One way to ensure more eggs year round is to choose the right breed of hen. Selecting a breed that satisfies your egg demands can be quite tricky. If you look in the books, at the adverts online or on notice boards in pet shops and places where you buy chicken feed, you can choose from a myriad fancy shapes and colours.

The fancier the hen, the less likely she is to lay many eggs, so beware of falling for a cute little chicken with fluffy feathers or a tall, rangy raptor of a beast. You still have to feed, water and care for this hen even when she's laying no eggs and she eats a similar amount of food to a hen that produces lots of eggs.

When you're selecting a hen for egg production, you need to pick a different breed than if you want a hen purely as an ornament to adorn your garden or are re-homing an ex-battery hen out of compassion.

The following list gives an idea about the egg-laying capability of some of the more common types of hen:

- **Commercial modern hybrid:** You buy these hens at *point-of-lay* (that is, at 16–18 weeks old and ready to start production). She's usually brown, perhaps with white tips to her tail and wings. In her first year of laying, she produces around 300 eggs. With only 65 days of rest, you get an egg a day nearly all year round and you can't do better than that. She moults approximately one year after first laying and stops producing eggs during this process. In her second year she lays about 25 per cent less eggs than the previous year, which is still a massive 225 eggs in a year.

    You can expect the spread of eggs to be concentrated round the spring and summer months with a more sporadic smattering during the cold, dark months. Of course, some of these hens go on and on but most are pretty worn out after two years of hard egg-laying work, so don't expect many more eggs on a regular basis after that.

    Hybrid laying birds are a specialist 'breed' and they lay lots of eggs and are easy to look after. If having your own freshly produced eggs is your aim, buy these birds at point-of-lay.

- **Traditional breeds:** Light Sussex, Rhode Island Red, Maran and Welsummers are some of the more common names. These breeds may give you a longer-lived hen starting with a respectable 200 odd eggs a year, dropping by 25 per cent year on year but compensating by laying larger eggs as time goes on. These hens may well grow up to be your 'granny hens' and, if you play your cards right, bring up a new flock of chicken for you too. Using eggs all year round from these birds means employing some of the eggs-tending facts in the later section 'Storing Eggs for the Future', because at certain periods of the year you're going to experience a scarcity of eggs.

- **Rare breeds and mixtures:** Some of these breeds are really cute and special, but rare is rare for a reason and if few are around they can't be laying much in the way of eggs. You can experience huge fluctuations in the number of eggs you get from a rare breed, from as low as 30 a year up to a similar number for traditional breeds. You can still have fun keeping these birds, but be philosophical on the egg-production side.

- **Ex-battery:** This type is a modern hybrid laying hen (see the first entry in this list) going into her second year of laying; the only difference is that she's been kept confined for most of her life. The hybrid egg-production figures still apply, but re-homing battery hens is a bit of a lottery: some do well in a new situation and some of the poor things are pretty worn out.

Lighting up

Light and day length affect the number of eggs a chicken lays, but she's still governed by the number of eggs she's born with. Although you can hurry some eggs forward in her life, you can't influence the total number that a hen can produce.

Commercial flocks are artificially lit to provide a minimum of 16 daylight hours a day. If you're really keen to have fresh eggs all year round, purchase a lighting set-up to help you achieve this end. If you buy a point-of-lay hybrid layer in her first flush of youth, she lays all year round without complicated lighting systems. Although you can artificially push her performance in the second year with lights, this practice is generally left to commercial businesses.

Staying 'au natural' and taking the consequences

Pushing hens beyond their natural egg-laying limits costs time and money, and because the hen can only produce a set number of eggs in her life you may as well go with the flow. You can, however, iron out large ups and downs in production, especially if you're committed to hen keeping and have the space to do so without putting too much pressure on your patch of land (you can keep your chickens indoors all the time, but they don't enjoy that much).

Make a plan to introduce new chickens every year, which means also working out what to do with the older ones. Some die natural deaths but hens can hang on until they're 7 or 8 years old without laying any eggs in the later (three!) years. You have to make hard decisions on that.

Buy in point-of-lay hens in the autumn, so that their first flush of eggs carries you through the winter months when the daylight length is decreasing and any older hens are moulting or dropping their production rate. If you breed your own replacement laying hens, aim to have chicks in March or April (around Easter); they're at point-of-lay at the right time and you've taken advantage of good weather and the best of the spring and summer greenery to grow healthy, hearty hens.

Easter time is the best time to have chicks and they start laying just before winter: a great win, win, win situation!

If you can only keep a few hens and yours are past their first year of laying (or have come to you as ex-battery hens in their second year) you have to put up with fluctuations in egg numbers. Expect to eat omelettes every day for the spring months of plenty but you may have to forgo that delicious fresh egg straight from the hen house for breakfast in winter when eggs are more scarce. As with all seasonal fruits, the wait is worthwhile when the time comes round again. At other times, you may have so many eggs that you may need to use them in ways you never dreamed of (and if you keep chickens, you may well end up dreaming about them and their eggs!).

Counting Up Hen and Egg Numbers

One problem you don't face when keeping your own hens is answering the age-old question of 'Which came first, the chicken or the egg?': you have to keep chickens first in order to have the eggs.

A commercially laid egg takes over a week, sometimes more, to get through all the sorting, grading, stamping, packing and transporting systems before it even hits the shops. That's so different from nipping down to the bottom of the garden, saying a quick hello and thank you to some curious little feathered friends while picking up an egg or two for breakfast.

If you're deciding whether keeping hens is right for your situation, take the following factors into consideration before you start:

- ✔ **Caring for them:** Have you got time every day to do the chores?
- ✔ **Cleaning out:** Can you deal with small but regular quantities of manure?
- ✔ **Finding hens:** Is a reputable source nearby?
- ✔ **Housing:** What size, and build your own or buy?
- ✔ **Ranging:** How much of your garden can you give over (the chickens would like it all)?
- ✔ **Safety from predators:** Can you protect your birds from foxes, rats or your pet dog?
- ✔ **Sourcing feed:** Is a shop nearby for all the necessary supplies?

Getting inside the egg

Have you noticed that hard-boiling and peeling the shell off one of your own freshly laid eggs is really difficult to do neatly? Chunks of the white come off in strips. Have you ever wondered why, and did you ever have this problem with shop-bought eggs?

Well, the egg has one layer of membrane just inside the eggshell and another encapsulating the liquid *albumen* (white runny bit) and yolk. The eggshell is porous, because the shell is designed to grow a baby chick that needs to breathe. Therefore, the liquid inside the egg begins to evaporate over time. Shrinking the liquid causes a tiny gap between the solid structure of the shell with its attached first membrane and the pliable second inner membrane. If you hard-boil and then peel an egg when the evaporation has taken place, this process is easy and your egg looks neat and tidy.

If you know that you're going to want to hard-boil your own eggs, put some to one side, write a date on them in pencil if you think that they may get muddled up with fresh ones – after five to seven days they peel easily.

When you've taken care of those aspects, you have to decide how many hens to get.

Chickens are flock creatures so always keep two or more. The *only* situation in which having a single hen on her own is acceptable is when the rest of the flock dies off and she's on her own home territory.

Assume that you buy modern hybrid laying hens (as I describe in the earlier section 'Eggs-tending your harvest by breed') and have sufficient room for six hens. In their first year, they're going to lay a total of 1,800 eggs. That's nearly 36 eggs each week. If you keep these same hens for another year, the production drops to nearer 24 a week (some 1,200 a year).

Now, ask yourself now many eggs do you buy normally to service your family's needs? Even if you've a big family and feed all the neighbours too, most people find 24 to 36 eggs a week overwhelming. You can, of course, sell some to workmates, friends and neighbours and recoup some of the cost of keeping your hens.

You aren't allowed to sell eggs to shops and bed and breakfast establishments unless you follow the food regulations laid out by the Department of the Environment, Food and Rural Affairs (DEFRA): visit www.defra.gov.uk to find out just how complicated life can become!

With so many eggs, you're going to have to think about storing them for future use (check out the later section 'Storing Eggs for the Future').

Watching Your Eggs Over Time

Whereas the earlier section 'Keeping Hens for Eggs' talks about knowing hens, this section provides some tips on dealing with the eggs themselves.

When you collect your own eggs every day, using them in rotation is really important. Piling them into a pretty bowl may look nice but if you don't make some attempt to organise them, you soon have a heap of eggs of all ages.

Use your eggs in date order. Here's an easy way to keep track of dates *and* have the pretty bowl: write a date on your eggs with a pencil. Pencils are non-toxic and write well on egg shell. Don't use a marker pen or biro.

You can also recycle egg boxes or an egg tray, which are made for the job though less aesthetically pleasing as the bowl. Papier-mâché boxes are a natural material that allows the eggs to breathe.

Take a look at the eggs stored this way coming from commercial egg packers: they always have the egg sitting rounded end up. Holding the egg air sac to the top stores them best for longest, up to five weeks. See the later section 'Checking age and freshness' for how to assess your egg for freshness.

If you like novelty items, you can buy something called an 'egg-skelter' that's good for holding up to 24 eggs at one time. As the name suggests, an egg-skelter is in the shape of a helter skelter and you add eggs at the top, taking the oldest from the bottom of the spiral each time.

Looking perfect

Check every egg all over before you store it, keeping only the perfect ones for a longer storage period. The shell and another invisible layer of *bloom* (the last protective coating produced by the hen as she lays the egg) are designed to repel bacteria.

Keeping your own hens allows you to see all the eggy flaws that you don't see in shop-bought eggs. Older hens in particular lay weird and wonderful eggs, all bumpy and wrinkled, but as long as the quality of the shell is good, these eggs store perfectly well.

Hens new to laying produce small eggs to begin with and then one day shock you (and probably themselves!) with a double-yolked whopper. Don't worry, they're just getting organised for laying perfect, smooth, oval eggs for months to come.

Cracking up and related problems

Finding broken or dirty eggs repeatedly may indicate a few problems in your hen house. Dirty and cracked eggs don't store as well because the shell barrier and its outer covering of bloom is breached, allowing bacteria to enter the egg.

- **Older hens:** As hens age, they lay larger eggs but their ability to form a perfect shell deteriorates.

- **Weak egg shells:** If you know that your hens are young, they may be ill or you aren't supplying enough extra calcium in the form of soluble grit. Sort this problem out quickly. Weak shells are prone to breaking, especially if other hens are clambering about in the nest boxes.

- **Egg eating:** Some hens pick up the bad habit of eating their own eggs, and they can 'teach' other hens to do the same. Nip this behaviour in the bud early: place the nest boxes in a darker corner of the hen house or drape a covering over the nest box entrance so that the eggs aren't as visible.

- **Dirty eggs:** If your hens are free range and the dirt is from muddy feet, don't worry too much. Store your eggs with the mud on and wash it off just before you use them. If you've particularly dirty 'poohy' eggs, check that a naughty hen isn't sleeping in the nest boxes and rearrange your housing to stop her. Use filthy eggs straightaway and don't store them for long periods.

Checking age and freshness

You normally know exactly how old your eggs are because you collect them every day. But sometimes things go a little awry and you get no eggs for a while – for example, when spring is in the air. Your hen is probably thinking that she should build a nest and raise a brood of chicks. This can't happen, of course, unless you've a cockerel around, but she lives in hope that she may get lucky and the cockerel of her dreams turn up at any moment. Therefore, hens start hunting around the garden in all the little nooks and crannies.

All well and good, but if you find a nest with 15 eggs in it, do you use them or not?

Eggs are fine for several weeks and without a cockerel they aren't fertile. The best thing to do is to keep these eggs separate from any others or mark them with a pencil.

If you need an egg for cooking, crack one of your mystery eggs into a cup. Looking and smelling gives you all the information you need. If it looks good and smells good, it's good. If you've a bad egg, you know it and your senses, evolved over thousands of years to help you eliminate dangerous food, come into play straightaway. I can guarantee that you recoil in horror, like when the pantomime monster from the deep marsh pops in for a visit, smelly and sulphurous and looking green and revolting!

Always crack one egg at a time into a cup before using it, so that if your mystery egg proves to be a rogue you don't spoil all your eggs.

But what about telling how fresh an egg is when you want to hard-boil it? Here's how to set your mind at rest as to whether you've a really old egg or an acceptably old egg. Remember, the egg is porous and has an air space at the rounded end.

- ✔ **Candling:** Holding a small torch to the end of your egg shows you what's inside. Look for a curved shadowy shape, which is the air sac that all eggs contain, at the rounded end of the egg. In a fresh egg, the sac is no more than a small dent, but the visible shadowy dent increases in size over time. At about 4 weeks old, the shadowy shape has grown to about 1 centimetre (half an inch) deep. The egg is still fine to use. (Take a look at Figure 17-1.)

- ✔ **Floating:** Place your egg in a bowl of water. A fresh egg sinks and a medium-aged egg tilts its air sac to the top of the water. A really old egg has converted some of its insides to gas and bobs about on the water. Watch out, you may be in for an exploding shock if you don't handle this egg carefully! (Check out Figure 17-2.)

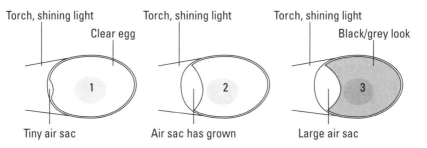

Figure 17-1: Checking eggs for freshness by candling.

1. The tiny air sac shows just how fresh this particular egg is.
2. The larger air sac up to 1 centimetre (1/2 inch) deep shows that this egg is probably 4 weeks old and is fine to use.
3. This egg is a bomb waiting to go off! Stand clear!

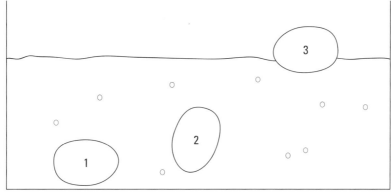

Figure 17-2: Checking eggs for freshness by floating.

1. This egg is very fresh. Use it for Chinese Salted Eggs.
2. This egg is old, but absolutely fine. Use for hard-boiled or pickled eggs, or use the whites for meringues.
3. Watch out! Stand clear! This egg is very old and full of gas!

Storing Eggs for the Future

When your own-produced eggs begin to pile up, don't panic. Store them at an ambient temperature, out of bright sunshine and away from strong smells, and they last a long time. On the supermarket shelves, eggs are allowed four weeks before the 'best before' date kicks in, and that only indicates that the eggs are 'best before' that date, not that they're off or bad for you. Look in the previous section 'Checking age and freshness' for one way to put your mind at ease if you aren't sure.

You can find some recipes and what to do to make your egg glut more manageable in this section. Enjoying your own eggs all year round may mean using them in different ways than frying, soft-boiling or in omelettes, but relish this experimentation – without your own hens you may never have come to enjoy these exciting, different flavours and textures.

Pickling your eggs

Home-made pickled eggs are quick and easy to make but don't treat them like the ones you see in chip shops and pubs (which include preservatives other than the basic vinegar treatment). Make room for these eggs in the fridge and they keep for months and months.

Picked eggs

Pickled eggs are great, and really easy to do. They make a great 'pub snack' when dropped into a packet of your favourite crisps to eat together. With a pint of beer, this combination makes a more substantial snack than you may realise! If you prefer something a little more upmarket, you can use pickled eggs to decorate salads. To understand more about what makes pickling and vinegar-proof lids work, take a look at Chapter 6. Chapter 3 has more on sterilisation.

The quantities for this recipe are purposely vague; it depends entirely on the number and size of eggs you want to pickle and the jars you've available.

Saving your eggs for five to seven days before hard-boiling makes them easy to peel, and they look neater.

Special tools required: *Sterilised jars, vinegar-proof lids*

Preparation time: *30 minutes peeling eggs*

Processing time: *25 minutes*

Yields: *As many eggs as you use*

Newly hard-boiled and peeled eggs

Vinegar of your choice (but not balsamic)

Any or none of the following as flavouring: fresh garlic, thinly sliced root ginger, pickling

Spices (peppercorns, black, red or green; coriander seeds; juniper berries; and so on). Use just 5 grams (one teaspoon) to each jar.

1 Pack the warm hard-boiled eggs into your sterilised jars.

2 Boil the vinegar in a non-ferrous pan (stainless steel is best) with the pickling spices and flavourings for about five minutes and pour into the jars to cover the eggs.

As soon as your eggs have boiled for the required length of time (six to eight minutes depending on the size of your eggs), run them under cold tap water. Doing so cools them quickly and you don't get a dark-grey ring round the yellow yolk.

3 Close the jars (using vinegar-proof lids) and allow to cool completely.

4 Mark with the date of making and store in the fridge. Be patient: pickled eggs (which keep for several months) taste much better if you allow them to mature. Leave them for one month before trying.

Per egg: 75 calories; 6 grams protein, 1 gram carbohydrate, 5 grams fat, 2 grams saturated fat, 213 milligrams cholesterol, 0 grams fibre, 63 milligrams sodium.

Picking up pickling tips

When I first made pickled eggs, I tried to stick to a recipe exactly; I soon found out that my eggs didn't 'go' with the recipe-suggested numbers. Anyway, sometimes I pickle duck eggs, which are really big, and sometimes pullet eggs, which are tiny by comparison.

Now I'm much more relaxed about pickling eggs. I do make sure that the jars are squeaky clean and sterilised in the oven at 120 degrees Celsius (250 degrees Fahrenheit) but I no longer measure anything. Instead, I go by eye.

I use cider vinegar because this vinegar is local to my area. I live in Devon, which has lots of orchards, and I like to support local growers. You can pickle eggs equally successfully with malt vinegar or wine vinegar.

After I fill my jars with eggs, I pour the boiled vinegar with its spices into the sterilised jars (making sure that some of the spices go into each jar, because they look pretty as much as for flavour-

ing) and then I put on the lids and leave the jars to cool completely before storing in the fridge. I store the jars in the fridge because eggs are such an excellent source of protein that they're a medium for bacteria to grow in. This method makes them slightly different from a pickle that you boil for a long time or a vegetable that's water-based. Eggs don't tolerate over-boiling: it makes the yolks go an unappetising colour (to avoid, run under cold tap water to cool them quickly).

I keep a 5-litre (around 1-gallon) plastic bottle of vinegar handy for topping up if I've under-estimated the amount of vinegar, and if I boiled up too much, I allow it to cool and return it, with any lingering spices, into my vinegar bottle so that I waste nothing.

I label my bottles clearly with the date they were made and my egg-eating family have to wait a month before using them, because they really do taste better when they've matured.

Solving egg storage

Solutions to egg storage are literally that: liquid mixtures or solutions. They work in different ways depending on the mix.

Here's an egg storage method that the Chinese have been using for thousands of years.

Saline solution

Make a supersaturated saline solution and immerse your eggs in it for 30 days before boiling and eating. The Chinese prefer duck eggs (Chinese salted duck eggs are on all the supermarket shelves in Asia) but you can do this process with chicken eggs too. To follow the Chinese tradition, after hard boiling your stored eggs, simply cut the whole egg in half lengthways and use a teaspoon to scoop out the middle.

The *supersaturated saline solution* (the highest proportion of salt that will dissolve in hot water) keeps bacteria from reaching the eggs but, because eggshell is porous, a *concentration gradient* (a higher density in one area compared to another) forms between the liquid inside the eggs and the saline solution on the outside. By a process of osmosis through the egg membranes, water from the egg moves into the saline solution, shrivelling the content.

Preparation time: *30 minutes*

Yield: *As many eggs as you use*

> Clean raw eggs in their shells (use fresh eggs)   2 litres (4 pints) water
> 230 grams (½ pound) rock salt

1 Boil the water and dissolve the salt in it; allow to cool.

2 Pack a jar with eggs and pour in the cooled liquid to completely cover the eggs; use a weight to keep them immersed.

3 Date and label your jar.

4 Leave for 30 days (or more) in the fridge before hard boiling the eggs for a truly global feast.

Per egg: *75 calories; 6 grams protein, 1 gram carbohydrate, 5 grams fat, 2 grams saturated fat, 213 milligrams cholesterol, 0 grams fibre, 1,183 milligrams sodium.*

Whisking up and separating out

Putting eggs straight into the freezer to store doesn't work: the liquid egg expands inside the shells, cracking them open and seeping liquid on thawing. Nevertheless, if you separate and whisk your eggs, you can use your freezer to preserve them so that you can use them later.

When you get the hang of it, separating eggs is easy and good fun:

1. **Hold your egg over a bowl (have another bowl ready too).**
2. **Tap it (with conviction) on the edge of the bowl to break it.**
3. **Pass the yolk from one half of the eggshell to the other several times, allowing the white to escape into the bowl.**
4. **Tip the yolk into another bowl when you've removed all the white.**

Separating eggs is like juggling, but you're allowed to drop bits!

When separated, store eggs as follows:

- **Egg whites:** Whisk and store in useful quantities for fools and other dishes (see the later section 'Cooking with eggs before storing' for how to make meringues).
- **Egg yolks:** Whisk, make ice cream or use to add richness and colour to dishes.
- **Whole eggs:** Whisk whole eggs and freeze in useful quantities for any kind of sweet or savoury cooking. (You can keep your eggs in this way for the Christmas cake or any special occasion.)

Chapter 7 gives you loads more freezer storage tips.

Cooking with eggs before storing

Not all 'eggy' dishes can withstand freezing: ones in which the egg is combined well with flour or something else come out of the freezer best. Here are a few ideas to use up eggs in times of surplus; in conjunction with your freezer, they last and last.

Make cakes using up your surplus eggs while they're fresh and freeze stacks of sponge bases. You can soon jolly up a well-made defrosted cake with an interesting fresh filling from your store of garden fruits.

Basic sponge

For this recipe, you need whole eggs. The best cakes have the same proportions of egg, flour, butter and sugar. Weigh your eggs first and use the result as a guide. If your mixing bowl is large enough, make several cakes at the same time using multiples of the ingredients and keeping the proportions the same. You may have to eat one immediately to test them out anyway!

The average medium egg weighs 56 grams (2 ounces) so the following recipe works with 225-gram (8-ounce) measures.

Preparation time: *20 minutes*

Cooking time: *20–25 minutes*

Serves: *6–8*

> *225 grams (8 ounces) butter, softened at room temperature*
>
> *225 grams (8 ounces) caster sugar*
>
> *4 medium eggs*

> *10 millilitres (2 teaspoons) vanilla extract*
>
> *225 grams (8 ounces) self-raising flour*
>
> *Milk, to loosen*

1 Preheat the oven to 180 degrees Celsius (350 degrees Fahrenheit)/Gas Mark 4.

2 Grease and line two 18-centimetre (7-inch) cake tins with baking paper.

3 Cream the butter and the sugar together in a bowl until pale and fluffy.

Old-fashioned butter makes the best cakes. If you use soft margarine or butter substitute (that's been whipped up with water to become that constituency – look at the ingredients panel) it may be easy to mix but the proportions of egg, flour, sugar and butter don't tally.

4 Beat in the eggs, a little at a time, and stir in the vanilla extract.

5 Fold in the flour using a large wooden spoon, adding a little extra milk if necessary, to create a batter with a soft dropping consistency.

6 Divide the mixture between the cake tins and gently spread out with a spatula.

7 Bake for 20–25 minutes, or until golden-brown on top and a skewer you insert into the middle comes out clean.

8 Remove from the oven and set aside for five minutes, and then remove from the tin and peel off the paper; place onto a wire rack.

9 Allow the cakes to cool completely and wrap up well for the freezer (if you make several, save one to eat straight away!). See Chapter 7 for more on freezing.

Per serving: 586 calories; 7 grams protein, 65 grams carbohydrate, 33 grams fat, 20 grams saturated fat, 207 milligrams cholesterol, 1 gram fibre, 492 milligrams sodium.

Simple meringue

For this recipe, you need the whites of the eggs only. You're going to appreciate this recipe if you take a liking to the homemade ice cream recipe that follows, because it leaves you with the whites to deal with. Master meringues and you've the perfect combination to hand for every special occasion that needs a fancy pud.

You can work out quantities by weighing your egg whites and doubling the weight for the sugar if you've odd amounts to use up.

Use egg whites from older eggs, because the whites have become more watery and whip up more easily.

Meringues store for ages at an ambient temperature if you wrap them in greaseproof paper and store in an airtight container or place them in a plastic bag. Keep them dry and safe from rough treatment or you may end up with meringue dust.

If you don't have caster sugar, you can make some by blasting granulated sugar in a food processor: caster sugar is just sugar in smaller crystals.

Successful meringue-making depends on starting out with scrupulously clean tools and equipment. Put your rubber gloves on and wash all your tools and bowls in scalding-hot, soapy water, and then rinse in clean water and allow to drain. Keeping plastic bowls really clean is more difficult than stainless steel or ceramic ones, because any tiny scratches trap residues of grease.

Special tools: Spotlessly clean, grease-free metal or ceramic bowl, whisk, piping bag

Preparation time: 40 minutes, less with electric whisk

Cooking time: 3–4 hours

Serves: 4–6

4 egg whites	100 grams (3½ ounces) caster sugar

1 Leave your egg whites to 'age' in the fridge for a week if they come from really fresh eggs, but keep them covered and clean. Allow them to come to room temperature before whipping and they create more volume (sieving them through a really clean sieve removes the little stringy bits if you're being pernickety).

You can whip up egg whites by hand, but doing so is jolly hard work; using an electric mixer is easier and quicker.

2 Beat eggs until stiff and then fold in a tablespoon (15 grams) caster sugar. Beat again until the mixture is smooth and satiny and can be pulled up into peaks. Using a metal spoon, fold in the rest of the sugar.

3 Pipe the mixture onto parchment paper laid on a baking sheet. Dredge with caster sugar.

4 Bake/dry out using a cool oven at 110 degrees Celsius (230 degrees Fahrenheit)/Gas Mark 1/4 for three or four hours or until the meringues are firm and crisp. Wedging open the oven door a little from time to time allows the steam to escape, speeding up the drying process.

5 Allow the meringues to cool completely. Peel off the parchment paper.

Per 30-gram serving: 118 calories; 4 grams protein, 25 grams carbohydrate, 0 grams fat, 0 grams saturated fat, 0 milligrams cholesterol, 0 grams fibre, 69 milligrams sodium. Based on 4 servings.

Basic ice cream

For this recipe you need egg yolks, and you'll find it easier with an ice-cream maker but making ice cream is possible without one. You can make rich ice creams and store them in the freezer; combine your own home-grown fruits for a double whammy storage solution.

This recipe is for basic ice cream and makes about 1 litre; you can find lots of recipe variations around so use the recipes that come with your machine (if you have one), fla-vouring plain ice cream with a splash of vanilla when you don't have any home- grown fruit handy.

Special tools required: *Mechanical ice-cream maker and electric whisk, ice cubes*

Preparation time: *40–50 minutes*

Processing time: *30 minutes mixing, then as per your ice-cream maker's instructions – or a few minutes stirring every 15 minutes (3 or 4 times) for the hand-made version.*

Yields: *About 1 litre (1¾ pints)*

500 millilitres (18 fluid ounces) double cream	*150 millilitres (5 fluid ounces) water*
100 grams (3½ ounces) caster sugar	*4 large egg yolks*

1 Scald the cream, bringing almost to the boil. Remove from the heat.

2 Dissolve the sugar in water over a low heat, and then whizz up the heat and boil rapidly making a light syrup (drop a little on a cold plate – the syrup is ready when stretching it between your fingers forms a thread). Leave to cool a little.

3 Whisk the egg yolks stirring in about 30–45 millilitres (2–3 tablespoons) of the cream to start with. Add the rest of the cream bit by bit, stirring and trickling in the hot syrup as you go. Keep whisking until the mixture is thick and creamy. Cool the mixture over a bowl of ice-cold water before pouring into the ice-cream maker and churn. (Follow the instructions for your machine carefully.)

4 Add any flavours, mixing in well and checking for sweetness. Add a little icing sugar if you find it too tart.

If you don't have the luxury of an ice-cream maker, follow the same steps, place mixture in a bowl and put this in the freezer. Leave for 15 to 20 minutes and then stir the mixture. Repeat several times to maintain an ice cream texture until the ice cream is well frozen.

Per 100-gram serving: *236 calories; 2 grams protein, 12 grams carbohydrate, 21 grams fat, 12 grams saturated fat, 154 milligrams cholesterol, 0 grams fibre, 22 milligrams sodium.*

Blowing eggs

You can preserve your egg shells (at least those with perfect shells) forever by blowing them. Using a tool such as an awl, bore a small hole in the top and bottom of the egg, big enough to insert a straw. Stick a bit of tape over the place where you're making the hole, because it stops the rest of the shell from cracking so easily. Loosen the inside of the egg by poking it with a skewer or thin knitting needle.

Blow air into the egg with the straw, so the contents come out through the other hole. To achieve the correct blowing pressure takes a little practice, and you need to be careful so that the shell doesn't crack. Clean the inside of the egg by immersing the whole thing in a mild bleach solution. Allow to dry well and decorate, making a delicate keepsake that lasts for years.

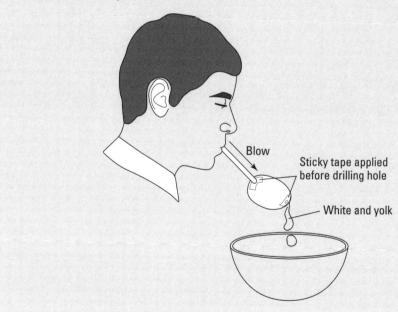

Blow

Sticky tape applied before drilling hole

White and yolk

Chapter 18

Going Wild in the Country

In This Chapter

▶ Collecting up the countryside's bounty

▶ Taking care in (and of) the countryside

▶ Storing and using nature's gifts

*T*aking a relaxing stroll in the countryside, or finding unspoilt places nearer to the urban sprawl, is infinitely more rewarding when you come away with a pocketful, or perhaps even arm-fuls, of something that you can turn into a delicious preserve or tasty tipple.

People have been gleaning food from the countryside for millennia – indeed it was the only shopping mall for our ancestors – and today no restrictions apply to the common free foods you find in hedgerows, woodlands, canal sides and other places, as long as you stick to public rights of way. In this chapter, I take you on a countryside walk, describing how to take care of yourself and the surroundings to ensure a pleasant, fruitful and safe day out collecting from nature's bounty.

I show that, with a bit of ingenuity and creativity, your larder can explode (lit-erally so, if your homemade wine gets too frisky!) with smells, tastes and the delicate colours of the natural bounty of the great outdoors.

Gathering Up Your Stores

Your trip into the countryside may be a casual walk. If, while out, you just happen upon something delicious by chance – perhaps a bank of wild straw-berries – eating them there and then is the best way to go. Preserve the delicate taste in your memory (they taste like strawberries with the cream already added!).

But imagine that you notice a crab-apple tree in full springtime bloom, and want to return later in the year to take advantage of the fruits. Or you're planning a more focused expedition, such as going out specifically to find blackberries. In these cases, you need to know what grows when and what's safe, which I tell you about in this section. And whatever your original impulse, you need to ensure that you're well equipped too.

Preparing to pick

Nature has a way of protecting herself, with stingers, thorns and prickles and by hanging fruits in inaccessible places. Here's some Scout-like advice on being prepared:

- ✔ Wear stout footwear and thorn-proof trousers and jacket.

- ✔ Put on just one stout glove (Michael Jackson style). Wearing two gloves for picking can be awkward and is probably more of a hindrance than a help. With one gloved hand you can grab a prickly or thorny bush and bend the branch gently, without breaking branches. Reaching and picking with your ungloved hand is then much easier.

    Put up with a few scratches and nettle stings – they're character-building and good for the circulation. Consider these minor brushes an occupational hazard; surface scratches heal quickly after a good wash when you're home. If you're the type whose minor scratches quickly turn septic, though, turn to Chapter 3 for a run through of First Aid equipment to keep handy for a quick clean up.

- ✔ Use a crooked stick for pulling high and awkward branches towards you. This excellent implement also helps with balance when wading through a prickly briar or bramble patch. Your stick is a handy tool for beating back the nettles when you're advancing deep into nature's bosom too.

- ✔ Carry a sensible basket or container for gathering flowers or fruits without crushing them. Plastic boxes with lids can stop your hard-earned harvest tipping out as you scramble back onto easier ground. Also, take a clean tea towel to lay gently over your collected produce in the basket; it stops flimsy flower heads and petals blowing away in the wind.

 When using the flowers of plants or trees – dandelions and elderflowers, for example – gather them in full sun at midday if you can; they're at their sweetest, driest and most 'nectarful'.

Familiarising yourself with new plants and their fruits is a wise move. A good, comprehensive, full-colour wild flower and plant identifier, however, is part of the countryside gleaner's toolkit. Look out for the Collins Complete Guides series, which offers titles that deal with wild flowers, trees and other wild topics like the birds and animals you may meet on your foraging journeys.

If you aren't certain what a plant is, leave it alone. Some flowers are poisonous – for example, foxglove and laburnum – and some leaves aren't good to eat – such as yew. Certain juicy-looking berries are poisonous (Arum Lily, also called Lords and Ladies) and some deadly (Deadly Nightshade). Some wild roots are killers – such as a Hemlock Water Dropwort – you need your identifier book to work out which this is from a similar bunch of plants. All fungi, bar the particularly common ones, are suspect unless you've made a comprehensive study of the subject.

Charting your way around the seasons

Planning specific collecting trips is going to be much more successful if you know when certain plants are right for picking. Here's a general guide:

- ✔ **Spring:** Young leaves, such as nettles, and early flower blossom, such as dandelions and ramsons; wild garlic and St. George's mushrooms
- ✔ **Summer:** Early flowering blossoms such as elderflower
- ✔ **Autumn:** Blackberry, crab apple, elderberry, rowan berries, field mushrooms, French hales, hips and haws and sloe
- ✔ **Winter:** Sloes after frost

Taking Care in the Countryside

In this section, you find helpful hints on staying safe in the countryside and leaving it so that you're welcomed back by the animals and people who live there full time.

If you already live in a rural area, no doubt you're familiar with the sights and sounds of the countryside and can skip this section. But visitors hoping to find some countryside items to jolly up the store cupboards may need to wise up on a few issues before marching out over the horizon in search of free food.

Stepping away from the beaten track

When you venture off into the unknown countryside, you need to treat what you find with respect and follow common-sense guidelines. What used to be called the Countryside Code is as good a set of sensible rules to follow as any: behave courteously and in a manner that brings no harm to you, wildlife (flora and fauna), any farmland that you walk over or domestic animals you come across.

Public footpaths, for walkers only, and public bridleways, for horses and riders as well as walkers, are well signposted tracks especially for you to use. In other places – seashore, heath or moorland, for example – you can roam around.

When you're out and about in the countryside:

✔ **Take your well-charged mobile phone with you.** Make use of technology! You can't guarantee to receive a signal, though, so as an added precaution tell someone what you're up to, and take a companion if possible.

✔ **Know where you are.** Your map – a good Ordinance Survey or similar large-scale one – tells you whether you're in a designated National Park. Official Nature Reserves have information boards showing which paths or areas you may use; don't pick anything from here. A wild bird or butterfly conservation job may be ongoing and even a common plant such as a nettle is important to such a fragile ecosystem.

Rare birds, butterflies and other wildlife need those plants more than you.

✔ **Carry a good pictorial wildflower and plant guide with you.** You can also use online identification sites such as www.botanicalkeys.co.uk that guide you towards identification easily, as long as you've enough accurate information. Note down any distinguishing features of a plant you suspect is the one you're looking for or avoiding. You can then look it up later.

Your mobile phone or digital camera helps you out here. Or sketch or write a note to yourself about leaf shape, size, how they're joined to the stem, colour, number of petals and any other little distinguishing features. Don't rely on memory.

You may be seeing the correct plant but at a time of year when the plant is not showing obvious features. Therefore, you may have to return when its fruits and flowers are ready, but at least now you know where to look. If you discover a rare plant, enjoy it *in situ* and leave it alone to flourish in its natural habitat.

✔ **Don't uproot any plants.** Taking a little from each plant and leaving the roots intact ensures a sustainable supply. After all, if your foray is a great success and you make an absolutely delicious meal, you want to return again knowing that more of the same is to be had in the future.

✔ **Leave gates as you find them, open or shut.** You may be on a relaxing stroll but other people are working in the area and animals and tractors may be moving from field to field. If you follow some people through a gate, enquire politely as to whether they found it open or shut so you know what to do with certainty.

An animal's life may depend on closing or leaving open a gate. The field may be shut to keep animals from straying onto the road, or left open to allow them access to a water supply.

✔ **Bring a snack or drink with you.** But make sure that you take every-thing home. Rubbish and litter looks unsightly and can cause serious harm to wildlife, perhaps when they fatally mistake a piece of nice-smell-ing plastic for food. Also, hard plastic and metal objects lodge between the *cleats* (splits between the toes) in cows' or sheep hooves, or punc-ture the sole of an animal's hoof, causing pain and infections. Hedgehogs starve to death if they get a plastic ring caught round their middle, and although a robin's nest in an old teapot looks cute on a calendar, leaving junk behind in the countryside is *fly tipping*: illegal littering.

✔ **Keep any dogs under control.** Keep your dog on a lead and never let them chase sheep; you don't know whether those sheep are heavily pregnant (in lamb) and you can cause a lot of misery to the animals and the shepherd caring for them. Farmers can legally shoot any dog that harasses his stock of cattle and sheep. Small dogs can get overexcited when they smell rabbits and disappear down a rabbit hole never to be seen again. Dogs don't understand about cliff edges either, and the bill for a helicopter rescue is expensive!

People are trained to clean up after their dogs – a wise thing in a heav-ily populated area – but if your dog leaves a deposit in the countryside, take the mess home with you or kick it discretely into the long grass and let nature dispose of it over time. Please don't bag it up in plastic and leave it hanging in a tree! Landowners hate having 'presents' of plastic-wrapped dog poop left on their land for weeks on end.

✔ **Believe and take seriously any 'Beware of the Bull' signs.** Don't wander into fields with bulls even when you see a fantastic clump of your chosen fruit right in front of you, no matter how tempting. Bulls guard their cows and you may well be considered the enemy. Don't risk it; bulls move surprisingly quickly when they're on a mission.

Keeping a weather eye open

The UK weather is famously changeable. If you're out foraging for goodies to add to your preserving repertoire, check the weather forecast. This section gives hints on beating the weather or using it to your own advantage.

Wear appropriate clothing – the saying 'There's no such thing as bad weather, only inappropriate clothing' applies to everyone. Trudging home soaking wet, cold and with damp feet is miserable when a pair of wellies and a raincoat can save you the trauma.

Also, although fruits pick well on sunny days, picking blackberries in your T-shirt and shorts is no fun, even in a blazing summer. Reaching the best ones in the middle of a briar patch is a prickly job. (Check out the early sec-tion on 'Preparing to pick' for some prickle-avoiding hints.)

If you're at the seaside and gleaning around the shores, pick up a 'Time of tides' booklet telling you exactly when the tides are in and out for that area; the booklet is available at small local shops and newsagents. Your life may depend on knowing when to turn for home without getting wet feet or worse.

Some plants preserve better depending on the weather around their fruiting time. For example, blackberries are no longer plump, delicious fruits after a heavy autumn shower – that is, 'after Old Nick spits (or worse) on them' as the saying goes! They become a pale imitation and don't make the best jellies and jams.

Combining watery blackberries with orchard or crab apples to brighten up your pots gives a better set. Chapter 5 has more jam and jelly talk.

St George's mushrooms (safe, white-gilled mushrooms that are traditionally ready to pick on 23 April) also deteriorate quickly after a downpour, giving off a stronger odour than in dryer times. If you're picking in the wet, deal with the mushrooms the same day before they become maggoty and unusable (flip to the later section 'Wild mushrooms' for more). After a wet spell, open freeze them (as I describe in Chapter 7) instead of attempting to dry – although in dry years half the work's already been done. Peruse Chapter 8 for tips on drying (the same advice applies to field mushrooms).

Conversely, making the best sloe gin depends on a good hard frost beating the sloes into submission, helping them to release their flavour. (The later section 'Sloes' contains a great Sloe Gin recipe.)

Choosing clean and safe food

Imagine that from the safety and comfort of your car you spot some particularly laden wild fruit trees or bushes. Open and shut case, you may think. But you need to ask yourself whether this place is really the best to be picking from. This section alerts you to some of the pitfalls of going for the seemingly easy option while seeking out your wild harvest. I also point you in the right direction for a clean and safe find.

Observing a few don'ts

Here are a few countryside food gathering no-nos:

✔ **Busy roads:** Although stopping in a lay-by on a busy road and whipping out your packed lunch box to pick nearby berries or fragrant flowers may seem like a good idea, stop and think. The busier the road, the more exhaust fumes and pollutants. And what about dirty spray from big lorries and cars that settles on the lovely, juicy fruits, even if the dirt isn't obvious?

In addition, lay-bys may well contain other human pollutants that you can't see and may not want to risk, especially at the below waist levels.

Fast and busy roads are really dangerous for you and other road users when you're out of your car; don't risk it for a pot of jam.

✔ **Cliffs:** Low bushes near the tops of cliffs are tempting but beware when reaching out for a particularly plump berry. Edges of cliffs can be deceptive with dense bushes hiding loose stones. People do fall down cliffs – don't let it be you.

✔ **Fields:** As well as taking note of any 'Beware of the Bull' signs, always reject the mushroom growing right in the middle of a cowpat too! The muck may wash off, but that's exactly the right place to pick up an invisible E. Coli bug (Chapter 3 explains in more detail why that's a problem).

Also, if the vegetation under or nearby where you want to pick looks brown, reddish, dry or shrivelled in a specific area, round a gateway for example, suspect that this vegetation has been sprayed with *herbicide* – a plant-killing chemical. Even if your chosen spot hasn't been targeted directly, the spray may have drifted, and so move to a different place. Beware also if you're picking fruit on the edge of a field full of crops and you don't know the spray history.

Better to wade through a few nettles to get to safe fruits than to eat poisoned ones!

✔ **Look down and up!** Animals, particularly foxes and farm dogs, scent-mark their territory with you know what; keep any picking to above knee height.

Keep an eye out when you're picking under a tree. Birds may use the same branches time and time again, and certain spots receive all the droppings – that's a flavour you don't want in your jam.

Following a few dos:

Here are a few definite do-dos (sorry, that didn't come out quite right!):

✔ Seek out places where the road traffic is light or non-existent. You can pick from hedgerows along the edges of public rights of way, unless signs say otherwise. Also, quiet country roads and tracks where only a few vehicles are driving about offer safe harvests from the hedgerows.

✔ Dress in light- or bright-coloured clothing to make you more obvious to unsuspecting road users. You're likely to meet tractors and people driving or riding animals on small country roads; be safe, be seen.

✔ Wear long trousers when going on a picking expedition; finding your bare legs becoming an insect meal along the way isn't much fun and it can lead to a more serious disease problem if you're in in areas where deer roam, such as moorland. Ticks don't want a mouthful of trouser, which is handy.

✔ Pick only obviously clean fruits and flowers.

✔ Look out for organic farms, which don't spray with chemicals. Chapter 21 contains ideas on getting access to areas that you can guarantee aren't contaminated with chemical crop sprays.

Staying on the right side of the law

Whose food is it anyway? Does wild food exist just for the picking and anybody can have it, or are things not quite as simple as that? Ultimately, individuals have to take responsibility for their actions and their own safety. Climbing into someone's orchard, no matter how abandoned and wild it looks, isn't going to do a person much good if a male goat lives there and is guarding his nanny goat wives with a good set of butting horns. In such a scenario, the human is bound to come off worse!

Common sense keeps nearly everybody on the right side of the law. Picking for home use is a tradition going back hundreds of years, but if you feel the need to understand more about your rights, the two principle acts of Parliament are the Countryside and Rights of Way Act 2000 (CROW) and the Wildlife and Countryside Act 1981 (WCA). Looking online at any good wild harvesting website introduces you to the details. Scotland's laws differ: visit www.forestharvest.org.uk for more information.

If an area looks like cultivated land – no matter how overgrown or scruffy – it belongs to someone and is private; hands off!

Respecting private property

Here's one example to illustrate the problem of scrumping/stealing. Our tiny farm has a disused railway – recently made into a cycle and recreational path – running through the middle of it. We're delighted that cycling safely is a possibility in the area and for people to enjoy the wonderful countryside here in Devon. Before we knew that the disused railway line was destined to become a public right of way, we planted several orchard trees along the banked edges of the track bed. These trees and the woodland alongside the track remain ours and are in full view of the track. As autumn approached, one of the trees, which we planted and have looked after since it was a scrappy sapling, looked like having a bumper crop of pears, and we were looking forward to home-made pear juice at least; sadly our harvest was not to be. Someone trespassed onto the land and stripped every pear; trampled ground all around the tree showed where the person had been.

Of course we welcome people walking along the path, but these trees aren't public property. They clearly look like a small private orchard and that appearance should have been respected. Please make sure that you only gather fruit from what's clearly common land.

Scrumping is stealing.

Sharing the bounty

Gathering wild produce from the hedgerows used to be a necessity for poor families, as well as delivering food flavours not found elsewhere. Whether you're wild harvesting to eke out a shrinking budget, as a newly found hobby, as a family tradition or just because you love the idea of using what nature has to offer, remember that you're not the only person who wants a share. Other humans do too and, more importantly, so does the wildlife.

You can probably go out and buy a bag of chips or a pizza if you're really hungry, but wild birds and animals rely on the wild harvest for all their food – even if you're feeding ones local to your garden – so please don't strip every last berry. The birds carry seeds and fertilise with their droppings: some seeds stick to beaks and the bird carries the seeds to a new spot and precious pollinators such as insects and bees feed on nectar while about their work. In the interest of future generations of both humans and wildlife, only take as much as you know you can use and never strip a whole plant.

Never uproot a plant and pick the fruit from it in that way.

Delighting in the Turning of the Seasons

In this section, I describe some of the fruits to keep an eye out for on your countryside gathering expeditions, fruits that humans have been using to bulk out their store cupboards for many, many generations. I also provide a few delicious recipes so that you can enjoy the tastes of the countryside. Remember that although most of your picking is autumn work, the enjoyment can last all year round.

I include here only the really obvious choices of plants that families have used time and time again. If you're a particularly adventurous soul, I advise finding a guided foraging tour. From tours such as these, you can really gain a good knowledge of the plants and fruits that are available 'out there'. Look online for foraging and bushcraft sites where you can meet plenty of like-minded people.

Hedgerow Jelly

I organise most of the fruits in this section alphabetically by fruit, but I just had to start with this recipe because it uses many (or as few) of the wild fruits you're likely to find on your travels.

You make this jelly from any combination of hedgerow fruits. Amass French hales, hips, haws, sloes and/or hazelnuts in any combination (though you may have to freeze a few of the ingredients while others come on stream; Chapter 7 gives frosty hints); just be sure to include the 900 grams (2 pounds) of crab apples to help with the setting and add blackberries to give the jelly a purple hue. The taste and colour of your finished jelly depends on the ingredients and will remind you of autumn every time you use it. This jelly is fantastic with savoury as well as sweet dishes or just straight onto a humble piece of toast.

Special tools required: Jelly bag, thermometer, sterilised jars

Preparation time: 30–40 minutes

Processing time: Straining about 4 hours, with 35 minutes cooking time (depending on fruits used)

Yield: 1.3–1.8 kilograms (3–4 pounds)

900 grams (2 pounds) ripe hedgerow fruit, mixed or single flavour

900 grams (2 pounds) crab apples (prepared weight)

450 grams (1 pound) granulated sugar per 600 millilitres (1 pint) liquid

1.8 litres (3 pints) water

1 Wash and pick over the berries, removing stalks, leaves and so on. Wash crab apples, and cut out any bruised or bad bits.

2 Place the fruit and water in a heavy-bottomed preserving pan or large saucepan; bring to the boil, cover and simmer for 20–25 minutes until the fruit is tender.

3 Strain through a clean, scalded jelly bag for at least four hours.

4 Heat the oven to 110 degrees Celsius (225 degrees Fahrenheit), Gas Mark ¼.

5 Measure the strained juice and weigh out 450 grams (1 pound) of granulated sugar for each 600 millilitres (1 pint) of juice. Put the sugar in an ovenproof dish and place in the centre of the oven to warm through for 10–15 minutes.

6 Heat the strained juice gently and add the warmed sugar, stirring until dissolved. Bring to the boil and boil rapidly for around ten minutes: test for set or use a sugar thermometer (check out Chapter 5 for testing set methods and Chapter 2 for the wonders of a sugar/jam thermometer).

7 Skim any scum and pot into sterilised jars; seal, label and store.

Tip: *Don't be tempted to squeeze the jelly bag to hurry the process, you just get cloudy jelly.*

Per 100-gram serving: 221 calories; 1 gram protein, 57 grams carbohydrate, 0 grams fat, 0 grams saturated fat, 0 milligrams cholesterol, 0 grams fibre, 2 milligrams sodium.

Blackberries

Blackberries are one of the most prolific wild plants. The clusters of tasty dark-purple berries contain lots of pips, so if you're 'pipophobic', make blackberry – also called bramble – jelly rather than jam; Chapter 5 takes you through the stages. Finding blackberries is easy: look in any uncultivated corner, urban or rural, for their scratchy, prickly, long tendrils whose delicately crumpled white to pink flowers, when pollinated, swell to the berries you're looking for.

Get dressed up for blackberry 'brambling'. The earlier section 'Gathering up your stores' has helpful hints and don't be afraid to wade intrepidly into the middle of a bramble patch: brambles give way quite easily and soon regenerate after such treatment.

Choosing the ripest plumpest berries, away from busy roadsides, gives the best results. Dry berries rolled in a little caster sugar respond well to open freezing (which I describe in Chapter 7). Make your jams/jellies straightaway or use frozen fruits at your leisure. Blackberries go delightfully well with apples, combining brilliantly in puddings, pies and crumbles, or make a syrup for pouring over ice cream (or down your throat in winter to ward off colds, because blackberries are an excellent source of vitamin C).

Blackberry and Apple Jam

With blackberries you get a wonderful free harvest and a unique 'country' taste that's so wonderful that plant breeders have cultivated blackberries without the prickles to grow in the garden (but I think that it's cheating if you don't get the odd scratch!). Apples help this jam to set, and if you hate the blackberry pips, remove them along the way. Chapter 3 has more on sterilisation.

Special tools required: *Muslin bag, jam thermometer, sterilised jars*

Preparation time: *30 minutes*

Processing time: *45–60 minutes, depending on whether you remove pips or not*

Yield: *4.5 kilograms (10 pounds), less if you remove the pips*

2 kilograms (4 pounds, 8 ounces) blackberries	*400 millilitres (13 fluid ounces) water*
1 kilogram (2 pounds, 4 ounces) cooking apples	*3 kilograms (6 pounds, 12 ounces) sugar*

1 Pick over the berries, removing any stalks. Peel, core and slice apples. (Save the stalks, peel and cores and put them into a muslin pouch for extra setting power.)

2 Simmer the blackberries and apples in separate pans with half the water each. (If you hate pips, now's the time to push the blackberry pulp through a sieve, leaving the pips behind.)

3 Mixing the two fruits and sugar together, simmer hard until the mixture reaches the setting point – use your jam thermometer (Chapter 2 explains more about that or turn to Chapter 5 for other set testing methods) to test the jam's set.

4 Pour into sterilised jars and then seal and label.

Per 100-gram serving: 292 calories; 0 grams protein, 75 grams carbohydrate, 0 grams fat, 0 grams saturated fat, 0 milligrams cholesterol, 3 grams fibre, 1 milligram sodium.

Blackberry Syrup

You can adapt this syrup recipe for any cultivated berries and currants you pick in the garden (Chapter 11 is berry informative). Straining the fruit removes the pips and skins. Freezing your syrup in ice cubes gives the opportunity to use just a small amount at a time – Chapter 7 has freezer hints. A warm blackberry-syrup drink trickling across painful tonsils soothes and adds a welcome a boost of vitamin C to a winter diet.

Special tools required: *Jelly bag*

Preparation time: *15 minutes*

Processing time: *5–6 hours with straining time*

Yield: *600–700 millilitres (1–1¼ pints)*

1.5 kilograms (3 pounds) blackberries

350 grams (12 ounces) caster sugar per 600 millilitres (1 pint) measured juice

150 millilitres (5 fluid ounces) water

1 Pick over the berries to remove stalks and put into a bowl with the water; place inside a large saucepan of gently boiling water.

2 Leave for about one hour, gently crushing the fruit against the sides of the bowl from time to time with the back of a wooden spoon to help the juices flow. This method avoids overcooking the fruit.

3 Strain the fruit through a jelly bag for a minimum of four hours, or overnight. Don't squeeze the jelly bag if you want clear jelly.

4 Measure the strained liquid and add the necessary amount of caster sugar – 350 grams (12 ounces) per 600 millilitres (1 pint) of strained juice. Stir until it dissolves.

5 Allow to cool slightly and bottle (I recommend the hot-bottling method that I describe in Chapter 5). Or freeze in ice-cube trays until hard; empty these into a plastic bag and store in the freezer until needed – Chapter 7 has lots more about freezers.

Tip: *As a variation to Step 2, place fruit and water in a large heavy-bottomed pan and simmer for one hour, crushing the fruit as in Step 2. Take great care with this method not to burn the fruit or evaporate too much of the juice.*

Per 100-millilitre serving: 356 calories; 2 gram protein, 90 grams carbohydrate, 0 grams fat, 0 grams saturated fat, 0 milligrams cholesterol, 0 grams fibre, 1 milligram sodium.

Coltsfoot

If you're looking on waste ground or in gravely places and find a brilliant yellow daisy-like flower that appears around March time – before the leaves – you've probably found coltsfoot.

Coltsfoot Wine

You make this wine with only the petals of the flowers. Take a measuring jug with you when gathering your flowers. You need the equivalent of 4 litres of petals; you can tip them into a bag when you've measured them. This way is the old-fashioned one to get the right amount. Remove petals using sharp scissors and take only as many as you need, but don't expect this job to be quick! For more alcoholic recipes see Chapter 9.

Special tools required: *Muslin, demijohn, airlock, thermometer*

Preparation time: *1 hour*

Processing time: *Fermentation until clear; use 2–3 months after bottling*

Yield: *About 3.6 litres (6 pints)*

3.6 litres (6 pints) (approx.) jugs of coltsfoot petals

1 kilogram (2 pounds, 4 ounces) granulated sugar

Juice of two lemons

Sachet of wine yeast – buy at a brewing shop

3.6 litres (6 pints) (approx.) water

1 Put petals into a large plastic bucket and pour on 1.5 litres (2½ pints) of water. Leave to soak for 24 hours, stirring from time to time.

2 Strain the liquid through a muslin-lined sieve. Press the flowers to extract maximum juice.

3 Add the lemon juice to the liquid. Start the yeast following instructions on the packet.

4 Stir the sugar into 1.5 litres (2½ pints) of water and bring to the boil. Stir well until the sugar dissolves.

5 Add the sugar solution to the liquid. Allow to cool to 21 degrees Celsius (70 degrees Fahrenheit), and then add yeast. Cover and leave to ferment for three days or until rapid fermentation reduces.

6 Transfer to a *demijohn* (a 4.5-litre/8-pint glass fermenting jar) fitted with an airlock and add water. Top the jar up to just below the neck with cold, boiled water.

7 Leave in warm place until fermentation stops. The gasses stop being released through the airlock and the wine clears; this process may take 4 months. Siphon or suck out the clear wine though a plastic tube into a clean jar, leaving any sediment behind. Seal and leave for another month. Siphon again and bottle. The wine is ready to drink after two to three months in storage.

Tip: *For Step 5, if you don't have a thermometer handy, use your (clean!) little finger. Dip it into the cooling liquid and wait until the liquid is a comfortable temperature that you're happy to feed to a baby (don't actually give it to a baby!). In other words, that's blood temperature, which jollies your yeast into life. Yeast works at a range of temperatures, but extreme hot or cold kill it.*

Per 100-millilitre serving: 121 calories; 1 gram protein, 31 grams carbohydrate, 0 grams fat, 0 grams saturated fat, 0 milligrams cholesterol, 0 grams fibre, 20 milligrams sodium.

Crab apple

Crab apple is the wild ancestor of today's orchard trees – many orchards have a crab apple tree in there too (go to Chapter 10 for more about cultivated orchard trees). Crab apple trees bear tiny, hard, sour fruit. Find these trees in wild woodland or as hedgerow trees.

Crab Apple Jelly

The excellent jam- and jelly-making qualities of crab apples make them indispensable on their own or to add to other fruits or tasty herbs and spices in the preserving tradition. You can be creative here by adding chopped-up mint or rosemary or your own fresh or dried spicy tastes at Step 5. Chapter 3 provides sterilisation methods.

Special tools required: *Jelly bag, sugar thermometer, sterilised jars*

Preparation time: *15 minutes*

Processing time: *Overnight straining and 1 hour cooking*

Yield: *Approximately 2 kilograms (4 pounds, 8 ounces)*

3 kilograms (6 pounds, 12 ounces) crab apples	*450 grams (1 pound) caster sugar per 600 millilitres (1 pint) juice*
Juice of one large lemon	*2 litres (3½ pints) water*

1 Wipe the apples and slice them roughly. Leave the peel, cores and pips to help the jelly to set.

2 Place the apples into a large pan with 2 litres of water and simmer gently until pulpy – approx 40 to 60 minutes.

3 Strain through a jelly bag. (Chapter 2 explains what a jelly bag is and what it does if you haven't already come across one.) Allow the liquid time to drip without forcing or your jelly becomes cloudy.

4 Measure the juice and, allowing 450 grams (1 pound) per 600 millilitres (1 pint), stir in the sugar and then the lemon juice; keep stirring until all the sugar dissolves.

5 Bring to the boil and continue to boil until the mixture reaches the setting point. (Read Chapter 5 for more about setting points.)

6 Pour the jelly into warm, sterilised jars, seal, label and store.

Per 100-gram: 193 calories; 1 gram protein, 50 grams carbohydrate, 0 grams fat, 0 grams saturated fat, 0 milligrams cholesterol, 0 grams fibre, 2 milligrams sodium.

Dandelion

Dandelions are one of the first abundant spring flowers setting you off on the wine-making trail early in spring. Look out for their bright yellow flowers on grassy lawns and the edges of fields; when you see one, you see lots. Avoid picking from the roadside – for more about perfect picking policies, flip to the earlier section 'Choosing clean and safe food'.

Dandelion Wine

This wine differs depending on the flowers and when you pick them, so choose a place where you know that no nasty chemicals are sprayed. It takes a while to clear, so don't give up on it and you're well rewarded. The wine is slightly different if you use only the petals and discard the *calyx* – the green 'cuppy' bit – or you use the whole dandelion head; both ways can make delicious wine.

Special tools required: *Demijohn, airlock*

Preparation time: *1 hour*

Processing time: *Fermentation until clear; use 2–3 months after bottling*

Yield: *3.6–4 litres (6–7 pints)*

2.5 litres (4 pints) dandelion heads gathered at midday when the sun is full and hot (see the earlier Coltsfoot recipe for picking hints)	Sachet of wine yeast – from a specialist brewing shop, or 15 grams (½ ounce) brewers' yeast from a health food shop
1.6 kilograms (3 pounds, 8 ounces) granulated sugar	2 oranges, juice and thinly pared skin, or 1 lemon and 1 orange prepared the same way
	4.5 litres (1 gallon) water

1 Wash and drain petals or dandelion heads through a fine sieve.

2 Put the clean petals/flowers in a large bowl and pour on 4.5 litres (1 gallon) of boiling water. Cover and allow to stand for three or four days, stirring daily.

3 Strain liquid into a large saucepan, and add the sugar and citrus peel. Heat gently, stirring until the sugar dissolves.

4 Simmer for 30 minutes.

5 Strain into the cleaned bowl and cool to 21 degrees Celsius (70 degrees Fahrenheit). Stir the citrus juice into the mixture.

6 Using a small quantity – in your favourite handy bowl – of the warm liquid, mix in the yeast until smooth and stir into the bulk, distributing evenly. Leave again for 3 (or more) days until rapid fermentation reduces.

7 Pour into a *demijohn* (a 4.5-litre, 1 gallon glass fermenting jar). (Turn to Chapter 2 for more on wine-making equipment and Chapter 9 for all about the full wine-making process.) Fit an airlock, and leave to ferment and clear (about four to five months).

8 Siphon off by sucking out the clear wine, when clear, though a plastic tube into bottles, leaving any sediment behind, and store.

Per 100-millilitre serving: 184 calories; 1 gram protein, 47 grams carbohydrate, 0 grams fat, 0 grams saturated fat, 0 milligrams cholesterol, 0 grams fibre, 14 milligrams sodium. Analysis is approximate.

Elder tree

You can gather a two-pronged bounty from this gracious tree, which grows like a rampant weed in some parts of the country and is much scarcer elsewhere:

- ✔ **Elderberries:** Add them to your Hedgerow Jelly (see the earlier recipe in this section) or make wine – flip to Chapter 9 for wine-making hints.
- ✔ **Elderflowers:** Gather these white flouncy clusters in May in the full sun for refreshing, delicate and delicious cordial and champagne recipes (check out Chapter 9 where they're the star performers).

Don't pick all the elderflowers; leave some to turn into elderberries.

Take heed of the picking instructions in the earlier section 'Gathering up your stores' for easy ways to reach your elder tree fruits.

French hales

Look out for clusters of tiny fruits – looking like miniature russet apples – hanging from these trees in autumn. Gather them when they're ripe but not overly squishy. If this tree isn't common in your area, substitute its family member Rowan berries – vivid red clusters of berries from the Rowan or Mountain Ash. You can use these fruits in the Hedgerow Jelly recipe at the beginning of this section.

French hales are wild bird food – take only what you've good use for.

Haws

Haws are the fruit of the hawthorn. They're great for adding to the Hedgerow Jelly recipe at the beginning of this section. The red berries add a delicate red hue to the finished results.

The availability of these berries differs from year to year and depends entirely on the weather in spring. When lots of Hawthorn flowers (this prickly bush has cascades of white blossom) are pollinated by the bees and other flying insects, you get a bumper crop with plenty of red berries, and the autumnal scene is amazing. Pick the berries ripe or after they've weathered a bit. They still perform in any hedgerow recipe.

Hips

These fading wild rose flowers (also called *dog rose*) leave a beautiful, rosy, bulbous fruit about 2.5 centimetres (1 inch) in diameter. Don't let the thorny branches put you off picking hips; read the earlier section 'Gathering up your stores' for hints on how to combat any picking problems. Children (or less mature!) adults can dry the inner, hairy, protective covering of the seeds to make effective 'itching powder'. You can add rosehips to the versatile Hedgerow Jelly recipe at the beginning of this section.

Rosehip Syrup

Traditionally the sweet wartime vitamin C drink for children with a slight rosy hue, imparting a delicate and unique flavour and great for keeping bad colds at bay. Country folk were paid to gather the wild fruits. (Chapter 3 gives you plenty of options on how to sterilise bottles.)

Special tools required: *Jelly bag, sterilised bottles*

Preparation time: *10–15 minutes*

Processing time: *Approximately 12 hours straining time, plus 10 minutes cooking*

Yield: *1.8 litres (3 pints)*

1 kilogram (2 pounds, 4 ounces) rosehips	1.8 litres (3 pints) water
600 grams (1 pound, 4 ounces) sugar	

1 Top and tail the rosehips and mince the fruit.

2 Put into a large pan with the boiling water. Bring liquid to the boil, and remove from heat. Allow to stand for 15 minutes.

3 Strain through a jelly bag. Leave for 12 hours or more.

4 Place strained juice in a pan with sugar. Stir over a low heat until sugar dissolves. Boil for five minutes.

5 Bottle in sterilised bottles and store.

> **Tip:** *Don't be tempted to squeeze the jelly bag to hurry the process, you just get cloudy juice. Leave fruit to drip its liquid through in its own time.*

> **Vary it!** *Use this syrup with ice creams and puddings or dilute in hot water as a soothing drink for sore throats.*

> **Per 100-millilitre serving:** *178 calories; 2 grams protein, 44 grams carbohydrate, 0 grams fat, 0 grams saturated fat, 0 milligrams cholesterol, 0 grams fibre, 81 milligrams sodium.*

Nettles

Who doesn't know what a nettle sting feels like? This potent little plant gets everywhere. Seek out fresh, young shoots early in the year. You can make Young Nettle Pesto by following the Wild Garlic Pesto recipe in the next section: just swap the main ingredients. Nettles lose their sting when cooked, so avoid eating nettles raw! And be sure to wear gloves when you're picking nettles.

Ramsons

Ramsons is another name for wild garlic. You find ramsons in and around woodlands and under hedgerows early in spring. With round sprays of white flowers, harvest the long, tapering leaves that have their own distinctive smell. You can use them in any dish in which you'd usually use onion or garlic; or add to bread for a savoury twist.

Wild Garlic Pesto

When the traditional basil pesto is out of season, use ramsons as an early spring replacement. Add to Bolognese sauces or straight onto pasta for a countryside twist to your meal or stay with the Italian theme and smear the base of your home-made pizza with it.

Special tools required: *Pestle and mortar or food processor*

Preparation time: *5 minutes*

Processing time: *20 minutes, less if you use a mechanical food processor*

Yield: *675 grams (1½ pounds)*

500 grams (1 pound, 2 ounces) ramson (wild garlic) leaves

200 millilitres (⅓ pint) olive oil

75 grams (3 ounces) walnuts

1 Finely chop the leaves and walnuts and then grind in a pestle and mortar, adding the olive oil bit by bit until everything is combined. If you're a food processor person, chop and mix in a blender, adding the olive oil in small quantities at a time.

2 Stores refrigerated for several weeks, or freeze in suitable quantities – Chapter 7 has freezer hints.

Per 30-gram serving: 102 calories; 1 gram protein, 2 grams carbohydrate, 10 grams fat, 1 gram saturated fat, 0 milligrams cholesterol, 0 grams fibre, 0 milligrams sodium.

Sloes

Sloes are the fruit of the blackthorn tree. They've small, dark, miniature, plum-like fruits, with a delicate bloom over their purple skins. Taking a bite from a raw sloe makes your eyes water – they're really astringent. But as the basis for a wine, and combined with other seasonal fruit such as the black-berry, they give great flavour.

When picking sloes, watch out for blackthorn attacks; they impart a distinc-tive, deep, throbbing pain with every injury (see the earlier section 'Gathering Up Your Stores' for some protective tips).

Try the following favourite recipe.

Sloe Gin

Sloe gin is a favourite Christmas tipple, and this gin recipe is easy to make and easy to drink. Wait until after the first frost to collect your sloes – the frost softens them up, releasing the flavour.

Special tools required: *Sterilised jars, muslin*

Preparation time: *15 minutes*

Processing time: *10 minutes, with storage for a minimum of 3 months*

Yield: *800 millilitres (1⅜ pints)*

450 grams (1 pound) sloes	*Few drops almond essence*
110 grams (4 ounces) caster sugar	*1 x 75-centilitre bottle London gin*

1 Wash sloes and prick with a thorn from the blackthorn tree (where you picked the fruits).

2 Put fruits into a screw or clamp-top sterilised jar.

3 Add the sugar and almond essence.

4 Fill the jar with gin, close the lid and shake well.

5 Leave in a dark place for three months.

6 After three months, strain the liquid through muslin until clear. Bottle and keep until required.

Per 100-millilitre serving: 288 calories; 0 grams protein, 21 grams carbohydrate, 0 grams fat, 0 grams saturated fat, 0 milligrams cholesterol, 0 grams fibre, 1 milligram sodium.

Wild mushrooms

If you love the idea of free fungi, consult a specialist book or go online to find yourself a 'Fungi Foray' close to home. Two clear mushroom favourites are in season at opposite ends of the year and worth looking out for:

✔ **St George's:** This white-gilled mushroom is ready around Easter time – 23 April to be precise.

At any other time of year, white gills on mushrooms are a danger signal.

✔ **Field mushrooms:** These may be as small as a button mushroom (closed over and with pinky gills on the underside) or as big as a dinner plate (open and 'raggy' with a dark brown set of gills).

Use these mushrooms straightaway or pick for storage. Chapter 8 helps out with techniques for drying, and you can find hints on freezing in Chapter 7.

Part VI
The Part of Tens

'O Great Guru – you know the
Secrets of Life – Why won't my jam set?'

In this part . . .

These three short and sweet chapters give you info in a top-ten fashion. In Chapter 19, you find information to whiz you through some sound ideas and practices for all storing and preserving tasks, and Chapter 20 is another quick read to troubleshoot your way through any worries or problems you may encounter along the way. Chapter 21 is all about pushing your boundaries, and offers information and ideas (close to home and globally) to stretch your horizons if you really catch the growing and preserving bug.

Chapter 19

Ten Pointers for Perfect Preserving

....

In This Chapter

▶ Choosing the right time for you and your home-grown produce

▶ Getting properly prepared with equipment and ingredients

▶ Avoiding safety hazards

....

*G*rowing, storing and (of course) eating your own fruit and veg are so satisfying that you really want to make the most of your efforts. This chapter contains a few hints to help you prepare for your preserving action in the kitchen; you can circumvent those annoying common pitfalls with a little foreknowledge.

Timing Is Key to Success

Timing is important in a couple of ways:

✔ **Picking your fruits and vegetables at the right time:** What the 'right' time actually is depends on the end result you want to achieve. For the most successful jams and jellies, pick early; you get the best results with slightly under-ripe firm fruits. On the other hand, if preserving seeds is your desired result, leave the seed heads (or pods, for beans and peas) on the plant until they're mature and the plant begins to wither.

✔ **Taking the time to study a recipe before diving in:** Having all the ingredients and equipment to hand is one vital aspect, but allowing enough time to get to the end of a task is also important. If you've to rush off to an appointment, don't start a time-consuming recipe. Although leaving a chutney to cool while you nip to the shops probably doesn't make any difference in the long run, the crucial last stage of setting jams and jellies requires no disturbances.

Preparing Yourself for Preserving

Preserves allow you to continue enjoying your own home-grown produce all year round, so don't let some silly omission or lack of planning cause you to miss out on the opportunity to fill up your store cupboard.

Make yourself a preparation checklist to follow:

- ✔ Save up sturdy jars, bottles and lids throughout the year.

- ✔ Stock up on the basic ingredients that you're likely to use in bulk; for example, buy sugar and vinegar in advance.

- ✔ Make sure that any equipment you like to use is well serviced and ready to go. Check your muslin cloth for holes and buy new if necessary: all good catering and cheese-maker's shops stock the cloth, or check online.

- ✔ Keep some inexpensive jam-top covers as spares, in case your recycled lids aren't perfect.

- ✔ Buy sticky labels that have enough room on them to write any necessary comments.

- ✔ Sharpen your knives . . . and get ready to chop.

Don't forget that Chapter 2 contains much more on equipment.

Sourcing Top-Quality Ingredients

Your home-made preserves can only ever be as good as the ingredients you add to them; in other words, you can't make a silk purse out of a sow's ear. Your home-grown fruit and veg are already undoubtedly the best you can have, deserving the best accompanying ingredients, and so choose things such as sugar and vinegar wisely. You're investing time and effort in the growing and processing, so also consider how much money you want to invest in these additional items.

If you make sure that your gardening is chemical-free, extend this lack of chemicals to your buying too; you know it makes sense in the long run.

Tooling Up for Work

Your kitchen supplies most of the everyday tools you need, and so adding a few extras to make life simple need not be expensive (as I describe in Chapter 2). Here are a few that can make a big difference to your efficiency when preserving:

- **Good purpose-made preserving pan:** Such a pan makes life easy. It needs to be large enough to hold up to a 4.5-kilogram (10-pound) batch of jam (finished weight) and open enough to allow efficient evaporation, which is a large part of the preserving secret. Choose a stainless steel preserving pan with measurement markings on the inside wall or borrow one in exchange for a jar of whatever you make. Remember that when you're on the preserving road, you're also developing some bargaining power, particularly if you freeze your produce in its prime to preserve in a different form at a later date when friends and neighbours have eaten up their stocks. Take advantage of it.

- **Wide-necked funnel (or jam funnel):** This inexpensive item makes filling jars quick, easy and much less sticky.

- **Roll of kitchen towel:** An inexpensive way to mop up any sticky patches as you go. Tear off a clean sheet every time and leave the bacteria-laden cloth behind.

- **Screw- and clamp-top preserving jars:** Save these jars whenever you can, but make sure that you buy new rubber seals if you're heat-treating any jars. Take a used rubber seal with you when you go shopping to match up sizes.

- **Strong rubber gloves:** Great for washing and rinsing jars thoroughly in scalding hot water before sterilising them, and for handling hot jars while filling them. If you go in for heat-treating, organise yourself 'industrial' strength rubber gloves one size too large, and fit thinner cotton gloves inside. The rubber gloves give grip as well as protection, or buy specialist jar-gripping tongs.

Reaping the Rewards of the Right Ripeness

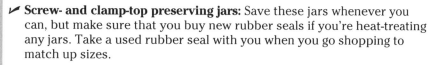

Jam works best with under-ripe fruit, so pick ahead of time and freeze some fruits for jam-making later in the year.

Don't just look to the perfect fruits: you can also make good use of *windfalls* (the blown-down fruit on the ground around your trees). For any preserve that calls for chopped-up fruits, just cut out the bad bits and use the good parts, making pectin stock with the rough ends and stalks from your currant bushes. (Chapter 5 holds the secret of pectin stock.)

Heating Up for Hygiene

Your hard work in preserving has the best chance of succeeding if all your equipment is scrupulously clean, which means proper sterilising. When you save recycled bottles and jars, steep them overnight (or even longer) in mildly soapy water to soak the old labels off. If you've really persistent glue, moisten a cloth with vinegar and give the label a rub. If that doesn't shift stubborn glue, nothing that's safe for food is going to: reject that jar (recycle it) and choose another.

Introduce an easy preserving routine that you can repeat when sterilising your jars and bottles, and have scalding hot water and a good pair of protective rubber gloves to hand. Begin the whole process by getting the sterilising underway, and keep your freshly sterilised jars warm in the oven; don't touch them until you want to fill them up.

Choose your sterilising method from the ones I present in Chapter 3, which also has loads more on keeping equipment safe and hygienic.

As for safety with frozen food, you're perfectly safe using produce that has already been frozen in preserving recipes as long as the food is then kept at boiling temperature (for example, simmering, rolling boil and so on) for 15 minutes or more.

Don't use frozen produce for a no-cook pickle preserve. For jams or chutneys, however, you're safe and you can also refreeze or preserve them perfectly safely.

Staying Safe

You work with high temperatures and dangerous equipment when preserving. Here are some areas in which to take care:

- **Boiling sugar:** Use a long-handled wooden spoon and keep children and pets out from under your feet, especially when lifting heavy pans from the heat.

- **Food and soil:** Your home-grown produce is bound to be dirty at some stage, so be aware that soil-borne bacteria can be dangerous. Remove dirty outer stalks and vegetable cleanings well away from the cooking area, preferably outdoors.

- **Kitchens:** If you ever deal with raw meat in your preserving area (vegetarians skip to the next point!), clean down thoroughly between jobs. Use separate, designated chopping boards and knives for meat and veg, at least while you're in preserving mode.

✔ **Pets and children:** Pets are known to carry bacteria, and you know how safe your children are likely to be around food and hot pans. Keep pets out of the area and dress youngsters up in aprons and encourage them to join in, after they've washed their hands thoroughly!

✔ **Sharp knives:** Sharp knives are safer than blunt knives, but all knives can be dangerous; treat them with respect.

Checking the Details Carefully

Recipes exist to make life easy, but they can't include every single aspect; they always contain a few assumptions. In the Introduction I state the assumptions I make about you in this book, so if you're wondering just how you're categorised, check it out now!

A few of the tiny details that make a big difference to the end result of your produce are:

✔ **Jelly bags:** Never squeeze a jelly bag unless the recipe advises it. Yes, waiting can be frustrating, but if you want clear jellies, leave well alone.

✔ **Racking:** Your wines are clearest if you *rack* them off (siphon off the clear liquid leaving the sediment behind) two or three times. (Flip to Chapters 9 and 18 for more tips on wine-making.)

✔ **Salt:** Follow the recipe precisely. Use sea salt if you're making a clear pickle, because free-running salt has an additive (sodium hexacyanoferrate) that makes your pickles cloudy.

✔ **Vacuum seal:** When you heat-treat any jars, always apply the 'lifting' test to every jar and check that the button is down on any recycled jars you use (as I describe in Chapter 8). Discard anything suspect.

✔ **Vinegar:** Your vinegar bottle states the acidity: use only 5 per cent acidity or more and the exact vinegar suggested in the recipe for the most precise results. (I discuss vinegar preserving in Chapter 6.)

Making What You Love to Eat

This advice may seem obvious but is worth stating: use only recipes that sound delicious when you read them, the ones that really make your mouth water. If you hate the taste of cloves, choose a recipe without them or omit from the recipe you have. If they turn out to have been a crucial part of that recipe, you discover this fact while tucking in! Add a note to yourself on the preserve label to remind yourself what you've done so that you know whether to avoid or repeat next time.

One way to make your home-grown produce go further is to freeze whole meals. When you make a favourite dish with ingredients fresh from your garden, double up quantities and squirrel some away in the freezer. Doing so takes a bit of self-discipline, but you can look forward to easy and delicious meals in future days.

Spreading the Preserved Wealth Around

If you're into your second year of home-grown produce and your freezer is still stuffed with, say, green beans that you haven't eaten, rethink your growing, preserving or using strategy. If you're surprised by how prolific your garden is, you've a decision to make: eat more beans next year, grow less, change how you preserve them or find new ways to use them. Perhaps Runner Bean (or French Bean Chutney – see Chapter 14 for the recipe) would go down with the family better?

When your store cupboards are chock-a-block with jams and jellies and a new harvest is ready to come in, rethink your eating patterns. If jam tarts (a base of pastry cut into rounds with a blob of home-made jam in the middle) were good enough for The Queen of Hearts, give them a go! They make a super snack or lunch-box treat and are surprisingly delicious. Train your children to make jam tarts themselves.

Alternatively, revive another stalwart pudding for cold winter evenings: jam roly-poly. You can find the simple recipe on the back of a suet packet (you can buy vegetarian suet as well); simply smother in home-made jam before rolling it up into the traditional shape.

Giving away your produce brings out the best in you, your friends and acquaintances. Don't ask for anything in return except the glowing feeling inside that genuine generosity engenders. One exception is that asking for the empty jars back is perfectly acceptable, and doing so is a lovely tradition.

Perhaps have a feast: make scones and host an old-fashioned cream tea afternoon in the sunshine while discussing preserving recipes new and old!

Chapter 20

Ten Troubleshooting Tips

*N*o matter how hard you try to stick to advice or recipes, unavoidable incidences can still get in the way of your storing and preserving, causing results that are less than perfect. Although frustrating, these efforts are only a waste of time if you fail to learn from the experience. Knowing what the problem is can help you be successful next time.

Therefore, in this chapter I describe some of the most common pitfalls in the world of preserving and how to avoid them.

Finding the Rotten Apple

Check your stored produce area regularly; make a habit of glancing at it critically whenever you're nearby and remove anything that's beginning to turn brown or mouldy. Remember that fungal spores travel through the air, and so take any rotting produce well out of the vicinity before the rot spreads.

Keep air circulating by opening windows on breezy days and shutting them if the rain can drive in. The sun's angle changes throughout the year, reaching through different windows at different times, so move your produce around (or protect with a layer of newspaper) to ensure that you avoid sun scorching or bleaching.

Check out Chapter 4 for much more on effective fruit storage.

Handling a Pest Crisis

Be vigilant around your storage areas; if you spot any suspicious-looking droppings or nibbled produce, take quick action. Invite a friendly dog or cat in to investigate, and call in professional advice if you've a serious problem with vermin.

Humans particularly dislike rats but somehow most people's reaction to mice is different. From a storage point of view, neither pest is welcome, but whereas rats visit your store nibbling their way into sacks and bags and removing goodies to a store of their own, mice have a really nasty personal problem: they're incontinent, and dribble their urine wherever they go – and that's all over your food. Treat any signs of these little creatures seriously. Chapters 3 and 4 contain more info on keeping pests at bay.

Freshening Up Freezer Space

Defrost your freezer in the spring before you start to fill it up again: it works more efficiently when not clogged up with ice.

If you open your freezer and it smells stale, you need to defrost it. But doing so immediately isn't always possible or convenient, so as an interim solution place some loose citrus fruit in there (lemons are best, but oranges work as well). Allow them to rattle around in the freezer when you're getting things in and out and they deodorise the freezer space.

You can find loads of nippy freezer advice in Chapter 7.

Working Out Why Your Jam Doesn't Set

Understanding the level of pectin in different fruits is crucial to making jam or jelly successfully. (Chapter 5 tells you how to check and work with various pectin levels.) Your jam needs a balance of acid with the pectin, so don't leave out lemon juice if the recipe asks for it.

When you use frozen fruit for jam-making, the freezing affects the pectin in the fruit. Therefore, add another amount (usually an eighth of the weight of the fruit does the job) or use a pectin stock with your frozen fruit.

Also, check that you've achieved the setting point: a jam thermometer helps to gauge the temperature, or use the flake test or wrinkle test – both are standard methods of knowing when your jam has set (as I discuss in Chapter 5).

Read your recipe carefully: most jam recipes call for an open, uncovered pan because evaporation is part of the process of concentrating flavours and colour. If you keep a lid on at the cooking stage, your jam turns out too watery and refuses to set or keep well. Some fruits don't require any additional water – for example, raspberries – whereas others do, such as plums. Adding unnecessary water is sure to affect the set adversely.

Gauging the Ripeness of Your Fruit

If your produce is over-ripe or wet when you start to make a preserve, it can only get sloppier. Use just-ripe or slightly under-ripe fruit for jams; fruit loses pectin as it gets older (I explain the importance of pectin in Chapter 5).

If you add the sugar to hard, undercooked fruit, it isn't going to soften any further. Check your cooking times with the recipe but add increments of five minutes and test again until you're sure that the fruit is soft.

Check your initial cooking times too: recipes can only guide you, so test your fruit often and believe the evidence of your eyes. For example, skins on fruits need a long cooking time, sometimes as long as an hour, to break down.

Cut up larger fruit so that it cooks evenly; for jelly-making, you need a long cooking time to break down fruit tissues.

Produce only small quantities when you're making jam at home: a maximum of 4.5 kilograms (10 pounds) when using a standard-sized preserving pan. Ensure that the jam pan is never more than two thirds full at any point.

Dealing with Bubbles and Crystals

Tiny bubbles on the surface of the boiling jam cause scum. You can avoid scummy jam by skimming the top with a slotted spoon or adding a small nut of butter when the jam's boiling. But you don't need to waste the skimmed-off bubbly bit of the jam; just put it into a bowl on the table and invite people to test your latest batch by having it on bread or scones.

Take care to use the type of sugar recommended in the recipe. Warm your carefully measured amount of sugar – jam-making always uses granulated sugar unless an individual recipe states differently – by placing it in a heat-proof bowl in the oven at 110 degrees Celsius (225 degrees Fahrenheit; gas mark ¼): doing so stops the fruit cooling when the sugar goes in and speeds up dissolving the sugar.

Another problem that can arise is tiny grains or crystals in your jam, owing to the sugar not totally dissolving before you begin the rapid boiling stage. To avoid, remove the boiling fruit from the heat (or turn it right down) while you add the sugar, stirring until it completely dissolves before turning the heat back up.

Sealing Containers Safely

The safety and longevity of your preserved produce relies on the way you seal containers:

✔ When heat-treating (something I discuss in Chapter 5), buy new rubber seals each time, whether online or at a catering/cook shop.

✔ If you re-use jam-pot lids, use the sort with the button on the top, in which a good vacuum forms when you press it down; if the button is up, discard the produce.

✔ Old-fashioned wax discs keep the air off the top of your preserves; cellophane tops, dampened and put securely over warm, just-filled pots, also work well.

✔ Check the rubber bands securing lids from time to time, and use the produce before these bands perish. Or use a belt and braces approach by tying a string around jars that you know you're keeping for a long time as well.

Deciding What to Do about Worrying Smells

If at any time you're unsure about a new preserve that you open, discard it. If this preserve is one of a batch, open another jar straightaway and compare smells: if one smells good and another doesn't, trust your nose (which has been honed by evolution to keep you safe from harm).

Never eat, or give to others, anything that you're dubious about. You may have an invisible flaw in a jar or a pinprick hole in a lid of which you're unaware. Always err on the side of caution.

If your chutney is shrinking or cracking inside the jar – if the contents of the jar are below the original level when you potted up or are coming away from the sides of the jar – the seal probably isn't airtight and moisture is evaporating: you may (or may not) detect an associated smell. If any of these things happen to you, check your potting and sealing method, and discard the produce in that jar as well as the rubber ring or lid for the jar. Make sure that the jar has absolutely no cracks or flaws, because even a small chip on the rim can break the seal.

In storage situations, always sniff the air: you may detect something going off and be able to limit the damage with quick action. Take any rotten produce right out of the vicinity, because the spores travel in the air.

Handling Hot Preserves

Protect your hands and work surfaces when dealing with any recipe involving a large proportion of sugar. Sugar boils at a higher temperature than water and takes more time to cool down; it can cause nasty burns on your skin. Avoid splashes by moving hot pans carefully, and work only in a safe environment (by which I mean without children or pets under your feet).

Put newspaper or wooden cutting boards on delicate surfaces to stop unsightly scorches on kitchen tops. When hot bottling (which I cover in Chapter 5), always ladle some of the water out of the pan before attempting to remove your heat-treated jars or bottles of preserve.

If you plan to heat-treat regularly, equip yourself with large tongs especially made for the job.

On another (but different sort of) hot topic, home-grown chilli is just as hot as the shop-bought varieties and the seeds are particularly volatile; you may surprise yourself at how little you need to heat up a large quantity of food. Chop up dried chilli particularly finely and use less than half a teaspoon per 450 grams (1 pound) of bulk until you understand the power of what you've grown. Some chilli heat increases over time too, and you don't want to frighten your family off from eating your lovingly made produce.

Maintaining a Sensible Storage Regime

Keep your produce in a dark, cool space; tempting as it may be to have all your produce on display, the colours fade in the light. Also, too much heat affects the rubber seals on preserving jars and if they fail you need to discard the produce. Always date and label your preserves clearly soon after you make something: if you wait a few days before labelling, you may well forget a vital ingredient.

Keeping well-stored preserves for more than one year is fine: lots of the savoury preserves improve over time and alcohol has a reputation for storing for ages. But be sensible about using a rotation system in the store cupboard, bringing older jars forward from time to time to remind you what's there and to use them up or give them away.

When you've opened a preserve, store it in the fridge. Some recipes recommend keeping the result in the fridge anyway: for example, pickled eggs (see Chapter 17) and fruiting vegetables preserved in oil (see Chapter 12) need to be refrigerated as part of safely preserving them.

Chapter 21

Ten (or So) Ways to Take Storing and Preserving Further

. . . .

In This Chapter

▶ Going beyond your normal grow-your-own boundaries

▶ Finding new ways to expand your knowledge without breaking the bank

▶ Discovering community projects

. . . .

*1*f you've caught the home-produce bug but need new challenges to expand your horizons, read on.

Perhaps you want to discover more growing and preserving skills from experts in the field, or want to put more time into the hobby but you've run out of space. You may want to understand just how much (or little) importance in the long term you want to give to the life-enhancing matter of growing your own safe, healthy food and making it last around the year.

Believe me, you're not the only one whose budget doesn't stretch to a house with a large garden or whose time is limited. All around you, people are stretching their imaginations and questioning the wisdom of paying for council land to be planted up with pretty flowers while also paying for food to be flown from around the world. Perhaps you want to take matters into your own hands and redress that balance by asking your council to rethink the planting strategy or hand over some land to people who can.

You may not want to eat runner beans grown on a busy roundabout in among the car exhaust fumes, but growing fruit and nut trees in the park makes positive use of a clean green space. So, if you're ready for a few new foody ideas, this chapter opens your eyes to established and more innovative projects.

Harvesting: To Boldly Go With the Stars

Tradition links sowing and planting times with the moon, and you can experience the benefits of this tradition in a more modern scientific context, going beyond only the moon's influence.

If you want the very best from your home-grown produce and are already a chemical-free zone, look to the *Biodynamic Sowing and Planting Calendar* compiled by Maria and Matthias Thun. More than 50 years of detailed scientific research has gone into working out which days favour different groupings of produce for sowing – and, more importantly for this book, harvesting – produce. Picking your produce at the optimum time aids better storage because healthy and disease-free produce won't have any sneaky bugs or bacteria festering away unseen in cracks and crevices – and the plain truth is that it tastes better too.

If you're keen on practical measures for gardening in tune with moon and the rest of the cosmos, buy the calendar from the Biodynamic Agriculture College (`www.bdacollege.org.uk`). It guides you day-by-day through the year of changing cosmic auspices affecting all growing plants. If reading about this globally accepted form of growing tickles your sensibilities, attending a practical course at the college on growing and harvesting fruit, vegetables and flowers may inspire you further.

Here's a brief summary of the theory. Biodynamically, produce is split into four main categories based on parts of the plant. The planting calendar assigns the best days and times for working with them, using observations and data to guide you towards perfect produce:

- **Flower:** Cut flowers have the strongest scent and last the longest if harvested on 'flower' days; dried flowers retain the most vivid colours.

- **Fruit:** Plants cultivated for their fruit or seeds belong to this category; choose this day to harvest fruits for the best storing and seeds for planting next year.

- **Leaf:** Includes the cabbage family, but harvesting on the 'leaf' day isn't the best for good storage results; leafy herbs are better harvested on 'fruit' and 'flower' days.

- **Root:** Includes radishes, swedes, beetroot, celeriac, carrots, potatoes and so on, as well as the bulb onion family. Harvesting these crops on a 'root' day gives top-quality storage results.

Extending Your Produce Range

You can top up with preserving produce that you can't grow for yourself at your nearby supermarket, outdoor market and, if you're lucky, a good farmers' market. But also try the following options:

- **Community Supported Agriculture (CSA):** As I describe in 'Getting Involved: Community Supported Agriculture', later in this chapter, the CSA is a good way to support both the farmer and yourself.

- **Gardening and allotment clubs and societies:** A fountain of knowledge, events and local lore.

- **Guerrilla gardening:** Discover like-minded individuals and groups that are making a difference and reclaim space in your local area (check out the later 'Finding Community Growing Spaces' section).

- **Mutual help schemes:** Find out about such schemes as Landshare (see the later section 'Looking into Landshare') and wwoofing, helpx and workaway (which I describe in 'Moving from Window Box to Part-Time Farmer', later in this chapter).

- **Open gardens:** Along with tiny one-off stalls selling seasonal produce, make a point of buying someone else's home-grown produce. Do check whether they spray their crops with anything you don't use at home, though, if that's important to you and your family.

- **Pick-your-own produce:** A great way to buy in quantity at competitive rates. Keep a look out for farms in your area that operate in this way. Roadside signs or ads in local papers can guide you to your nearest pick-your-own farm. If you're aiming for a picking session with a bulk jam- or chutney-making day ahead of you, remember to get your other stores, sugar, vinegar, pots and tops ready for the occasion in advance.

- **Seedy Sunday (or Saturday):** A free seed swap (see the later section 'Enjoying Seedy Sunday: A Free Seed Bonanza'). Don't forget to take your own stored seeds, too.

- **'SwapCrop' pages:** Seek out at the Guild of Jam and Preserve Makers' website (`www.jamguild.co.uk`) and become united with someone else's glut for the price of a jar or two of whatever you make.

- **Transition Town schemes:** Sign up (as I discuss in the later section 'Joining Your Transition Town Movement') for a lower carbon input way of life, starting at the eating end with the Food Group – nearly every town has one – and you'll soon be swapping top preserving tips and jam-making recipes. The cut and thrust of this movement is a 'waste-not, want-not' approach to food growing, which is exactly what preserving skills can do for you.

- **Vegetable box schemes:** Search out one as close to home as possible; often word of mouth is the only way to find out where they are. Speak to friends and neighbours (some smaller schemes only operate during part of the year). These schemes are the ones with truly seasonal produce just waiting for you to transform it into lovely chutneys, jams and jellies.

- **Village fetes:** Usually a good source of fresh garden produce, but do ask whether the produce is spray-free. You see the veterans in action here, and you can often find competitive classes for making the best jams, jellies and chutneys. Go on, enter! Competitions are a fun way to show off your new skills, and you may even win a rosette!

Moving from Window Box to Part-Time Farmer

If you're looking glumly at a small window box of salad leaves and are aching to experience the world of growing and processing food on a wider scale, don't despair. Change your whole world by investigating the following organisations, and discover a lot along the way:

- **HelpX:** The website www.helpX.net takes you worldwide, matching up people who want to travel with people who're willing to accommodate and feed them in exchange for help. On average, you're required to work 4 hours per day, but each host has a different requirement and it may be a house-sitting venture where you're essentially on duty 24 hours a day. The website allows you to liaise with hosts before committing yourself; use this interaction to make sure that the jobs on offer are up your street. If you hate animals, obviously don't choose a smallholding-sitting job; on the other hand if the help is to do with harvesting soft fruit and making preserves, you've the opportunity to put theory into practice and perfect your technique in a short time alongside more experienced hands.

- **Workaway:** This sharing website offers you the opportunity to work your way round the world and find out about different cultures and ways of life for a few hours of work a day in their communities. Choose places where the food culture includes harvesting, storing and preserving as part of their way of life and you can tap into generations of knowledge. The website www.workaway.info matches you with friendly hosts.

- **WWOOFing:** World Wide Opportunities on Organic Farms is a worldwide organisation matching hosts who run a business along organic lines with willing workers. Investigate more or even join at www.wwoof.org. Reading other's experiences on the website shows just what opportunities are out there for the adventurous, and as long as you can organise your own travel arrangements, your board and lodgings are guaranteed: you even have insurance cover while working. Make sure that you liaise with your hosts beforehand; don't just turn up! The arrangements you make have to suit both host and willing worker, but are generally five to six hours per day with an agreement over meals for days when you're not working to leave you time for sightseeing too. Plenty of opportunities exist to expand on your growing and preserving skills, which are all part and parcel of what most hosts do.

Hosts and jobs vary; taking pot luck on the jobs you do is one way to experience WWOOFing. Or with a little prior research, you can, say, work your way around the vineyards of the world or look into growing olive trees and processing oil; the themes are limited by your imagination only. You find yourself working alongside highly experienced organic growers, and may soon be helping to make organic wine in Australia, France or Italy, gleaning ideas from all over the world.

WWOOFing your way around the world – safe in the knowledge that the work you willingly undertake may be tiring, muddy or dusty but doesn't include spraying dangerous chemicals onto the land or yourself – is a tried and tested formula.

Enjoying Seedy Sunday: A Free Seed Bonanza

Traditionally, seed swapping days are held on the first Sunday (or Saturday) in the month of February each year, but check when your nearest one takes place. Gardeners' clubs, health food shops and local vegetable box schemes are likely to know the location, or look online at www.seedysunday.org for your closest event location.

Just when gardeners everywhere are studying their seed catalogues beside a roaring fireside, anticipating the spring and new gardening season, people who've successfully stored seeds from previous harvests are parcelling them up in home-made seed packets for a give-away. Even if you've nothing to swap this year, visit a seed swap anyway and see what the fuss is all about; you're welcome to have seeds in the hope that you become hooked.

Some complicated rules exist about selling seeds, as well as issues about large corporations having a stranglehold on legitimate seed selling. By giving or swapping seeds, you get around any legislation and all the great heritage seeds and seeds that are successful in a particular geographic area are freely circulated. Seedy days are brilliant fun you can take part in and enjoy.

You can receive free seeds on seedy Sundays even if you've not saved or stored any yourself, but you can't give any until you've at least one successful session of seed saving and storing under your belt. Chapter 8 gives you information you need to start seed saving.

Investing in Containers

Even if your space is limited, you can make room for a pot or two. Be inventive with containers: use everything from milk cartons with drainage holes punched in the bottom to old leather boots. You can make or buy *growbags* (plastic bags with a growing medium in them); use them as they are or empty them into a pot, container or even a stack of tyres for growing root vegetables in a non-garden place (and then turn to Chapter 13 for the information you need to make optimum preserving use of roots). Or go 'posh' and make a feature of matching tubs bursting with your home-grown produce.

Use hanging baskets and wall containers to hold tumbling tomato and pepper plants (Chapter 12 gives plenty of scope for preserving these foods); they've the added advantage of being more difficult (but not impossible) for snails and slugs to reach. Or build wigwams of canes out of containers to grow your beans up (and visit Chapter 14 for inventive beany ideas); just keep it all pegged down when the wind blows.

Growing on the Rooftops

Roof gardens are a long-used solution to lack of space in urban settings. Charles Dickens mentions them and even has an illustration of one in *Our Mutual Friend*. Make sure that your space is sturdy enough for heavy pots. Wet compost or growing medium weighs heavier than dry fluffy compost that you buy and if you want to grow the heaviest pumpkin in your city (some can grow to over 25 kilograms (56 pounds) with care and attention), ensure that you've room and structural strength for the spreading tentacles and weighty fruits. You may be keen on pumpkin but your neighbours may not want one appearing through their ceiling uninvited!

Look in the earlier 'Investing in Containers' section for ideas that also suit roof spaces (and balconies) in urban settings.

If you take over roof space not designed purposely as a roof garden, be particularly aware of the possibility of structural failure. Keep within the weight limits of the space and structure.

Digging Up Your Lawn

If you're a home-produce grower, lawns are passé. The wartime 'Dig for Victory' mentality is back in a sense, but with a modern twist. You just need enough space to set out a chair for resting while admiring your new raised bed, at first neat and tidy, full of secret seeds and promise, and later blossoming forth goodness with dinners to come.

Who needs the hassle of cutting a lawn when you can spend the same time tending to a garden and later in the kitchen turning that home-grown fare into preserves to last the year round? You can never buy the same high quality that you grow yourself; even your own wobbly carrots and freshly picked peas just aren't available anywhere else.

Allotmenteering, If You Aren't Already

If you already have a space on an allotment, treasure it. You may not be able to make a living from your allotment growing but you can reduce your household bills, provide a great deal of fresh food immediately from the plot and preserve a good portion for future food, gifts and bartering power! At one time the domain of old men with their rules and regulations, nowadays all genders, ages, creeds and colours are welcome. Allotment waiting lists are months, sometimes years long, and yes, rules are in place, but often alongside a fantastic community spirit and sharing of outdoor healthy time, ideas, produce and seeds that cross the cultural divide. You can find your own sense of expression in an allotment, without judgement; an allotment is as much an extension of your personality as your clothing and reflects the time you're able to give it.

Get in touch with your local council to find out about local allotment availability. Because of the shortage of council allotment space, some private landowners have designated land using the allotment template. Depending on where this land is situated, you may be able to put up your own shed. Sharing water facilities is the norm and some regulation on the water use is necessary; for example, using as much water as you can carry with a watering can is fine, but you may not be allowed to siphon water onto your patch.

Keeping paths between allotment patches clear is a common sense courtesy, but there may be a communal lawn mower or shared tool borrowing store to help you manage, or in certain cases someone takes responsibility for supplying certain items. Sharing farmyard manure drops or municipal compost drops make sense; if you haven't got anyone willing to organise such things, become the organiser, finding out your hidden talents.

With plenty of room for collective benefits, your own allotment also reflects your personality. Some are set out like mini gardens with seating areas, a play area for visiting children and a hut with kettle and stove for entertaining and holding whole working party days. Others are more 'make do and mend' and recycle materials, old windows acting as cold frames, upturned plastic bottles for protective cloches and skip-gleanings of broken scaffold planks for the sides of raised beds.

Along with such a generous growing space comes the responsibility of using all that allotment-grown produce and turning it into a whole year's worth of preserves for your own family, and if you haven't grown a certain fruit or vegetable you're perfectly positioned to swap your successes with another 'allotmenteer'. You may find yourself preserving a greater variety of fruits and vegetables than you've grown yourself.

Speak to your local town council to find out how to get in touch with your allotment representative or look online for information (www.allotment.org).

Finding Community Growing Spaces

Tired of the bland, mass-produced, over-chemicalised ranks of uniform fruit and vegetables you see in supermarkets? Why not join the individuals and communities who are taking back space, in unofficial groups or officially by approaching their councils when they identify a piece of underused land. This so-called 'guerrilla gardening' is a trendy new hobby for some people.

If your subversive side needs venting in this productive way, sneak your leek plants into the roundabout flowerbeds and park gardens. Parks are a feature of all big towns and cities and even the smallest village has a playing field or green: join in with the voices who want to reuse this land for food growing as a statement for better food security in the country. With enough will, you can find community growing projects or be the innovator and start one yourself.

Even in such unorthodox places, wherever there's growing, there's harvesting, and with harvesting comes storing and preserving, too, Whatever you grow and wherever you grow it, don't waste the triumph by letting your produce go to waste. Preserve it.

Wild spaces are for wildlife too and your chemical-free gardening needs a balance of pollinators in the form of bees and other flying creatures as well as an army of feathery and creeping pest controllers. Before you grab any old piece of land, do your research; you need to keep a balance.

Some industrial or 'brown field' land has been polluted with heavy metals, which affects the quality of the food you can grow there, so avoid such areas.

Looking into Landshare

Landshare's role is the mixing and matching of responsible people who have land, with responsible people without land. You can join in by looking at www.landshare.net and logging your interest. You may be able to expand from a tiny plot to a field's worth of growing space in a short time, which will really challenge your storing and preserving abilities. By using the land together, it becomes more productive, and people can grow great food on a larger scale while forging great friendships.

Getting Involved: Community Supported Agriculture

If you feel thwarted by your space constraints, look beyond the boundaries of your town or city. Community Supported Agriculture (CSA) isn't a new idea; it started in continental Europe and is alive and kicking in the UK too. Some CSA farms are legally set up to benefit the community; if you're lucky enough to have one of these farms near you, then joining in ensures your future food supply if ever the supermarket shelves run dry. Sometimes you can even buy up shares in the farm, becoming a proper landowner!

The basic idea of CSA is that a food growing farmer – maybe close to your town, but the principle can work for farms farther afield too – gains some money in advance from a number of willing people, allowing the farmer to buy seeds, machinery or whatever to grow crops specifically for the community that financially supports that farm.

At harvest time, your money entitles you to share the harvest. In addition, you follow and understand the ongoing running and growing of the crops through newsletters, websites, blogs and so on, and perhaps have some say in which crops to grow. Your hands-on experiences on that farm with weeding, picking and harvesting days (farms farther afield may offer weekend or holiday breaks in exchange for some work) are valuable assets for the project too. Joining in with cider-making or apple-pressing or other farm processing may be part of the bargain – you get to take home some of the produce you help to preserve and develop practical skills and confidence in these areas along the way – or you may only contribute from afar financially, and enjoy a box of vegetables regularly or as a one-off for your input. The details are for you and your CSA farmer to work out between you.

Usually, the types of farm willing to extend their hands beyond the boundary of the farm are environmentally aware ones that may need to call on a larger workforce from time to time and recognise the value (sadly unrecognised by supermarket buyers) of growing healthy food while protecting the environment for future generations; they often welcome families and children as workers.

You benefit by finding a legitimate way to get out into the fresh air onto a farm, building a relationship with the person who grows your food, understanding the problems and seasonal influences of food growing and, if you have children, enjoying a great way to reconnect them with the earth, which is a positive grounding in these days of over-industrialised food and virtual living. Of course, you come home with food to eat and share in the seasonal gluts, which you can then turn into delicious home preserves.

The farmer benefits from being able to call upon people when necessary and, because farming is a full-time, sometimes lonely, occupation, your friendship is a valuable asset. Look up 'Community Supported Agriculture' on the Internet to find a farm near you, or approach your local organic box scheme to find out whether it runs such a CSA project.

The types of farms hosting this kind of scheme are likely to be small family-run farms working on a tight budget.

Joining Your Transition Town Movement

All over the world, but more pertinently just around the corner from where you live right now, a new movement of sensible people is stepping up to the plate and asking the question, 'What will we do when the oil runs out?' Bearing in mind that most of the food due to be in every supermarket in the country tomorrow is likely to be in a lorry driving down a road near you today, food transportation needs a lot of oil!

If this question ever bothers you, whether for your own or your children's future, the Transition Town Movement can help you steer a way through the thought processes and start preparing for a less oil-fuelled tomorrow now. Reading this book is one kind of new beginning: you're already growing, or planning to start growing, your own food for storing and preserving to eat throughout the year. Every single item that you use in this way is one less piece of produce that needs transporting. Join with like-minded people by discovering exactly who they are and where they hang out; visit www. transitionnetwork.org for contacts at a local level.

The Transition Town Movement members hope to educate each other by swapping experiences, rethinking living spaces for whole towns and cities, studying places that are already living low carbon lifestyles and putting this experience into place in a harmonious and joyful manner. Discovering how to grow, store and preserve your own food is so often the starting point.

Index

••

FOR DUMMIES®

Making Everything Easier! ™

UK editions

BUSINESS

978-0-470-97626-5

978-0-470-97211-3

978-1-119-97527-4

REFERENCE

978-0-470-68637-9

978-0-470-97450-6

978-0-470-74535-9

HOBBIES

978-0-470-69960-7

978-0-470-68641-6

978-0-470-68178-7

Asperger's Syndrome For Dummies
978-0-470-66087-4

Basic Maths For Dummies
978-1-119-97452-9

Boosting Self-Esteem For Dummies
978-0-470-74193-1

British Sign Language
For Dummies
978-0-470-69477-0

Cricket For Dummies
978-0-470-03454-5

Diabetes For Dummies, 3rd Edition
978-0-470-97711-8

English Grammar For Dummies
978-0-470-05752-0

Flirting For Dummies
978-0-470-74259-4

IBS For Dummies
978-0-470-51737-6

Improving Your Relationship
For Dummies
978-0-470-68472-6

Keeping Chickens For Dummies
978-1-119-99417-6

Lean Six Sigma For Dummies
978-0-470-75626-3

Management For Dummies,
2nd Edition
978 0 470-97769-9

Neuro-linguistic Programming
For Dummies, 2nd Edition
978-0-470-66543-5

Nutrition For Dummies, 2nd Edition
978-0-470-97276-2

FOR DUMMIES®

A world of resources to help you grow

UK editions

SELF–HELP

978-0-470-66541-1

978-1-119-99264-6

978-0-470-66086-7

Origami Kit For Dummies
978-0-470-75857-1

Overcoming Depression For Dummies
978-0-470-69430-5

Positive Psychology For Dummies
978-0-470-72136-0

PRINCE2 For Dummies, 2009 Edition
978-0-470-71025-8

Project Management For Dummies
978-0-470-71119-4

Psychometric Tests For Dummies
978-0-470-75366-8

Reading the Financial Pages
For Dummies
978-0-470-71432-4

STUDENTS

978-0-470-68820-5

978-0-470-74711-7

978-1-119-99134-2

Rugby Union For Dummies, 3rd Edition
978-1-119-99092-5

Sage 50 Accounts For Dummies
978-0-470-71558-1

Self-Hypnosis For Dummies
978-0-470-66073-7

Study Skills For Dummies
978-0-470-74047-7

Teaching English as a Foreign Language
For Dummies
978-0-470-74576-2

Time Management For Dummies
978-0-470-77765-7

Training Your Brain For Dummies
978-0-470-97449-0

HISTORY

978-0-470-68792-5

978-0-470-74783-4

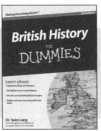

978-0-470-97819-1

Work-Life Balance For Dummies
978-0-470-71380-8

Writing a Dissertation For Dummies
978-0-470-74270-9

**Available wherever books are sold. For more information or to order direct go to
www.wiley.com or call +44 (0) 1243 843291**

32812 (p2)

FOR DUMMIES®

The easy way to get more done and have more fun

LANGUAGES

978-0-470-68815-1
UK Edition

978-1-118-00464-7

978-0-470-90101-4

MUSIC

978-0-470-97799-6
UK Edition

978-0-470-66603-6
Lay-flat, UK Edition

978-0-470-66372-1
UK Edition

SCIENCE & MATHS

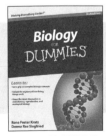

978-0-470-59875-7

978-0-470-55964-2

978-0-470-55174-5

Art For Dummies
978-0-7645-5104-8

Bass Guitar For Dummies, 2nd Edition
978-0-470-53961-3

Criminology For Dummies
978-0-470-39696-4

Currency Trading For Dummies,
2nd Edition
978-1-118-01851-4

Drawing For Dummies, 2nd Edition
978-0-470-61842-4

Forensics For Dummies
978-0-7645-5580-0

Guitar For Dummies, 2nd Edition
978-0-7645-9904-0

Hinduism For Dummies
978-0-470-87858-3

Index Investing For Dummies
978-0-470-29406-2

Knitting For Dummies, 2nd Edition
978-0-470-28747-7

Music Theory For Dummies, 2nd Edition
978-1-118-09550-8

Piano For Dummies, 2nd Edition
978-0-470-49644-2

Physics For Dummies, 2nd Edition
978-0-470-90324-7

Schizophrenia For Dummies
978-0-470-25927-6

Sex For Dummies, 3rd Edition
978-0-470-04523-7

Sherlock Holmes For Dummies
978-0-470-48444-9

Solar Power Your Home
For Dummies, 2nd Edition
978-0-470-59678-4

FOR DUMMIES®

Helping you expand your horizons and achieve your potential

COMPUTER BASICS

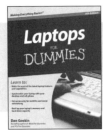

978-0-470-57829-2

978-0-470-61454-9

978-0-470-49743-2

DIGITAL PHOTOGRAPHY

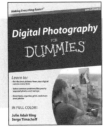

978-0-470-25074-7

978-0-470-76878-5

978-1-118-00472-2

MICROSOFT OFFICE 2010

978-0-470-48998-7

978-0-470-58302-9

978-0-470-48953-6

Access 2010 For Dummies
978-0-470-49747-0

Android Application Development
For Dummies
978-0-470-77018-4

AutoCAD 2011 For Dummies
978-0-470-59539-8

C++ For Dummies, 6th Edition
978-0-470-31726-6

Computers For Seniors For Dummies,
2nd Edition
978-0-470-53483-0

Dreamweaver CS5 For Dummies
978-0-470-61076-3

iPad For Dummies 2nd Edition
978-1-118-02444-7

Macs For Dummies, 11th Edition
978-0-470-87868-2

Mac OS X Snow Leopard For Dummies
978-0-470-43543-4

Photoshop CS5 For Dummies
978-0-470-61078-7

Photoshop Elements 9 For Dummies
978-0-470-87872-9

Search Engine Optimization
For Dummies, 4th Edition
978-0-470-88104-0

The Internet For Dummies,
12th Edition
978-0-470-56095-2

Visual Studio 2010 All-In-One
For Dummies
978-0-470-53943-9

Web Analytics For Dummies
978-0-470-09824-0

Word 2010 For Dummies
978-0-470-48772-3

WordPress For Dummies, 4th Edition
978-1-118-07342-1

32812 (p4)